SPEECHES
THAT SHAPED
SOUTH AFRICA

SPEECHES
THAT SHAPED
SOUTH AFRICA
From Malan to Malema

MARTHA EVANS

PENGUIN BOOKS

Published by Penguin Books
an imprint of Penguin Random House South Africa (Pty) Ltd
Reg. No. 1953/000441/07
The Estuaries No. 4, Oxbow Crescent, Century Avenue, Century City, 7441
PO Box 1144, Cape Town, 8000, South Africa
www.penguinrandomhouse.co.za

Penguin
Random House
South Africa

First published 2017

1 3 5 7 9 10 8 6 4 2

PUBLISHER: Marlene Fryer
MANAGING EDITOR: Robert Plummer
EDITOR: Dane Wallace
PROOFREADER: Bronwen Maynier
COVER AND TEXT DESIGNER: Ryan Africa
TYPESETTER: Monique Cleghorn
INDEXER: Sanet le Roux

Set in 11 pt on 14 pt Minion

Printed by **novus print**, a Novus Holdings company

MIX
Paper from
responsible sources
FSC® C022948

Penguin Random House is committed to a sustainable future
for our business, our readers and our planet. This book is made from
Forest Stewardship Council® certified paper.,

ISBN 978 1 77609 141 6 (print)
ISBN 978 1 77609 142 3 (ePub)

Contents

Preface

In contrast with books on South African writing, there are few works about speech in the country[1] and even fewer about speeches – this, despite our rich oral tradition and the relatively high number of South African orators whose words are revered in international compilations of great twentieth-century speeches. This collection is an attempt to gather some of our most important addresses in one book.

The speeches in this collection span nearly seventy years and represent a selection of the spoken words from some of South Africa's influential political traditions. While selecting them, it became clear that there are actually relatively few speeches whose historical influence was immediate. One or two addresses changed the course of history as they were uttered: F.W. de Klerk's 2 February speech (page 209) and Thabo Mbeki's resignation speech (page 270) stand as somewhat unique examples. And the historic importance of certain speeches is immediately apparent. Nelson Mandela's speech from the dock (page 65), for instance, in addition to being covered in all major newspapers, was widely reprinted and distributed as part of the anti-apartheid struggle. It changed the international perception of the African National Congress and became one of the founding documents of the nation's civic religion.

But the influence of other speeches is less easy to determine. It's not known, for example, how many listeners tuned in to hear Walter Sisulu on the first Radio Freedom broadcast in the middle of the night in 1963 (page 61), or whether the audience at Steve Biko's 'White Racism, Black Consciousness' talk (page 117) accepted his challenges. Helen Suzman (page 107) claimed that, after railing in Parliament for no fewer than twenty-five years, she hadn't managed to prevent the passing of a single apartheid law,[2] and even the influence of a speech such as Mandela's televised address in the wake of Chris Hani's assassination (page 230) is difficult to measure.

But if there is anything that an examination of decades' worth of powerful speeches reveals, it is this: speeches do not exist in isolation. They may begin as a whisper, but they gather volume and form a powerful chorus of utterance that ultimately helps to shape history. Speech begets speech, sometimes with literal intertextual references: Harold Macmillan's 'Wind of Change' (page 31) makes its way into Albert Luthuli's Nobel lecture (page 50), and Luthuli is quoted in Mandela's speech from the dock. Likewise, Pixley ka Isaka Seme's proud declaration 'I am an African' is resurrected in Thabo Mbeki's speech of the same title (page 253). In addition, the voices of various traditions carry through and are echoed by their heirs. The ideas of Robert Sobukwe (page 21) thread through Steve Biko and together find their way into Mbeki's 'I am an African' speech, which emphasises African agency and self-reliance. Moreover, many of the speakers in this collection have established foundations (e.g. Helen Suzman, Steve Biko, Nelson Mandela, F.W. de Klerk, Thabo Mbeki and Ahmed Kathrada), which preserve the traditions and morals they espoused.

Of course, the afterlife of speeches is dependent on their being known, and one of the major constraints in selecting influential addresses from the apartheid era is the imbalance in archiving. The words of many apartheid leaders were carefully and systematically recorded as part of the Afrikaner nationalist project to 'build a nation from words',[3] and, in this collection, the speeches of Verwoerd (page 44) and Vorster (page 139) were found in already existing volumes published in their honour. This was not always true of the discourse of the liberation movement, not least because of the apartheid state's attempts to silence the voices of the opposition.

Prior to 1994, an ever-increasing variety of interlinked laws conspired to drive dissident speech underground, ensuring its near erasure from history. Most vicious was the Suppression of Communism Act of 1950, which gave the state the power to create a uniquely South African category of individual, the so-called 'banned person'. At its heart, the arbitrarily served 'banning order' was an attempt to stop people from giving speeches. While there were various permutations of the law, banned persons were usually confined to non-public spaces and forbidden to attend gatherings of more than a permitted number of people – usually determined by the perceived threat posed by that banned person.

To some extent, these bannings were successful. A hunt for Winnie Madikizela-Mandela's oft-referenced 'fiery' speeches, for instance, resulted in the sum total of two recorded addresses – one of which was incorrectly archived in an academic library. Madikizela-Mandela was banned for nearly thirty years, with a short period of 'freedom' of just over a year between 1975 and 1976. When she gave her first speech of which there is a transcribed record (page 129), she had endured an enforced silence of thirteen years.

In a country where it was in fact dangerous to keep copies of words uttered by dissidents, it is remarkable that any have survived at all. Some of the texts that have endured are available only because they were seized and produced in criminal trials as incriminating evidence against activists. These documents were thus subsumed into the apartheid state's official archives. This was the case with the only surviving speech by Lilian Ngoyi[4] (page 14), which was found in the home of Paul Joseph and used as evidence in the much-publicised Treason Trial, when the state attempted to convict 156 activists of treason.

For many years, in fact, the courtroom became the only site that permitted dialogue between the state and dissidents, and there have been some interesting works on the speech acts that emerged in this space.[5] Following Luthuli and Mandela's examples, defendants began to use the court as a stage from which to deliver speeches that would otherwise have been outlawed. Two years after the Rivonia Trial, Communist Party leader Bram Fischer (page 79) used the same platform to broadcast his political vision. In this way, political trials became an important means of communicating to audiences outside the country.

Parliament was also influential in this respect, and, before 1974, this was solely because of Helen Suzman, who for thirteen years was the only real voice of opposition in the House. She made a remarkable contribution to countering the dominant narrative of Afrikaner nationalism in its self-created structures, using her position to force leaders to listen to letters, narratives and perspectives that they had tried to silence.

As communication between liberation leaders and 'the people' became an increasingly clandestine affair, activists developed South Africa's own version of *samizdat*, finding new and creative ways to make themselves heard. For example, an early innovator, Yusuf Dadoo (page 7), eluded the police on at least one occasion by playing a tape-recorded speech over a loudspeaker instead of delivering it personally. And Oliver Tambo's much-anticipated 8 January addresses (page 158) were not only broadcast routinely on Radio Freedom, but cassette recordings were also distributed via underground networks.

Frustratingly, sometimes major speeches referred to in popular accounts of important events remained elusive. There appears to be no record of Ngoyi's keynote speech at the 1956 Women's March or of any of the speeches given at Matthew Goniwe's funeral. Other speeches, identified as influential in newspaper coverage from the time, appear to have been delivered off the cuff and have left little more than a trail of hearsay. There is no full version of the Munsieville speech in which Madikizela-Mandela broke her banning order to say, 'Together, hand in hand, with our matches and our necklaces, we shall liberate this country', making it difficult to interrogate her defence that she was quoted out of context. The words of great township rally speakers, such as Chris Hani, are also difficult to trace. Ironically, individuals described as great orators have left a remarkably thin paper trail. Such speakers (Eugène Terre'Blanche also springs to mind) belong to a different tradition of speech delivery – one that depends very much on reading and responding to the crowd.

In addition to the carefully scripted and official speeches from heads of state, the collection includes a large number of speeches given by speakers whose oratory skills were perfected at the pulpit. From Malan to Boesak to Tutu to Maimane, some of the country's most skilled speakers illustrate the extent to which successful speech delivery benefits from the techniques of religious rhetoric.

The year 1990, and F.W. de Klerk's 2 February parliamentary address, ushered in a new era in which speeches blossomed as the charismatic Mandela returned to the world stage, magically speaking the new South Africa into being.[6] Also important in this respect was Archbishop Desmond Tutu (page 202), whose conjuring of the 'rainbow people of God' worked towards creating a new national identity. Soon after 1994, the space was also created to hear the stories that had been silenced for so many years, and between 1996 and 1998 the often-painful hearings of the Truth and Reconciliation Commission (page 244) dominated headlines, television and especially radio.

Insofar as possible, rather than relying on the speeches' written forms, this collection has adhered to their original audio and video recordings, which grew more common as technology advanced. From the 1980s onwards, it became easier to find video footage of speeches, which allowed for an enhanced sense of the context of their delivery and sometimes the reactions of the audience. Something quite magical happens when a speech that exists in audio or video format alone is transcribed, allowing one to reread lines and fully grasp the implications of the content. This is particularly the case with individuals considered to be skilled orators. There is a vast difference between watching Julius Malema speak to crowds in Marikana, for instance, and reading the transcribed version of his speech (page 280).

There was sometimes difficulty in determining who to credit for an address, and it became clear that the very best speeches were produced by collective efforts. Harold Macmillan's 'Wind of Change' and Robert Kennedy's 'Ripple of Hope' speeches (page 95) were researched, drafted, revised and fine-tuned by a team of advisors, and the success of this practice is more recently seen with Mmusi Maimane's 'Broken Man' speech at the 2015 State of the Nation debate (page 308).

In some cases, the influence of a speech drew strength from the charismatic or symbolic power of its speaker, whose identity was inscribed into the rhetoric of the address. Mandela is an obvious example here, and this is probably the case whenever he spoke. It did not matter that he sometimes sounded – in Desmond Tutu's opinion – 'deadly dull' as an orator;[7] by the time of his release, he had acquired such immense moral capital that he brought 'Madiba magic' to any occasion. Many of his speeches, including his famous inauguration speech (page 237), were actually written by Thabo Mbeki, whose legendary speechwriting skills thread through much of the ANC tradition. Another fine example of the success of both collective composition and strategic use of speaker is the 'My Father Says' speech, attributed in this book to Mandela's daughter Zindzi (page 173). Drawing on the symbolism of the speaker (a young woman denied a father), the speech claims to deliver Mandela's words, but it was in fact written by a team of writers in Pollsmoor Prison. Nkosi Johnson's address at the 13th International AIDS Conference in 2000 (page 263) is the only speech by a child that is included in this collection. Here, too, the speaker's identity is as important as the words of the speech, which were written by his adoptive mother, Gail Johnson.

The collection also includes speeches that became famous for what they did *not* say – when speakers missed the opportunity to shape history. P.W. Botha's Rubicon speech (page 179) is the most infamous in this respect, and Jacob Zuma's 2015 State of the Nation Address (page 297) is remembered for all the wrong reasons.

Many have decried the seeming devaluation of the political speech in our current context. Stephen Grootes points out that for a speech to inspire and 'move a nation', there are a few necessary ingredients: good speechwriters, a conducive political context and a skilled orator. Moreover, 'that person needs to understand why it is important for it to be delivered well', something that 'seldom happens in our politics'.[8] S'thembiso Msomi describes the all-too-familiar mode of delivery well: 'In some cases the audience could be forgiven for suspecting that the politician is encountering his or her speech for the first time as they disjointedly read each sentence as if it had no connection with the previous one or the one that comes after it.'[9] Although this is true of many staid government addresses, in recent years we have witnessed the delivery of some remarkably rousing speeches. During the ten-day period alone in which the nation mourned the loss of Nelson Mandela, dozens of inspiring speeches were given (page 289), many more of which would have been included here were it not for space constraints. More importantly, the various memorial services held after Ahmed Kathrada's death saw the return of the political funeral and a proliferation of stirring speeches calling for moral introspection and change (page 319). These events made it clear that there will always be times that call for influential speeches, and speakers who rise to the occasion.

There are no doubt countless gaps in this collection, not only because of the problem of unequal archiving and the state's suppression of speech between 1948 and 1990, but also because the selection has been limited to speeches delivered mainly in English. There is much scope for research into the speeches and spoken traditions of other languages. The attempt to 'cover' history also made for some omissions. A few of these were notable speeches clustered around the year 1985, but the need to move through time inevitably meant that not all of them could be included.

It is hoped that by bringing together a collection of spoken words that inspired, enraged, comforted and in some cases disappointed South Africans, this collection will lead to additional research into speeches that have shaped our nation.

D.F. Malan

National Party campaign speech,
Paarl, 29 March 1948

In the years following World War II, few South Africans believed that the white
supremacist National Party (NP) would defeat the ruling United Party (UP)
in the general election. For one, the two leaders were incomparable. The UP
was led by the charismatic Field Marshal Jan Christiaan Smuts – basking in
post-war glory and popular with both English- and Afrikaans-speaking whites.
The newly formed NP, on the other hand, had opposed the war effort and was
led by the podgy Dr Daniel François Malan, whose thick-rimmed glasses and
unsmiling demeanour were off-puttingly austere.

The UP's experience in international relations was also sure to give it the
edge. The electorate, Smuts surmised, would have confidence in his party's
ability to navigate the increasingly tense global situation. The seventy-eight-
year-old Anglo-Boer War hero had led the country since 1939 and was one
of the high-profile founders of the United Nations Organisation. The NP, in
contrast, favoured an insular form of ethno-nationalism in a world that was
celebrating the defeat of Nazism, the birth of television, increased international travel, and a renewed sense of commitment to shared global values.

The UP was confident about its much-criticised handling of race relations
in the country, even though it had come under attack from both sides. While
The Economist, for instance, pointed to the hypocrisy of its so-called 'Christian
trusteeship' of black South Africans,[1] the opposition accused it of not taking
the 'native question' seriously enough. Buoyed by the findings of its own-
appointed Fagan Commission, which dismissed the idea of total segregation
and recommended a relaxation of legislation controlling urban influx control,
Smuts was vague about how the UP would deal with the mass movement of
black South Africans to the cities – referred to as 'swamping'[2] by the Nats. On
the one hand, he acknowledged the necessity of cheap black labour to keep
the wartime economy afloat; on the other, his assurance that the black prole-
tariat was simply made up of 'temporary sojourners' contradicted statements
about the experience of 'accelerated' African urbanisation, a process about
which he had also said, 'You might as well try to sweep the ocean back with a
broom.' Overall, he sidestepped the issue of a race policy, saying, 'Generations
to come will decide their own policy.'[3]

Popular accounts suggest that this was a grave mistake, and that one of the main reasons Smuts lost out to the Nats was because he failed to read white fear of black majority rule. He and others with a more Anglophile stance dismissed the word 'apartheid' (the Nat term for segregation) as a campaign buzzword. Indeed, in a 1948 report, Sir Evelyn Baring, the British High Commissioner in Pretoria, accused Malan and his cohorts of having few 'constructive suggestions' when it came to the race question.[4]

To a certain extent, this was true; it would take many years before the NP's apartheid 'ideal' was fully realised. But Baring and others underestimated the NP's visceral appeal to the hearts and minds of rural Afrikaners. Ultimately, it was this group that would vote Smuts out. Afrikaners were fast losing faith in the UP's ability to protect their interests. They were impatient with continued wartime rationing, fearful of the rise in crime that accompanied urbanisation, concerned about diminished labour on the farms, and they disliked, in particular, the liberal Jan Hendrik Hofmeyr, who was pinned as Smuts's successor. The radical-sounding promise of 'apartheid', even if vague on detail, addressed many of their concerns.

The term 'apartheid' had entered the NP lexicon soon after the party's loss in the 1943 election, and it found fuller expression in the campaign discourse for 1948, particularly after Malan chose to focus the party's promotion on race.[5] On 29 March, two months before the election, a determined Malan read out an NP campaign statement to a Paarl constituency in the Western Cape. The speech is a terrifying outline of a policy of social engineering that few would have thought possible in the heady post-war years.

There are two sections of thought in South Africa in regard to the policy affecting the non-European community. On the one hand there is the policy of equality, which advocates equal rights within the same political structure for all civilized and educated persons, irrespective of race or colour, and the gradual granting of the franchise to non-Europeans as they become qualified to make use of democratic rights.

On the other hand there is the policy of separation (apartheid) which has grown from the experience of established European population of the country, and which is based on the Christian principles of justice and reasonableness.

Its aim is the maintenance and protection of the European population of the country as a pure White race, the maintenance and protection of the indigenous racial groups as separate communities, with prospects of developing into self-supporting communities within their own areas, and the stimulation of national pride, self-respect, and mutual respect among the various races of the country.

We can act in only one of two directions. Either we must follow the course of equality, which must eventually mean national suicide for the White race, or we must take the course of separation (apartheid) through which the character and the future of every race will be protected and safeguarded with full opportunities for development and self-maintenance in their own ideas, without the interests of one clashing with the interests of the other, and without one regarding the development of the other as undermining or a threat to himself.

The party therefore undertakes to protect the White race properly and effectively against any policy, doctrine or attack which might undermine or threaten its continued existence. At the same time the party rejects any policy of oppression and exploitation of the non-Europeans by the Europeans as being in conflict with the Christian basis of our national life and irreconcilable with our policy.

The party believes that a definite policy of separation (apartheid) between the White races and the non-White racial groups, and the application of the policy of separation also in the case of the non-White racial groups, is the only basis on which the character and future of each race can be protected and safeguarded and on which each race can be guided so as to develop his own national character, aptitude and calling.

All marriages between Europeans and non-Europeans will be prohibited.

In their areas the non-European racial groups will have full opportunities for development in every sphere and will be able to develop their own institutions and social services whereby the forces of the progressive non-Europeans can be harnessed for their own national development (*volkeepbou*). The policy of the country must be so planned that it will eventually promote the ideal of complete separation (*algehele apartheid*) in a national way.

A permanent advisory body of experts on non-European affairs will be established.

The State will exercise complete supervision over the moulding of the youth. The party will not tolerate interference from without or destructive propaganda from the outside world in regard to the racial problems of South Africa.

The party wishes all non-Europeans to be strongly encouraged to make the Christian religion the basis of their lives and will assist

3

churches in this task in every possible way. Churches and societies which undermine the policy of apartheid and propagate doctrines foreign to the nation will be checked.

The Coloured community takes a middle position between the European and the Natives. A policy of separation (apartheid) between the Europeans and Coloureds and between Natives and Coloureds will be applied in the social, residential, industrial and political spheres. No marriage between Europeans and Coloureds will be permitted. The Coloureds will be protected against unfair competition from the Natives in so far as where they are already established.

The Coloured community will be represented in the Senate by a European representative to be appointed by the Government by reason of his knowledge of Coloured affairs.

The present unhealthy system which allows Coloureds in the Cape to be registered on the same voters' roll as Europeans and to vote for the same candidate as Europeans will be abolished and the Coloureds will be represented in the House of Assembly by three European representatives.

These Coloured representatives will be elected by a Coloured representative council. They will not vote on:

(1) Votes on confidence in the Government.

(2) A declaration of war, and

(3) A change in the political rights of non-Europeans.

A State Department of Coloured Affairs will be established.

The Coloured community will be represented in the Cape Provincial Council by three Europeans elected by the Coloured representative council.

A Coloured representative council will be established in the Cape Province consisting of representatives elected by the Coloured community, divided into constituencies with the present franchise qualifications, the head of the Department of Coloured Affairs and representatives nominated by the Government. In their own areas the Coloured community will have their own councils with their own public services which will be managed by themselves within the framework of the existing councils with higher authority.

Attention will be given to the provision of social, medical and welfare services in which the efforts of the Coloured themselves can be harnessed, and in which they will be taught as far as possible to be self-supporting.

The speech, like the NP campaign overall, presented a radical 'all or nothing' vision of a completely segregated South Africa. While there were, at this point, many paths the country might have chosen, Malan appealed to the white audience's fear of black domination by claiming, dramatically, that there were only two: '*algehele apartheid*' or 'national suicide'.

A former editor of the Afrikaner nationalist newspaper *Die Burger*, Malan had a talent for encapsulating ideals and coining catchphrases and slogans.[6] Without qualification, the speech repeats the verb 'will' in a reassuring presentation of a known future: interracial marriage 'will be prohibited'; 'The party will not tolerate interference'; 'doctrines foreign to the nation will be checked'. In a shifting and uncertain political environment, Malan's totalising discourse – his appeal to 'definite policy', 'full opportunity' and 'complete separation' – appealed to Afrikaners' impatience with half-hearted socio-political measures.

As would become typical of apartheid justifications in the years to come, Malan sugar-coated the idea of segregation as a Christian policy of 'mutual respect' addressing the needs of all racial groups in South Africa. 'The future of every race will be protected and safeguarded with full opportunities' and 'Coloured citizens', who formed a minority alongside whites, will be 'protected' from 'unfair competition', Malan claims. In a misguided reading of religious doctrine, the party promised that 'oppression and exploitation of non-Europeans' would be irreconcilable with the 'Christian basis' of their policy.

Here, Malan's closeness to the church must have been influential. Historically, his role in the 1948 general election has been underplayed. Yet, as his biographer Lindie Koorts points out,[7] his unique brand of charisma helped to persuade Afrikaners, many also deeply religious, to place their trust in the NP. A former minister of the Dutch Reformed Church, Malan was earnest, hard-working and devout (embracing celibacy until the age of fifty-two). No doubt influenced by his time at the pulpit, his oratory style was famously zealous, his voice 'deep and vibrant'.[8] While he appeared dour and tight-lipped to an international audience, to the Afrikaner electorate he was a reassuring, prophet-like figure of authority. An English journalist summed up Malan's influence:

He smiles rarely – and wanly – and the only indulgence he permits himself in his speeches is an occasional exercise in elaborate irony. Nevertheless, in a land of sunshine, where men laugh loudly, none – not even Smuts – enjoys higher prestige among his own people than this stern, implacable, isolated man of God.[9]

The seventy-three-year-old Malan campaigned energetically in the months leading up to the election, delivering similar speeches at a range of civic venues. In contrast, Smuts was preoccupied with post-war affairs and only appeared to take serious interest in the election a few days before citizens were due to go to the polls.

By this time, however, it was too late: the electorate had been lost. The world watched with widening astonishment as the results trickled in. By Friday morning on 28 May, it was clear that Smuts had been voted out. Although Smuts had secured the popular vote, the Nats (in alliance with N.C. Havenga's Afrikaner Party) won more parliamentary seats. Because of the country's electoral system, the more sparsely populated rural constituencies weighed more in Parliament. Ironically, given the focus on African urbanisation in the election campaign, Smuts supporters were clustered in urban areas. In the end, only 39.85 per cent of the electorate voted for Malan, compared to 53.49 per cent for Smuts and his allies. The biggest surprise was the Transvaal, which nearly tripled Nationalist representation in Parliament, increasing it from eleven seats (in 1943) to thirty-two (in 1948).

The Smuts constituencies and British press were shocked. *The Times* referred to the subsequent 'anxious discussions and long lists of sharp falls in the prices of South African mining and industrial shares' in a piece titled 'The shock from South Africa'.[10] From London, former prime minister Sir Winston Churchill lamented the outcome, stating in *Time* magazine, 'A great world statesmen has fallen and with him his country will undergo a period of anxiety and perhaps a temporary eclipse.'[11]

In many respects, Smuts did react as if the defeat were a 'temporary eclipse', assuming that the narrowness of the victory would see Malan ejected from office before long.[12] This wasn't to be. Two years later, Smuts would be dead, fracturing the opposition and providing fertile ground for Afrikaner nationalism to extend its roots. Apartheid was not, as Baring had dismissed it, a 'vague and woolly theory' at all,[13] and the NP would keep all but one of their campaign promises. Over the course of the next four decades, they set about instituting the policy of apartheid at every level of life. To do so, however, they had to employ draconian measures that were totally irreconcilable with Christian doctrine.

Yusuf Dadoo

'Apartheid over our dead bodies' speech,
Red Square, Johannesburg, 10 July 1948

To the majority of South Africans, the handover of power from the United Party to the National Party seemed like business as usual. The UP's 1948 campaign likewise supported segregation and white minority rule, even if the party appeared willing to consider minor concessions. Despite the shockwaves elicited by Smuts's defeat, it wasn't as if the Nats had ousted a party proposing radical change. Oliver Tambo remembers that at a press conference held in the wake of the election, then president-general of the African National Congress (ANC) Dr A.B. Xuma stated that the supposedly new apartheid policies came as no surprise to anybody vaguely familiar with South Africa's history.[1] Indeed, pre-1948 legislation such as the Urban Areas Act (1923) and the Ghetto Act (1946) bore all the hallmarks of apartheid thinking, and in February 1948, Smuts had unequivocally stated in Parliament that he didn't support the principle of equality between races. That the white electorate voted in the NP was therefore less surprising to oppressed South Africans than it was to the rest of the world.

Despite this, important changes were on the way. The organisations fighting for the rights of the variously disenfranchised racial groups in the country were beginning to work together. A year before the election, the ANC, the Transvaal Indian Congress and the Natal Indian Congress had already agreed to unite in opposition to government policies through the Xuma-Naicker-Dadoo Pact (the so-called Doctors' Pact). Unity would prove to be one of the most powerful defences against apartheid, and the pact served as a prelude to the adoption of the Freedom Charter in 1955.

One of the signatories to the pact was the widely travelled Dr Yusuf Mohamed Dadoo, a general practitioner and president of the Transvaal Indian Congress. Influenced by Mohandas Gandhi (who had saved Dadoo's father from losing his shop in court when Dadoo was a child) and, sometimes conflictingly, Marx, Dadoo was an ardent supporter of mass passive resistance and non-racialism. He, and G.M. 'Monty' Naicker, succeeded in radicalising the Indian resistance organisations, which had previously adopted a more moderate and self-serving approach to politics in the country. As E.S. Reddy points out, Dadoo's most valuable contribution to the fight against apartheid was his focus on unity, across class and race, and in 'persuading the Indian community to link its destiny with that of the African majority'.[2]

Dadoo had a strong distaste for hypocrisy. He disliked, in particular, the extent to which some of the Indian congresses focused only on the aspirations of wealthier Indians,[3] and when Smuts denounced his support for the principle of racial equality, Dadoo sent out a press release, pointing to the prime minister's double standards; while preaching a human rights message in Europe, Smuts reverted to oppressive tactics in his own country. Smuts's comment, said Dadoo, 'does not bring any credit' to his 'international reputation'.[4]

The thirty-nine-year-old father-of-one missed the rest of the election debacle, however, as he was serving a six-month sentence along with Naicker, Sundra Pillay and Manilal Gandhi (son of Mohandas Gandhi, who had been assassinated just one month prior). They had all been arrested for their part in orchestrating phase two of the passive resistance campaign.

By the time of his release four and a half months later, Dadoo had discovered that he had a new opponent in the newly elected Malan. Initially, the Passive Resistance Council was relieved to see the end of Smuts's rule, even sending Malan a congratulatory note expressing new hope about the future treatment of Indians. The NP quickly made it known that they viewed Indian South Africans as a 'foreign element', however, by repealing sections of the much-hated Ghetto Act – for all the wrong reasons – and introducing new regressive legislation such as the Asiatic Law Amendment Act. Malan also publicly stated that the NP planned to resurrect repatriation policies (abandoned by the Union government in the mid-1930s) and that it would be persuading as many Indians as possible to return to their motherland.[5]

Dadoo responded to these threats by spreading the message of the Doctors' Pact, speaking first at a post-release reception held at the People's Square in Pietermaritzburg and then delivering what famously became known as the 'apartheid over our dead bodies' speech on 10 July. The speech was given at a mass welcome meeting at Red Square in the Johannesburg suburb of Fordsburg organised in his honour by the Transvaal Passive Resistance Council. In these stirring excerpts, the call to unity gathers urgent momentum:

> Dr Naicker and I return and are with you again after a period of four and a half months. During those four and a half months a great deal has happened, great changes have taken place.
>
> During the last four and a half months the high walls of prison had cut us off completely from the outside world. We did not know what was happening in South Africa. We only knew of the food we got, the work

we had to do and the cold we had to bear. During those four and a half months the leadership of the Natal and Transvaal Indian Congresses and the Joint Passive Resistance Council was called upon to take decisions to meet with the demands of the situation.

[...]

Important Events

As far as South Africa is concerned, two important events have taken place in the last two or three months.

Firstly, the great People's Assembly which assembled here in Johannesburg, representing vast masses of the Non-European people of the Transvaal and Orange Free State – representatives of more people than those who voted in the Transvaal and Orange Free State in the last General Election – declared quite clearly to the South African Government that as far as the vast masses of the people are concerned, they demand immediately and now full franchise for all sections of the South African population; that this country faces a very dark future unless the franchise is extended to all sections of the population. To my mind, it was a very important and momentous event.

The other very important event was the coming into power of the Nationalist Party. These two important events must be analysed.

[...]

High Priest of Imperialism

General Smuts, the ex-Prime Minister, soon after delivering his country into the hands of the Nationalists, flew over to Britain. There, as the High Priest of Imperialism, he delivered an oration in which he warned the people of the dark menace of Communism. General Smuts talked of freedom! He who denied franchise to four-fifths of the population of his own country – he warned the world of the menacing forces of Communism in Western Europe. So General Smuts, the spokesman for the Imperialist camp, talks of freedom of the people. And just the other day Dr Malan went to a function to celebrate American Independence Day and there Dr Malan praised American imperialism as a great saviour of mankind.

Nationalist Government due to United Party

This policy is detrimental to the interests of South Africa. We have had a change of Government in this country from the United Party to the Nationalist Party. It was a surprise. But if the Nationalists have assumed power then it is the logical outcome of the rotten policies pursued by General Smuts and his United Party Government. Their policy of repressing the Non-European people, cheap labour, colour bars and Ghetto Acts was a policy of segregation. If General Smuts and the United Party stand for segregation, then who is more capable than the Nationalist Party of putting that policy into effect? This we must understand quite clearly because on it will be based the future policy of South Africa. On this basis Dr Malan and his Government have come into power.

[...]

Grave Danger

From all these utterances come out the facts that important changes in high offices, Defence Department, are being conducted by the Nats. Today, they constitute a grave danger to the people of South Africa and as far as the Indian people are concerned, the Nationalist Party's rotten policy put before South Africa is known to us all. They declare that the Indian people are outlandish.

We the Indian people – a quarter of a million Indian people born in South Africa – we whose home is in South Africa – we who are the sons of the soil, we who have contributed our share in the prosperity and making of South Africa, we are declared outlandish elements. We say to the Government of South Africa, South Africa is our home cradle, and South Africa will be our grave – no one dare put us out.

If the Indian people are repatriated, then what of other sections of the population tomorrow? What of the Jews, the English people? Let us make it quite clear that we are South Africans – we are going to stay in South Africa and we are going to play our part in making South Africa a progressive and democratic State.

Time to Act

That is the most important path before us. It is no use making speeches, the time has come in South Africa for everyone to act and here we must all act together. Now we must talk of a Democratic People's Front in South Africa. We must bring it about in this country – it must include not only Indians, Africans and Coloureds but the vast masses of the Europeans as well.

The Democratic People's Front is absolutely vital and necessary at the present stage of South Africa. It must fight for the preservation of democracy in South Africa or else we are doomed.

Communist Bogey

We must be very careful because the Government is using a bogey. The Communist bogey is the highest political fraud perpetrated by any Government or any Party because it is done with the criminal intent to destroy the cherished principles of democracy and the democratic way of life. When they talk of crushing the Communist menace they do not mean what you mean by Communism. Under the guise of this Communist bogey, they want to come down on the legitimate organisations of the European and Non-European people, organisations which fight for democratic rights of the people.

There is no such menace. If Communism exists, it exists as the legitimate movement of the people because they fight for democracy, for a happy South Africa for all, but when Dr Malan and Smuts talk about the Communist menace, they use it as the thin edge of the wedge to divide the people first and then go on to a further oppression of the vast masses of the people.

Meaning of Apartheid

They want to tell us, the Non-Europeans, that they are going to put us into separate compartments in our own interests. The application of the policy of apartheid can only mean further repression and oppression for the Non-European people of this country. Policy of apartheid means creating by brute force a permanent force of cheap migratory labour for the mines and on the farms. That is apartheid.

In order to bring about this policy greater force and greater violence will be used and eventually the outcome of such a policy can only lead to a fascist police State in South Africa. That is a danger which is inherent in allowing the present policy to continue and therefore what we require at the present moment is a Democratic People's Front on a minimum programme.

Programme

It will consist of a programme which must include such fundamental demands as Votes for All. The right of all workers to organise, to skilled jobs, freedom of movement of the people, repeal of colour bar laws, Pass Laws, Ghetto Act, a minimum living wage for all, homes for all – these are some of the vital demands which affect every section of our multi-racial population. These are the demands on which a Democratic People's Front must be started. Under these demands the people must go into action in order to save the country from the attacks on their rights and for the bringing about of a democratic State in this country.

These demands must be carried into effect and therefore I wish to make an appeal, first to the African National Congress as the National movement of the African people. I make an appeal to the leadership that they must have the courage to come out on such a declared policy and work for it and if such leadership is found wanting then those leaders must be ousted and the African national movement must be placed in the hands of a progressive leadership which enjoys the confidence of the masses.

I say to the Natal Indian Organisation and the Transvaal Indian Organisation, that they must fold up their organisations at the present moment. They must come within the ranks of the legitimate organisations of the Indian people, of the Transvaal and Natal Indian Congresses. There is no time at the present moment for the Natal Indian Organisation and the Transvaal Indian Organisation. In asking for an interview with Dr Malan they say that their organisation excludes communists. They have sunk to the lowest level. It means that they are saying to Dr Malan 'We are with you.' Such a policy is not only a great danger to the Indian people; such a policy is suicide for the Indian community. There is no time for such organisations to exist at the present moment.

We the Indian people demand that if you want to become leaders of the people you must serve the people. I say to the leaders of the Coloured people, that the time has come for them to see where they sit. I say to the members of the C.A.C. when they talk so much about Coloured rights, they still sit in the chairs of the C.A.C. The time has come when they must come out and challenge the rotten policy pursued by the present Government of attacking the political rights little as they are, of the Coloured people.

I say to those democratic organisations among the European people – they must not create the illusion in the minds of the European people that the United Party is pushing back the undemocratic attacks of Malan. This is all nonsense. The time has come for European democrats to come out if they want to save democracy.

The hour has struck for serious and hard work. The time has come when on this policy we must go forward. That is the only policy which at the present moment can meet the dangers which face us in this country. We have vast and progressive forces throughout the world. If we can unite the progressive forces in South Africa we can beat back the reactionary forces in this country. Let us not panic. We have the strength and power in our hands if we act rightly. It may entail suffering and sacrifice and plenty of hard work, but we must realise that these reactionary forces can be defeated and must be defeated in South Africa. On those lines, we must go forward. My warning to the people, both Europeans and Non-Europeans, is this:

In the present circumstances, either we hang together or we hang separately. That is the question before South Africa.

That is the lesson which every democrat in South Africa must learn at the present moment.

Finally, in thanking you for this warm reception which you have given me, I would like to express my fullest confidence in the ability, in the strength, of the vast masses of the European and Non-European people to prevent fascism, attacks on the rights and liberties which exist today and in order to move forward to democracy for all. And I have the confidence in the ability and strength of the masses, to say to the tyrants that be that democracy for all or apartheid and fascism over our dead bodies.

Seldom photographed without his pipe, Dadoo is remembered as being modest, well read and naturally shy.[6] He was also a dynamic orator, however, using his charisma to draw crowds to rallies. He cleverly evaded the authorities on more than one occasion. Once, when he was due to deliver a keynote speech at a public meeting, he was tipped off that the security police were hunting for him. He shrewdly recorded his speech with what was then a new invention: the tape recorder. Dadoo's words were subsequently played over a loudspeaker to the assembled crowd without him physically being there.[7]

A master rhetorician, Dadoo drafted concise retorts and coined memorable phrases. The power in this speech resides in the principle 'an injury to one is an injury to all'. He points out that the likely result of an anti-Indian stance would be the adoption of anti-Jewish and anti-English policies – everybody would be regarded as 'outlandish' at some point. To prevent this, he calls for unity among Indians, Africans, coloureds and indeed the 'vast masses of Europeans' under one umbrella: a Democratic People's Front. Unity, he suggests, is the most powerful defence against the NP's plan to divide and rule, stating 'either we hang together or we hang separately' – recalling a remark reportedly made by Benjamin Franklin at the signing of the Declaration of Independence. Dadoo also warns against any form of collaboration with the NP, saying that to seek special treatment for some at the expense of others would be 'suicide'.

The concluding phrase 'over our dead bodies' became a popular slogan in the unfolding battle against apartheid. Most notably, the ANC Youth League used an amended version – 'removal over our dead bodies' – during the Sophiatown campaign in 1954.[8] The phrase was also tragically prophetic, for in the years to come many would lose their lives in the fight for freedom.

Lilian Ngoyi

Presidential address to the Transvaal ANC
Women's League, 11 November 1956

The 1956 Women's March was a turning point in the struggle against apartheid, particularly in bringing women into the fold. During the 1950s, the call to unity in the fight against apartheid began to cross gender boundaries, and the ANC Women's League started to play an increasingly important role in campaigns and protests. Formed in 1948, the Women's League participated in the Defiance Campaign of 1952 and went on to assist with the organisation of the Freedom Charter in 1955.

But the Women's League really came into its own with the issue of passbooks. Attempts to restrict the movement of African women already had a long history in the country. There had been an outcry in 1913 when government officials declared that African women living and working in the urban townships of the Orange Free State would need to buy a new entry permit every month. Sporadic outbreaks of civil disobedience and demonstrations continued for several years until the permit requirement for women was finally abandoned. It was resurrected by the apartheid state in the 1950s, and when Hendrik Verwoerd, then minister of native affairs, announced that the government would begin issuing passbooks to women the following year, the Women's League responded with a small but ardent protest on 27 October 1955. A total of 2 000 women marched to the Union Buildings in Pretoria and handed bundles of signed petitions to the leaders of the campaign, Rahima Moosa, Helen Joseph, Lilian Ngoyi and Sophia Williams. The Afrikaner nationalist newspaper *Die Vaderland* tried to downplay the success of the protest by suggesting that it would never have seen the light of day were it not for the involvement of white women leaders[1] – an obvious deception, disproved by the activities of Lilian Ngoyi in particular.

Ngoyi, who had been elected as president of the Transvaal Women's League in 1954, was one of a growing number of influential women in the resistance movement. Together with Moosa, Joseph, Maggie Resha and Dora Tamana, as well as many of the wives of the struggle leaders, she helped to dispel the perception that the struggle was the preserve of men. In pursuit of international collaboration, Tamana and Ngoyi travelled to Europe to attend the World Congress of Mothers in Switzerland. A visit to Germany, and the sites of the

Nazi concentration camps, had been particularly stirring for her. When she returned to South Africa, she stated that she would fight for freedom 'to the bitter end'.[2]

A young widow and mother of two, Ngoyi worked in the clothing industry as an industrial machinist. She had proven her leadership skills as a union steward and officer with the radical Garment Workers' Union and joined the ANC during the Defiance Campaign. Despite a deprived educational background – she exited formal schooling at the age of eleven – within three years she became the first woman to be elected to the organisation's National Executive Committee in December 1955.

In the wake of the small but motivating 1955 protest, and in the absence of any clear directive from the ANC parent body on how to respond to the issuing of passes, Ngoyi and others began to travel the country to galvanise women into action. Although government officials had met with little resistance when they began issuing passbooks in rural areas in early 1956, this soon changed. In Winburg, where the state had first tried to issue passes to African women in 1913, a group of defiant protestors burnt their passes outside the magistrate's office. They were arrested, and some refused to post bail.[3]

The Winburg revolt was followed by several defiant protests, culminating in one of the most successful resistance marches of the decade. Under the umbrella of the Federation of South African Women, a broad multiracial alliance of women's groups, an estimated 20 000 women marched to the Union Buildings on 9 August 1956 to express their dissatisfaction to Prime Minister J.G. Strijdom.

The women had come from all over the country, some at great personal expense, and despite state officials' petty attempts to derail the protest by cancelling buses that had been booked by the organisers.[4] The crowd was especially colourful since the women had been encouraged to dress in appropriate uniforms: traditional attire, nurses' pinafores and caps, and the red-and-white uniform of Methodist church members.

The women, although sizeable in number, presented an orderly, patient and unified mass, with placards stating, 'Passes mean destitute children' and 'With passes we are slaves'. The march was noted for its display of immense discipline, and although Ngoyi delivered a key speech[5] (of which there appears to be no record), the occasion is remembered mainly for silence and song. The words of a new Zulu freedom song reverberated throughout the Union Buildings amphitheatre: '*Strijdom uthitta abafazi, uthinti imbokotho*' ('Strijdom, you've tampered with the women, you've struck against a rock'). After the delegation's leaders had delivered a list of women's demands to Strijdom's office, the entire crowd, at Ngoyi's suggestion, stood in complete silence for a full half-hour. This was partly a protest against the prime minister's new banning order that prevented rally speeches,[6] but it was also a display of immense stoicism and passive resistance. Maggie Resha remembers the climax to this half-hour of deafening silence: 'Before the day was wound up with "*Nkosi Sikelel' iAfrica*," Lilian's voice echoed from the walls of the Union Buildings as she cried out: "*A . . . frika!*" The atmosphere seemed electrified by the power of her voice, and the crowd responded: "*Mayibuye!*" (May it [r]eturn!).'[7]

A few months after the women's protest, Ngoyi addressed the Transvaal members of the ANC Women's League, building on the strength of the march by mobilising for continued resistance against the government. In this, her only surviving speech,[8] she again focused attention on pass laws:

> The principal and most pressing task of the Women's League at the present moment is to mobilise all the women of South Africa to fight against the extension of the passes to African women. Hardly any other South African Law has caused so much suffering and hardship to Africans as the pass laws. Hardly any other measure has created so much suffering and racial friction and hostility between black and white. Any policeman may at any time demand to see your pass, and failure to produce it for any reason means imprisonment or a fine. It makes it permissible to violate the sanctity and privacy of our homes. An African, sleeping peacefully in his house, may be woken up at night and asked to produce one, and failure to do so may lead to his arrest and imprisonment even though he has committed no crime whatsoever. Before an African is issued with a railway ticket, especially when travelling from one province to another, he must produce his pass to the booking clerk. No trading licence may be given to an African unless his pass shows that he is lawfully resident in the area where he wants to trade. Attempts were made recently by marriage officers to refuse to solemnise African marriages unless a reference book was produced. All sorts of restrictions are imposed upon Africans under the pass laws. For example, in almost every municipal area Africans are not allowed to be in the streets after 11 p.m. unless they have a special pass from an employer. Under this system, thousands of innocent and respectable Africans are arrested, flung into kwela-kwelas, detained in jail and cruelly ill-treated.
>
> The pass law is the basis and cornerstone of the system of oppression and exploitation in this country. It is a device to ensure cheap labour for

the mines and the farms. It is a badge of slavery in terms whereof all sorts of insults and humiliations may be committed on Africans by members of the ruling class. It is because of these reasons that the Congress has always regarded the pass laws as the principal target of the struggle for freedom. It is because of these reasons that African leaders, progressives, Liberals, and even Government Commissions have repeatedly condemned the system as the source of dangerous, explosive and racial tensions. It is also because of this fact that the Congress has chosen the extension of the pass laws to African women as a major issue of national importance. The issue is perfectly clear. The government has decided that we shall carry passes. Must we accept this deception? Definitely not! To do so, would be to expose the African Women to all the evils that we have referred to above. We would lose our honour, betray our comrades at Winburg, Lichtenburg and in numerous other towns and villages throughout the country where the daughters of Africa are putting up a glorious struggle in defence of their rights. When the rights of a people are taken away from them and even liberties are being crushed, the only way that is open to them is to mobilise the masses of the people affected to stand up and fight those injustices. *The immediate issue facing us, therefore, is to organise all the various organisations of African women and individuals against this inhuman and wicked decision of the Government. Only direct mass action will deter the Government and stop it from proceeding with its cruel laws.* It is in recognition of these women of South Africa who have launched a National Campaign against the extension of the Pass Laws [that] numerous local and national demonstrations have already been staged with amazing success. In the face of numerous difficulties, more than 50 000 women of all races from town and village took part in these demonstrations. The remarkable successes we have gained and victories we have achieved so far, and the extent in which the women have entered the campaign, reveal that the democratic forces in this country can stop and even defeat the forces of reaction if we work hard enough. We have made an excellent start. The historic Pretoria demonstrations of October last year including 30 000 women constitute an important landmark in our struggle against injustice and will remain the source of tremendous inspiration for many years to come. STRIJDOM, STOP AND THINK FOR YOU HAVE AROUSED THE WRATH OF THE WOMEN OF SOUTH AFRICA and that wrath might put you and your evil deeds out of action sooner than you expect. In spite of the remarkable victories we have won, there are still some serious weaknesses in our movement. 50 000 women is still a very small number in a population of 12½ million. More women must be brought into the anti-pass movement in order that the fight should be organised and concerted. The movement against the passes is still primarily centered in the big cities and sufficient work has not been done on the country dorps, on the farms and in the reserves. In these places the organisation is comparatively weak and the government has taken advantage of the situation and is busy issuing reference books. The aim is to isolate the stronger areas and thereafter to concentrate all its resources to crush opposition in the cities. We must immediately deal with this situation. I would suggest the appointment in each province of a number of full-time organisers who will visit various areas, talk to women, establish committees and bring out mass opposition to the scheme. We strongly condemn and reject the passes and we shall fight it with all the resources at our disposal to the bitter end, [and] at the same time we must, as far as possible, avoid reckless and isolated action. Action taken in one isolated place and without sufficient work being done and without proper co-ordination may be disastrous to the movement. It may give the government the opportunity to concentrate all its resources in crushing resistance in that local place, in the victimisation of the active fighters in that area and the crushing of resistance before it begins in other areas. We must learn to place and to co-ordinate beforehand so that we might strike fatal blows at the enemy when the time comes.

To ensure the defeat of the nationalist government we must work together for greater unity amongst the African people and the broadest possible alliance embracing the Congress movement, the non-Congressites and all those who oppose apartheid. The Manyano women, the National Council for African Women, the Mothers Welfare Organisation, religious, sporting, political and otherwise, should be invited to enter the campaign against the Nationalist government. In this way our movement will become a mighty movement for the defeat of the Nationalist government during our lifetime.

The Minister of Native Affairs has announced that African women will in future be requested to pay poll-tax. This decision has three objectives: firstly it is intended to force the African Women to pay for the cost of Apartheid. Secondly, it is intended to answer the attack on Nationalists by the United Party to the effect that the Nationalists are spending more money on Africans than the U.P. ever spent. Thirdly and most important it is an election stunt on the part of the Nationalists. We will fight against this move.

We [live] in momentous times. We [live] at a time when the oppressed people all over the world are rebelling against colonialism and oppression. We are going through a period when some of these people have bravely fought and won their independence. But there are also hours of serious danger. The imperialists, reading that their days are numbered, are becoming more desperate and restless. The unlawful aggression in Egypt by the English, French and Israelite armies is an act of aggression and brings the danger of fear very close to our shores. In such dangerous times it becomes the duty of the women of our country to put the question of peace [forward]. We stand for peace in Africa and the rest of the world. We stand for disarmament and the abolition of atomic weapons; we are against military blocks and pacts. We ask the executive Committee of the Congress to demand the withdrawal of foreign troops from Egypt, and the end of military operations which seek to end the independence of Egypt.

[...]

It is fitting that I should close this address by rendering our heartiest congratulations to the brave daughters of Winburg who put up such a united and gallant fight against the passes earlier this year. It is in Winburg that the passes for women were introduced. It is also in this place that direct mass action was taken for the first time against the passes for women. The whole of South Africa was impressed by the heroism of the women of Winburg. The reverses we suffered there were more than compensated by the historic Pretoria march of 20 000 women on August the 9th this year. Strijdom! Your government now preach and practice colour discrimination. It can pass the most cruel and barbaric laws, it can deport leaders and break homes and families, but it will never stop the women of Africa in their forward march to FREEDOM DURING OUR LIFETIME.

To you daughters of Africa I say '*MALIBONGWE IGAMA BAKAKO-SIKAZI MALI-BONGWE!*' [Praise the name of women; praise them!]

In a 1956 *Drum* profile, Ezekiel Mphahlele described Ngoyi as a 'brilliant orator' who can 'toss an audience on her little finger' and 'get men grunting with shame and a feeling of smallness'. Ngoyi's discourse, he added, 'always teems with vivid figures of speech: Mrs Ngoyi will say: "We don't want men who wear skirts under their trousers. If they don't want to act, let us women exchange garments with them.'"[9]

In this more formal address, Ngoyi resurrects the phrase 'badge of slavery' to describe the passbook.[10] The image deftly exposes the reprehensible nature of the government's proposed pass laws, which they had tried to defend as a means of managing urbanisation.

The speech presents a mix of both practical solutions and inspiring rhetoric, with Ngoyi emphasising the need for women to 'get to work'. The words are infused with a sense of 'busyness', which mirrors the 'bundles on bundles of energy' she reportedly displayed. Ngoyi, Mphahlele asserted, may not have been 'much of a political thinker', but she 'gets down to the job'.[11] In this address, she sets out a clear path of action, calling for the establishment of communication networks and cautioning against solitary protest. The tactic – of staging simultaneous protests in different geographic regions – proved to be one of the key strategies of the liberation movement.

At the same time, the defiant, direct address to Strijdom echoes the statements made at the Pretoria buildings, ensuring that the historic moment continued to gather momentum. 'STRIJDOM,' Ngoyi warns, 'STOP AND THINK FOR YOU HAVE AROUSED THE WRATH OF THE WOMEN OF SOUTH AFRICA'. The speech is also notable for its optimistic tone; for its focus on women's successes, however small; for the hope that Strijdom will be neutralised sooner than he expects; and for the ardent call for 'freedom during our lifetime'.

Despite this defiant optimism and the fact that by 1958 there had been no fewer than forty-five anti-pass demonstrations,[12] the government did not repeal the detested pass laws for another thirty years – an event that Ngoyi didn't live to witness. Her European tour and the glorious 1956 protest were likely the high points of her life. In the period that followed, the state made her existence increasingly difficult. At the end of the year, she was arrested and accused of treason along with another 156 dissidents. During the four-year-long Treason Trial, she endured a harsh period of solitary confinement. Thereafter the state proceeded to silence her by imposing one banning order after another. Hilda Bernstein notes that 'for 18 years, this brilliant and beautiful woman spent most of her time in a tiny house, silenced, struggling to earn money by doing sewing and with her great energies totally suppressed'.[13] Hers was indeed a fight to the 'bitter end'.

Robert Sobukwe

Opening address at the Africanist inaugural convention,
Orlando Communal Hall, Johannesburg, 4 April 1959

The figure of Robert Sobukwe hovers on the outskirts of history. During his
lifetime, he was also always set apart. He was held under a specially created
clause, the 'Robert Sobukwe Clause', which allowed the state to detain him
indefinitely for no reason at all. And on Robben Island, where he was imprisoned between 1963 and 1969, he was separated from other political prisoners,
because he was deemed too dangerous. He occupied an isolated two-roomed
dwelling on a fenced-off, bleak part of the island. Similarly, his role in the
country's history doesn't fit neatly into mainstream narratives; as Grahame
Hayes points out, the ANC government has 'done much to airbrush him out of
the freedom struggle'.[1] But as the founder of the Pan Africanist Congress (PAC),
whose ideas influenced Steve Biko and the Black Consciousness Movement,
his role is important, if only for the impact these movements had on the
ANC's trajectory.

Born in 1924 in Graaff-Reinet, Sobukwe overcame his humble beginnings
(his father worked as a labourer and his mother was a domestic worker and
cook) and he received a bursary from the Department of Education after
completing his schooling. This opened the door to Fort Hare University, where
the twenty-three-year-old Sobukwe developed a keen interest in literature
and enrolled in a BA, majoring in English, Xhosa and Native Administration
in 1947. As it had for a number of other African leaders (Govan Mbeki, Oliver
Tambo and Nelson Mandela had preceded him), Fort Hare provided an induc-
tion into politics for the 'serious-minded' Sobukwe.[2] By his own admission,
he had little interest in politics before attending Fort Hare, but a mere year
after enrolling – the same year in which the NP defeated Smuts – he joined
the newly established ANC Youth League and launched a daily newsletter,
Beware, along with three peers. The newsletter, which called for action against
apartheid, was stuck up on campus noticeboards late at night so that all
students could read the calls for mobilisation the following morning.

He also became known for holding radical weekend and evening meetings,
where he delivered fiery speeches. A fellow student, Dennis Siwisa, remembers
him as an 'orator of mean repute' who 'was always called up to make speeches,
and no meeting ... would be regarded as having ended until or unless Robert

had spoken.[3] A natural leader, Sobukwe was elected as president of the Students' Representative Council in 1949. That same year, in the first major speech of which there is a record, Sobukwe spoke with passion about the need to fight for the liberation of Africa 'within our lifetime'. 'We are pro-Africa,' he told his audience. 'We breathe, we dream, we live Africa.'[4] These kinds of events resulted in the eventual banning of the ANC Youth League on campus.

After university, he worked first as a teacher and then as a lecturer in African Studies at the University of the Witwatersrand (where he acquired the nickname 'Prof'). He played a pivotal role in the Defiance Campaign (for which he was temporarily suspended from his teaching post), and in 1957 he became the editor of *The Africanist* newspaper, using this position to criticise the ANC for its collaboration with what he termed 'liberal-left-multi-racialists'.[5]

Sobukwe's stance led to his gradual dissociation from the ANC, and the formation of the breakaway PAC. In the late 1950s, the Congress leadership was compromised by the Treason Trial and the organisation was beginning to show signs of strain. Beset with administrative and financial challenges, it also had to contend with internal ideological conflict. Together with Josias Madzunya and Potlako Leballo, Sobukwe became increasingly disillusioned with the ANC's cooperation with white communists in particular, believing that its multiracial approach was ineffective in fostering unity among Africans and amounted to collaboration in their own oppression. The ANC Africanists were further concerned that the tension in the organisation would make it vulnerable to communist opportunists. The ANC had, in their view, strayed from the organisation's original policy and adopted a class struggle at the expense of African nationalism. After a failed leadership coup at a Transvaal conference in 1948, where the chairman Oliver Tambo outwitted them, the Africanists announced their intention to split from the ANC, seeing themselves as the custodians of the movement's original beliefs.

The following year, at the culmination of a three-day conference, the PAC was launched. The inaugural event was held, no doubt deliberately, at the Orlando Community Hall, a favoured site for official ANC meetings. Both Hastings Banda and Kenneth Kaunda had been invited to open the conference – a symbolic gesture, since both were in British colonial prisons at the time. In acknowledgement of his de facto leadership status, it fell on Sobukwe to give the opening address. In it, he delivered what would become some of the founding tenets of the new organisation's political policy:

22

We are living today. Sons and Daughters of the Soil, fighters in the cause of African freedom, in an era that is pregnant with untold possibilities for good and evil. In the course of the past two years we have seen man breaking asunder, with dramatic suddenness, the chains that have bound his mind, solving problems which for ages it has been regarded as sacrilege even to attempt to solve. The tremendous epoch-making scientific achievements in the exploration of space, with man-made satellites orbiting the earth, the new and interesting discoveries made in the Geophysical Year, the production of rust-resistant strains of wheat in the field of agriculture, the amazing discoveries in the fields of medicine, chemistry and physics – all these mean that man is acquiring a better knowledge of his environment and is well on the way to establishing absolute control over that environment.

However, in spite of all these rapid advances in the material and physical world, man appears to be either unwilling or unable to solve the problem of social relations between man and man. Because of this failure on the part of man, we see the world split into two large hostile blocks represented by the USA and the Soviet Union respectively. These two blocks are engaged in terrible competition, use tough language and tactics, and employ brinkmanship stunts which have the whole world heading for a nervous breakdown. They each are armed with terrible weapons of destruction and continue to spend millions of pounds in the production of more and more of these weapons. In spite of all the diplomatic talk of co-existence, these blocks each behave as though they did not believe that co-existence was possible.

Africa's position

The question then arises, where does Africa fit into this picture and where, particularly, do we African nationalists, we Africanists in South Africa, fit in?

There is no doubt that with the liquidation of Western imperialism and colonialism in Asia, the Capitalist market has shrunk considerably. As a result, Africa has become the happy hunting ground of adventuristic capital. There is again a scramble for Africa, and both the Soviet Union and the United States of America are trying to win the loyalty of the African states. Africa is being wooed with more ardour than she has ever been. There is a lot of flirting going on, of course, some Africans flirting with the Soviet camp, and others with the American camp. In some cases, the courtship has reached a stage where the parties are going out together, and they probably hold hands in the dark, but nowhere has it yet reached a stage where the parties can kiss in public without blushing.

This wooing occurs at a time when the whole continent of Africa is in labour, suffering the pangs of a new birth, and everybody is looking anxiously and expectantly towards Africa to see, as our people so aptly put it, *ukuthi iyozala nkomoni* (what creature will come forth). We are being wooed internationally at a time when in South Africa, the naked forces of savage *Herrenvolkism* are running riot; when a determined effort is being made to annihilate the African people through systematic starvation; at a time when brutal attempts are being made to retard, dwarf and stunt the mental development of a whole people through organised 'miseducation'; at a time when thousands of our people roam the streets in search of work and are being told by the foreign ruler to go back to a 'home' which he has assigned them, whether that means the break-up of their families or not; at a time when the distinctive badge of slavery and humiliation, the '*dom* pass' is being extended from the African male dog to the African female bitch. It is at this time, when fascist tyranny has reached its zenith in South Africa, that Africa's loyalty is being competed for. And the question is, what is our answer?

The African leaders of the continent have given our answer, Mr Speaker and children of the soil. Dr Kwame Nkrumah has repeatedly stated that in international affairs, Africa wishes to pursue a policy of positive neutrality, allying herself to neither the existing blocks but, in the words of Dr Nnamdi Azikiwe of Nigeria, remaining 'independent in all things but neutral in none that affect the destiny of Africa'. Mr Tom Mboya of Kenya has expressed himself more forthrightly, declaring that it is not the intention of African states to change one master (western imperialism) for another (Soviet hegemony).

We endorse the views of African leaders on this point. But we must point out that we are not blind to the fact that the countries – which pursue a policy of planned state economy – have outstripped, in industrial development, those that follow the path of private enterprise. Today, China is industrially far ahead of India. Unfortunately, however, this rapid industrial development has been accompanied in all cases by a rigid totalitarianism notwithstanding Mao Tse Tung's 'Hundred Flowers' announcement. Africanists reject totalitarianism in any form and accept political democracy as understood in the west. We also reject the economic exploitation of the many for the benefit of a few. We accept as policy the equitable distribution of wealth aiming, as far as I am concerned, to equality of income which to me is the only basis on which the slogan 'equal opportunities' can be founded.

Borrowing then the best from the East and the best from the West, we nonetheless retain and maintain our distinctive personality and refuse to be the satraps or stooges of either power block.

Relation to states in Africa

Quoting George Padmore's book, *Pan Africanism or Communism*, may state our relation to the States of Africa precisely and briefly. Discussing the future of Africa, Padmore observes that 'there is a growing feeling among politically conscious Africans throughout the continent that their destiny is one, that what happens in one part of Africa to Africans must affect Africans living in other parts'.

We honour Ghana as the first independent state in modern Africa which, under the courageous nationalist leadership of Dr Nkrumah and the Convention People's Party, has actively interested itself in the liberation of the whole continent from White domination, and has held out the vision of a democratic United States of Africa. We regard it as the sacred duty of every African state to strive ceaselessly and energetically for the creation of a United States of Africa, stretching from Cape to Cairo, Morocco to Madagascar.

The days of small, independent countries are gone. Today we have, on the one hand, great powerful countries of the world; America and Russia cover huge tracts of land territorially and number hundreds of millions in population. On the other hand, the small weak independent countries of Europe are beginning to realise that for their own survival, they have to form military and economic federations, hence NATO and the European market.

Besides the sense of a common historical fate that we share with the other countries of Africa, it is imperative, for purely practical reasons, that the whole of Africa be united into a single unit, centrally controlled. Only in that way can we solve the immense problems that face the continent.

National movements in Africa

It is for the reasons stated above that we admire, bless and identify ourselves with the entire nationalist movements in Africa. They are the core, the basic units, the individual cells of that large organism envisaged, namely, the United States of Africa; a union of free, sovereign independent democratic states of Africa.

For the lasting peace of Africa and the solution of the economic, social and political problems of the continent, there needs must be a democratic principle. This means that White supremacy, under whatever guise it manifests itself, must be destroyed. And that is what the nationalists on the continent are setting out to do. They all are agreed that the African majority must rule. In the African context, it is the overwhelming African majority that will mould and shape the content of democracy. Allow me to quote Dr Du Bois, the father of Pan Africanism: 'Most men in the world,' writes Du Bois, 'are coloured. A belief in humanity means a belief in coloured men. The future of the world will, in all reasonable possibility, be what coloured men make it.' As for the world, so for Africa. The future of Africa will be what Africans make it.

The race question

And now for the thorny question of race. I do not wish to give a lengthy and learned dissertation on race. Suffice it to say that even those scientists who do recognise the existence of separate races have to admit that there are borderline cases which will not fit into any of the three races of mankind.

All scientists agree that all men can trace their ancestry back to the first Homo Sapiens, that man is distinguished from other mammals and also from earlier types of man by the nature of his intelligence. The structure of the body of man provides evidence to prove the biological unity of the human species. All scientists agree that there is no 'race' that is superior to another, and there is no 'race' that is inferior to others.

The Africanists take the view that there is only one race to which we all belong, and that is the human race. In our vocabulary, therefore, the word 'race' as applied to man, has no plural form. We do, however, admit the existence of observable physical differences between various groups of people, but these differences are the result of a number of factors, chief among which has been geographical isolation.

In Africa, the myth of race has been propounded and propagated by the imperialists and colonialists of Europe, in order to facilitate and justify their inhuman exploitation of the indigenous people of the land. It is from this myth of race with its attendant claims of cultural superiority that the doctrine of white supremacy stems. Thus it is that an ex-engine driver can think of himself as fully qualified to be the head of the government of an African state, but refuse to believe that a highly educated black doctor, more familiar with Western culture than the

White premier is, cannot even run a municipal council. I do not wish to belabour this point. Time is precious. Let me close discussion of this topic by declaring, on behalf of the Africanists, that with UNESCO we hold that 'every man is his brother's keeper. For every man is a piece of the continent, a part of the main, because he is involved in mankind'.

In South Africa

In South Africa we recognise the existence of national groups which are the result of geographical origin within a certain area as well as a shared historical experience of these groups. The Europeans are a foreign minority group which has exclusive control of political, economic, social and military power. It is the dominant group. It is the plotting group, responsible for the pernicious doctrine of White Supremacy which has resulted in the humiliation and degradation of the indigenous African people. It is this group which has dispossessed the African people of their land and with arrogant conceit, has set itself up as the 'guardians', the 'trustees' of the Africans. It is this group which conceives the African as a child nation composed of Boys and Girls, ranging in age from 120 years to one day. It is this group which, after 300 years, can still state with brazen effrontery that the Native, the Bantu, the Kaffir is still backward and savage etc. But they still want to remain 'guardians', 'trustees' and what have you, of the African people. In short, it this group which has mismanaged affairs in South Africa just as their kith and kin are mismanaging affairs in Europe. It is from this group that the most rabid race baiters and agitators come. It is members of this group who, whenever they meet in their Parliament, say things which agitate the hearts of millions of peace-loving Africans. This is the group which turns out thousands of experts on that new South African Science – the Native mind.

Then there is the Indian foreign minority group. This group came to this country not as imperialists or colonialists, but as indentured labourers. In the South African set-up of today, this group is an oppressed minority. But there are some members of this group, the merchant class in particular, who have become tainted with the virus of cultural supremacy and national arrogance. This class identifies itself by and large with the oppressor but, significantly, this is the group which provides the political leadership of the Indian people in South Africa. And all that the politics of this class have meant up to now is the preservation and defence of the sectional interests of the Indian merchant class. The downtrodden, poor 'stinking coolies' of Natal, who, alone, as a result of the pressure of material conditions, can identify themselves with the indigenous African majority in the struggle to overthrow White supremacy, have not yet produced their leadership. We hope they will do so soon.

The Africans constitute the indigenous group and form the majority of the population. They are the most ruthlessly exploited and are subjected to humiliation, degradation and insult.

Now it is our contention that true democracy can be established in South Africa and on the continent as a whole, only when White supremacy has been destroyed. And the illiterate and semi-literate African masses constitute the key and centre and content of any struggle for true democracy in South Africa. And the African people can be organised only under the banner of African nationalism in an All-African Organisation, where they will by themselves formulate policies and programmes and decide on the methods of struggle without interference from either so-called left-wing or right-wing groups, of the minorities who arrogantly appropriate to themselves the right to plan and think for Africans.

We wish to emphasise that the freedom of the African means the freedom of all in South Africa, the European included, because only the African can guarantee the establishment of a genuine democracy in which all men will be citizens of a common state and will live and be governed as individuals and not as distinctive sectional groups.

Our ultimate goals

In conclusion, I wish to state that the Africanists do not at all subscribe to the fashionable doctrine of South African exceptionalism. Our contention is that South Africa is an integral part of the indivisible whole that is Africa. She cannot solve her problems in isolation from and with utter disregard of the rest of the continent.

It is precisely for that reason that we reject both apartheid and so-called multi-racialism as solutions of our socio-economic problems. Apart from the number of reasons and arguments that can be advanced against apartheid, we take our stand on the principle that Africa is one and desires to be one, and nobody, I repeat, nobody has the right to balkanise our land.

Against multi-racialism we have this objection: that the history of South Africa has fostered group prejudices and antagonisms, and if we have to maintain the same group exclusiveness, parading under the term of multi-racialism, we shall be transporting to the new Africa these very antagonisms and conflicts. Further, multi-racialism is in fact a pandering to European bigotry and arrogance. It is a method of safeguarding white interests irrespective of population figures. In that sense it is a complete negation of democracy. To us the term 'multi-racialism' implies that there are such basic insuperable differences between the various national groups here that the best course is to keep them permanently distinctive in a kind of democratic apartheid. That to us is racialism multiplied, which probably is what the term truly connotes.

We aim, politically, at government of the Africans by the Africans for Africans, with everybody who owes his only loyalty to Africa and who is prepared to accept the democratic rule of an African majority being regarded as an African. We guarantee no minority rights, because we think in terms of individuals, not groups.

Economically we aim at the rapid extension of industrial development in order to alleviate pressure on the land, which is what progress means in terms of modern society. We stand committed to a policy guaranteeing the most equitable distribution of wealth.

Socially, we aim at the full development of the human personality and a ruthless uprooting and outlawing of all forms or manifestations of the racial myth. To sum it up, we stand for an Africanist Socialist Democracy.

Here is a tree rooted in African soil, nourished with waters from the rivers of Africa. Come and sit under its shade and become, with us, the leaves of the same branch and the branches of the same tree.

Sons and Daughters of Africa, I declare this inaugural Convention of the Africanists open. *IZWE LETHU!*

The speech drew 'tumultuous applause'[6] from the audience and is regarded as an incisive clarification of the philosophy of Africanism. Sobukwe identifies two enemy targets: apartheid and the contemporary approach to the fight against apartheid. To stress the urgency of the situation – and in turn portray the reaction to it as inadequate – he uses strong language to describe the current context. The African faces annihilation on account of 'miseducation', foreign rule and dehumanisation. As did Lilian Ngoyi, he focuses on the pass system, referring to the 'distinctive badge of slavery' or '*dom* pass' (literally 'dumb pass') currently being 'extended from the African male dog to the African female bitch'. The pass system would later launch the PAC's most significant political protest – culminating in the Sharpeville massacre the following year.

As a lecturer, Sobukwe was of course accustomed to public speaking. His deep love of literature is evident in the many literary conventions that animate this speech. He refers to the whole world 'heading for a nervous breakdown' in reaction to global politics, and he appeals to his audience's sense of humour with the extended metaphor of Africa's wooing by the East and the West: 'In some cases, the courtship has reached a stage where the parties are going out together, and they probably hold hands in the dark, but nowhere has it yet reached a stage where the parties can kiss in public without blushing.'

The Africanist position on race – dismissed out of hand as crude reverse racism in local reports – is elucidated in a much-quoted line by admirers of the speech: 'There is only one race to which we all belong, and that is the human race.' Recognising and focusing on race, Sobukwe suggests, plays into the hands of the oppressor, allowing for the growth of sectional interests that undermine the nationalist project. Instead, the Africanists call for a 'government of the Africans by the Africans for Africans, with everybody who owes his only loyalty to Africa and who is prepared to accept the democratic rule of an African majority being regarded as an African'. In a deft play on words, Sobukwe concludes that Africanists support non-racialism over multiracialism since the latter is in fact 'racialism multiplied'.

The speech also embraces pan-Africanism, paying homage to intellectual forefathers such as Du Bois and Nkrumah. 'The days of small, independent countries are gone', Sobukwe claims, dismissing the 'fashionable doctrine of South African exceptionalism'. The pan-African theme was mirrored in the hall decor, which was adorned with slogan-bearing banners from the speech, including 'Africa for Africans. Cape to Cairo, Morocco to Madagascar' and 'Forward to the United States of Africa'.[7]

The breakaway conference was covered by *The Times* of London, which positioned the PAC as 'extremist black nationalists' in relation to the more 'moderate' ANC.[8] It's likely that, over the next few decades, with the radical PAC in the shadows, the international community found it easier to accept the ANC as the liberation movement of choice.

According to Benjamin Pogrund, a new 'strength and stature' was evident in Sobukwe's inaugural speech, due perhaps to his eventual acceptance of his political calling. Just prior to the conference, he'd been offered a full and handsomely paid professorship from Rhodes University, and he was divided over whether to pursue an academic or political career. The Rhodes offer came with conditions – that Sobukwe refrain from political activities – but it was also a significant promotion from his current position. He chose politics, and the certainty over his new path is reflected in the confidence of the speech: '[H]e was scholarly as always,' Pogrund claimed, 'but there was now also a fluency and passion which put it among the finest oratory I had heard.'[9]

Harold Macmillan

'Wind of Change' speech, address to Parliament,
3 February 1960[1]

The early months of 1960 were full of drama in South Africa – a presage of what the decade held in store for the country. On 20 January, the National Party's third prime minister, Hendrik Verwoerd, announced that the NP government, now firmly entrenched after winning a clear majority in the 1958 election, would hold an all-white referendum to gauge the country's view on becoming a republic. This was a significant departure from the 1948 policy, when, strategically, the NP didn't campaign for a republic. Interestingly, Verwoerd withheld his party's position on whether the country was to become a republic inside or outside the Commonwealth until a later date.

Relations between Britain and South Africa grew increasingly tense during the following months, triggered no doubt by British prime minister Harold Macmillan's frank remarks about South Africa's domestic policies in his famous 'Wind of Change' speech.

The speech was the much-anticipated culmination of Macmillan's six-week tour of British Africa, undertaken to influence future relations between the Commonwealth and African nations. The tour, reminiscent of those by British royalty, was a counterpart to Macmillan's Asian and Australasian tour undertaken in 1958, and it was the first of its kind by a British prime minister in Africa.

Macmillan's reception on the continent was mixed. While Nigeria's welcome had been cordial, the Ghanaian press was reportedly hostile, and there were demonstrations outside the building of his official welcome in Blantyre in Nyasaland (now Malawi).[2] During his visits to the northern countries, Macmillan met with a range of representatives, including African nationalists – although this wasn't the case when he travelled down to South Africa, where a combination of excessive security control, and a likely desire to avoid offending his hosts, prevented him from doing so.

Instead, under tight rein, an 'irritated'[3] Macmillan was taken down a mineshaft, to the Voortrekker Monument, and to Meadowlands, the 'model' township to which Sophiatown residents had been forcibly relocated. He was treated to a range of artificial cultural displays, including a Sotho choir performance of Purcell and a kingly offering of a leopard-skin kaross from a supposed Sekukuni paramount chief.[4] This attempt to extol the virtues of apartheid was not altogether successful, however, and there were reports of protestors bearing placards with slogans such as 'Mac, we've never had it so bad',[5] in reference to the prime minister's speech in which he famously stated that Britons 'have never had it so good', describing the UK's post-war economic boom. Others urged him to 'please visit our leaders' and declared that 'Apartheid will fail. Not even Mac can save it.'[6] It seems clear that both parties viewed the tour as a PR opportunity to gain Britain's approval.

The sixty-five-year-old prime minister spent a few days in Cape Town at Verwoerd's official residence, Groote Schuur, before delivering what is sometimes described as the finest speech of his career – a 'fitting climax to a historic tour', according to the *Rand Daily Mail*.[7] Macmillan spoke on 3 February to both Houses of Parliament in the Old Assembly dining room, a dark wood-panelled room overlooked by paintings commemorating South Africa's unification. The occasion was expected to be celebratory, because it coincided with the fiftieth anniversary of the Union. There was a festive air in Cape Town and the streets were full of flags.[8] Macmillan began with an appropriate tribute:

It is a great privilege to be invited to address the Members of both Houses of Parliament in the Union of South Africa. It is a unique privilege to do so in 1960 just half a century after the Parliament of the Union came to birth. I am most grateful to you all for giving me this opportunity and I am especially grateful to your Prime Minister who invited me to visit this country and arranged for me to address you here today.

My tour of Africa – parts of Africa – the first ever made by a British Prime Minister in office, is now alas nearing its end, but it is fitting that it should culminate in the Union Parliament here in Cape Town, in this historic city so long Europe's gateway to the Indian Ocean, and to the East.

As in all the other countries that I have visited my stay has been all too short.

I wish it had been possible for me to spend a longer time here, to see more of your beautiful country and to get to know more of your people, but in the past week I have travelled many hundreds of miles and met many people in all walks of life.

I have been able to get at least some idea of the great beauty of your countryside, with its farms and its forests, mountains and rivers, and the clear skies and wide horizons of the veldt. I have also seen some of your great and thriving cities, and I am most grateful to your Government for all the trouble they have taken in making the arrangements which have enabled me to see so much in so short a time.

Some of the younger members of my staff have told me that it has been a heavy programme, but I can assure you that my wife and I have enjoyed every moment of it. Moreover, we have been deeply moved by the warmth of our welcome.

Wherever we have been in town or in country, we have been received in a spirit of friendship and affection which has warmed our hearts, and we value this the more because we know it is an expression of your goodwill, not just to ourselves but to all the people of Britain.

It is, as I have said, a special privilege for me to be here in 1960 when you are celebrating what I might call the golden wedding of the Union. At such a time it is natural and right that you should pause to take stock of your position, to look back at what you have achieved, to look forward to what lies ahead.

In the 50 years of their nationhood the people of South Africa have built a strong economy founded upon a healthy agriculture and thriving and resilient industries. During my visit I have been able to see something of your mining industry, on which the prosperity of the country is so firmly based. I have seen your Iron and Steel Corporation and visited your Council of Scientific and Industrial Research at Pretoria.

These two bodies, in their different ways, are symbols of a lively, forward-looking and expanding economy. I have seen the great city of Durban, with its wonderful port, and the skyscrapers of Johannesburg, standing where 70 years ago there was nothing but the open veldt. I have seen, too, the fine cities of Pretoria and Bloemfontein. This afternoon I hope to see something of your wine-growing industry, which so far I have only admired as a consumer.

No one could fail to be impressed with the immense material progress which has been achieved. That all this has been accomplished in so short a time is a striking testimony to the skill, energy and initiative of your people. We in Britain are proud of the contribution we have made to this remarkable achievement. Much of it has been financed by British capital. According to the recent survey made by the Union Government, nearly two-thirds of the overseas investment outstanding in the Union at the end of 1956 was British. That is after two staggering wars which have bled our economy white.

But that is not all. We have developed trade between us to our common advantage, and our economies are now largely interdependent. You export to us raw materials, food and gold. We in return send you consumer goods or capital equipment. We take a third of all your exports and we supply a third of all your imports. This broad traditional pattern of investment and trade has been maintained in spite of the changes brought by the development of our two economies, and it gives me great encouragement to reflect that the economies of both our countries, while expanding rapidly, have yet remained interdependent and capable of sustaining one another.

If you travel round this country by train you will travel on South African rails made by Iscor. If you prefer to fly you can go in a British Viscount. Here is a true partnership, living proof of the interdependence between nations. Britain has always been your best customer and, as your new industries develop, we believe that we can be your best partners too.

In addition to building this strong economy within your own borders, you have also played your part as an independent nation in the world.

As a soldier in the first world war, and as a Minister in Sir Winston Churchill's Government in the second, I know personally the value of the contribution which your forces made to victory in the cause of freedom. I know something too, of the inspiration which General Smuts brought to us in Britain in our darkest hours.

Again in the Korean crisis you played your full part. Thus in the testing times of war or aggression your statesmen and your soldiers have made their influence felt far beyond the African continent. In the period of reconstruction, when Dr Malan was your Prime Minister, your resources greatly assisted the recovery of the sterling area. In the post-war world now, in the no less difficult tasks of peace, your leaders in industry, commerce and finance continue to be prominent in world affairs to-day. Your readiness to provide technical assistance to the less well-developed parts of Africa is of immense help to the countries that receive it.

It is also a source of strength to your friends in the Commonwealth and elsewhere in the Western world. You are collaborating in the work of the Commission for Technical Co-operation in Africa South of the Sahara, and now in the United Nations Economic Commission for Africa. Your Minister for External Affairs intends to visit Ghana later this year. All this proves your determination, as the most advanced industrial country of the continent, to play your part in the new Africa of today.

Sir, as I have travelled round the Union I have found everywhere, as I expected, a deep preoccupation with what is happening in the rest of the African continent. I understand and sympathise with your interest in these events, and your anxiety about them. Ever since the break-up of the Roman Empire one of the constant facts of political life in Europe has been the emergence of independent nations. They have come into existence over the centuries in different forms, with different kinds of Government, but all have been inspired by a deep, keen feeling of nationalism which has grown as the nations have grown.

In the twentieth century and especially since the end of the war, the processes which gave birth to the nation states of Europe have been repeated all over the world. We have seen the awakening of national consciousness in peoples who have for centuries lived in dependence upon some other Power. Fifteen years ago this movement spread through Asia. Many countries there of different races and civilisations pressed their claim to an independent national life.

Today the same thing is happening in Africa and the most striking of all the impressions I have formed since I left London a month ago is of the strength of this African national consciousness. In different places it takes different forms but it is happening everywhere. The wind of change is blowing through this continent and, whether we like it or not, this growth of national consciousness is a political fact. We must all accept it as a fact, and our national policies must take account of it.

Of course you understand this better than anyone. You are sprung from Europe, the home of nationalism, and here in Africa you have yourselves created a new nation. Indeed, in the history of our times yours will be recorded as the first of the African nationalisms, and this tide of national consciousness which is now rising in Africa is a fact for which you and we and the other nations of the Western world are ultimately responsible.

For its causes are to be found in the achievements of Western civilisation, in the pushing forward of the frontiers of knowledge, in the applying of science in the service of human needs, in the expanding of food production, in the speeding and multiplying of the means of communication, and perhaps, above all, the spread of education.

As I have said, the growth of national consciousness in Africa is a political fact and we must accept it as such. That means, I would judge, that we must come to terms with it. I sincerely believe that if we cannot do so we may imperil the precarious balance between the East and West on which the peace of the world depends. The world today is divided into three main groups. First there are what we call the Western Powers. You in South Africa and we in Britain belong to this group, together with our friends and Allies in other parts of the Commonwealth. In the United States and in Europe we call it the Free World.

Secondly there are the Communists – Russia and her Satellites in Europe and China, whose population will rise by the end of the next

10 years to the staggering total of 800 million. Thirdly, there are those parts of the world whose people are at present uncommitted either to Communism or to our Western ideas.

In this context we think first of Asia and then of Africa. As I see it the great issue in this second half of the Twentieth Century is whether the uncommitted peoples of Asia and Africa will swing to the East or to the West. Will they be drawn into the Communist camp? Or will the great experiments in self-government that are now being made in Asia and Africa, especially within the Commonwealth, prove so successful, and by their example so compelling that the balance will come down in favour of freedom and order and justice? The struggle is joined and it is a struggle for the minds of men. What is now on trial is much more than our military strength or our diplomatic and administrative skill. It is our way of life. The uncommitted nations want to see before they choose.

What can we show them to help them choose right? Each of the independent members of the Commonwealth must answer that question for itself. It is a basic principle of our modern Commonwealth that we respect each other's sovereignty in matters of internal policy. At the same time we must recognise that in this shrinking world in which we live to-day the internal policies of one nation may have effects outside it. We may sometimes be tempted to say to each other 'mind your own business', but in these days I would myself expand the old saying so that it runs: 'mind your own business but mind how it affects my business, too'.

Let me be very frank with you, my friends. What Governments and Parliaments in the United Kingdom have done since the war in according independence to India, Pakistan, Ceylon, Malaya and Ghana, and what they will do for Nigeria and other countries now nearing independence, all this, though we take full and sole responsibility for it, we do in the belief that it is the only way to establish the future of the Commonwealth and of the Free World on sound foundations.

All this of course is also of deep and close concern to you for nothing we do in this small world can be done in a corner or remain hidden. What we do today in West, Central and East Africa becomes known tomorrow to everyone in the Union, whatever his language, colour or traditions. Let me assure you, in all friendliness, that we are well aware of this and that we have acted and will act with full knowledge of the responsibility we have to all our friends.

Nevertheless I am sure you will agree that in our own areas of responsibility we must each do what we think right. What we think right derives from a long experience both of failure and success in the management of our own affairs. We have tried to learn and apply the lessons of our judgment of right and wrong.

Our justice is rooted in the same soil as yours – in Christianity and in the rule of law as the basis of a free society. This experience of our own explains why it has been our aim in the countries for which we have borne responsibility, not only to raise the material standards of living, but also to create a society which respects the rights of individuals, a society in which men are given the opportunity to grow to their full stature – and that must in our view include the opportunity to have an increasing share in political power and responsibility, a society in which individual merit and individual merit alone is the criterion for a man's advancement, whether political or economic.

Finally in countries inhabited by several different races it has been our aim to find means by which the community can become more of a community, and fellowship can be fostered between its various parts. This problem is by no means confined to Africa. Nor is it always a problem of a European minority. In Malaya, for instance, though there are Indian and European minorities, Malays and Chinese make up the great bulk of the population, and the Chinese are not much fewer in numbers than the Malays. Yet these two peoples must learn to live together in harmony and unity and the strength of Malaya as a nation will depend on the different contributions which the two races can make.

The attitude of the United Kingdom towards this problem was clearly expressed by the Foreign Secretary, Mr Selwyn Lloyd, speaking at the United Nations General Assembly on the 17th September, 1959. These were his words:

'In those territories where different races or tribes live side by side the task is to ensure that all the people may enjoy security and freedom and the chance to contribute as individuals to the progress and well being of these countries. We reject the idea of any inherent superiority of one race over another. Our policy therefore is non-racial. It offers a future in which Africans, Europeans, Asians, the peoples of the Pacific and others with whom we are concerned, will all play their full part as citizens in the countries where they live, and in which feelings of race will be submerged in loyalty to new nations'.

I have thought you would wish me to state plainly and with full candour the policy for which we in Britain stand. It may well be that in trying to do our duty as we see it we shall sometimes make difficulties

37

for you. If this proves to be so we shall regret it. But I know that even so you would not ask us to flinch from doing our duty.

You, too, will do your duty as you see it. I am well aware of the peculiar nature of the problems with which you are faced here in the Union of South Africa. I know the differences between your situation and that of most of the other States in Africa. You have here some 3 million people of European origin. This country is their home. It has been their home for many generations. They have no other.

The same is true of Europeans in Central and East Africa. In most other African States those who have come from Europe have come to work, to contribute their skills, perhaps to teach, but not to make a home.

The problems to which you as members of the Union Parliament have to address yourselves are very different from those which face the Parliaments of countries with homogenous populations. These are complicated and baffling problems. It would be surprising if your interpretation of your duty did not sometimes produce very different results from ours in terms of Government policies and actions.

As a fellow member of the Commonwealth it is our earnest desire to give South Africa our support and encouragement, but I hope you won't mind my saying frankly that there are some aspects of your policies which make it impossible for us to do this without being false to our own deep convictions about the political destinies of free men to which in our own territories we are trying to give effect.

I think we ought, as friends, to face together, without seeking to apportion credit or blame, the fact that in the world of today this difference of outlook lies between us.

I said that I was speaking as a friend. I can also claim to be speaking as a relation, for we Scots can claim family connexions with both the great European sections of your population, not only with the English-speaking people but with the Afrikaans-speaking as well. This is a point which hardly needs emphasis in Cape Town where you can see every day the statue of that great Scotsman, Andrew Murray. His work in the Dutch Reformed Church in the Cape, and the work of his son in the Orange Free State, was among Afrikaans-speaking people. There has always been a very close connexion between the Church of Scotland and the Church of the Netherlands. The Synod of Dort plays the same great part in the history of both. Many aspirants to the Ministry of Scotland, especially in the 17th and 18th Centuries, went to pursue their theological studies in the Netherlands.

Scotland can claim to have repaid the debt in South Africa. I am thinking particularly of the Scots in the Orange Free State. Not only the younger Andrew Murray, but also the Robertsons, the Frasers, the McDonalds – families which have been called the Free State clans who become burghers of the old Free State and whose descendants still play their part there.

But though I count myself a Scot my mother was an American, and the United States provides a valuable illustration of one of the main points which I have been trying to make in my remarks to-day. Its population, like yours, is of different strains and over the years most of those who have gone to North America have gone there in order to escape conditions in Europe which they found intolerable.

The Pilgrim Fathers were fleeing from persecution as Puritans and the Marylanders from persecution as Roman Catholics. Throughout the 19th Century a stream of immigrants flowed across the Atlantic to escape from poverty in their homelands, and in the 20th Century the United States have provided asylum for the victims of political oppression in Europe.

Thus for the majority of its inhabitants America has been a place of refuge, or place to which people went because they wanted to get away from Europe. It is not surprising, therefore, that for so many years a main objective of American statesmen, supported by the American public, was to isolate themselves from Europe, and with their great material strength, and the vast resources open to them, this might have seemed an attractive and practicable course. Nevertheless in the two world wars of this century they have found themselves unable to stand aside.

Twice their manpower in arms has streamed back across the Atlantic to shed its blood in those European struggles from which their ancestors thought they would escape by emigrating to the New World; and when the second war was over they were forced to recognise that in the small world of today isolationism is out of date and offers no assurance of security.

The fact is that in this modern world no country, not even the greatest, can live for itself alone. Nearly 2 000 years ago, when the whole of the civilised world was comprised within the confines of the Roman Empire, St. Paul proclaimed one of the great truths of history – we are all members one of another. During this 20th Century that eternal truth has taken on a new and exciting significance.

It has always been impossible for the individual man to live in isolation from his fellows, in the home, the tribe, the village, or the city. Today it is impossible for nations to live in isolation from one another.

What Dr John Donne said of individual men 300 years ago is true today of my country, your country, and all the countries of the world: 'Any man's death diminishes me, because I am involved in Mankind. And therefore never send to know for whom the bell tolls; it tolls for thee.'

All nations now are interdependent one upon another and this is generally realised throughout the Western world. I hope in due course the countries of Communism will recognise it too.

It was certainly with that thought in mind that I took the decision to visit Moscow about this time last year. Russia has been isolationist in her time and still has tendencies that way, but the fact remains that we must live in the same world with Russia and we must find a way of doing so. I believe that the initiative which we took last year has had some success, although grave difficulties may arise.

Nevertheless; I think nothing but good can come out of its extending contacts between individuals, contacts in trade and from the exchange of visitors.

I certainly do not believe in refusing to trade with people because you may happen to dislike the way they manage their internal affairs at home. Boycotts will never get you anywhere, and may I say in parenthesis that I deprecate the attempts that are being made to-day in Britain to organise the consumer boycott of South African goods. It has never been the practice, as far as I know, of any Government of the United Kingdom of whatever complexion to undertake or support campaigns of this kind designed to influence the internal politics of another Commonwealth country, and my colleagues in the United Kingdom deplore this proposed boycott and regard it as undesirable from every point of view. It can only have serious effects on Commonwealth relations, on trade, and lead to the ultimate detriment of others than those against whom it is aimed.

I said I was speaking of the interdependence of nations. The members of the Commonwealth feel particularly strongly the value of interdependence. They are as independent as any nation in this shrinking world can be, but they have voluntarily agreed to work together. They recognise that there may be and must be differences in their institutions; in their internal policies, and their membership does not imply the wish to express a judgment on these matters, or the need to impose a stifling uniformity. It is, I think, a help that there has never been question of any rigid constitution for the Commonwealth. Perhaps this is because we have got on well enough in the United Kingdom without a written constitution and tend to look suspiciously at them.

Whether that is so or not, it is quite clear that a rigid constitutional framework for the Commonwealth would not work.

At the first of the stresses and strains which are inevitable in this period of history, cracks would appear in the framework and the whole structure would crumble.

It is the flexibility of our Commonwealth institutions which gives them their strength.

Mr President, Mr Speaker, Honourable Ministers, Ladies and Gentlemen, I fear I have kept you a long time. I much welcome the opportunity to speak to this great audience. In conclusion may I say this. I have spoken frankly about the differences between our two countries in their approach to one of the great current problems with which each has to deal within its own sphere of responsibility.

These differences are well known. They are matters of public knowledge, indeed of public controversy, and I should have been less than honest if by remaining silent on them I had seemed to imply that they did not exist. But differences on one subject, important though it is, need not and should not impair our capacity to co-operate with one another in furthering the many practical interests which we share in common.

The independent members of the Commonwealth do not always agree on every subject. It is not a condition of their association that they should do so.

On the contrary the strength of our Commonwealth lies largely in the fact that it is a free association of independent sovereign States, each responsible for ordering its own affairs but co-operating in the pursuit of common aims and purposes in world affairs. Moreover these differences may be transitory. In time they may be resolved. Our duty is to see them in perspective against the background of our long association.

Of this at any rate I am certain – those of us who by grace of the electorate are temporarily in charge of affairs in your country and in mine, we fleeting transient phantoms in the great stage of history, we have no right to sweep aside on this account the friendship that exists between our countries, for that is the legacy of history. It is not ours alone to deal with as we wish. To adapt a famous phrase, it belongs to those who are living, but it also belongs to those who are dead and to those who are yet unborn. We must face the differences, but let us try to see beyond them down the long vista of the future.

I hope – indeed, I am confident – that in another 50 years we shall look back on the differences that exist between us now as matters of historical interest, for as time passes and one generation yields to another, human problems change and fade. Let us remember these truths. Let us resolve to build not to destroy, and let us remember always that weakness comes from division, strength from unity.

The speech's courteous discourse was matched by both its delivery and Macmillan's appearance. With his clipped sentences and clipped moustache, the aristocratic Macmillan was the epitome of the English gentleman. He spent the first quarter of his speech bestowing every manner of praise upon his hosts – complimenting the beauty of the country, the warmth and initiative of its people, the strength of its economy (although also reminding the audience that many initiatives were British funded). He goes on to celebrate the trade relationship between the two countries, before acknowledging South Africa's role in the Second World War and praising the country for helping to develop other African nations.

But as the speech progresses, it becomes clear that Macmillan is in fact engaging the art of softening the blow, and the many compliments are really a means of preparing his audience for the true and brutal message of the speech, which is that South Africa is falling out of step with the rest of the world and can no longer rely on Britain's support.

For anybody with an ear for suspense, the over-the-top remarks ('No one could fail to be impressed with the immense material progress which has been achieved' and 'Of course you understand this better than anyone') beg to be followed by a resounding 'but'. With each successive commendation, it becomes clearer that Macmillan is building up to a grand thematic turn.

After a misleading turn ('But that is not all'), it finally comes with a direct address to Verwoerd: 'Sir, as I have travelled round the Union I have found everywhere, as I expected, a deep preoccupation with what is happening in the rest of the African continent.' Hereafter, Macmillan turns his attention to the changing politics in Africa and the implications for South Africa.

Perhaps heeding the *Rand Daily Mail*'s warning, made almost a month before, that one mention of apartheid 'might start a crisis'[9] – Macmillan never refers to apartheid or the country's racial policies directly. The insinuation in what is perhaps the speech's most damning line is nevertheless clear: 'I hope you won't mind my saying frankly that there are some aspects of your policies which make it impossible for us to do this [give support and encouragement] without being false to our own deep convictions about the political destinies of free men'.

In an attempt to persuade his audience into his way of thinking, Macmillan flits between use of the inclusive pronoun ('we must come to terms with it', 'whether we like it or not', 'we must all accept it as a fact', 'we must face the differences') and, less frequently, second person in a more accusatory vein ('there are some aspects of *your* policies'). This sometimes results in some spurious connections, particularly when he tries to number South Africa as one of the free nations of the world: 'Indeed, in the history of our times yours will be recorded as the first of the African nationalisms. And this tide of national consciousness which is now rising in Africa is a fact for which you and we and the other nations of the Western world are ultimately responsible.' Despite the verbal gymnastics and excessive flattery, the speech cannot veil its patronising tone. Philippe-Joseph Salazar describes it 'as a sort of command to lesser beings'.[10] And like any godly decree it contains a stern warning, particularly clear in Macmillan's words: 'We may sometimes be tempted to say to each other "mind your own business", but in these days I would myself expand the old saying so that it runs: "mind your own business but mind how it affects my business, too".'

Macmillan and his team of advisors had two aims in delivering the speech. First, they wished to signal to South Africa and the rest of the world that Britain's rule in Africa was coming to an end. (Indeed, over the next decade, Britain granted independence to all of its colonies.) The second aim was more challenging: to prompt Afrikaners to rethink apartheid policies in light of changing events in Africa, and to do so without offending them.

Reactions suggest that Macmillan was successful on the first front. The speech was widely reported internationally, making the front page of the *New York Times*.[11] In South Africa, the *Rand Daily Mail* claimed that 'there has probably never been so polished, so adroit a speech made within those walls',[12] and for the first time in four years the Soviet bloc opened its airwaves especially to transmit the address.[13]

In addition, although the resistance movement in South Africa was more interested in Britain's actions, they nevertheless found the speech encouraging. ANC leader Albert Luthuli claimed it gave 'oppressed people some inspiration and hope'.[14]

The African people did not constitute Macmillan's primary audience, however. The primary audience, the white men in power at Parliament, remained unmoved, perhaps 'dazed', suggested Anthony Sampson, 'by the rhetoric and historical scope of the speech', so very different from the 'usual noisy debating' of Parliament.[15] For the most part, they tolerated the speech in silence, cheering only when Macmillan rejected the boycott.[16] The speech's failure to achieve its second aim became apparent immediately after its delivery, when Verwoerd delivered an abrupt and defiant response.

H.F. Verwoerd

Speech of thanks to Harold Macmillan,
Parliament, 3 February 1960

Prime Minister H.F. Verwoerd's response to Macmillan's 'Wind of Change' speech was off-the-cuff – a sore point among Afrikaner nationalists, who at every opportunity bemoaned the fact that the South African prime minister did not receive an advance copy of the great speech. A.N. Pelzer says in his hallowed collection of Verwoerd's addresses that Macmillan was thanked 'despite Dr Verwoerd not having received, as is customary, a copy of Mr Macmillan's speech beforehand'[1] – a moot point considering how Verwoerd would have appeared had he *not* thanked the statesman.

The Netherlands-born Verwoerd took office shortly after J.G. Strijdom died in 1958. Like Malan, he had studied abroad (in Germany) and achieved academic success very young, receiving offers to study further at Oxford University. Driven by an unwavering sense of purpose, Verwoerd was not content to remain in the world of ideas; he returned to South Africa and worked tirelessly to uplift poor white Afrikaners. Like Robert Sobukwe, he gave up an offer of tenured professorship to pursue politics, choosing to edit a poorly funded Afrikaner nationalist newspaper, *Die Transvaler*,[2] which, under his editorship, took a pro-Nazi stance during World War II. As editor, he was also known for virtually ignoring the much-celebrated 1947 royal tour of King George VI and his family, save for a few remarks about resultant traffic congestion.

There was no love lost between Verwoerd and Macmillan. Verwoerd remained morose and distant throughout Macmillan's state visit,[3] and the British prime minister later claimed that Verwoerd was unyielding, despite his quiet, reasonable-sounding voice. In an obituary for *Life* magazine, Anthony Sampson noted a similar combination of traits:

> To meet, Dr. Verwoerd seemed a man of unusual gentleness. He was tall, with a tubby face, turned-up nose and direct gray eyes. Only in repose could you see the stern lines of his mouth, the strain in his eyes. He spoke in a soft, schoolmasterly way, as if reassuring anxious students, and he smiled with cherubic innocence, which seemed to say, 'It's all so simple.'[4]

Verwoerd's remarkable lack of self-doubt stands out in assessments of his personality. The journalist Stanley Uys, who wrote for a number of American and UK newspapers in the 1950s and 60s, noted, 'Dr Verwoerd differs from you and me in this important way: we allow ourselves the conceit of thinking we are right. He knows he is right.'[5] Indeed, in response to a question about his ability to sleep given the burden and far-reaching effects of his policies, Verwoerd stated, 'You see, one does not have the problem of worrying whether one perhaps could be wrong.'[6]

In light of these reports, the standard claim that Verwoerd was incensed by his guest's speech is surprising. Reporters made much of his physical reactions during Macmillan's speech, with the *Rand Daily Mail* saying that it made the 'heavier, less-well tailored figure of Dr. Verwoerd grow slowly pale and tense'[7] and the *Guardian* reported that the speech 'clearly took Dr Verwoerd by surprise' and that he 'appeared less confident and assertive than he usually is'.[8]

In the BBC recording of the speech, Verwoerd's opening comment – a peculiar combination of flattery and insult – does indeed sound awkward, as if Verwoerd is sputtering, although he recovers quickly and goes on to give what *Die Burger* described as a 'small masterpiece'.[9]

Mr Prime Minister, you have set me a considerable task. We have problems enough in South Africa without you coming to add to them by making such an important statement and expecting me to thank you in a few brief words.

There are two ways in which one can approach a motion of thanks, as you very well know. The first is practically to repeat and endorse every statement that you made. But that, of course, presupposes that one can endorse all you said, which I cannot do in all instances, but it also presupposes a somewhat boring repetition and that I do not wish to inflict you [*sic*]. A second possible method is to comment on every point you put before us. That would be worse still. It would mean an interdebate between you and myself on this occasion, which is certainly not suited to that. So I will not inflict that upon you either.

All that I wish to do is thank you very heartily for coming to South Africa and putting before us here your point of view – your philosophy, as you see it – as that philosophy may be applicable particularly to the areas for which you are responsible. I am glad you were frank. We are a people who are capable of listening with great pleasure to what others have to say even though they differ from us. I think it is an attribute of civilization that one should be capable of discussing matters with friends with great frankness and even in spite of difference, great or small, remain friends after that and be able to co-operate in all that remains of mutual interest.

May I say that we can understand your outlook on the picture of the world and on the picture of Africa in that world. I also do not find fault with the major object you have in view. South Africa has the same objects: peace, to which you have made a very considerable contribution and for which I also wish to thank you today. The survival of Western ideas, of Western civilization; throwing in your weight on the side of the Western nations in this possibly increasing division which exists in the world today – we are with you there. Seeing Africa as making possible balance between the two world groupings, and hoping to develop the mind of man as it exists in Africa in the above-mentioned direction – that too can be of the greatest value in your search for a goodwill between all men and for peace and prosperity on earth. It is only a matter of how that can best be achieved. How can Africa be won? There we do not see eye to eye very often.

You believe, as I gather, that policies which we deem not only advisable for South Africa but which we believe, if rightly understood, should make an impact upon Africa and upon the world, are not to the advantage of those very ideals for which you strive and we strive too! If our policies were rightly understood, we believe, however, that it would be seen that what we are attempting to do is not at variance with a new direction in Africa but is in the fullest accord with it. We never presume to criticize the application of other policies in the areas for which you are responsible, but when on an occasion such as this, on which we are perfectly frank, we look at them critically, then we see, differing from you, that there may be great dangers inherent in those policies. The very object at which you are aiming may be defeated by them.

The tendency in Africa for nations to become independent and, at the same time, the need to do justice to all, does not only mean being just to the black man of Africa, but also being just to the white man of Africa. We call ourselves Europeans but actually we represent the white men of Africa. They are the people, not only in the Union but throughout major portions of Africa, who brought civilization here, who made possible the present development of black nationalism by bringing the natives education, by showing them the Western way of life, by bringing to Africa industry and development, by inspiring them with the ideals which Western civilization has developed for itself. The white man who came to Africa, perhaps to trade, and in some cases, perhaps to bring the Gospel, has remained and we particularly, in this southernmost portion of Africa, have such a stake here that this has become our only motherland. We have nowhere else to go. We settled [in] a country which was bare. The Bantu too came to this country and settled certain portions for themselves. It is in line with thinking on Africa to grant them there, those fullest rights which we with you, admit all people should have. We believe in providing those rights for those people in the fullest degree in that part of southern Africa which their forefathers found for themselves and settled in. But we also believe in balance. We believe in allowing exactly those same full opportunities to remain within the grasp of the white man in the areas he settled, the white man who has made all this possible.

We see ourselves as a part of the Western world, a true white state in Africa, notwithstanding the possibility of granting a full future to the black men in our midst. We look upon ourselves as indispensable to the white world. If there is a division in the future, how can South Africa best play its part? It should both co-operate with the white nations of the world and, at the same time, make friends with the black states of Africa in such a way that they will provide strength to the arm of those who fight for the civilization in which we believe. We are the link. We are white, but we are in Africa. We have links with both and that lays upon us a special duty and we realize that.

I do not wish to pursue this matter any further but do wish to assure you that in the Christian philosophy which you endorse, we find a philosophy which we too wish to follow. If our methods should be different, let us try to understand one another and may we at least find in the world at large that trust in our sincerity which must be the basis of all goodwill and true understanding.

I wish to thank you for coming to South Africa, not in order to commit yourself to our policies, not in order to become either the mediator or the judge in our problems or between the various racial groups which we have in this country. We thank you for coming to see us simply because that shows that you wish to be our friend, as we wish to be yours. It also shows quite clearly that between us and Great Britain there exists now, and should, and I hope will exist in the future, the best co-operation on those many matters in which we can co-operate. You mentioned the economic relations which exist between our two countries. We know they are very good; we know they go very far. We, members of the present Government, would be the last to wish to deduct in the slightest from that. We wish to increase our prosperity and yours by good co-operation, and I can truly endorse the wise words you uttered when you said: 'Nothing can be gained by trying to harm each other economically, in the political or theoretical fields.'

Here, at least, we have a sphere of activity in which we not only think fully alike, but in which we are equally interested: the economic world, the prosperity of South Africa, the prosperity of Great Britain, the prosperity of Africa. I pledge myself and my Government to the fullest co-operation in seeking that prosperity and happiness for all.

If you have done no more by coming here than to make it possible for that principle to penetrate everywhere: that no one can do any good by trying to hurt somebody with whose point of view he differs, but that only good can come from trying to do good to others, then your journey so far southwards will have been very well rewarded.

I thank you from the depth of my heart for your presence in South Africa. I bid you on behalf of the Parliament of South Africa Godspeed on your return. May you find in Great Britain less problems to deal with than we, unfortunately, have here.

In many respects, the two speeches embody the appearance of their respective speakers. The elegant and flowing sentences of 'Wind of Change' personify Macmillan, whom a *Star* reporter described as 'lean Edwardian, carelessly elegant in dress',[10] whereas Verwoerd – described as 'stocky, precise and purposeful'[11] in flesh – is similarly direct and forceful in word, partly, no doubt, because English was his second language.

The speech moves joltingly between obsequious thanks ('All that I wish to do is thank you very heartily'; 'I thank you from the depth of my heart'), repetition of Macmillan's words (the 'white man who came to Africa' has 'nowhere else to go'; 'Nothing can be gained by trying to harm each other economically') and direct retort ('There we do not see eye to eye very often').

The opening barbed compliment – 'We have problems enough in South Africa without you coming to add to them by making such an important statement and expecting me to thank you in a few brief words' – is echoed in Verwoerd's parting shot, 'May you find in Great Britain less problems to deal with than we, unfortunately, have here.' The argument that South Africa's race problem was somehow unique and understandable only to white South Africans became part of the narrative of apartheid exceptionalism in years to come.

While Macmillan had tried to pre-empt this response with references to South Africa's specialised knowledge on the topic, his attempt to persuade Verwoerd and his cohort to take a longer view of history ultimately failed – contrary to John Maud's assessment of the effect of Macmillan's speech.

Maud, who was Macmillan's advisor and one of the main contributors to the text of 'Wind of Change', interpreted Verwoerd's response as a fumbled statement that served only to glorify Macmillan: 'Dr V's effort, after yours,' he conveyed in a letter, 'was all that was needed to make the effect of your triumph certain. The whole thing will have done untold good, out here.'[12]

Yet, while the speech may have served as a warning of the isolation that was to come, it made no dent in the obstinacy of the apartheid cabinet. If anything, it caused them to dig in their heels. This became chillingly clear two months later, when the situation in South Africa came to a head.

On 21 March, at the behest of Robert Sobukwe, a 6 000-strong crowd of PAC supporters engaged in protest action outside Sharpeville police station, offering themselves up for arrest by not carrying passbooks or by burning the hated documents. The police opened fire, killing 69 unarmed demonstrators and wounding a further 180. When, a few days later, more protests began to erupt around the country, the government clamped down, declaring a nationwide state of emergency on 30 March and banning the PAC and the ANC on 8 April.

One day later, an English businessman and farmer named David Pratt, driven, he later confessed, by a desire to eliminate 'the epitome of apartheid',[13] made an attempt to assassinate Verwoerd. Firing two shots at the prime minister, who was opening the Union Exposition in Milner Park, Pratt succeeded only in puncturing Verwoerd's right cheek and ear. It would be another six years before a second assassin fulfilled Pratt's aim.

Albert Luthuli

Nobel Peace Prize lecture, 'Africa and Freedom',
Oslo University, 11 December 1961

When ANC leader Albert Luthuli was awarded the 1960 Nobel Peace Prize, it was a sign that the wind of change was blowing not only through Africa but also through the world. In addition to being the first African laureate, he was also the first person outside of Europe and the Americas to receive the honour.

The wind of change was not stirring in Luthuli's home country, however. In 1960 the South African government committed a number of brutal and self-isolating acts. In the wake of the Sharpeville massacre, during which sixty-nine unarmed protestors were shot dead outside a police station, the government banned the ANC and the PAC and passed draconian legislation that allowed it to detain individuals while withholding their access to legal counsel for a period of twelve days. When the United Nations Security Council adopted Resolution 134, calling for an end to apartheid, the state proceeded to withdraw from the Commonwealth and declared itself an independent republic – despite only garnering 52 per cent of the electorate's support in a white referendum.

Against this backdrop, the 1960 Nobel Prize signalled the Anglo-Western world's growing disapproval of South Africa's increasingly repressive policies, while applauding Luthuli's unwavering commitment to non-violent struggle.

The government must have been less than impressed when, a year after banning the ANC, the organisation's leader was feted with this worldwide honour. Luthuli's movement in his own country was severely restricted, and he was under house arrest in the rural village of Groutville. His request for permission to travel to the 1961 ceremony was initially refused by the state, a petty act that created sympathetic media hype over whether Luthuli would be able to attend the award ceremony at all.

It was, as Scott Couper points out in his biography of Luthuli, a 'lose/lose proposition'[1] for the apartheid government. After much pressure, particularly from US assistant secretary of state G. Mennen Williams,[2] the authorities capitulated and granted Luthuli and his wife, Nokukhanya, a ten-day travel pass. Minister of justice B.J. Vorster begrudgingly remarked that he would allow the sixty-two-year-old Christian leader to travel 'notwithstanding the fact that the government fully realises that the award was not made on merit.[3] The passports came with conditions, however; Luthuli was not to make any political statements, nor to tarnish South Africa's image in any way.[4]

Although Luthuli was awarded the prize for 1960, he only received it the following year. The Norwegian Nobel Committee felt that none of the original 1960 nominations met the criteria outlined in Alfred Nobel's will. Luckily, the Nobel Foundation's statutes allowed for the prize to be reserved until the following year, so Luthuli was nominated for the 1960 prize in February 1961 and received it later that year, delivering a short acceptance speech in the Great Hall at Oslo University.

In this first speech, Luthuli was diplomatic, paying homage to several European luminaries, including David Livingstone and Alfred Nobel, as well as the 1961 Peace Prize winner, United Nations Secretary-General Dag Hammarskjöld. Two months earlier, the Swede had died in a tragic and suspicious plane crash en route to the Congo. Hammarskjöld had played a pivotal role in the UN resolution denouncing apartheid, so the posthumous award was a double blow for the South African government.

While graciously acknowledging the award's significance, Luthuli couldn't resist the opportunity to chide Europe for its own transgressions. With the mischievous proviso that 'it is not time to speak about that here', he nevertheless went on to intimate that Africa's offer of 'the hand of friendship' hadn't always been warmly received.

About affairs in South Africa, he was both light-hearted and oblique. In a modest dismissal of his Nobel worthiness, and in reference to Vorster's comment, he quipped, 'Such is the magic of a peace prize, that it has even managed to produce an issue on which I agree with the government of South Africa.'

But the acceptance speech made no mention of 'apartheid', and Luthuli's criticism of conditions in his home country was veiled; the focus instead was on hope and the need for global peace and freedom. The awards ceremony wasn't, Luthuli seems to have decided, a space for direct attack.

Rhetoric aside, the leader made a clear statement through his sartorial choices for the evening, electing to wear a Zulu warrior king's headpiece that was cut from leopard skin and a necklace made from lion's teeth (borrowed, apparently, from Mangosuthu Buthelezi).[5] While this traditional attire might have appeared exotic to the Oslo audience, it was unusual for Luthuli too, and it was perhaps an overt act of defiance against the apartheid state, which had stripped him of his chiefdom in 1952, claiming that he couldn't hold the office (paid for by the government) because of his involvement with the ANC. Some local newspapers responded to this tactic appropriately. The *Star* consistently referred to Luthuli as 'the king' in its report on the event and emphasised his decision to wear the royal regalia in its headline 'Luthuli, dressed as Zulu Chief, gets his prize'.[6]

The Nobel committee also requests recipients to deliver a lecture on a subject connected to the award. While many laureates give this lecture on separate occasions, Luthuli, constrained by his travel pass, grabbed the small window of opportunity to address an international audience and delivered his lecture the following day.

This lecture was far more solemn and substantial than the acceptance speech. In it, Luthuli presented a scathing attack on apartheid South Africa, calling it a 'museum piece' and a 'relic of an age which everywhere else is dead'. Here are several excerpts:

> In years gone by, some of the greatest men of our century have stood here to receive this award, men whose names and deeds have enriched the pages of human history, men whom future generations will regard as having shaped the world of our time. No one could be left unmoved at being plucked from the village of Groutville, a name many of you have never heard before and which does not even feature on many maps – to be plucked from banishment in a rural backwater, to be lifted out of the narrow confines of South Africa's internal politics and placed here in the shadow of these great figures. It is a great honour to me to stand on this rostrum where many of the great men of our times have stood before.
>
> The Nobel Peace Award that has brought me here has for me a threefold significance. On the one hand, it is a tribute to my humble contribution to efforts by democrats on both sides of the colour line to find a peaceful solution to the race problem. This contribution is not in any way unique. I did not initiate the struggle to extend the area of human freedom in South Africa; other African patriots – devoted men – did so before me. I also, as a Christian and patriot, could not look on while systematic attempts were made, almost in every department of life, to debase the God-factor in man or to set a limit beyond which the human being in his black form might not strive to serve his Creator to the best of his ability. To remain neutral in a situation where the laws of the land virtually criticised God for having created men of colour was the sort of thing I could not, as a Christian, tolerate.
>
> On the other hand, the award is a democratic declaration of solidarity with those who fight to widen the area of liberty in my part of the world. As such, it is the sort of gesture which gives me and millions who think

as I do, tremendous encouragement. There are still people in the world today who regard South Africa's race problem as a simple clash between black and white. Our government has carefully projected this image of the problem before the eyes of the world. This has had two effects. It has confused the real issues at stake in the race crisis. It has given some form of force to the government's contention that the race problem is a domestic matter for South Africa. This, in turn, has tended to narrow down the area over which our case could be better understood in the world.

From yet another angle, it is welcome recognition of the role played by the African people during the last 50 years to establish, peacefully, a society in which merit and not race would fix the position of the individual in the life of the nation.

This award could not be for me alone, nor for just South Africa, but for Africa as a whole. Africa presently is most deeply torn with strife and most bitterly stricken with racial conflict. How strange then it is that a man of Africa should be here to receive an award given for service to the cause of peace and brotherhood between men. There has been little peace in Africa in our time. From the northernmost end of our continent, where war has raged for seven years, to the centre and to the south there are battles being fought out, some with arms, some without. In my own country, in the year 1960, for which this award is given, there was a state of emergency for many months. At Sharpeville, a small village, in a single afternoon 69 people were shot dead and 180 wounded by small arms fire, and in parts like the Transkei, a state of emergency is still continuing. Ours is a continent in revolution against oppression. And peace and revolution make uneasy bedfellows. There can be no peace until the forces of oppression are overthrown.

[...]

There is a paradox in the fact that Africa qualifies for such an award in its age of turmoil and revolution. How great is the paradox and how much greater the honour that an award in support of peace and the brotherhood of man should come to one who is a citizen of a country where the brotherhood of man is an illegal doctrine, outlawed, banned, censured, proscribed and prohibited; where to work, talk, or campaign for the realisation in fact and deed of the brotherhood of man is hazardous, punished with banishment, or confinement without trial, or imprisonment; where effective democratic channels to peaceful settlement of the race problem have never existed these 300 years;

and where white minority power rests on the most heavily armed and equipped military machine in Africa. This is South Africa.

[...]

It is not necessary for me to speak at length about South Africa; its social system, its politics, its economics, and its laws have forced themselves on the attention of the world. It is a museum piece in our time, a hangover from the dark past of mankind, a relic of an age which everywhere else is dead or dying. Here the cult of race superiority and of white supremacy is worshipped like a god. Few white people escape corruption, and many of their children learn to believe that white men are unquestionably superior, efficient, clever, industrious, and capable; that black men are, equally unquestionably, inferior, slothful, stupid, evil, and clumsy. On the basis of the mythology that 'the lowest amongst them is higher than the highest amongst us', it is claimed that white men build everything that is worthwhile in the country – its cities, its industries, its mines, and its agriculture and that they alone are thus fitted and entitled as of right to own and control these things, while black men are only temporary sojourners in these cities, fitted only for menial labour, and unfit to share political power. The prime minister of South Africa, Dr Verwoerd, then minister of Bantu Affairs, when explaining his government's policy on African education had this to say: 'There is no place for him in the European community above the level of certain forms of labour.'

[...]

There is nothing new in South Africa's apartheid ideas, but South Africa is unique in this: the ideas not only survive in our modern age but are stubbornly defended, extended, and bolstered up by legislation at the time when, in the major part of the world, they are now largely historical and are either being shamefacedly hidden behind concealing formulations or are being steadily scrapped. These ideas survive in South Africa because those who sponsor them profit from them. They provide moral whitewash for the conditions which exist in the country: for the fact that the country is ruled exclusively by a white government elected by an exclusively white electorate which is a privileged minority; for the fact that eighty-seven percent of the land and all the best agricultural land within reach of town, market, and railways are reserved for white ownership and occupation, and now through the recent Group Areas legislation non-whites are losing more land to white greed; for the fact that all skilled and highly paid jobs are for whites only; for the fact that all universities of any academic merit are exclusively preserves of whites; for the fact that the education of every white child costs about £64 per year while that of an African child costs about £9 per year and that of an Indian child or coloured child costs about £20 per year; for the fact that white education is universal and compulsory up to the age of sixteen, while education for the non-white children is scarce and inadequate; and for the fact that almost one million Africans a year are arrested and jailed or fined for breaches of innumerable pass and permit laws, which do not apply to whites.

I could carry on in this strain and talk on every facet of South African life from the cradle to the grave. But these facts today are becoming known to all the world. A fierce spotlight of world attention has been thrown on them. Try as our government and its apologists will, with honeyed words about 'separate development' and eventual 'independence' in so-called 'Bantu homelands', nothing can conceal the reality of South African conditions. I, as a Christian, have always felt that there is one thing above all about 'apartheid' or 'separate development' that is unforgivable. It seems utterly indifferent to the suffering of individual persons, who lose their land, their homes, their jobs, in the pursuit of what is surely the most terrible dream in the world. This terrible dream is not held on to by a crackpot group on the fringe of society or by Ku Klux Klansmen, of whom we have a sprinkling. It is the deliberate policy of a government, supported actively by a large part of the white population and tolerated passively by an overwhelming white majority, but now fortunately rejected by an encouraging white minority who have thrown their lot with non-whites, who are overwhelmingly opposed to so-called separate development.

Thus it is that the golden age of Africa's independence is also the dark age of South Africa's decline and retrogression, brought about by men who, when revolutionary changes that entrenched fundamental human rights were taking place in Europe, were closed in on the tip of South Africa – and so missed the wind of progressive change.

In the wake of that decline and retrogression, bitterness between men grows to alarming heights; the economy declines as confidence ebbs away; unemployment rises; government becomes increasingly dictatorial and intolerant of constitutional and legal procedures, increasingly violent and suppressive; there is a constant drive for more policemen, more soldiers, more armaments, banishments without trial, and penal whippings. All the trappings of medieval backwardness and cruelty come to the fore. Education is being reduced to an instrument of subtle indoctrination; slanted and biased reporting in the organs of public information, a creeping censorship, book banning, and blacklisting – all these spread their shadows over the land. This is South Africa today, in the age of Africa's greatness.

[...]

Through all this cruel treatment in the name of law and order, our people, with a few exceptions, have remained non-violent. If today this peace award is given to South Africa through a black man, it is not because we in South Africa have won our fight for peace and human brotherhood. Far from it. Perhaps we stand farther from victory than any other people in Africa. But nothing which we have suffered at the hands of the government has turned us from our chosen path of disciplined resistance. It is for this, I believe, that this award is given.

[...]

It is this vision which prompted the African National Congress to invite members of other racial groups who believe with us in the brotherhood of man and in the freedom of all people to join with us in establishing a non-racial, democratic South Africa. Thus the African National Congress in its day brought about the Congress Alliance and welcomed the emergence of the Liberal Party and the Progressive Party, who to an encouraging measure support these ideals.

[...]

In their fight for lasting values, there are many things that have sustained the spirit of the freedom-loving people of South Africa and those in the yet unredeemed parts of Africa where the white man claims resolutely proprietary rights over democracy – a universal heritage. High among them – the things that have sustained us – stand: the magnificent support of the progressive people and governments throughout the world, among whom number the people and government of the country of which I am today guest; our brothers in Africa, especially in the independent African states; organisations who share the outlook we embrace in countries scattered right across the face of the globe; the United Nations Organisation jointly and some of its member nations singly. In their defence of peace in the world through actively upholding the quality of man, all these groups have reinforced our undying faith in the unassailable rightness and justness of our cause. To all of them I say: Alone we would have been weak. Our heartfelt appreciation of your acts of support of us we cannot adequately express, nor can we ever forget, now or in the future when victory is behind us and South Africa's freedom rests in the hands of all her people.

We South Africans, however, equally understand that, much as others might do for us, our freedom cannot come to us as a gift from abroad. Our freedom we must make ourselves. All honest freedom-loving people have dedicated themselves to that task. What we need is the courage that rises with danger.

[...]

In bringing my address to a close, let me invite Africa to cast her eyes beyond the past and to some extent the present, with their woes and tribulations, trials and failures, and some successes, and see herself an emerging continent, bursting to freedom through the shell of centuries of serfdom. This is Africa's age – the dawn of her fulfilment, yes, the moment when she must grapple with destiny to reach the summits of sublimity, saying: Ours was a fight for noble values and worthy ends, and not for lands and the enslavement of man.

Africa is a vital subject matter in the world of today, a focal point of world interest and concern. Could it not be that history has delayed her rebirth for a purpose? The situation confronts her with inescapable challenges, but more importantly with opportunities for service to herself and mankind. She evades the challenges and neglects the opportunities, to her shame, if not her doom. How she sees her destiny is a more vital and rewarding quest than bemoaning her past, with its humiliations and sufferings.

The address could do no more than pose some questions and leave it to the African leaders and peoples to provide satisfying answers and responses by their concern for higher values and by their noble actions that could be

> Footprints on the sands of time.
> Footprints, that perhaps another,
> Sailing o'er life's solemn main,
> A forlorn and shipwrecked brother,
> Seeing, shall take heart again.[7]

Still licking the scars of past wrongs perpetrated on her, could she not be magnanimous and practise no revenge? Her hand of friendship scornfully rejected, her pleas for justice and fair play spurned, should she not nonetheless seek to turn enmity into amity? Though robbed of her lands, her independence, and opportunities – this, oddly enough, often in the name of civilisation and even Christianity – should she not see her destiny as being that of making a distinctive contribution to human progress and human relationships with a peculiar new African flavour enriched by the diversity of cultures she enjoys, thus building on the summits of present human achievement an edifice that would be one of the finest tributes to the genius of man?

She should see this hour of her fulfilment as a challenge to her to labour on until she is purged of racial domination, and as an opportunity of reassuring the world that her national aspiration lies not in overthrowing white domination to replace it by a black caste but in building a non-racial democracy that shall be a monumental brotherhood, a 'brotherly community' with none discriminated against on grounds of race or colour.

What of the many pressing and complex political, economic, and cultural problems attendant upon the early years of a newly independent state? These, and others which are the legacy of colonial days, will tax to the limit the statesmanship, ingenuity, altruism, and steadfastness of African leadership and its unbending avowal to democratic tenets in statecraft. To us all, free or not free, the call of the hour is to redeem the name and honour of Mother Africa.

In a strife-torn world, tottering on the brink of complete destruction by man-made nuclear weapons, a free and independent Africa is in the making, in answer to the injunction and challenge of history: 'Arise and shine for thy light is come.' Acting in concert with other nations, she is man's last hope for a mediator between the East and West, and is qualified to demand of the great powers to 'turn the swords into ploughshares' because two-thirds of mankind is hungry and illiterate; to engage human energy, human skill, and human talent in the service of peace, for the alternative is unthinkable – war, destruction, and desolation; and to build a world community which will stand as a lasting monument to the millions of men and women, to such devoted and distinguished world citizens and fighters for peace as the late Dag Hammarskjöld, who have given their lives that we may live in happiness and peace.

Africa's qualification for this noble task is incontestable, for her own fight has never been and is not now a fight for conquest of land, for accumulation of wealth or domination of peoples, but for the recognition and preservation of the rights of man and the establishment of a truly free world for a free people.

Luthuli's lecture echoes and builds on Macmillan's words, particularly in his reference to the 'wind of progressive change', which had missed South Africa, a country still in the 'dark age' of 'decline and retrogression'.

To emphasise the point, Luthuli appeals to human rights discourse as well as to Christian doctrine and liberal values. Despite his limited context, he had a canny understanding of the changing values of the Western world and he referred to them throughout the lecture. His reference to the indignity of his personal situation – a grown, educated Christian man confined to the rural 'backwater' of Groutville – exposed the state's 'honeyed' suggestion that apartheid was simply a policy of 'good neighbourliness'. At the same time, his emphasis on 'the brotherhood of man', on dignity and equality, and on apartheid's ability to 'debase the God-factor in man' moved the audience.

But some of the speech's more militant references must have come as a surprise, given that the award celebrated Luthuli's belief in non-violence. He refers to peace and revolution as 'uneasy bedfellows' and emphasises, almost in warning, the impossibility of peace 'until the forces of oppression are overthrown'.

The award in fact put Luthuli in an extremely difficult and lonely position. It came, as Nelson Mandela points out in his autobiography, at an 'awkward' time in the ANC's history.[8] After Sharpeville, sections of the party began to doubt the effectiveness of non-violent resistance, and younger leaders – led by Mandela – were beginning to shift the focus towards armed struggle. Just months prior to the award ceremony, a decision was taken at a joint congress meeting to form Umkhonto we Sizwe (MK), the armed wing of the ANC, a decision that his biographer said 'must have weighed on Luthuli's conscience'.[9]

In light of these events, many believe that the prize was an implicit message not only to the NP but also to the resistance movement. Writer Ezekiel Mphahlele certainly read it as such, stating in *Africa Today* that the award may be interpreted as 'implying that the Scandinavians were investing in non-violence in South Africa'.[10] Publicly, Luthuli himself was less sceptical, telling the *Sunday Tribune* that the award was 'not trying to buy me for peace'.[11]

Motivation aside, the ANC leader nevertheless found himself upon the world stage, receiving a prize for what Mphahlele says was 'a religious-political creed his organisation now found irrelevant'.[12] The awkwardness of Luthuli's situation is reflected when he notes: 'Africa presently is most deeply torn with strife and most bitterly stricken with racial conflict. How strange then it is that a man of Africa should be here to receive an award given for service to the cause of peace'.

Other comments appear to have been directed towards Luthuli's own party. His emphasis on the 'chosen path of disciplined resistance' can be seen perhaps as a plea for continued non-violence in a brewing power battle over the movement's strategies.

Reactions to the lecture around the world were overwhelmingly positive. Both *The Times* of London[13] and the *New York Times*[14] devoted almost a full page to unedited speech excerpts, and a Norwegian newspaper celebrated Luthuli as Africa's 'exceptional' representative in Europe, saying 'in his words, his voice, his smile, his strength, his spontaneity, a whole continent speaks'.[15]

The South African authorities, on the other hand, responded with disdain. When Luthuli requested an extension of his travel pass so that he could take up an invitation to visit Sweden, minister of foreign affairs Eric Louw said that South Africa had no wish to allow Luthuli 'further opportunity to carry on his propaganda and incitement in Europe',[16] a comment that the ANC leader said struck a 'lonely, jarring note' amid 'a worldwide demonstration of unity in the cause of peace'.[17]

Luthuli's Nobel lecture stands as a rare, relatively unmediated message from the South African oppressed to an international audience that was beginning to pay increasing attention to the country. Its appeal, however, for the ongoing embrace of non-violent resistance failed. The launch of MK was announced on 16 December, the day after Luthuli returned from Oslo.

Walter Sisulu

First Radio Freedom broadcast,
Johannesburg, 26 June 1963

Umkhonto we Sizwe was literally launched with a bang. On the night of 15 December 1961, several bombs were detonated in Durban, and more exploded the following day in Johannesburg and Port Elizabeth. At the same time, posters appeared on the city streets, declaring the organisation's intent: 'The time comes in the life of any people when there remain two choices: to submit or fight. That time has now come to South Africa. We will not submit but will fight back with all means at our disposal in defence of our rights, our people and our freedom.' In the months that followed, over 200 acts of sabotage were planned and executed in urban centres around the country. (In keeping with the organisation's policy, there were no fatalities, save for one MK soldier who was killed by his own bomb.)

But the newly formed organisation, led by Joe Slovo, Walter Sisulu, Nelson Mandela and Govan Mbeki (the so-called high command of MK), struggled to find focus and there was no real strategy to their actions.[1] Their task was complicated by the fact that the high-command members were under constant surveillance and often got into trouble with the law, largely because of the ever-amended Suppression of Communism Act.

As the most senior ANC member still at liberty in the country,[2] Walter Sisulu was one of the state's main targets. He was continually harassed by the police; yet although he was arrested six times in 1962, he was charged only once. In March 1963, he was finally convicted to six years' imprisonment for furthering the aims of the ANC and for playing a part in organising the 1961 May stayaway – a nationwide strike that was held on the day that South Africa became an independent republic.

Sisulu was released on bail, pending an appeal, but the magistrate declared that he was to remain under twenty-four-hour house arrest at his home in Orlando. House arrest became one of the most hated tools of repression used by the apartheid state; in effect, dissidents were made prisoners in their own homes and at their own expense. Sisulu was forbidden to communicate 'in any manner whatsoever' with anybody but his immediate family and representatives of the state.

On the night of 19 April 1963, he decided to skip his bail conditions and go underground so that he could devote his efforts to MK. After bidding his children farewell, he surveyed the exterior of his home for police presence and then, judging it to be clear, disappeared into the darkness. His wife, Albertina, had no idea where he'd gone – so intense interrogations from the security police the following morning proved fruitless, as did her arrest under the newly promulgated General Law Amendment Act or 'No Trial' Act, which extended the power to detain arrestees for up to ninety days without charging them or giving them access to legal counsel. There was widespread speculation about Sisulu's movements, with some reports stating that he'd taken the 'secret escape route' to Botswana and others claiming that he'd been spotted in Lourenço Marques in Mozambique.[3] But there were no leads in the weeks following his escape; he appeared to have vanished without a trace, a prospect that was as worrying to his loved ones as it was to the security police.

Then, at eight o'clock on the night of 26 June 1963, a familiar voice crackled over the airwaves in and around Johannesburg. To those who knew him, it was instantly recognisable as Sisulu's.

Sons and Daughters of Africa:
I speak to you from somewhere in South Africa.
I have not left the country.
I do not plan to leave.

Many of our leaders of the African National Congress have gone underground. This is to keep the organisation in action; to preserve the leadership; to keep the freedom fight going. Never has the country, and our people, needed leadership as they do now, in this hour of crisis.
Our house is on fire.
It is the duty of the people of our land – every man and every woman – to rally behind our leaders. There is no time to stand and watch. Thousands are in jail including our dynamic Nelson Mandela. Many are banished to remote parts of the country. Robben Island is a giant concentration camp for political prisoners. Men and women, including my wife, rot in cells under Vorster's vicious laws to imprison without trial. Men wait in the death cells to be hanged. Men die for freedom.
South Africa is in a permanent state of emergency. Any policeman may arrest any South African – and need not bring him to trial. People may be hanged for appealing to the United Nations to intervene. Under the Bantu Laws Amendment Bill, the pass laws will turn children into orphans, wives into widows, men into slaves. We must intensify the attack

on the pass laws. We must fight against the removal of the Africans from the Western Cape. We must reject once and for all times, the Bantustan fraud. No act of Government must go unchallenged. The struggle must never waver. We the African National Congress will lead with new methods of struggle. The African people know that their unity is vital. Only by united action can we overthrow this Government. We call on all our people to unite and struggle. Workers and peasants; teachers and students; Ministers of Religion and all Churches. We call upon all our people, of whatever shade of opinion. We say: The hour has come for us to stand together. This is the only way to freedom. Nothing short of unity will bring the people their freedom. We warn the Government that drastic laws will not stop our struggle for liberation. Throughout the ages men have sacrificed – they have given their lives for their ideals. And we are also determined to surrender our lives for our freedom.

In the face of violence, men struggling for freedom have had to meet violence with violence. How can it be otherwise in South Africa? Changes must come. Changes for the better, but not without sacrifice. Your sacrifice. My sacrifice.

We face tremendous odds. We know that. But our unity, our determination, our sacrifice, our organisation are our weapons. We must succeed! We will succeed!

Amandla!

Before Sisulu's speech, an unknown speaker, addressing the audience in Zulu, Sesotho and English, introduced 'Freedom Radio: the broadcasting service of the African National Congress' speaking from 'our underground head-quarters ... somewhere in South Africa'. The clandestine nature of the address was heightened by the fact that Sisulu was never formally introduced, nor did he openly declare his identity, although any listeners familiar with recent events would easily have inferred the significance of his announcement that he had not left the country and decoded the references to 'my wife' imprisoned 'without trial' (Albertina Sisulu was in fact the first woman detained under the 'No Trial' Act).[4]

Sisulu reassures potentially dispirited listeners of the necessity for the ANC leadership to work underground 'to keep the freedom fight going'. With so many leaders in exile, and with the state's repressive clamp-down on resistance activities, the organisation must have seemed diminished in the eyes of its followers. But Sisulu assures listeners of the movement's continuing sacrifice and determination, claiming that the current crisis calls for unity, fortitude and an intensification of the struggle.

Because a live broadcast would have been too risky, the address, and a similar one read out by Ahmed Kathrada, had been recorded by Denis Goldberg, the movement's 'Mr Technico', a week or two earlier. Initially, Sisulu, Govan Mbeki and Kathrada had written over forty-five minutes of material, but Goldberg persuaded them that this was far too dangerous, so they agreed to limit the broadcast to fifteen minutes.

The address was not, in fact, transmitted from the ANC's underground headquarters but from the home of Fuzzy and Archie Levitan in Parktown, a white Johannesburg suburb. The Levitans were supportive of the struggle but had fallen off the police radar, and so their residence was deemed safe. On the night in question, Goldberg, Ivan Schermbrucker and Cyril Jones travelled to the Levitans' home, where Goldberg erected an aluminium aerial that had been custom-built by Lionel Gay, a physics lecturer at the University of the Witwatersrand. The aerial was spray-painted black to blend into the night, and, while Goldberg assembled it, Schermbrucker and Jones stood sentry, ready to signal to him with a walkie-talkie and torchlight in the event of police interception.[5]

Although there appears to have been no large-scale attempt to publicise the broadcast beforehand,[6] most likely for security reasons, Goldberg has said that it 'created quite a stir in the country and was widely reported'.[7] It was also mentioned in both the *New York Times*[8] and the London *Times*.[9] *The Times*'s report suggests that the police had knowledge of the transmission, citing anonymous 'expert radio opinion' that 'said that the broadcast could have come from a radio transmitter anywhere within 250 miles of Johannesburg'.

While it's not known who first had the idea to begin broadcasting, nor how wide the range or audience was, according to Goldberg, this first address was important in giving a sense of technology's potential to communicate with the people in an era of intense suppression.[10] In the 1970s and 80s, Radio Freedom proved to be one of the most effective means of keeping the spirit of the liberation movement alive from beyond South Africa's borders. It was particularly successful in connecting the exile community with the people back home.

Goldberg recalls the rush of adrenaline that came with orchestrating the broadcast, describing Sisulu's speech as 'inspiring and brave, a deviant call to unity in the face of tremendous oppression'.[11] This triumph was short-lived, however, and Radio Freedom did not broadcast again for nearly a decade. Within two weeks, Sisulu, Kathrada and Goldberg would all be arrested.

Nelson Mandela

Statement from the dock during the Rivonia Trial,
Pretoria Supreme Court, 20 April 1964

By 1963 – at the time of Walter Sisulu's disappearance – the ANC's other high-profile leader, Nelson Mandela, had already been imprisoned. Tall, charismatic and self-assured, Mandela was one of the most wanted men in the country at the time of his arrest in 1962. Together, Sisulu and Mandela presented a formidable combination. They complemented one another, with Sisulu content to play a 'back room' role,[1] grooming Mandela 'like a boxer manager with a champ'.[2] 'You can't talk about Mandela without Sisulu,'[3] Ahmed Kathrada later claimed. It was Sisulu who first realised the young Mandela's potential, saying of their first encounter in 1941: 'He happened to strike me more than any person I had met.'[4] An amateur heavyweight boxer, who was always stylishly dressed, Mandela combined the moral stature of a king with the sharp intellect of a lawyer. 'I had no hesitation, the moment I met him, that this is the man I need,'[5] Sisulu recalls. As it turned out, Mandela was the man the entire country would need.

But the Mandela the world came to know and adore in the post-apartheid era differed markedly from the Mandela of the 1960s. Described as an impatient 'hot-head',[6] he had been the leader of the Transvaal ANC since 1952 and had spearheaded the activities of MK along with Joe Slovo. He began establishing regional commands in the main centres immediately after receiving the ANC's half-granted permission to launch the armed struggle. MK, it was initially agreed, would be an autonomous organisation, utilising alliances but ultimately separate from the ANC.

In February 1962, Mandela embarked on his own Africa tour, meeting with leaders and securing support, training and funds from a range of countries, including Ethiopia, Egypt, Morocco and Liberia. He also travelled to London, where he met with Oliver Tambo, anti-apartheid activists, high-profile journalists (including David Astor of the *Observer*) and prominent liberal politicians (Hugh Gaitskell and Denis Healey of the Labour Party, and Jo Grimond, leader of the Liberal Party).

Having escaped conviction during the highly publicised and lengthy Treason Trial (1956–61) – when the state attempted, and failed, to convict 156 dissidents – Mandela was again arrested in August 1962. The circumstances of his arrest remain unclear. Nicknamed 'the Black Pimpernel', Mandela was a master of disguise, but his luck ran out when, dressed as a chauffeur, he was apprehended near Howick en route to Johannesburg from Durban. According to Donald Rickard, the US vice-consul in Durban, a CIA agent had tipped off the authorities, but this account remains unsubstantiated and Rickard had no formal association with the CIA.[7] It's equally possible that Mandela, who some say lacked caution,[8] was already under police surveillance.

In court, Mandela was accused of inciting strikes, leaving the country without permission and evading arrest. At his trial, he cut an impressive figure. Mirroring Luthuli's decision to wear traditional attire in Oslo, Mandela emphasised his aristocratic status by wearing a royal Thembu kaross and took every opportunity to undermine the authority of the court, stating outright: 'I consider myself neither legally nor morally bound to obey laws made by a parliament in which I have no representation.' Despite the negative international publicity that the trial attracted, on 25 October he was found guilty and convicted to five years' imprisonment – a devastating indictment for the forty-four-year-old husband and father.

But a far worse fate awaited. One year into Mandela's sentence, on 11 July 1963, the South African security police raided a seemingly sleepy farm in the residential suburb of Rivonia in northern Johannesburg. The farm, called Liliesleaf, stretched across twenty-eight acres and had been bought with South African Communist Party (SACP) funds to serve as a hideout and meeting place for the leaders of banned organisations. SACP member Arthur Goldreich and his wife fronted as its white owners, and many political fugitives sought refuge there. It was at Liliesleaf that Sisulu had been hiding after he skipped bail three weeks earlier, and Mandela, disguised as a gardener and using the alias David Motsamayi, had resided there between 1961 and 1962. According to Thula Simpson, the MK high command had planned to transfer its operations to a new safe-house but hadn't yet made the move,[9] and Liliesleaf held a number of implicating documents, including Mandela's Africa diary, a document titled 'How to be a good communist' and drafts in which sabotage plans were laid out.

The identity of the person who alerted the security police to the activities on the farm also remains a mystery. According to the state's official account,[10] a random arrest led to a tip-off and dramatic late-night search for a suburb named 'Ivon' – in reference to a Rivonia sign that had lost its first and last letters. The person's identity has never been made public, although many years later Ahmed Kathrada claimed he'd been told it was an ANC member.[11]

Whoever raised the flag on Liliesleaf has a lot to answer for: the tip-off saw the arrest of nineteen individuals. The state had expected only Sisulu to be there and were delighted to find Kathrada and Mbeki among the 'catch'. 'Here, in one fell swoop,' the official account boasts, 'they had rounded up all the key men of the underground movement.'[12]

Thirteen of the initial arrestees were detained for several months before being formally charged with various counts of sabotage. In a dramatic turn of events, two of them, Arthur Goldreich and Harold Wolpe, escaped from prison and managed to flee the country disguised as priests. Of the remaining eleven, Bob Hepple turned state witness before also fleeing the country, leaving ten accused. They were Walter Sisulu, Ahmed Kathrada, Govan Mbeki, Denis Goldberg, Raymond Mhlaba, Elias Motsoaledi, Rusty Bernstein, Andrew Mlangeni, James Kantor and Nelson Mandela – virtually the full senior leadership of the ANC and the SACP.

The remaining accused appeared in court on 30 October, and over the course of the next few months the state called on 174 witnesses – many of them imprisoned and interrogated under the newly promulgated 'No Trial' Act. A damning case was established against Mandela and his co-accused.

When the time came for the defence to present its case, there was no question of a not-guilty verdict. The defence team called no witnesses and abandoned the bid for freedom, deciding instead to use the courtroom as a platform to address the rest of the world.

As the first accused, Mandela opened the defence on 20 April 1964. In consultation with his co-accused, he elected to give up his right to cross-examination and to deliver a statement from the dock instead. This was an incredibly risky decision. It meant that his statement would hold very little weight in court, since the prosecutor couldn't interrogate him. But it also meant that Mandela could speak unconstrained by the usual interruptions. The decision to deliver a statement from the dock was therefore a stroke of genius on the part of the defendants. Although Elias Motsoaledi and Andrew Mlangeni would do the same, it was Mandela's electrifying three-hour speech that captured the imagination of the watching world. His opening words, in which he emphasised his legal credentials, proud heritage and political ambitions, have become historic:

I am the First Accused.

I hold a Bachelor's Degree in Arts and practised as an attorney in Johannesburg for a number of years in partnership with Oliver Tambo. I am a convicted prisoner serving five years for leaving the country without a permit and for inciting people to go on strike at the end of May 1961.

At the outset, I want to say that the suggestion made by the State in its opening that the struggle in South Africa is under the influence of foreigners or communists is wholly incorrect. I have done whatever I did, both as an individual and as a leader of my people, because of my experience in South Africa and my own proudly felt African background, and not because of what any outsider might have said.

In my youth in the Transkei I listened to the elders of my tribe telling stories of the old days. Amongst the tales they related to me were those of wars fought by our ancestors in defence of the fatherland. The names of Dingane and Bambata, Hintsa and Makana, Squngthi and Dalasile, Moshoeshoe and Sekhukhuni, were praised as the glory of the entire African nation. I hoped then that life might offer me the opportunity to serve my people and make my own humble contribution to their freedom struggle. This is what has motivated me in all that I have done in relation to the charges made against me in this case.

Mandela goes on to candidly confess to some of the charges levelled against him, before giving a cogent and detailed account of the conditions and events that led to the establishment of MK and the adoption of the armed struggle. Instead of focusing on legal intricacies, Mandela used the courtroom as a platform to address the watching world, asking for the question of his guilt or innocence to be judged in the broadest moral sense. The violence adopted by MK, he explained, was not terrorism, as the zealous state prosecutor Percy Yutar had been at pains to prove. Mandela recounts, in some detail, the ANC's history of passive resistance and chronicles the long, patient and painful journey towards a departure from this policy, pointing out 'that fifty years of non-violence had brought the African people nothing but more and more repressive legislation, and fewer and fewer rights'.

The formation of MK was, he also argued, actually an attempt to curb violence in South Africa, because the ANC's followers 'were beginning to lose confidence in this policy [of non-violence] and were developing disturbing ideas of terrorism'. They needed an outlet of some sort, a source of hope. Yet, he claimed, the 'dominant idea' of MK 'was that loss of life should be avoided', despite the reality that 'violence had, in fact, become a feature of the South African political scene' and that ever-repressive legislation sought to prevent Africans from realising their rights. Upholding this view, MK launched a clear and targeted attack, not on white South Africans but on the country's economy in an attempt to pressurise the state:

> I must deal immediately and at some length with the question of violence. Some of the things so far told to the court are true and some are untrue. I do not, however, deny that I planned sabotage. I did not plan it in a spirit of recklessness, nor because I have any love of violence. I planned it as a result of a calm and sober assessment of the political situation that had arisen after many years of tyranny, exploitation, and oppression of my people by the whites.
>
> I admit immediately that I was one of the persons who helped to form Umkhonto we Sizwe, and that I played a prominent role in its affairs until I was arrested in August 1962.
>
> [...]
>
> I deny that Umkhonto was responsible for a number of acts which clearly fell outside the policy of the organisation, and which have been charged in the indictment against us. I do not know what justification there was for these acts, but to demonstrate that they could not have been authorised by Umkhonto, I want to refer briefly to the roots and policy of the organisation.
>
> [...]
>
> I, and the others who started the organisation, did so for two reasons. Firstly, we believed that as a result of government policy, violence by the African people had become inevitable, and that unless responsible leadership was given to canalise and control the feelings of our people, there would be outbreaks of terrorism which would produce an intensity of bitterness and hostility between the various races of this country which is not produced even by war. Secondly, we felt that without violence there would be no way open to the African people to succeed in their struggle against the principle of white supremacy. All lawful modes of expressing opposition to this principle had been closed by legislation, and we were placed in a position in which we had either to accept a permanent state of inferiority, or to defy the government. We chose to defy the law. We first broke the law in a way which avoided any recourse to violence; when this form was legislated against, and then the government resorted to a show of force to crush opposition to its policies, only then did we decide to answer violence with violence.
>
> But the violence which we chose to adopt was not terrorism. We who formed Umkhonto were all members of the African National Congress,

and had behind us the ANC tradition of non-violence and negotiation as a means of solving political disputes. We believe that South Africa belongs to all the people who live in it, and not to one group, be it black or white. We did not want an interracial war, and tried to avoid it to the last minute. If the court is in doubt about this, it will be seen that the whole history of our organisation bears out what I have said, and what I will subsequently say, when I describe the tactics which Umkhonto decided to adopt.

[...]

Four forms of violence were possible. There is sabotage, there is guerrilla warfare, there is terrorism, and there is open revolution. We chose to adopt the first method and to exhaust it before taking any other decision.

In the light of our political background the choice was a logical one. Sabotage did not involve loss of life, and it offered the best hope for future race relations. Bitterness would be kept to a minimum and, if the policy bore fruit, democratic government could become a reality. This is what we felt at the time, and this is what we said in our Manifesto (Exhibit AD):

'We of Umkhonto we Sizwe have always sought to achieve liberation without bloodshed and civil clash. We hope, even at this late hour, that our first actions will awaken everyone to a realisation of the disastrous situation to which the Nationalist policy is leading. We hope that we will bring the government and its supporters to their senses before it is too late, so that both the government and its policies can be changed before matters reach the desperate state of civil war.'

The initial plan was based on a careful analysis of the political and economic situation of our country. We believed that South Africa depended to a large extent on foreign capital and foreign trade.

We felt that planned destruction of power plants, and interference with rail and telephone communications, would tend to scare away capital from the country, make it more difficult for goods from the industrial areas to reach the seaports on schedule, and would in the long run be a heavy drain on the economic life of the country, thus compelling the voters of the country to reconsider their position.

At the same time, the organisation planned sabotage on government buildings and other 'symbols of apartheid' to 'serve as a source of inspiration to our people'. In addition, Mandela claimed, steps were taken for the possibility of guerrilla warfare, even though the organisation hoped that this would not be necessary. Experience, however, had suggested to them that it might be. Here, Mandela cited various attacks on the African people, beginning with the killing of twenty-four protestors who had been demonstrating for the release of union leader Samuel Masabalala in 1920 and concluding with the recent Sharpeville massacre: 'How many more Sharpevilles would there be in the history of our country?' he asked. 'And how many more Sharpevilles could the country stand without violence and terror becoming the order of the day?'

> Experience convinced us that rebellion would offer the government limitless opportunities for the indiscriminate slaughter of our people. But it was precisely because the soil of South Africa is already drenched with the blood of innocent Africans that we felt it our duty to make preparations as a long-term undertaking to use force in order to defend ourselves against force. If war were inevitable, we wanted the fight to be conducted on terms most favourable to our people. The fight which held out prospects best for us and the least risk of life to both sides was guerrilla warfare. We decided, therefore, in our preparations for the future, to make provision for the possibility of guerrilla warfare.

Mandela pointed out that since all white men underwent compulsory military training, it seemed expedient for MK members to seek military training abroad. He admits that he started to equip himself for the role that he might have to play 'if the struggle drifted into guerrilla warfare'.

The speech gains much of its power from the fact that Mandela identifies the truths of the case and dispels the lies against the backdrop of the broad history and vision of the ANC. He acknowledges many of the larger, and in most cases legally damning, accusations but also takes time to correct seemingly trivial inaccuracies. At the outset, he confesses to establishing MK, engaging in acts of sabotage, and planning for the possibility of guerrilla warfare, but he also takes time to deny that MK was responsible for particular incidents involving civilians and denounces the state's belief that the ANC's headquarters had been located at Liliesleaf. The tactic – of frank confession and denial – creates an impression of his trustworthiness as a speaker.

In the second half of the speech, Mandela spent a good deal of time refuting Percy Yutar's repeated attempt to conflate the SACP and the ANC. Invoking the Freedom Charter, which he said was 'by no means a blueprint for a socialist state', Mandela called 'for redistribution, but not nationalisation, of land' and pointed out that 'the ANC has never at any period of its history advocated a revolutionary change in the economic structure of the country'.

He went on to explain that although the parties are united against a common enemy and seek similar short-term solutions, they have different goals. While 'the Communist Party sought to emphasise class distinctions', Mandela claimed, 'the ANC seeks to harmonise them', and the parties cooperate in their quest for 'the removal of white supremacy'. He then cited a host of similar historical precedents:

> The history of the world is full of similar examples. Perhaps the most striking illustration is to be found in the co-operation between Great Britain, the United States of America, and the Soviet Union in the fight against Hitler. Nobody but Hitler would have dared to suggest that such co-operation turned Churchill or Roosevelt into communists or communist tools, or that Britain and America were working to bring about a communist world.

Mandela's dealing with the issue of communism was strategic and likely influenced by his travels abroad, where he had witnessed the zeitgeist of the Cold War first hand. He had also approached journalist Anthony Sampson, asking him to ensure that the speech would appeal to an international audience.[13] Understanding the fears of both white citizens and Western powers that were concerned that South Africa would serve as the gateway to communist revolution in Africa, Mandela's most convincing point came when he defined his own beliefs, describing himself as an 'African patriot' with a very different set of beliefs to his communist comrades:

> From my reading of Marxist literature and from conversations with Marxists, I have gained the impression that communists regard the parliamentary system of the West as undemocratic and reactionary. But, on the contrary, I am an admirer of such a system.
>
> The Magna Carta, the Petition of Rights, and the Bill of Rights are documents which are held in veneration by democrats throughout the world.
>
> I have great respect for British political institutions, and for the country's system of justice. I regard the British Parliament as the most democratic institution in the world, and the independence and impartiality of its judiciary never fail to arouse my admiration.
>
> The American Congress, that country's doctrine of separation of

powers, as well as the independence of its judiciary, arouses in me similar sentiments.

The final section of the speech analyses the political and socio-economic landscape in South Africa. Here, the ANC clearly held the moral high ground, and Mandela let the statistics speak for themselves:

> South Africa is the richest country in Africa, and could be one of the richest countries in the world. But it is a land of extremes and remarkable contrasts. The whites enjoy what may well be the highest standard of living in the world, whilst Africans live in poverty and misery. Forty per cent of the Africans live in hopelessly overcrowded and, in some cases, drought-stricken Reserves, where soil erosion and the overworking of the soil makes it impossible for them to live properly off the land. Thirty per cent are labourers, labour tenants, and squatters on white farms and work and live under conditions similar to those of the serfs of the Middle Ages. The other 30 per cent live in towns where they have developed economic and social habits which bring them closer in many respects to white standards. Yet most Africans, even in this group, are impoverished by low incomes and high cost of living.
>
> The highest-paid and the most prosperous section of urban African life is in Johannesburg. Yet their actual position is desperate. The latest figures were given on 25 March 1964 by Mr Carr, Manager of the Johannesburg Non-European Affairs Department. The poverty datum line for the average African family in Johannesburg (according to Mr Carr's department) is R42.84 per month. He showed that the average monthly wage is R32.24 and that 46 per cent of all African families in Johannesburg do not earn enough to keep them going.

In addition to the destructive results of poverty – malnutrition, tuberculosis, pellagra, kwashiorkor, gastro-enteritis, scurvy and high infant mortality – Mandela targets the evil logic of the apartheid state with devastating moral clarity:

> The complaint of Africans, however, is not only that they are poor and the whites are rich, but that the laws which are made by the whites are designed to preserve this situation. There are two ways to break out of poverty. The first is by formal education, and the second is by the worker acquiring a greater skill at his work and thus higher wages. As far as

Africans are concerned, both these avenues of advancement are deliberately curtailed by legislation.

The present government has always sought to hamper Africans in their search for education. One of their early acts, after coming into power, was to stop subsidies for African school feeding. Many African children who attended schools depended on this supplement to their diet. This was a cruel act.

There is compulsory education for all white children at virtually no cost to their parents, be they rich or poor. Similar facilities are not provided for the African children, though there are some who receive such assistance. African children, however, generally have to pay more for their schooling than whites. According to figures quoted by the South African Institute of Race Relations in its 1963 journal, approximately 40 per cent of African children in the age group between seven to fourteen do not attend school. For those who do attend school, the standards are vastly different from those afforded to white children. In 1960–61 the per capita government spending on African students at state-aided schools was estimated at R12.46. In the same years, the per capita spending on white children in the Cape Province (which are the only figures available to me) was R144.57. Although there are no figures available to me, it can be stated, without doubt, that the white children on whom R144.57 per head was being spent all came from wealthier homes than African children on whom R12.46 per head was being spent.

The quality of education is also different. According to the *Bantu Educational Journal*, only 5 660 African children in the whole of South Africa passed their Junior Certificate in 1962, and in that year only 362 passed matric. This is presumably consistent with the policy of Bantu education about which the present Prime Minister said, during the debate on the Bantu Education Bill in 1953: 'When I have control of Native education I will reform it so that Natives will be taught from childhood to realise that equality with Europeans is not for them ...

People who believe in equality are not desirable teachers for Natives. When my Department controls Native education it will know for what class of higher education a Native is fitted, and whether he will have a chance in life to use his knowledge.'

The other main obstacle to the economic advancement of the African is the industrial colour-bar under which all the better jobs of industry are reserved for Whites only. Moreover, Africans who do obtain employment in the unskilled and semi-skilled occupations which are open to them are not allowed to form trade unions which have recognition under the Industrial Conciliation Act. This means that strikes of African workers are illegal, and that they are denied the right of collective bargaining which is permitted to the better-paid White workers. The discrimination in the policy of successive South African governments towards African workers is demonstrated by the so-called 'civilised labour policy' under which sheltered, unskilled government jobs are found for those white workers who cannot make the grade in industry, at wages which far exceed the earnings of the average African employee in industry.

Mandela goes on to pre-empt the government's defence that black South Africans enjoy the highest standard of living in Africa, arguing that this point is 'irrelevant' in light of a political system designed to keep the African underfoot. Such a system will ensure the continuing existence of inequality in the country:

> Our complaint is not that we are poor by comparison with people in other countries, but that we are poor by comparison with the white people in our own country, and that we are prevented by legislation from altering this imbalance.

The final section of the speech is a heartfelt appeal to white South Africans to recognise the dignity of their fellow citizens, to embrace non-racialism and not to fear the consequences of democracy:

> The lack of human dignity experienced by Africans is the direct result of the policy of white supremacy. White supremacy implies black inferiority. Legislation designed to preserve white supremacy entrenches this notion. Menial tasks in South Africa are invariably performed by Africans. When anything has to be carried or cleaned the white man will look around for an African to do it for him, whether the African is employed by him or not. Because of this sort of attitude, whites tend to regard Africans as a separate breed. They do not look upon them as people with families of their own; they do not realise that they have emotions – that they fall in love like white people do; that they want to be with their wives and children like white people want to be with theirs; that they want to earn enough money to support their families properly, to feed and clothe them and send them to school. And what 'house-boy' or 'garden-boy' or labourer can ever hope to do this?

Pass laws, which to the Africans are among the most hated bits of legislation in South Africa, render any African liable to police surveillance at any time. I doubt whether there is a single African male in South Africa who has not at some stage had a brush with the police over his pass. Hundreds and thousands of Africans are thrown into jail each year under pass laws. Even worse than this is the fact that pass laws keep husband and wife apart and lead to the breakdown of family life.

Poverty and the breakdown of family life have secondary effects. Children wander about the streets of the townships because they have no schools to go to, or no money to enable them to go to school, or no parents at home to see that they go to school, because both parents (if there be two) have to work to keep the family alive. This leads to a breakdown in moral standards, to an alarming rise in illegitimacy, and to growing violence which erupts not only politically, but everywhere. Life in the townships is dangerous. There is not a day that goes by without somebody being stabbed or assaulted. And violence is carried out of the townships in the white living areas. People are afraid to walk alone in the streets after dark. Housebreakings and robberies are increasing, despite the fact that the death sentence can now be imposed for such offences. Death sentences cannot cure the festering sore.

Africans want to be paid a living wage. Africans want to perform work which they are capable of doing, and not work which the government declares them to be capable of. Africans want to be allowed to live where they obtain work, and not be endorsed out of an area because they were not born there. Africans want to be allowed to own land in places where they work, and not to be obliged to live in rented houses which they can never call their own. Africans want to be part of the general population, and not confined to living in their own ghettoes. African men want to have their wives and children to live with them where they work, and not be forced into an unnatural existence in men's hostels. African women want to be with their menfolk and not be left permanently widowed in the Reserves. Africans want to be allowed out after eleven o'clock at night and not to be confined to their rooms like little children. Africans want to be allowed to travel in their own country and to seek work where they want to and not where the Labour Bureau tells them to. Africans want a just share in the whole of South Africa; they want security and a stake in society.

Above all, we want equal political rights, because without them our disabilities will be permanent. I know this sounds revolutionary to the whites in this country, because the majority of voters will be Africans. This makes the white man fear democracy.

But this fear cannot be allowed to stand in the way of the only solution which will guarantee racial harmony and freedom for all. It is not true that the enfranchisement of all will result in racial domination. Political division, based on colour, is entirely artificial and, when it disappears, so will the domination of one colour group by another. The ANC has spent half a century fighting against racialism. When it triumphs it will not change that policy.

This then is what the ANC is fighting. Their struggle is a truly national one. It is a struggle of the African people, inspired by their own suffering and their own experience. It is a struggle for the right to live.

During my lifetime I have dedicated myself to this struggle of the African people. I have fought against white domination, and I have fought against black domination. I have cherished the ideal of a democratic and free society in which all persons live together in harmony and with equal opportunities. It is an ideal which I hope to live for and to achieve. But if needs be, it is an ideal for which I am prepared to die.

Joel Joffe, who served on the Rivonia defence team, remembers that Mandela, before delivering his final defiant lines, paused for a long time and looked squarely at the judge. 'You could hear a pin drop in the court,'[14] Joffe said, claiming that the audience maintained silence for nearly half a minute while Mandela's final words reverberated throughout the room. Mandela's legal team had in fact urged him to exclude the last line, fearing it was too much of a provocation. Mandela insisted on keeping it, however, agreeing only to add the phrase 'if needs be' at lawyer George Bizos's suggestion.[15]

Denis Goldberg, sitting alongside the defendants, claims that at the conclusion of the speech 'he knew it was a moment of history', the moment when Mandela 'emerged as a great leader'.[16]

The world agreed. Several international newspapers printed unedited excerpts from the speech, giving Mandela a platform to address their readers directly. The *New York Times* later claimed that most of the world regarded the Rivonia trialists as the 'George Washingtons and Benjamin Franklins of South Africa'.[17] In response, *Die Burger* grumbled that 'the aim of "selling" the accused to a rather broad overseas public as freedom fighters against an unbearable tyranny succeeded admirably'.[18]

The speech changed the focus of the court proceedings, at least in the eyes of the international community, putting apartheid on trial and drawing attention to the illegitimacy of the state. The world rallied around the Rivonia men, lobbying for clemency and for the trial to be overturned. Two days before sentencing, the United Nations passed a resolution calling for the emancipation of the trialists and all other political prisoners in South Africa.

The pleas fell on deaf ears. On 11 June 1964, exactly eleven months after the Liliesleaf raid, Judge Quartus de Wet announced his verdict: all but one of the accused were found guilty of various counts of sabotage. Although expected, the judgment, broadcast live on radio, was a blow; sabotage had recently been decreed a capital offence, and the state had already hanged several men found guilty of lesser acts than those committed by the accused. The liberal writer Alan Paton came forward to deliver a moving testimony in mitigation of sentence, claiming that he felt compelled to do so as a 'lover of my country',[19] and for a torturous twenty-four hours, the trialists and their loved ones waited to hear their fate.

The following morning, 12 June, De Wet delivered his sentence. Dressed in black and red robes, he began with the damning words that the crime before him was 'in essence one of high treason', leading the courtroom to expect the worst, but he quickly went on to say, 'in his usual quiet voice',[20] that he'd decided not to 'impose the supreme penalty'. Instead, the sentence he delivered was life imprisonment.[21]

Under any other circumstances, this would have been grim news indeed. The courtroom fell quiet for 'what seemed like a full minute'[22] before the trialists turned to face their supporters, breaking out into smiles of relief. They had escaped the noose.

Bram Fischer
'What I did was right', statement from the dock,
Supreme Court, Pretoria, 28 March 1966

One of the lawyers defending Nelson Mandela and his fellow Rivonia trialists could just as easily have been in the dock with them. Abram 'Bram' Fischer[1] was a trusted member of the Rivonia inner circle, who by coincidence was not at Liliesleaf farm on the afternoon of the raid in 1963. Unbeknown to the police officials, many of the incriminating documents seized during the raid were written by his hand.

Fischer was an anomaly in apartheid South Africa: a devout communist from the finest Afrikaner pedigree. His grandfather, Abraham Fischer, was prime minister of the Orange River Colony and, after 1910, minister of lands in the Union of South Africa, while his father, Percy, was judge president of the Orange Free State. A distinguished scholar, Fischer won a Rhodes Scholarship and studied at Oxford University between 1931 and 1934, at the height of the intellectual movement against fascism. In the years that followed, the great writers of the time – W.H. Auden, George Orwell, Ernest Hemingway – would travel to the Continent to support the Republican cause in the Spanish Civil War. These intellectual currents, and Fischer's own trip to the Soviet Union in 1932, influenced his lifelong embrace of communism.

The role of the Communist Party in South Africa was also important. In the 1940s, it was the only political home for white men and women seeking to oppose the racial injustices of the apartheid state.[2] Fischer had joined their ranks by 1942 and swiftly moved into leadership positions. By now he was married – to the independent-minded Molly Krige, who was also from a prominent Afrikaner family – and his law career was soaring, with many saying that he might one day become chief justice.

The Communist Party's alliance with the African National Congress grew and, in 1943, Fischer helped to revise the ANC's constitution. It wasn't long before the lawyer got into trouble with the law, however, and in 1946 he was charged with incitement because of the role he'd played as a Communist leader in the African Mineworkers' strike.

In the era of oppression that came with the National Party's 1948 victory, Fischer increasingly turned down lucrative work in order to appear for the defence in political trials. For a time, his communist beliefs appeared not to affect his law career – perhaps because of his Afrikaner background or perhaps because his peers were awed by his sheer brilliance. 'He comes from the right stock,' Nadine Gordimer wrote in 1966, 'with not only the brains but the intellectual *savoir-faire* coveted by people who sometimes feel, even at the peak of their political power, some veld-bred disadvantage in their dealings with the sophistications of the outside world.'[3] When the Communist Party was banned in 1950, he and his wife Molly found that they themselves were increasingly targets of the state.[4]

In 1956, Fischer formed part of the defence counsel for Nelson Mandela and others in the high-profile Treason Trial, which dragged on for five years but ultimately resulted in the defendants' acquittals. There was to be no such victory at the end of the Rivonia Trial, however, and on 11 June 1964 Fischer sat helplessly as the top leaders of the ANC and Communist Party were sentenced to life imprisonment.

Personal tragedy struck a few days after the trialists were sentenced. Bram and Molly, along with their friend Elizabeth Lewin, were heading to Cape Town to celebrate their daughter Ilse's twenty-first birthday. It was twilight, and Fischer was driving the couple's grey Mercedes-Benz through Koolspruit in the Orange Free State when a cow wandered into the road. Fischer braked and swerved to avoid hitting the animal, causing the car to veer down an incline into a deep pool of water. Fischer and Lewin were able to wind down their windows and escape, but Molly was trapped in the back of the sinking car. Despite Fischer's efforts to dive down and rescue her, she drowned.

Devastated by the loss of his wife of nearly thirty years, he channelled his grief into his political work. When he went to discuss the possibility of an appeal with the Rivonia trialists on Robben Island a few days after Molly's funeral service, a stoic Fischer didn't mention the incident, and since the prisoners were denied news material, they had no way of knowing about the tragedy.

A few days later, Fischer was himself arrested and held in detention. This was met with an outcry; the international legal community was particularly damning of the apartheid's detention-without-trial laws, and he was released after just three days. But it was only a matter of time before he was arrested again, and on 23 September 1964, along with Eli Weinberg and ten others, he was charged under the Suppression of Communism Act.

Before his arrest, Fischer's expertise had been requested at a patent case in London, and he asked the court for permission to attend, stating, 'I am an Afrikaner. My home is in South Africa. I will not leave my country because my political beliefs conflict with those of the Government ruling the country.'[5]

His legal credentials were so highly respected that the magistrate, calling him a 'son of our soil and an advocate of good standing', released him on bail of R10 000.

While attending to the case in London, Fischer was pressured to go into exile, but he kept his word and returned to South Africa for the start of his own trial in November 1965. He was facing a possible five years' imprisonment for participating in and furthering the aims of the Communist Party – and, despite being betrayed by colleagues, the charges remained 'relatively mild'. There was thus some surprise when, after a ten-day recess, Fischer did not appear on 23 January. His counsel Harold Hanson soon explained why, reading out a letter from Fischer:

> By the time this reaches you I shall be a long way from Johannesburg and shall absent myself from the remainder of the trial. But I shall still be in the country to which I said I would return when I was granted bail. I wish you to inform the Court that my absence, though deliberate, is not intended in any way to be disrespectful. Nor is it prompted by any fear of the punishment which might be inflicted on me. Indeed I realise fully that my eventual punishment may be increased by my present conduct ...
>
> My decision was made only because I believe that it is the duty of every true opponent of this Government to remain in this country and to oppose its monstrous policy of apartheid with every means in his power. That is what I shall do for as long as I can ...

Given that Fischer could have gone into exile just a few months earlier, the decision to go into hiding made little sense. It was a defiant political gesture that put him at great personal risk. Outraged by his absconding, the Johannesburg Bar Council lobbied to have him struck off the advocates' roll on the grounds that his 'recent conduct was unbefitting that of an advocate', and in a trial held in his absence, Judge Quartus de Wet, who'd presided over the Rivonia Trial, agreed. The case reportedly crushed Fischer, whose only solace came from De Wet's implicit acknowledgement that law and justice in South Africa weren't identical, conveyed in his referral to Fischer's possible readmission at 'some future time'.[6]

Under the name Douglas Black – which hinted at the 'absurdities of racial assignations'[7] – and wearing a goatee for disguise, Fischer remained underground for a lonely 290 days, during which time his communist colleagues in London took a prolonged period to provide him with a passport. He didn't get the opportunity to use it, however, mainly because the death of Molly, the isolation of living underground and his disillusionment with the political situation appeared to have resulted in a stymieing depression. Then, one evening in November 1965, after several misleading apprehensions of lookalikes, a Lieutenant Rudolf van Rensburg recognised Fischer, who was then driving home. The lieutenant immediately contacted his colleagues, who swooped in quickly.[8] In Fischer's hideout, the police officials found several incriminating documents, including a copy of the journal *African Communist*. Fischer's game was up.

This time the charges were more serious and had multiplied from four to fifteen. In March 1966 he was accused of furthering the aims of communism and conspiring to overthrow the government. If found guilty, the sentence, as he well knew, would likely be life imprisonment. Following the example set by Mandela, he gave up his right to cross-examination and the prospect of a not-guilty verdict, and chose instead to give a speech from the dock.

I am on trial for my political beliefs and for the conduct to which those beliefs drove me. Whatever labels may be attached to the fifteen charges brought against me, they all arise from my having been a member of the Communist Party and from my activities as a member. I engaged upon those activities because I believed that, in the dangerous circumstances which have been created in South Africa, it was my duty to do so.

When a man is on trial for his political beliefs and actions, two courses are open to him. He can either confess to his transgressions and plead for mercy or he can justify his beliefs and explain why he acted as he did. Were I to ask for forgiveness today I would betray my cause. That course is not open to me. I believe that what I did was right. I must therefore explain to this Court what my motives were: why I hold the beliefs that I do and why I was compelled to act in accordance with them.

My belief, moreover, is one reason why I have pleaded not guilty to all the charges brought against me. Though I shall deny a number of important allegations made, this Court is aware of the fact that there is much in the State case which has not been contested. Yet, if I am to explain my motives and my actions as clearly as I am able, then this Court was entitled to have had before it the witnesses who testified in chief and under cross-examination against me. Some of these, I believe, were fine and loyal persons who have now turned traitors to their cause and to their country because of the methods used against them by the State – vicious and inhuman methods. Their evidence may therefore in important respects be unreliable.

There is another and more compelling reason for my plea and why I persist in it. I accept the general rule that for the protection of a society laws should be obeyed. But when the laws themselves become immoral and require the citizen to take part in an organised system of oppression – if only by his silence or apathy – then I believe that a higher duty arises. This compels one to refuse to recognise such laws.

The laws under which I am being prosecuted were enacted by a wholly unrepresentative body, a body in which three-quarters of the people of this country have no voice whatever. These laws were enacted, not to prevent the spread of communism, but for the purpose of silencing the opposition of the large majority of our citizens to a government intent upon depriving them, solely on account of their colour, of the most elementary human rights: of the right to freedom and happiness, the right to live together with their families wherever they might choose, to earn their livelihoods to the best of their abilities, to rear and educate their children in a civilised fashion, to take part in the administration of their country and obtain a fair share of the wealth they produce; in short, to live as human beings.

My conscience does not permit me to afford these laws such recognition as even a plea of guilty would involve. Hence, though I shall be convicted by this Court, I cannot plead guilty. I believe that the future may well say that I acted correctly.

My first duty then is to explain to the Court that I hold and have for many years held the view that politics can only be properly understood and that our immediate political problems can only be satisfactorily solved without violence and civil war by the application of that scientific system of political knowledge known as Marxism.

[...]

When I consider what it was that moved me to join the Communist Party, I have to cast my mind back for more than a quarter of a century to try and ascertain what precisely my motives at that time were.

Marxism is a system of philosophy which covers and seeks to explain the whole range of human activity, but looking back, I cannot say that it was Marxism as a social science that drew me originally to the Communist Party, just as little, presumably, as a doctor would say that he was originally drawn to his own field of science by its scientifically demonstrable truths. These only become apparent later.

In my mind there remain two clear reasons for my approach to the Communist Party. The one is the glaring injustice which exists and has existed for a long time in South African society, the other, a gradual realisation as I became more and more deeply involved with the Congress Movement of those years, that is, the movement for freedom and equal human rights for all, that it was always members of the Communist Party who seemed prepared, regardless of cost, to sacrifice most; to give of their best, to face the greatest dangers, in the struggle against poverty and discrimination.

[...]

Though nearly forty years have passed, I can remember vividly the experience which brought home to me exactly what this 'white' attitude is and also how artificial and unreal it is. Like many young Afrikaners I grew up on a farm. Between the ages of eight and twelve my daily companions were two young Africans of my own age. I can still remember their names. For four years we were, when I was not at school, always in each other's company. We roamed the farm together, we hunted and played together, we modelled clay oxen and swam. And never can I remember that the colour of our skins affected our fun or our quarrels or our close friendship in any way.

Then my family moved to town and I moved back to the normal white South African mode of life where the only relationship with Africans was that of master to servant. I finished my schooling and went to university. There one of my first interests became a study of the theory of segregation, then beginning to blossom. This seemed to me to provide the solution to South Africa's problems and I became an earnest believer in it. A year later, to help in a small way to put this theory into practice, because I do not believe that theory and practice can or should be separated, I joined the Bloemfontein Joint Council of Europeans and Africans, a body devoted largely to trying to induce various authorities to provide proper (and separate) amenities for Africans. I arrived for my first meeting with other newcomers. I found myself being introduced to leading members of the African community. I found I had to shake hands with them. This, I found, required an enormous effort of will on my part. Could I really, as a white adult, touch the hand of a black man in friendship?

That night I spent many hours in thought trying to account for my strange revulsion when I remembered I had never had any such feelings towards my boyhood friends. What became abundantly clear was that it was I and not the black man who had changed; that despite my growing interest in him, I had developed an antagonism for which I could find no rational basis whatsoever.

I cannot burden this Court with personal reminiscences. The result of all this was that in that and in succeeding years when some of us ran literacy classes in the old Waaihoek location in Bloemfontein, I came to understand that colour prejudice was a wholly irrational phenomenon and that true human friendship could extend across the colour bar once the initial prejudice was overcome. And that I think was lesson No. 1 on my way to the Communist Party, which has always refused to accept any colour bar and has always stood firm on the belief, itself two thousand years old, of the eventual brotherhood of all men.

The other reason for my attraction to the Communist Party, the willingness to sacrifice, was a matter of personal observation. But there could be no doubt of its existence. By that time the Communist Party had already for two decades stood avowedly and unconditionally for political rights for non-whites and its white members were, save for a handful of courageous individuals, the only whites who showed complete disregard for the hatred which this attitude attracted from their fellow white South Africans. These members, I found, were whites who could have taken full advantage of all the privileges open to them and their families because of their colour, who could have obtained lucrative employment and social position, but who, instead, were prepared for the sake of their consciences, to perform the most menial and unpopular work at little or sometimes no remuneration. These were a body of whites who were not prepared to flourish on the deprivations suffered by others.

But apart from the example of the white members, it was always the communists of all races who were at all times prepared to give of their time and their energy and such means as they had, to help those in need and those most deeply affected by discrimination. It was members of the Communist Party who helped with night schools and feeding schemes, who assisted trade unions fighting desperately to preserve standards of living and who threw themselves into the work of the national movements. It was African communists who constantly risked arrest or the loss of their jobs or even their homes in locations, in order to gain or retain some rights. And all this was carried on regardless of whether it would be popular with the authorities or not.

Without a question this fearless adherence to principle must always exercise a strong appeal to those who wish to take part in politics, not for personal advantage, but in the hope of making some positive contribution. The Court will bear in mind that at that stage, and for many years afterwards, the Communist Party was the only political party which stood for an extension of the franchise. To this day, the elimination of discrimination and the granting to all of normal, human rights remain its chief objective. [...] It is the objective for which I have lived and worked for nearly thirty years.

But I have to tell this Court not only why I joined the Communist Party when it was a legal party – when at times it had representatives in Parliament, the Cape Provincial Council and the City Council of Johannesburg. I must also explain why I continued to be a member after it was declared illegal. This involves what I believe on the one hand to be the gravely dangerous situation which has been created in South Africa from about 1950 onwards, and, on the other, the vital contribution which socialist thought can make towards its solution. I shall start with the latter.

This is neither the time nor the place in which to embark upon an exposition of a system of philosophy. I want to refer, however, to a few well-recognised principles which demonstrate the nature of the extremely dangerous situation into which South Africa is being led, by those who choose to ignore these principles, and which also demonstrate the desperate urgency for reversing this direction. I should add that most of the Marxist principles to which I shall refer are today accepted by many historians and economists who are by no means themselves Marxists. It is clear for instance that during the course of its development, human society assumes various forms. There is a primitive kind of communism found in early stages, best illustrated today by the Bushman society still in existence in parts of South Africa. There have been slave-owning societies and feudal societies. There is capitalism and socialism, and each of these types of society develops its own characteristic form of government, of political control.

Fischer goes on to outline, in orthodox Marxist terms, how societies develop from one form to another and how a political system must necessarily change when the economic system changes.

The political changes, therefore, are as inevitable as the economic changes, and ultimately both depend upon that slow but ever accelerating process of change in the methods of production. It is these political changes which, in the Marxist language, are known as 'revolutions', whether they take place by violent or by peaceful means, and this again depends on the circumstances at any given stage of history. It is not difficult to illustrate this proposition either, if one merely compares the French

Revolution with the evolution of capitalist democracy in England during the nineteenth century.

[...]

History therefore becomes something which can be rationally understood and explained. It ceases to be a meaningless agglomeration of events or a mere account of great men wandering in haphazard fashion across its stage. Similarly, modern society itself assumes a meaning as well. It has not appeared on the scene by mere chance; it is not final or immutable and in its South African form it contains its own contradictions which must irresistibly lead to its change.

Fischer adds that 'Marxism is not something evil or violent or subversive', in spite of the 'unbridled and unscrupulous' propaganda against it, and points out that 'socialism has already been adopted by fourteen states with a population of over 1000 million people'. He reminds his audience of 'those four years when the Soviet State, then the only socialist State, stood as one of the main bastions between civilisation and the Nazi armies'.

He then turns his attention to capitalism, a system in which the means of production (such as factories, mines and land) are owned by a small handful of people, a system that depends on competition for markets, raw materials and cheap labour – which led to imperialism and the division of the world into colonies in the nineteenth century. For the vast majority of people, this system is based on fear of unemployment and poverty, and this fear is fertile soil for racialism and intolerance. The 'ultimate remedy for [these] evils ...' he posits, 'lies in a change to a socialist system', where 'the means of production are owned by the people', where 'production takes place not for profit but for the benefit of the people', and which 'can ensure full employment at all times and will therefore abolish fear'. As society transforms from socialism to true communism, 'a superabundance of wealth entitles all to receive according to their needs', and this is accompanied by 'an ever widening democracy and an ever-increasing degree of individual freedom and participation in the control of the country'.

But, as far as South Africa is concerned, there are matters that the future will settle.

As I have already indicated, we have never put forward socialism as our immediate solution. What we have said is that immediate dangers can be avoided by what we always refer to as a national democratic revolution, that is by bringing our state at this stage into line with the needs of today, by abolishing discrimination, extending political rights and then allowing our peoples to settle their own future.

Fischer talks about the decolonisation movement that has swept through Africa and elsewhere in the world:

Four empires have had to dissolve themselves and have been compelled to grant political independence to some thirty or forty states, just as Britain was compelled to grant the vote to the so-called 'lower' classes last century. But with three or four notable exceptions these States have achieved their independence peacefully and without having to resort to any form of violence.

South African State propaganda suggests that this was due to some mystical decadence in the West. Nothing could be further from the truth. Britain, France, Holland and Belgium have not in a couple of decades become soft or decadent. Far deeper forces have come into play which left them with no alternative but to do what they have done. The combination of the new nationalism and the urge to take control of their own economic future proved in the new States to be irresistible.

It should indeed not be difficult for South Africans to understand this process. In one sense we Afrikaners were the vanguard of this liberation movement in Africa. Of all former colonies we displayed the greatest resistance to imperial conquest, a resistance which a handful of freedom fighters carried on for three years against the greatest Empire of all time. We failed then. A few decades later, without having once more to resort to arms, we succeeded in gaining our independence because it was impossible to stop us. [...] Now, as we communists see it, those who rule South Africa are trying to do just those things which imperialism could achieve in the nineteenth century but which are impossible in the second half of the twentieth. That attempt must lead inevitably to disaster.

To further explain why he was impelled to break the law, Fischer warns about the dangers of intensifying the system of segregation at precisely the time when decolonisation had become unstoppable:

This has far-reaching consequences for South Africa, which is in effect trying to establish a 'colonial' system of its own brand at this stage of history, complete with 'indirect' rule and even with the re-establishment of tribalism. This can never succeed for one cannot move backwards in history.

I am not trying to dramatise this situation. I am stating nothing but plain simple fact: It is there for anyone to see – for anyone whose vision is not totally obscured by the myopia of the white South African:

There is a strong and ever growing movement for freedom and for basic human rights amongst the non-white people of the country – i.e. amongst four-fifths of the population. This movement is supported not only by the whole of Africa, but by virtually the whole membership of the United Nations as well – both West and East.

However complacent and indifferent white South Africa may be, this movement can never be stopped. In the end it must triumph. Above all, those of us who are Afrikaans and who have experienced our own successful struggle for full equality should know this.

The sole questions for the future of all of us therefore are not whether the change will come, but only whether the change can be brought about peacefully and without bloodshed; and what the position of the white man is going to be in the period immediately following on the establishment of democracy – after the years of cruel discrimination and oppression and humiliation, which he has imposed on the non-white people of this country.

[...]

I must now deal further with the allegations made in the evidence led by the State. Before doing so, I have one more thing to say as to my motives. I entreated bail on the 25th January of last year. Had I wanted to save myself, I could have done so by leaving the country or simply by remaining in England in 1964. I did not do so because I regarded it as my duty to remain in this country and to continue with my work as long as I was physically able to do so. The same reasons which induced me to join the illegal Communist Party induced me to entreat bail. By 1965 they had been magnified a hundred-fold. All protest had been silenced. The very administration of justice had been changed by the 90-day law and by the 'Sobukwe' clause, which, in a vital respect, had usurped the functions even of the court trying me. My punishment was no longer in the sole discretion of that court.

During the previous decade too – and now I speak as an Afrikaner – something sinister for the future of my people had happened. It is true that 'apartheid has existed for many decades' with all that it entails in shapes ranging from segregation and the deprivation of rights, to such apparently trivial things as the constant depicting in our Afrikaans newspaper cartoons of the African as a cross between a baboon and a

19th century American coon. What is not appreciated by my fellow Afrikaner, because he has cut himself off from all contact with non-whites, is that the extreme intensification of that policy over the past fifteen years is laid entirely at his door. He is now blamed as an Afrikaner for all the evils and humiliation of apartheid.

Hence today the policeman is known as a 'Dutch'. That is why too, when I give an African a lift during a bus boycott, he refuses to believe that I am an Afrikaner.

All this bodes ill for our future. It has bred a deep-rooted hatred for Afrikaners, for our language, our political and racial outlook amongst all non-whites – yes, even amongst those who seek positions of authority by pretending to support apartheid. It is rapidly destroying amongst non-whites all belief in future co-operation with Afrikaners.

To remove this barrier will demand all the wisdom, leadership and influence of those Congress leaders now interned and imprisoned for their political beliefs. It demands also that Afrikaners themselves should protest openly and clearly against discrimination. Surely, in such circumstances there was an additional duty cast on me, that at least one Afrikaner should make this protest actively and positively, even though, as a result, I now face fifteen charges instead of four.

It was to keep faith with all those dispossessed by apartheid that I broke my undertaking to the Court, separated myself from my family, pretended I was someone else, and adopted the life of a fugitive. I owed it to the political prisoners, to the banished, to the silenced and those under house arrest, not to remain a spectator, but to act. I knew what they expected of me and I did it. I felt responsible, not to those who are indifferent to the sufferings of others, but to those who are concerned. I knew that by valuing, above all their judgment, I would be condemned by people who are content to see themselves as respectable and loyal citizens. I cannot regret any condemnation that may follow me.

Fischer goes on to deal with the evidence against him, which in some cases he says is inaccurate. Then, like Mandela before him, he outlines the history of the struggle and the reasons for MK's formation.

In these circumstances history will not blame those Congress leaders who, in some way or other, came together in July 1961 and devised the scheme by which the Spear of the Nation was to be brought into existence under the control of one of its ablest and most responsible leaders, Nelson Mandela.

[...]

The Congresses and the Communist Party did not wish to have their membership held liable for every act of sabotage nor, and this was of crucial political importance, did they want their members to gain the idea that once sabotage commenced, political work should cease. This separation of organisations was always maintained. I had no hand in the founding of uMkhonto and I was never a member. I became aware of its existence, and I did not disapprove.

[...]

I should say, at this stage, that the Communist Party has always, in this country and elsewhere, been rigidly opposed to individual acts of violence. Such acts are regarded by communists as acts of terrorism, which achieve nothing. Communists are not, of course, opposed to violence on principle. They are not pacifists. They do, however, believe that, in general, it is the working class which suffers most from violence and war, and hence that wherever possible this is to be avoided.

We in the Communist Party never believed that South Africa was ripe for a socialist revolution. That is precisely why in our programme we aim in the first place only at democracy and the abolition of racial discrimination and leave entirely open the manner in which, and the time when, socialism may eventually be achieved in this country, for, of course, it is clear from all the theoretical Marxist statements today, that communists do not believe that violence is the only method by which socialism can be achieved.

He concludes with a personal reminiscence about events during the First World War, when he was a young boy.

The last subject I want to mention is personal. Therefore I hesitated before deciding to do so. But I shall not be giving evidence or making a statement in mitigation and perhaps I should acquaint the Court with one aspect of my background.

I was a Nationalist at the age of six, if not before. I saw violence for the first time when, sitting on my father's shoulder, I saw business premises with German names burned to the ground in Bloemfontein, including those of some of my own family. I can still remember the weapons collected by my father and his friends who were bent on preventing a second outbreak. I saw my father leave with an ambulance unit to try and join the rebel forces. I remained a Nationalist for over twenty years thereafter and became, in 1929, the first Nationalist Prime Minister of a student parliament.

I never doubted that the policy of segregation was the only solution to this country's problems until the Hitler theory of race superiority began to threaten the world with genocide and with the greatest disaster in all history. The Court will see that I did not shed my old beliefs with ease.

It was when these doubts arose that, one night, when I was driving an old ANC leader to his house far out to the west of Johannesburg, that I propounded to him the well-worn theory that if you separate races you diminish the points at which friction between them may occur, and hence ensure good relations. His answer was the essence of simplicity. If you place races of one country in two camps, said he, and cut off contact between them, those in each camp begin to forget that those in the other camp are ordinary human beings, that each lives and laughs in the same way, that each experiences joy or sorrow, pride or humiliation for the same reasons. Thereby each becomes suspicious of the other and each eventually fears the other, which is the basis of all racialism.

I believe no-one could more effectively sum up the South African position today. Only contact between the races can eliminate suspicion and fear; only contact and co-operation can breed tolerance and understanding. Segregation or apartheid, however genuinely believed in, can produce only those things it is supposed to avoid: inter-racial tension and estrangement, intolerance and race hatreds.

All the conduct with which I have been charged has been directed towards maintaining contact and understanding between the races of this country. If one day it may help to establish a bridge across which white leaders and the real leaders of the non-white can meet to settle the destinies of all of us by negotiation and not by force of arms, I shall be able to bear with fortitude any sentence which this Court may impose on me. It will be a fortitude strengthened by this knowledge at least, that for twenty-five years I have taken no part, not even by passive acceptance, in that hideous system of discrimination which we have erected in this country, and which has become a by-word in the civilised world today.

In prophetic words, in February 1881, one of the great Afrikaner leaders addressed the President and Volksraad of the Orange Free State.

His words are inscribed on the base of the statue of President Kruger in the square in front of this Court. After great agony and suffering after two wars they were eventually fulfilled without force or violence for my people.

President Kruger's words were:

'Met vertrouwen leggen wij onze zaak open voor de geheele wereld. Het zij wij overwinnen, het zij wij sterven: de vrijheid zal in Afrika rijzen als de zon uit de morgenwolken.' ['With confidence we place our case before the entire world. Whether we are victorious or whether we die, freedom will arise in Africa like the sun from the morning clouds.']

In the meaning which those words bear today they are truly prophetic, as they were in 1881. My motive in all I have done has been to prevent a repetition of that unnecessary and futile anguish which has already been suffered in one struggle for freedom.

The speech from the dock, described by Fischer's biographer as a 'revolutionary's definitive moment',[9] gave Fischer the opportunity to explain all of the questions surrounding his case: why, when he might have been free in exile or suffered a lesser sentence, did he choose to go into hiding? As an advocate, he must have been aware of the likely outcome. He spoke for a full five hours – through the tea and lunch breaks – and presented the court with a detailed account of his life and principles.

Fischer's speech combines doctrinaire Marxism and humanism, and pleads for a moral revolution. In addition to the immorality of apartheid, Fischer speaks 'as an Afrikaner' and warns of its danger for his people. 'It has bred a deep-rooted hatred for Afrikaners,' he says, 'for our language, our political and racial outlook'. This position and Fischer's story would later appeal to dissident South African novelists and, in the 1970s, he was fictionalised in André Brink's *Rumours of Rain* and Nadine Gordimer's *Burger's Daughter*, both of which reproduced parts of his speech, which was banned days after its delivery.

Newspaper reports on Fischer's speech emphasised his lone position, frequently mentioning that the dock in which he stood had been especially built for the Rivonia trialists.[10] Whereas Mandela and his colleagues had stood together, Fischer faced his fate alone. He was also, says Stephen Clingman, 'no Nelson Mandela ... and there was no obvious drama or passion; but the effect none the less was transfixing'.[11] The success of the speech no doubt owed much to Fischer's identity. Here was a man of the law, an Afrikaner who many had said could one day become chief justice, standing in the courtroom and declaring 'what I did was right' with the prospect of a life sentence hanging over his head. There could be no greater indictment of the country's laws.

On 4 May 1966, as expected, he was found guilty and sentenced to life imprisonment five days later. The night before sentencing, he'd written to his children to say, '[J]ust as there is a last night as an awaiting trial prisoner, so there will come a "last night" for me as a prisoner. Just think what a night that will be.'[12]

But there would be no such reunion with his son, Paul, who died of cystic fibrosis at the age of twenty-three in 1971. Fischer wasn't allowed to attend the funeral. Then, in 1974, Fischer was diagnosed with cancer and, after growing increasingly weak, he suffered a fall while struggling to get into the shower with his crutches. It left him with a fractured femur, partial paralysis and an inability to talk. Helen Suzman spearheaded the campaign for clemency in South Africa, pointing out that a sixty-six-year-old in his condition would hardly be capable of political incitement, but the authorities remained unmoved. During this time, Fischer was largely cared for by Rivonia trialist Denis Goldberg, who was also serving a life sentence.

In December of that year, the authorities finally transferred him to hospital, where he fell into a brief coma. When he recovered, he was placed under house arrest at his brother's home in Bloemfontein. There, after two months with friends and family, Fischer died on 8 May 1975. In an act of what Helen Suzman called 'sheer vindictiveness',[13] minister of justice Jimmy Kruger dictated the terms of the funeral arrangements and demanded that Fischer's ashes be returned to the prison department.

Although his ashes were never recovered, in 2003 – in recognition of his principled stand against injustice – the Johannesburg High Court passed a new law specifically for the purpose of reinstating certain deceased legal practitioners. Under what instantly became known as the 'Bram Fischer Act', some forty years after being struck from the roll, Fischer became the first South African ever to be posthumously reinstated to the Bar.[14]

Robert F. Kennedy

'Ripple of Hope' speech, University of Cape Town,
6 June 1966

When Senator Robert F. Kennedy made the decision to travel to South Africa in 1966, the world came along with him. The younger brother of the recently assassinated John F. Kennedy was the next best thing to the former US president himself, and the historic visit put South Africa in the global spotlight.

The National Union of South African Students (NUSAS) invited the forty-year-old junior New York senator to speak at their Day of Reaffirmation of Academic and Human Freedom – an annual event held as a reminder of academia's moral commitments. In the 1960s, the multiracial NUSAS became increasingly vocal in its opposition to apartheid. They organised protests against the 1962 Sabotage Act and the extension of the General Law Amendment Act, and they resisted racial segregation in universities and in sport.[1] When an earlier plan to have Martin Luther King Jr address their annual convention was thwarted because the government refused to grant him a visa,[2] NUSAS's president, the twenty-one-year-old Ian Robertson, came up with the idea, in 'the middle of the night', to invite Kennedy. NUSAS was looking to 'reach outside the country', said Robertson, and Kennedy, who had established a reputation as a civil rights advocate serving as Attorney-General during his brother's presidency, was an obvious choice because 'he captured the idealism, the passion, of young people all over the world'.[3] To the student organisation's great surprise,[4] the statesman accepted the invitation.

Although Kennedy's visa application was approved – presumably because the government feared slighting a potential future president – over forty applications from journalists and photographers wanting to document the visit were denied[5] and the trip was restricted to five days. The government dismissed the visit as 'presidential publicity-seeking build-up',[6] and B.J. Vorster, then minister of justice, claimed that it was 'provocative of NUSAS to have invited the senator and provocation of him to have accepted'.[7] The government was partly right; Kennedy's trip to Africa no doubt helped to raise his political profile, but attempts to control the media were ultimately self-defeating: 'The Government is always sensitive to anything that it fears will result in adverse publicity,' *The Times* of London reported at the time, 'but it is probable that its banning action will do more damage in this direction than any inflating of Senator Kennedy's visit.'[8] Indeed, the *Cape Times* went on to lament that the government's 'prim talk about dislike of publicity stunts is foolish while taking precisely the action to ensure the success of the stunt.'[9]

While Kennedy's acceptance of the invitation must have seemed a coup to the young Robertson, he paid a heavy price for it. A few weeks before the senator was due to arrive, the government slapped him with a five-year banning order under the Suppression of Communism Act. The order forbade the young law student to attend any social or political meetings (apart from his 'bona fide' lectures for his LLB degree) or to converse with groups of more than three people at a time. In addition, he was unable to teach or attend courtroom proceedings unless subpoenaed. The ban crippled Robertson's career prospects and meant that he was unable to attend Kennedy's address.

Kennedy, his wife Ethel and his speechwriter Adam Walinsky arrived shortly before midnight on 4 June at Jan Smuts Airport in Johannesburg. Despite the late hour, he was welcomed with great fanfare, and a crowd of over three thousand people broke into a rendition of 'For he's a jolly good fellow'.[10] Over the following few days, he met with businesspeople, newspaper editors and opposition leaders, including Helen Suzman of the Progressive Party and S.J. Marais Steyn of the United Party. His requests to meet with government representatives were declined, however.[11]

Two days after his arrival, Kennedy made his way to the University of Cape Town to give the first of his university addresses (with subsequent speeches planned for the universities of Stellenbosch, Natal and the Witwatersrand). This first speech attracted a good deal of media attention, and the university arranged for loudspeakers to extend its range. The steps leading up to the campus's Jameson Hall were so packed with hopeful listeners that it took half an hour for Kennedy to make his way through the doors. Inside, an all-white audience of mainly students filled the hall, with a chair to the left of the lectern left empty for Robertson in symbolic protest against his imposed absence.

Kennedy began his speech by misleading the audience – a favoured rhetorical device of his, which drew amused applause from the crowd:

> I come here this evening because of my deep interest and affection for a land settled by the Dutch in the mid-seventeenth century, then taken over by the British, and at last independent; a land in which the native inhabitants were at first subdued, but relations with whom remain a problem to this day; a land which defined itself on a hostile frontier; a land which has tamed rich natural resources through the energetic application of modern technology; a land which was once the importer

of slaves, and now must struggle to wipe out the last traces of that former bondage. I refer, of course, to the United States of America.

But I am glad to come here, and my wife and I and all of our party are glad to come here to South Africa and we are glad to come here to Cape Town. I am already greatly enjoying my stay and my visit here. I am making an effort to meet and exchange views with people from all walks of life, and all segments of South African opinion, including those who represent the views of the government. Today I am glad to meet with the National Union of South African Students. For a decade, NUSAS has stood and worked for the principles of the Universal Declaration of Human Rights – principles which embody the collective hopes of men of good will all around the globe.

Your work, at home and in international student affairs, has brought great credit to yourselves and to your country. I know the National Student Association in the United States feels a particularly close relationship with this organisation. And I wish to thank especially Mr Ian Robertson, who first extended the invitation on behalf of NUSAS. I wish to thank him for his kindness to me in inviting me. I am very sorry that he cannot be with us here this evening.

I was happy to have had the opportunity to meet and speak with him earlier this evening and I presented him with a copy of *Profiles in Courage* which was a book that was written by President John Kennedy and was signed to him by President Kennedy's widow, Mrs John Kennedy.

This is a Day of Affirmation, a celebration of liberty. We stand here in the name of freedom. At the heart of that Western freedom and democracy is the belief that the individual man, the child of God, is the touchstone of value, and all society, all groups, and states, exist for that person's benefit. Therefore the enlargement of liberty for individual human beings must be the supreme goal and the abiding practice of any Western society.

The first element of this individual liberty is the freedom of speech: the right to express and communicate ideas, to set oneself apart from the dumb beasts of field and forest; the right to recall governments to their duties and to their obligations; above all, the right to affirm one's membership and allegiance to the body politic – to society – to the men with whom we share our land, our heritage, and our children's future.

Hand in hand with freedom of speech goes the power to be heard, to share in the decisions of government which shape men's lives. Everything that makes man's life worthwhile – family, work, education, a place to

97

rear one's children and a place to rest one's head – all this depends on the decisions of government; all can be swept away by a government which does not heed the demands of its people, and I mean all of its people. Therefore, the essential humanity of man can be protected and preserved only where government must answer – not just to the wealthy, not just to those of a particular religion, not just to those of a particular race, but to all of the people.

And even government by the consent of the governed, as in our own Constitution, must be limited in its power to act against its people; so that there may be no interference with the right to worship, but also no interference with the security of the home; no arbitrary imposition of pains or penalties on an ordinary citizen by officials high or low; no restriction on the freedom of man to seek education or to seek work or opportunity of any kind, so that each man may become all he is capable of becoming.

These are the sacred rights of Western society. These were the essential differences between us and Nazi Germany, as they were between Athens and Persia.

They are the essence of our differences with communism today. I am unalterably opposed to communism because it exalts the state over the individual and over the family, and because its system contains a lack of freedom of speech, of protest, of religion, and of the press, which is characteristic of a totalitarian regime. The way of opposition to communism is not to imitate its dictatorship, but to enlarge individual freedom, in our own countries and all over the globe. There are those in every land who would label as Communist every threat to their privilege. But may I say to you as I have seen on my travels in all sections of the world, reform is not communism. And the denial of freedom, in whatever name, only strengthens the very communism it claims to oppose.

Many nations have set forth their own definitions and declarations of these principles. And there have often been wide and tragic gaps between promise and performance, ideal and reality. Yet the great ideals have constantly recalled us to our own duties. And – with painful slowness – we in the United States have extended and enlarged the meaning and the practice of freedom to all of our people.

For two centuries, my own country has struggled to overcome the self-imposed handicap of prejudice and discrimination based on nationality, on social class, or race – discrimination profoundly repugnant to the theory and to the command of our Constitution. Even as my father grew up in Boston, Massachusetts, signs told him No Irish Need Apply. Two generations later President Kennedy became the first Irish-Catholic and the first Catholic to head the nation; but how many men of ability had, before 1961, been denied the opportunity to contribute to the nation's progress because they were Catholic, or because they were of Irish extraction? How many sons of Italian or Jewish or Polish parents slumbered in the slums – untaught, unlearned, their potential lost forever to our nation and to the human race? Even today, what price will we pay before we have assured full opportunity to millions of Negro Americans?

In the last five years we have done more to assure equality to our Negro citizens, and to help the deprived both white and black, than in the hundred years before that time. But much, much more remains to be done.

For there are millions of Negroes untrained for the simplest of jobs, and thousands every day denied their full and equal right under the law; and the violence of the disinherited, the insulted, the injured, looms over the streets of Harlem and of Watts and of the South Side Chicago.

But a Negro American trains as an astronaut, one of mankind's first explorers into outer space; another is the chief barrister of the United States government, and dozens sit on the benches of our court; and another, Dr Martin Luther King, is the second man of African descent to win the Nobel Peace Prize for his non-violent efforts for social justice between all of the races.

We have passed laws prohibiting discrimination in education, in employment, in housing, but these laws alone cannot overcome the heritage of centuries – of broken families and stunted children, and poverty and degradation and pain.

[...]

In some, there is concern that change will submerge the rights of a minority, particularly where that minority is of a different race from that of the majority. We in the United States believe in the protection of minorities; we recognise the contributions they can make and the leadership they can provide; and we do not believe that any people – whether minority or majority, or individual human being – are 'expendable' in the cause of theory or of policy. We recognise also that justice between men and nations is imperfect, and that humanity sometimes progresses very slowly indeed.

All do not develop in the same manner, and at the same pace. Nations, like men, often march to the beat of different drummers, and the precise solutions of the United States can neither be dictated nor transplanted to others, and that is not our intention. What is important is that all nations must march toward increasing freedom; toward justice for all; toward a society strong and flexible enough to meet the demands of all of its people, whatever their race, and the demands of a world of immense and dizzying change that face us all.

In a few hours, the plane that brought me to this country crossed over oceans and countries which have been a crucible of human history. In minutes we traced the migration of men over thousands of years; seconds, the briefest glimpse, and we passed battlefields on which millions of men once struggled and died. We could see no national boundaries, no vast gulfs or high walls dividing people from people; only nature and the works of man – homes and factories and farms – everywhere reflecting man's common effort to enrich his life. Everywhere new technology and communications brings men and nations closer together, the concerns of one inevitably become the concerns of all. And our new closeness is stripping away the false masks, the illusion of difference which is at the root of injustice and of hate and of war. Only earthbound man still clings to the dark and poisoning superstition that his world is bounded by the nearest hill, his universe ends at river shore, his common humanity is enclosed in the tight circle of those who share his town or his views and the colour of his skin. It is your job, the task of young people in this world, to strip the last remnants of that ancient, cruel belief from the civilisation of man.

Each nation has different obstacles and different goals, shaped by the vagaries of history and of experience. Yet as I talk to young people around the world I am impressed not by the diversity but by the closeness of their goals, their desires and their concerns and their hope for the future. There is discrimination in New York, the racial inequality of apartheid in South Africa, and serfdom in the mountains of Peru. People starve to death in the streets of India, a former prime minister is summarily executed in the Congo, intellectuals go to jail in Russia, and thousands are slaughtered in Indonesia; wealth is lavished on armaments everywhere in the world. These are different evils; but they are the common works of man. They reflect the imperfections of human justice, the inadequacy of human compassion, the defectiveness of our sensibility toward the sufferings of our fellows; they mark the limit of our ability to use knowledge for the well-being of our fellow human beings throughout the world. And therefore they call upon common qualities of conscience and indignation, a shared determination to wipe away the unnecessary sufferings of our fellow human beings at home and around the world.

[...]

In the world we would like to build, South Africa could play an outstanding role and a role of leadership in that effort. This country is without question a preeminent repository of the wealth and knowledge and skill of this continent. Here are the greater part of Africa's research scientists and steel production, most of its reservoirs of coal and of electric power. Many South Africans have made major contributions to African technical development and world science; the names of some are known wherever men seek to eliminate the ravages of tropical disease and of pestilence. In your faculties and councils, here in this very audience, are hundreds and thousands of men and women who could transform the lives of millions for all time to come.

But the help and the leadership of South Africa or of the United States cannot be accepted if we – within our own countries or in our relationships with others – deny individual integrity, human dignity, and the common humanity of man. If we would lead outside our own borders, if we would help those who need our assistance, if we would meet our responsibilities to mankind, we must first, all of us, demolish the borders which history has erected between men within our own nations – barriers of race and religion, social class and ignorance.

Our answer is the world's hope; it is to rely on youth. The cruelties and the obstacles of this swiftly changing planet will not yield to obsolete dogmas and outworn slogans. It cannot be moved by those who cling to a present which is already dying, who prefer the illusion of security to the excitement and danger which comes with even the most peaceful progress.

This world demands the qualities of youth; not a time of life but a state of mind, a temper of the will, a quality of the imagination, a predominance of courage over timidity, of the appetite for adventure over the life of ease, a man like the chancellor of this university. It is a revolutionary world that we all live in, and thus, as I have said in Latin America and in Asia, and in Europe and in my own country the United States, it is the young people who must take the lead. Thus you, and your young compatriots everywhere, have had thrust upon you a greater burden of responsibility than any generation that has ever lived.

'There is,' said an Italian philosopher, 'nothing more difficult to take in hand, more perilous to conduct, or more uncertain in its success than

to take the lead in the introduction of a new order of things.' Yet this is
the measure of the task of your generation, and the road is strewn with
many dangers.

First is the danger of futility: the belief there is nothing one man
or one woman can do against the enormous array of the world's ills –
against misery, against ignorance, or injustice and violence. Yet many of
the world's great movements, of thought and action, have flowed from the
work of a single man. A young monk began the Protestant Reformation,
a young general extended an empire from Macedonia to the borders of
the earth, and a young woman reclaimed the territory of France. It was a
young Italian explorer who discovered the New World, and 32-year-old
Thomas Jefferson who proclaimed that all men are created equal.

'Give me a place to stand,' said Archimedes, 'and I will move the
world.' These men moved the world, and so can we all. Few will have
the greatness to bend history, but each of us can work to change a small
portion of the events, and in the total of all those acts will be written in
the history of this generation. Thousands of Peace Corps volunteers are
making a difference in the isolated villages and the city slums in dozens
of countries. Thousands of unknown men and women in Europe
resisted the occupation of the Nazis and many died, but all added to the
ultimate strength and freedom of their countries. It is from numberless
diverse acts of courage such as these that the belief that human history is
thus shaped. Each time a man stands up for an ideal or acts to improve
the lot of others, or strikes out against injustice, he sends forth a tiny
ripple of hope, and crossing each other from a million different centres
of energy and daring, those ripples build a current which can sweep
down the mightiest walls of oppression and resistance.

'If Athens shall appear great to you,' said Pericles, 'consider then that
her glories were purchased by valiant men, and by men who learned
their duty.' That is the source of all greatness in all societies, and it is the
key to progress in our time.

The second danger is that of expediency; of those who say that hopes
and beliefs must bend before immediate necessities. Of course, if we
would act effectively we must deal with the world as it is. We must get
things done. But if there was one thing that President Kennedy stood
for that touched the most profound feelings of young people around
the world, it was the belief that idealism, high aspirations, and deep
convictions are not incompatible with the most practical and efficient of
programmes – that there is no basic inconsistency between ideals and

realistic possibilities, no separation between the deepest desires of heart and of mind and the rational application of human effort to human problems. It is not realistic or hardheaded to solve problems and take action unguided by ultimate moral aims and values, although we all know some who claim that it is so. In my judgement, it is thoughtless folly. For it ignores the realities of human faith and of passion and of belief – forces ultimately more powerful than all of the calculations of our economists or of our generals. Of course to adhere to standards, to idealism, to vision in the face of immediate dangers takes great courage and takes self-confidence. But we also know that only those who dare to fail greatly can ever achieve greatly.

It is this new idealism which is also, I believe, the common heritage of a generation which has learned that while efficiency can lead to the camps at Auschwitz, or the streets of Budapest, only the ideals of humanity and love can climb the hills of the Acropolis.

A third danger is timidity. Few men are willing to brave the disapproval of their fellows, the censure of their colleagues, the wrath of their society. Moral courage is a rarer commodity than bravery in battle or great intelligence. It is the one essential, vital quality of those who seek to change a world which yields most painfully to change. Aristotle tells us: 'At the Olympic Games it is not the finest or the strongest men who are crowned, but those who enter the lists …

'So too in the life of the honorable and the good it is they who act rightly who win the prize.' I believe that in this generation those with the courage to enter the conflict will find themselves with companions in every corner of the world.

For the fortunate among us, the fourth danger, my friends, is comfort, the temptation to follow the easy and familiar paths of personal ambition and financial success so grandly spread before those who have the privilege of an education. But that is not the road history has marked out for us. There is a Chinese curse which says 'May he live in interesting times.' Like it or not we live in interesting times. They are times of danger and uncertainty; but they are also the most creative of any time in the history of mankind. And everyone here will ultimately be judged – will ultimately judge himself – on the effort he has contributed to building a new world society and the extent to which his ideals and goals have shaped that effort.

So we part, I to my country and you to remain. We are – if a man of forty can claim the privilege – fellow members of the world's largest younger generation. Each of us have our own work to do. I know at times you must feel very alone with your problems and difficulties. But I want to say how impressed I am with what you stand for and for the effort that you are making; and I say this not just for myself, but men and women all over the world. And I hope you will often take heart from the knowledge that you are joined with your fellow young people in every land, they struggling with their problems and you with yours, but all joined in a common purpose; that, like the young people of my own country and of every country I have visited, you are all in many ways more closely united to the brothers of your time than to the older generations in any of these nations; and that you are determined to build a better future. President Kennedy was speaking to the young people of America, but beyond them to young people everywhere, when he said, 'The energy, the faith, the devotion which we bring to this endeavour will light our country and all who serve it – and the glow from that fire can truly light the world.'

And he added, 'With a good conscience our only sure reward, with history the final judge of our deeds, let us go forth to lead the land we love, asking His blessing and His help, but knowing that here on earth God's work must truly be our own.' I thank you.

Margaret Marshall, NUSAS's vice president, who hosted Kennedy in Robertson's stead, remembers that at the end of the speech, Kennedy 'stopped and looked around as if to say, "Was that enough?"'[12] – and the crowd answered with a resounding 'yes' by breaking into applause. The epic address, which later became known as the 'Ripple of Hope' speech, is considered by many to be one of Kennedy's finest.

The speech's appeal with its audience was likely a result of the combined effort of its composition. As with Macmillan's 'Wind of Change' speech and Mandela's speech from the dock, several individuals contributed to the address. The first draft – written by Kennedy's speechwriter Adam Walinsky – was rejected by Kennedy, who was then advised to seek the assistance of Allard K. Lowenstein, a young Democrat familiar with southern African politics. Lowenstein, in turn, sought feedback from the very best minds: a group of South African students studying in the US.[13] According to Walinsky, Lowenstein's intervention necessarily 'blew the whole thing up'[14] and jolted him and his team into a better understanding of what was needed.

The inspiring breadth of the address comes from the wide references to cultures, nations and historical periods well beyond the confines of the university hall. From the hills of the Acropolis and the mountains of Peru to Joan of Arc and Archimedes, Kennedy encouraged his young audience to take the longer view of history. Although he never directly advises them to resist apartheid, he encourages them, in broad strokes, to effect political change – even though doing so may at times seem futile and inexpedient and require one to overcome timidity and overlook personal comfort. *The Times* of London claimed that Kennedy denounced apartheid and urged young people to 'take a stand'.[15]

The South African audience was particularly appreciative of two points: Kennedy's remarks about communism and his call for both the US and South Africa to respect human dignity in their own countries before seeking to lead or assist other nations. About communism, he claimed to be 'unalterably opposed', and his call to fight it by enlarging freedom, instead of imitating its dictatorship, was loudly cheered. Here, the speech spoke directly to the situation of many young activists because of the state's pernicious attempt to conflate opposition to apartheid with promoting a communist agenda. Robertson himself had been banned for supposedly furthering 'the achievement of the objects of communism'.[16]

In the days after the address, Kennedy continued to meet with South African representatives around the country, most famously taking a helicopter ride to Groutville to meet with Albert Luthuli. The media had little forewarning of this encounter, and the South African public was delighted when Kennedy returned with the first news they had received about their Nobel Peace Prize winner in years. 'He is one of the most impressive men I have met in my travels round the world,'[17] the statesman told reporters. Although Kennedy's request to visit with Luthuli was granted by the authorities, his attempts to secure meetings with government representatives remained unanswered.

The US senator's visit prompted a 'ripple of hope' in South Africa during one of the darkest periods of its history. The *Rand Daily Mail* exalted the visit in epic terms: 'Senator Robert Kennedy's visit is the best thing that has happened to South Africa for years ... Suddenly, it is possible to breathe again without feeling choked.'[18]

This reprieve was short-lived, however. A few months afterwards, a forty-eight-year-old parliamentary messenger by the name of Dimitri Tsafendas stabbed Prime Minister Hendrik Verwoerd to death in the House of Assembly. The motivation for the assassination remains unclear.

And a year later, Luthuli was killed when he was struck by a freight train while crossing a railway bridge in Stanger near his homestead. The exact details of his death remain unknown.

In addition, little did Kennedy know that at the Cape Town speech, he was reciting words that would soon be engraved on his own tombstone. In 1968, having won the Democratic presidential primary election in California, one of history's great 'what ifs' was also assassinated – by a twenty-four-year-old Palestinian, Sirhan Bishara Sirhan, who had become enraged with the senator's advocacy for US support of Israel.

Kennedy's tombstone at Arlington National Cemetery commemorates the most famous speech of his short career: 'Each time a man stands up for an ideal or acts to improve the lot of others, or strikes out against injustice, he sends forth a tiny ripple of hope, and crossing each other from a million different centres of energy and daring, those ripples build a current which can sweep down the mightiest walls of oppression.'

Helen Suzman

Speech in Parliament on the NP's race policy,
22 July 1970

For thirteen years (1961–74), Helen Suzman was the lone voice of the Progressive Party in Parliament – the 'bright star in a dark chamber', as Albert Luthuli described her. More than this, she was the only effective voice of opposition. As *The Times* of London pointed out on the eve of the 1974 election, Sir De Villiers Graaff and his United Party, which frequently voted alongside the NP, 'entirely accept[ed] the racialist basis of South Africa'[1] and had done little to advance the fight for freedom. Although Suzman's parliamentary career had begun with the UP in 1953, she, along with several colleagues, soon realised that the backward-looking party was no opponent for the Nats, and they broke away to form the Progressive Party. When her colleagues lost their seats in the 1961 election, it was left to Suzman to draw government's attention to the injustices of apartheid. Despite sexist and anti-Semitic jeering from the mainly Afrikaner Calvinist men in Parliament, as well as a steady supply of frightening hate mail, she did this with tireless enthusiasm – attacking, with 'penetrating criticism',[2] everything from segregation in sport, Bantu education, and unequal wages for black and white workers, to separate development, forced removals and detention laws.

Her achievement, 'hard to overstate' according to J.M. Coetzee,[3] was partly the result of her being, in Phyllis Lewsen's words, an 'outstandingly eloquent speaker, a hard-working incisive debater, with the gifts of brevity, wit and repartee – invaluable in handling the heckling she would have to face'.[4] With a degree in economics and statistics, she proved a formidable opponent in Parliament. But she also spent time visiting political prisoners, speaking to communities affected by apartheid legislation, and attending activists' funerals, giving her a more-than-academic understanding of the frustrations of the black majority in the country.

Suzman's role as a parliamentarian was twofold. She continually drew the House's attention to perspectives that most members preferred to ignore or of which they were unaware. She read out letters from activists, banned persons and political prisoners who had written to her, often anonymously for fear of victimisation, appealing for her to help improve their personal circumstances. She described her desk, which was full of such pleas, as a 'sad harvest of the seeds of apartheid'.[5] When these failed to move her fellow MPs, she read out damning newspaper reports from abroad. In 1962, she recited part of Mandela's defence speech, which meant, because of parliamentary privilege, that the *Rand Daily Mail* could report its content.[6]

Suzman undercut the apartheid state's pride in its Western-based parliamentary and judicial frameworks. As J.M. Coetzee points out, she used the platform granted to her as an MP to maximum effect:

> Operating within a near-totalitarian political system, she cannily exploited a structural weakness of that system – parliamentary privilege – to bring into the open abuses of power which, by means of bans on public speech and restrictions on reporting, the government would otherwise successfully have kept hidden.[7]

A meticulous researcher, Suzman delivered speeches brimming with statistics that disputed the state's official narratives. Helped by the English-language liberal press, she ensured that important debates dominated news headlines, and these in turn served as sources for foreign reports, keeping the country on the international agenda. This was particularly the case with prison conditions and the government's detention-without-trial legislation, which received much negative publicity overseas.

Although she was still the lone representative of her party in 1970, the Nats were beginning to feel pressure from all sides. International condemnation of apartheid was growing, and the government's insistence on segregation in sport meant that South Africa was banned from the Davis Cup tennis tournament and barred from participating in a highly anticipated cricket tour in Britain. What's more, in the April election, the party lost support for the first time since 1948, largely because of the formation of the Herstigte Nasionale Party (Reconstituted National Party) under Albert Hertzog. This far-right party was formed by disgruntled NP members a year earlier in protest against the government's decision to allow a Maori member of the All Blacks rugby team to compete in a match in South Africa.[8]

Balthazar Johannes Vorster had succeeded the insular and zealous Verwoerd in 1966, but despite being a more pragmatic and outward-looking prime minister, his main focus was still the maintenance of white domination, and his leadership, according to Suzman, merely meant that there 'might be changes in emphasis'.[9] At the time of Suzman's speech, Vorster – the most widely travelled apartheid prime minister – had just returned from a supposedly 'private' trip to Portugal, Spain, France and Switzerland, where he had nevertheless held 'low-key' diplomatic talks with leaders.[10] Suzman's speech was mainly a response to the announcement made by minister of Bantu administration and development M.C. Botha that the government intended to accelerate its Bantustan policy, offering 'privileges' to urban blacks who accepted homeland citizenship in an attempt to speed up what was referred to as their 'endorsing out' of urban areas.[11] The proposal met with Suzman's exasperated ire, and the extract here gives a sense of the spirited, insightful and cutting debate that she brought to Parliament for thirty-six years:[12]

Mrs H. Suzman: Mr Speaker, the honourable the Minister of Bantu Administration and Development brings a dangerous enthusiasm with him for his hopeless task. He has a crusading spirit which I personally find rather frightening ... and in his hands there is a dangerous amount of power. That is why I have found the words he acted this afternoon distinctly frightening. He talks about a dynamic third decade of the National Party's regime.

The Minister of Bantu Administration and Development: I hope you will see it.

Mrs H. Suzman: Yes, I hope I will, but what I see at the moment is a shrinking economy ... simply because of the policies which this country has been following for the last 23 years. The honourable the minister says that the shortage of labour is caused by the prosperity of this country. He does not know what he's talking about. If he had listened to any of the experts ... he would know that all of them have stated the shortage of labour is an artificial one ... The entire economy is being hindered by the Government's policy of refusing to let up on labour restrictions ... I do not believe he has made any study of economics. If he had ... he would know that labour is not a unit which can be substituted, one man for the other, as happens in a migratory system of labour, which in any case is unsuited to an economy that is highly industrialised and which requires more and more skilled and semi-skilled labour ...

However, there is another aspect which is brought to the attention of this House this afternoon, namely his grandiose schemes for creating dozens of governments in South Africa. As I remember it, there are to be 11 in Southwest Africa, eight in South Africa for the Africans, one for the coloureds, one for the Indians and one for the white people. That makes 22 governments for 20 million people. One government, roughly, for every million people is not a bad average. When one remembers that something like 36 per cent ... of the gainfully employed white population in South Africa is directly or indirectly in state employment in this so-called free enterprise country of ours, one's mind absolutely boggles to think of the number of people who will now be absorbed in unproductive occupations in manning 22 governments ... and 22 civil services ...

There was the third point that the honourable minister made on which I want to take issue with him ... The third point ... was that he, Merlin the magician, will give to every single African a tribal identity. He will link him to his tribe. Each one will have his own country. How does the honourable the minister know that the African wants this? Who is he to tell the urbanised African that he has to go back to tribal culture? How does the honourable the minister know this?

The Minister of Bantu Administration and Development: Because I am in contact with them.

Mrs H. Suzman: The honourable the minister's contact with urban Africans consists of telling them what he wants them to do and telling them what they must do. It does not consist of asking them or consulting them. Nothing of the kind. I want to tell the honourable the minister that he has forgotten that among the three-and-a-half million urban Africans there are at least two generations that were born in the urban areas, that have lost their tribal contact and that want to have nothing whatsoever to do with all these ethnic groupings that he is forcing on them. The honourable the minister is forgetting all about 150 years of contact with Christianity ... They do not retain their tribal culture once they have adopted Christianity ... The honourable the minister cannot promote Christianity and tribalism any more than he can promote tribalism and the modern system of agriculture, for those are incompatible as well. The honourable the minister has forgotten that the African has had decades of contact with Western civilisation and with modern industrial systems. He has forgotten that those people do not want to return to the tribal culture and tribal customs. If the honourable the minister does not believe me, why does he not ask them? Why does he not give them the choice? Why does he insist on imposing his will on people who may not want it? ...

I want to say that I am disappointed in this debate ... We did not even have an interesting little travelogue from the honourable Prime Minister. I was looking forward to some sort of account of his travels ... He should have mixed with some of the common people [overseas]. It might have been difficult for him, because he says he does not speak other languages. But that does not matter. He could have gone heavily disguised as an ordinary human being, if necessary, and sat himself down at a table at the boulevard cafe and watched the world go by. He would have learnt a great deal from that. One of the things that he would have learnt is that it is completely irrelevant to bring in examples of what happened in the pre-war world ... The whole world has changed ... Not only geographically, it has changed politically and sociologically. Most of all perhaps, it has changed in its attitude to race ... It is for that reason that we appear to be so weird to the outside world. That is one of the reasons why the honourable the Prime Minister finds it so difficult to sell separate development or apartheid or South Africa's colour policy to the outside world. We are the only country that has moved backwards. Every other country in the world has been extending rights to people of colour. But this is not the position in South Africa. This is the only country where there has been a steady whittling away of the rights of the non-white people. Any independent observer ... will come to the conclusion that what has been substituted for those rights – the territorial authorities that we heard so much about, the Coloured Representative Council, the Indian Council or the Transkeian assembly – do not mean anything. How can they measure up to the rights in the Parliament which legislates for, or rather, against those people who do not have any representation in this House any more ...?

I was hoping that there would be some sort of dramatic change and that the Honourable Prime Minister and his cabinet would come back with some sort of fresh attitudes after the election. We all know they were severely affected earlier this year. The whole lot of them had a dread disease known as Hertzogitis ... However, that is over now. Honourable members need not be so upset. They are recovering from this disease. I was hoping we would have a bit of a new outlook. However, it is the same old mixture as before. And it seems to me from what the honourable the Minister of Bantu Administration has been saying that it is going to get worse. It is going to be a stronger mixture ...

The honourable the Prime Minister has an idea – and he got it I think from the honourable the Minister of Bantu administration – that if we only stop calling the country 'multiracial' and start calling it 'multinational', we will be able to pull the wool over the world's eyes ...

Then we will apparently get over this whole business of a minority government, because it almost puts the whites in the majority in this country. In this way it is thought that that argument would be disposed of.

Does he really think that the world judges us by the myths that keep Nationalists happy? Or does the world judge us by the realities of the South African scene? The honourable the Prime Minister found the policy difficult to explain, because the world judges us by the realities ... You cannot explain away the treatment of the urbanised Africans [to people] overseas. People do not believe that urbanised people want tribal culture. And they are quite right in not believing that. You cannot explain away the harshness of the policy as it is implemented today, by telling people that in the future there are going to be rewards from the policy ... It is no use trying to give explanations to the outside world, as its views on race have moved miles ahead of South Africa. You cannot explain the obvious unfairness of separate amenities, when there are not even pretensions that these amenities are 'separate' but 'equal' ... We cannot explain our sporting policy away at all, because it is based on a completely unacceptable principle. People do not realise in South Africa what a highly emotive issue the race issue is overseas ... They do not consider an all-white team sent by South Africa as a team that comes from a country whose policies they disapprove of. They consider a South African all-white team – and now I quote from a newspaper – 'as a roving embassy for racialism'. And that is why we will never get our sporting policy accepted even though we offer to send two teams to the Olympic Games. It is not going to work that way ... South Africans must stop bluffing themselves that the cancellation of the cricket tour [to Britain] was the work of what they care to think of as long-haired demos and a bloody-minded [British] Labour Party government. Nothing of the sort. This issue became something far greater. It had become a race relations issue inside Britain itself. It had become a Commonwealth relations issue. That position will remain until we change our actual attitude inside South Africa ... We have to change fundamentally our attitude on sport. We have got to have multiracial sport and we will have to pick our teams on merit. Otherwise we are out of sport internationally. We can forget about it. The tide which has swept us out of the Olympic Games, out of the Davis Cup, out of international soccer and out of international athletics is simply going to roll on and sweep us out of any remaining international contests in which we hope to participate.

Do you know what you also cannot explain in England or elsewhere, irrespective of whether you call this country multiracial or multinational? You cannot explain away why a country, which is not in an emergency situation, cannot control its population, presumably, without the use of acts, such as the Terrorism Act, particularly Section 6 thereof, and the 180 day detention law. You cannot explain why there are powers still in force allowing ministers to detain people without trial. It is obvious that many more people are being detained without trial than any of us know anything about. Why is this so in a country where there is no emergency situation? Why should this be in a country where we are spending millions on the army and the police force? Can we not control any attacks that might come from abroad? Only the other day the Prime Minister was telling us that not only could we control people that attacked us, but if necessary we could arm ourselves to attack other people. He, however, hastened to add that we have no intention of doing so. Why do we need these powers which are only taken in democratic countries under the most stringent emergencies? ...

The Minister of Community Development: You are against a white government in this country.

Mrs H. Suzman: I do not want a black government either. I want a multiracial government for a multiracial country. That is exactly what I want.

What cannot be explained away is why a young, vigorous country like South Africa, with natural resources that are the envy of the world, should be running into economic difficulties, as it is. How do you explain that the Government absolutely ignores all the cries about bottle-necks, and the crippling effects of the industrial colour bar? This is what you cannot explain to people overseas. It all seems mad to them, and you know what, Sir? It all is mad.

I have not even touched on petty apartheid, which is humiliating and disgusting ... I want to stick to ... major apartheid. This is what is ripping the very fabric of society in South Africa. What concerns me particularly is what we are doing in this all-white Parliament of ours ... the gay abandon with which we pass laws that wreak havoc in the lives of ordinary people ... This honourable minister ... said that the Government has brought stability. Stability of what? Stability to whom? Could it bring stability to non-whites who know that they are doomed to poverty and second-class citizenship? Is that the sort of stability that people want? We have heard talk again of all being quiet and peaceful in South Africa.

Does nobody take any notice of the fact that we have the highest daily average prison population in the Western world? Does this mean anything to these honourable members when they talk about peace and quiet in South Africa?

The Prime Minister stated that the coloured people are contented. He says they like their Coloured Representative Council. Do they? They are complaining it has not been called together, [that] they have never been consulted ... They have put in a resolution wherein they asked for equal pay for equal work, particularly as far as teachers, nurses and other civil servants are concerned. What is going to happen to that cry of equal pay for equal work? Is this Government going to listen to it? ... I wonder whether the honourable Prime Minister has seen the statement made by Mr Justice [J.H.] Steyn the other month wherein he stated that 50 per cent of the coloured people are living below the poverty datum line. Are these people satisfied with their conditions? I wonder if he thinks that the coloured people enjoy being shunted around under the Group Areas Act. Certain areas are proclaimed for them where they can build their houses and where they can settle down again in a sort of new community, then suddenly they are deproclaimed ... Does he think that people like this sort of stability? I wonder if he thinks that the coloured people really think of their Representative Council as anything other than a facade when everything that is significant in their lives is ruled by this Parliament ... I wonder whether the honourable the Prime Minister really thinks that the Indians are really satisfied with what they got, and the treatment they are getting under the Group Area proclamations.

[...]

What employment is there in his resettlement areas the honourable Minister has been talking about so proudly? What must these women, many of whom are widows, or children do when they are sent back to the resettlement areas? Many of these widows were in gainful employment: they are endorsed out of the urban areas, where they are not allowed to have houses, but there is no employment for them in the resettlement areas with the result that there are no means of maintaining the family in those areas at all. In other societies the aged, the sick, the widows and the very young are treated with special care. In our society they were singled out for especially harsh treatment ... They are the famous 'superfluous appendages'. What does the honourable the minister think the endorsing out of African families does to them? He is very proud of the number of people he has kept out of the urban areas, but he never

stops to think what ... they live on and what their family lives are like ...
The urban Africans are in a constant state of apprehension, because
they have a very shrewd idea of what is going to happen to them ...
The 30-year leases [of houses] have gone, showing that permanency
is not considered to be an intrinsic part of the urban Africans.

There is also the question of the building of high schools in the
towns. The Africans know that schools are being built in the rural
areas and in their homelands in order to orientate their children
towards the homelands. I would like to know what sort of jobs are
going to be provided for the new generation of urban-born Africans if
the Physical Planning Act is carried out to its fullest extent. Where are
the job opportunities going to come from for the young generation of
urban-born Africans who do not want to go back to live in their
homelands? What is going to happen if the Bantu Laws Amendment
Act is in fact enforced on the educated Africans, the white collar
Africans, who have dragged themselves up by their own efforts?

Suzman's animated speech, while obviously off the cuff, gives a sense of
why Vorster once told her that she was worth ten United Party MPs.[13] She
raises question after question to highlight the weaknesses of the various
policies proposed, exposing their expense, impracticality and moral vacu-
ousness. The invective of her attack is softened only by her use of inclusive
pronouns ('What concerns me particularly is what we are doing in this
all-white Parliament of ours'; 'We cannot explain our sporting policy away
at all'; 'the world judges us by the realities'; etc.).

Suzman urges her fellow parliamentarians to look at South Africa
through two sets of eyes. Firstly, she conjures the West's view of the country. Familiar with the state's peculiar combination of arrogance and low
self-esteem – its disregard of global opinion and its simultaneous desire
for inclusion in the family of nations – she paints a precise picture of how
backward and 'mad' South Africa appears to the rest of the world. The use
of detention without trial, she explains, makes no sense to democratic
countries elsewhere in the world, and nor does the idea of 'separate amenities'. Most importantly, she says, the state's expensive attempt to position
itself as a majority government by assigning different tribal identities and
homelands to citizens will not fool anyone.

Secondly, she brings to bear the perspective of the voiceless majority – the
urban black South Africans who have no desire to live in homelands, coloured
families whose lives are torn apart by forced removals, and the people who,

one year earlier, deputy minister of justice, mines and planning G.F. van L. Froneman had referred to as 'superfluous appendages' – the widows, children and elderly dependants of the black labour force who were 'endorsed out' to barren resettlement areas.

Suzman correctly predicted the country's sporting future. Three months later, South Africa was expelled from the International Olympic Committee, and its attempts to circumvent the 1970s cricket ban by competing in the hastily assembled 'Rest of the World' team were never officially recognised. Over the next two decades, South Africa would find itself further and further condemned into the sporting wilderness.

Liberal to the core, Suzman opposed isolation in sport, largely because she saw it as a precursor to sanctions, which, she argued, would affect poorer black workers before having repercussions for white South Africans[14] – a view that attracted criticism from various quarters as support for more revolutionary responses grew. She herself acknowledged in 1977 that during her twenty-five years in Parliament, she'd not managed to halt one oppressive law,[15] and eventually events overtook her. She was prevented from giving an address that she'd been invited to deliver at Robert Sobukwe's funeral in 1978, after Black Consciousness leaders began to reject white liberalism as paternalistic and irrelevant. By the end of the decade, liberalism, too, was gradually isolated.

Steve Biko
'White Racism, Black Consciousness' address,
Abe Bailey Institute, University of Cape Town,
January 1971

While the state's crackdown on activism turned the 1960s into South Africa's
'dark decade', new passion characterised the 1970s, as workers and students –
following university uprisings the world over – began to mobilise. The renewed
hope for 'freedom in our lifetime' drew much energy from the emergence of
a new youth movement, led by the South African Students' Organisation
(SASO). The organisation in turn owed its existence to a twenty-one-year-
old medical student who would become one of anti-apartheid's most famous
martyrs: Stephen Bantu Biko.

Raised primarily by his mother, a young widow, Biko was the third of
four children. His education, both formal and political, was largely due to
the efforts of his brother, Khaya – a member of the PAC who was convicted
to two years' imprisonment for his involvement in Poqo, the PAC's armed
wing. Khaya saw to it that when Biko was expelled from Lovedale College ('for
absolutely no reason', Khaya claimed),[1] he was able to continue his education
at St Francis College in Mariannhill, Natal. Biko had a sharp analytical mind
and he shone academically, serving as vice chair of St Francis's debate society
and going on to enrol for medicine at Wentworth (Natal University's school
for black students). After he was elected to the student council, he attended
a NUSAS conference at Rhodes University in 1967. NUSAS had attracted
many black student members because of its sympathetic anti-apartheid
stance, but it was still a mainly white organisation and had never had a black
leader. Although Biko had already raised the question of white paternalism
within NUSAS, it was this experience that provided the spark for the formation
of SASO.

En route to Grahamstown, Biko was angry to discover that the host university had refused to allow racially integrated accommodation and eating
facilities for the student delegates. Opening his point of order in Xhosa to
illustrate that the organisation's structure had become exclusive, he put
forward a motion for NUSAS to disband the conference and reconvene at a
non-racial venue in the townships. The motion was debated all night, but it
was ultimately rejected, leading a disappointed Biko and others to question

the effectiveness of liberalism and multiracialism as well as the organisation's ability to act in the interests of black students.

In their view, NUSAS was hamstrung by the political structure of the country, and its overly gentle approach did little to advance the struggle. Barney Pityana, Biko's colleague, went on to explain that the split was necessary because black people needed to 'build themselves into a position of non-dependence on whites' and 'work towards a self-sufficient political, social and economic unit' and that '[t]o hope that change might come through existing political parties in South Africa [was] a pipedream'.[2] Over the next few years, Biko, Pityana and a black caucus from the University Christian Movement formed SASO – an all-black student organisation, advocating, ironically, racially separate protest organisations in the land of separate development.

Initially, the state underestimated SASO's importance, viewing its formation as evidence of the logic of apartheid thinking.[3] But they didn't account for the widespread appeal of its approach in uniting the oppressed groups within South Africa. With the formation of SASO, a new ideology known as Black Consciousness swept through the country. More than a political doctrine, it promoted a philosophy that sought the psychological liberation of black people, the rediscovery of black culture and values, and the complete rejection of apartheid-created systems.

While Biko outlined his position in several important essays and writings, and although he spoke at various meetings and events as well as in a court, few full accounts of his spoken addresses have been preserved. One, 'White Racism, Black Consciousness: The Totality of White Power in South Africa', given at the Abe Bailey Institute of Inter-Racial Studies in Cape Town in 1971, outlines his early thinking.

Now the Centre for Conflict Resolution, the Abe Bailey Institute was founded in 1968 by sociologist Professor H.W. van der Merwe. Its main objective was to 'promote greater knowledge, contact and understanding between the various population groups';[4] to this end, it arranged a workshop on student activism in South Africa in January 1971. Student representatives from both ends of the political spectrum were invited in their personal capacity, from the 'conservative' Afrikaanse Studentebond (ASB) on the right through to the newly formed 'militant' SASO on the left. As vice president and president of SASO, Biko and Pityana – the only black representatives – were invited to give papers, both of which received much coverage in the white press.[5] Extracts from Biko's paper are reproduced here.

'No race possesses the monopoly of beauty, intelligence, force, and there is room for all of us at the rendezvous of victory.' I do not think Aimé Césaire was thinking about South Africa when he said these words. The whites in this country have placed themselves on a path of no return. So blatantly exploitative in terms of the mind and body is the practice of white racism that one wonders if the interests of blacks and whites in this country have not become so mutually exclusive as to exclude the possibility of there being 'room for all of us at the rendezvous of victory'.

The white man's quest for power has led him to destroy with utter ruthlessness whatever has stood in his way. In an effort to divide the black world in terms of aspirations, the powers that be have evolved a philosophy that stratifies the black world and gives preferential treatment to certain groups. Further, they have built up several tribal cocoons, thereby hoping to increase inter-tribal ill-feeling and to divert the energies of the black people towards attaining false prescribed 'freedoms'. Moreover, it was hoped, the black people could be effectively contained in these various cocoons of repression, euphemistically referred to as 'homelands'. At some stage, however, the powers that be had to start defining the sphere of activity of these apartheid institutions. Most blacks suspected initially the barrenness of the promise and have now realised that they have been taken for a big ride. Just as the Native Representative Council became a political flop that embarrassed its creators, I predict that a time will come when these stooge bodies will prove very costly not only in terms of money but also in terms of the credibility of the story the Nationalists are trying to sell. In the meantime the blacks are beginning to realise the need to rally around the cause of their suffering – their black skin – and to ignore the false promises that come from the white world.

Then again the progressively sterner legislation that has lately filled the South African statute books has had a great effect in convincing the people of the evil inherent in the system of apartheid. No amount of propaganda on Radio Bantu or promises of freedom being granted to some desert homeland will ever convince the blacks that the government means well, so long as they experience manifestations of the lack of respect for the dignity of man and for his property as shown during the mass removals of Africans from the urban areas. The unnecessary harassment of Africans by police, both in towns and inside townships, and the ruthless application of that scourge of the people, the pass laws, are constant reminders that the white man is on top and that the blacks are only tolerated – with the greatest restraints. Needless to say, anyone finding himself at the receiving end of such deliberate (though uncalled for) cruelty must ultimately ask himself the question: what do I have to lose? This is what the blacks are beginning to ask themselves.

To add to this, the opposition ranks have been thrown into chaos and confusion. All opposition parties have to satisfy the basic demands of politics. They want power and at the same time they want to be fair. It never occurs to them that the surest way of being unfair is to withhold power from the native population. Hence one ultimately comes to the conclusion that there is no real difference between the United Party and the Nationalist Party. If there is, a strong possibility exists that the United Party is on the right of the Nationalists. One needs only to look at their famous slogan, 'White supremacy over the whole of South Africa', to realise the extent to which the quest for power can cloud even such supposedly immortal characteristics as the 'English sense of fair play'. Africans long ago dismissed the United Party as a great political fraud. The Coloured people have since followed suit. If the United Party is gaining any votes at all it is precisely because it is becoming more explicit in its racist policy. I would venture to say that the most overdue political step in South African White politics is a merger between the United and Nationalist Parties.

The flirtation between the Progressive Party and blacks was brought to a rude stop by legislation. Some blacks argue that at that moment the Progressives lost their only chance of attaining some semblance of respectability by not choosing to disband rather than lose their black constituents. Yet I cannot help feeling that the Progressives emerged more purified from the ordeal. The Progressives have never been a black man's real hope. They have always been a white party at heart, fighting for a more lasting way of preserving white values in this southern tip of Africa. It will not be long before the blacks relate their poverty to their blackness in concrete terms. Because of the tradition forced onto the country, the poor people shall always be black people. It is not surprising, therefore, that the blacks should wish to rid themselves of a system that locks up the wealth of the country in the hands of a few. No doubt Rick Turner was thinking of this when he declared that 'any black government is likely to be socialist', in his article on 'The Relevance of Contemporary Radical Thought'.

We now come to the group that has longest enjoyed confidence from the black world – the liberal establishment, including radical and leftist groups. The biggest mistake the black world ever made was to assume that whoever opposed apartheid was an ally. For a long time the black world has been looking only at the governing party and not so much at the whole power structure as the object of their rage. In a sense the very political vocabulary that the blacks have used has been inherited from the liberals. Therefore it is not surprising that alliances were formed so easily with the liberals.

Who are the liberals in South Africa? It is that curious bunch of non-conformists who explain their participation in negative terms; that bunch of do-gooders that goes under all sorts of names – liberals, leftists, etc. These are the people who argue that they are not responsible for white racism and the country's 'inhumanity to the black man'; these are the people who claim that they too feel the oppression just as acutely as the blacks and therefore should be jointly involved in the black man's struggle for a place under the sun; in short, these are the people who say that they have black souls wrapped up in white skins.

The liberals set about their business with the utmost efficiency. They made it a political dogma that all groups opposing the status quo must necessarily be non-racial in structure. They maintained that if you stood for a principle of non-racialism you could not in any way adopt what they described as racialist policies. They even defined to the black people what the latter should fight for.

With this sort of influence behind them, most black leaders tended to rely too much on the advice of liberals. For a long time, in fact, it became the occupation of the leadership to 'calm the masses down', while they engaged in fruitless negotiation with the status quo. Their whole political action, in fact, was a programmed course in the art of gentle persuasion through protests and limited boycotts and they hoped the rest could be safely left to the troubled conscience of the fair-minded English folk.

[...]

It never occurred to the liberals that the integration they insisted upon as an effective way of opposing apartheid was impossible to achieve in South Africa. It had to be artificial because it was being foisted on two parties whose entire upbringing had been to support the lie that one race was superior and others inferior. One has to overhaul the whole system in South Africa before hoping to get black and white walking hand in hand to oppose a common enemy. As it is, both black and white walk into a hastily organised integrated circle carrying with them the seeds of destruction of that circle – their inferiority and superiority complexes.

The myth of integration as propounded under the banner of the liberal ideology must be cracked and killed because it makes people believe that something is being done when in reality the artificially integrated circles are a soporific to the blacks while salving the consciences of the guilt-stricken white. It works from the false premise that, because it is difficult to bring people from different races together in this country, achievement of this is in itself a step towards the total liberation of the blacks. Nothing could be more misleading.

How many white people fighting for their version of a change in South Africa are really motivated by genuine concern and not by guilt? Obviously it is a cruel assumption to believe that all whites are not sincere, yet methods adopted by some groups often do suggest a lack of real commitment. The essence of politics is to direct oneself to the group which wields power. Most white dissident groups are aware of the power wielded by the white power structure. They are quick to quote statistics on how big the defence budget is. They know exactly how effectively the police and the army can control protesting black hordes – peaceful or otherwise. They know to what degree the black world is infiltrated by the security police. Hence they are completely convinced of the impotence of the black people. Why then do they persist in talking to the blacks? Since they are aware that the problem in this country is white racism, why do they not address themselves to the white world? Why do they insist on talking to blacks?

[...]

The limitations that have accompanied the involvement of liberals in the black man's struggle have been mostly responsible for the arrest of progress. Because of their inferiority complex, blacks have tended to listen seriously to what the liberals had to say. With their characteristic arrogance of assuming a 'monopoly on intelligence and moral judgement', these self-appointed trustees of black interests have gone on to set the pattern and pace for the realisation of the black man's aspirations.

I am not sneering at the liberals and their involvement. Neither am I suggesting that they are the most to blame for the black man's plight. Rather I am illustrating the fundamental fact that total identification with an oppressed group in a system that forces one group to enjoy privilege and to live on the sweat of another, is impossible. White society collectively owes the blacks so huge a debt that no one member should automatically expect to escape from the blanket condemnation that needs must come from the black world. It is not as if whites are allowed to enjoy privilege only when they declare their solidarity with the ruling party. They are born into privilege and are nourished by and nurtured in the system of ruthless exploitation of black energy. For the 20-year-old white liberal to expect to be accepted with open arms is surely to overestimate the powers of forgiveness of the black people. No matter how genuine a liberal's motivations may be, he has to accept that, though he did not choose to be born into privilege, the blacks cannot but be suspicious of his motives.

[...]

What I have tried to show is that in South Africa political power has always rested with white society. Not only have the whites been guilty of being on the offensive but, by some skilful manoeuvres, they have managed to control the responses of the blacks to the provocation.

Not only have they kicked the black but they have also told him how to react to the kick. For a long time the black has been listening with patience to the advice he has been receiving on how best to respond to the kick. With painful slowness he is now beginning to show signs that it is his right and duty to respond to the kick in the way he sees fit.

Black Consciousness

'We Coloured men, in this specific moment of historical evolution, have consciously grasped in its full breath, the notion of our peculiar uniqueness, the notion of just who we are and what, and that we are ready, on every plane and in every department, to assume the responsibilities which proceed from this coming into consciousness. The peculiarity of our place in the world is not to be confused with anyone else's. The peculiarity of our problems which aren't to be reduced to subordinate forms of any other problem. The peculiarity of our history, laced with terrible misfortunes which belong to no other history. The peculiarity of our culture, which we intend to live and to make live in an ever realler manner.' (Aimé Césaire, 1956, in his letter of resignation from the French Communist Party.)

At about the same time that Césaire said this, there was emerging in South Africa a group of angry young black men who were beginning to 'grasp the notion of (their) peculiar uniqueness' and who were eager to define who they were and what. These were the elements who were disgruntled with the direction imposed on the African National Congress by the 'old guard' within its leadership. These young men were questioning a number of things, among which was the 'go slow' attitude adopted by the leadership, and the ease with which the leadership accepted coalitions with organisations other than those run by blacks. The 'People's Charter' adopted in Kliptown in 1955 was evidence of this. In a sense one can say that these were the first real signs that the blacks in South Africa were beginning to realise the need to go it alone and to evolve a philosophy based on, and directed by, blacks. In other words, Black Consciousness was slowly manifesting itself.

[…]

The importance of the SASO stand is not really to be found in SASO per se – for SASO has the natural limitations of being a student organisation with an ever-changing membership. Rather it is to be found in the fact that this new approach opened a huge crack in the traditional approach and made the blacks sit up and think again. It heralded a new era in which blacks are beginning to take care of their own business and to see with greater clarity the immensity of their responsibility.

The call for Black Consciousness is the most positive call to come from any group in the black world for a long time. It is more than just a reactionary rejection of whites by blacks. The quintessence of it is the realisation by the blacks that, in order to feature well in this game of power politics, they have to use the concept of group power and to build a strong foundation for this. Being an historically, politically, socially and economically disinherited and dispossessed group, they have the strongest foundation from which to operate. The philosophy of Black Consciousness, therefore, expresses group pride and the determination by the blacks to rise and attain the envisaged self. At the heart of this kind of thinking is the realisation by the blacks that the most potent weapon in the hands of the oppressor is the mind of the oppressed. Once the latter has been so effectively manipulated and controlled by the oppressor as to make the oppressed believe that he is a liability to the white man, then there will be nothing the oppressed can do that will really scare the powerful masters. Hence thinking along lines of Black Consciousness makes the black man see himself as a being, entire in himself, and not as an extension of a broom or additional leverage to some machine. At the end of it all, he cannot tolerate attempts by anybody to dwarf the significance of his manhood. Once this happens, we shall know that the real man in the black person is beginning to shine through.

[...]

The attitude of some rural African folk who are against education is often misunderstood, not least by the African intellectual. Yet the reasons put forward by these people carry with them the realisation of their inherent dignity and worth. They see education as the quickest way of destroying the substance of the African culture. They complain bitterly of the disruption in the life pattern, non-observation of customs, and constant derision from the nonconformists whenever any of them go through school. Lack of respect for the elders is, in the African tradition, an unforgivable and cardinal sin. Yet how can one prevent the loss of respect of child for father when the child is actively taught by his know-all white tutors to disregard his family's teachings? How can an African avoid losing respect for his tradition when in school his whole cultural background is summed up in one word: barbarism?

To add to the white-oriented education received, the whole history of the black people is presented as a long lamentation of repeated defeats. Strangely enough, everybody has come to accept that the history of South Africa starts in 1652. No doubt this is to support the often-told lie that blacks arrived in this country at about the same time as the whites. Thus, a lot of attention has to be paid to our history if we as blacks want to aid each other in our coming into consciousness. We have to rewrite our history and describe in it the heroes that formed the core of resistance to the white invaders. More has to be revealed and stress has to be laid on the successful nation-building attempts by people like Chaka, Moshoeshoe and Hintsa.

[...]

It is often claimed that the advocates of Black Consciousness are hemming themselves in into a closed world, choosing to weep on each other's shoulders and thereby cutting out useful dialogue with the rest of the world. Yet I feel that the black people of the world, in choosing to reject the legacy of colonialism and white domination and to build around themselves their own values, standards and outlook to life, have at last established a solid base for meaningful cooperation amongst themselves in the larger battle of the Third World against the rich nations. As Fanon puts it; 'The consciousness of the self is not the closing of a door to communication. ... National consciousness, which is not nationalism, is the only thing that will give us an international dimension.' This is an encouraging sign, for there is no doubt that the black–white power struggle in South Africa is but a microcosm of the global confrontation between the Third World and the rich white nations of the world which is manifesting itself in an ever more real manner as the years go by.

Thus, in this age and day, one cannot but welcome the evolution of a positive outlook in the black world. The wounds that have been inflicted on the black world and the accumulated insults of oppression over the years were bound to provoke reaction from the black people. Now we can listen to the Barnett Potters concluding with apparent glee and with a sense of sadistic triumph that the fault with the black man is to be found in his genes, and we can watch the rest of the white society echoing 'amen', and still not be moved to the reacting type of anger. We have in us the will to live through these trying times; over the years we have attained moral superiority over the white man; we shall watch as time destroys his paper castles and know that all these little pranks were but frantic attempts of frightened little people to convince each other that they can control the minds and bodies of indigenous people of Africa indefinitely.

Biko pulled no punches in attacking the culture and institutions of colonialism and apartheid, calling the Native Representative Council – Prime Minister J.B.M. Hertzog's dismal answer to African representation in the Union – a 'political flop' and claiming that there was not much distinction between the UP and the NP. But what must have been surprising to the audience was Biko's attack on organisations sympathetic to black suffering.

He dismisses, out of hand, the efforts of the Progressive Party as a fight 'for a more lasting way of preserving white values in this southern tip of Africa'. About liberals, he is equally disdainful, describing them as a bunch of 'do-gooders', motivated by guilt and incapable of transcending their white privilege. In Biko's view, liberals maintained the status quo instead of dis- mantling it, as the ideal of multiracialism is 'soporific to the blacks while salving the consciences of the guilt-stricken white'.

The paper, which even Biko later conceded was 'overkill',[6] must have made for difficult listening for the other, predominantly white, participants.[7] Despite the institute's aim to promote tolerance, Van der Merwe noted that some students had to agree to disagree: 'One thing became increasingly clear: that while it is hoped that better understanding will contribute to better relations this is not always the case. This became very obvious when we hear the dia- metrically-opposed thoughts of the Afrikaans students and the Blacks.'[8]

Perhaps the most famous line from the speech is Biko's assertion that 'the most potent weapon in the hands of the oppressor is the mind of the oppressed'. It neatly summed up the Black Consciousness Movement's focus on the psychological transformation of those who identify as black.

Pityana, who spoke after Biko, made a similar call for the oppressed to stand on their own feet, concluding with the famous line 'Black man, you're on your own', which became a kind of slogan for the movement. The workshop gave Pityana and Biko a chance to formalise their thinking, and the two papers provide an important synthesis of their discussions at the time. 'We felt certain of the capacity of black people to participate in their own struggle,' Pityana recalls, 'but that needed to be said in a challenging and in a critical way.'[9]

This tactic was successful. For academic papers, the addresses received a surprising amount of press attention, sparking long-overdue national conversation about race relations. Some publications responded fearfully; the *Cape Times* foregrounded Biko's warnings about whites being on a 'path of no return',[10] while another paper cautioned against a local version of the American 'Black Power' movement.[11]

Other (white) newspapers were more interested in the participants' ability to shed light on black thinking: 'How representative of local African opinion are these students?' asked the *Financial Mail*, adding, 'The sad reply is that the limitations on freedom of thought and expression in this country make an answer impossible.'[12] (This lament did not stop the government from banning Biko two years later.)

While Biko's comments might have seemed radical, they gave an accurate representation of the mounting impatience with the state of affairs, and they account for the success of the Black Consciousness Movement in capturing the imagination of the 1970s generation. Biko said black South Africans were beginning to ask themselves, 'What do I have to lose?', a truth that was borne out by the protests that swept through the country in 1976.

Beginning on 16 June in Soweto as a student rebellion against Prime Minister B.J. Vorster's insistence on Afrikaans as a medium of instruction in schools, the protests spread to over 160 townships nationwide after police opened fire on the youths. Ultimately, it is estimated that up to 700 people, many of them children, died during what became known as the Soweto uprising. More and more young South Africans joined the fight against apartheid, often beyond South Africa's borders, leading to the perception of a 'lost generation' of young people who had abandoned education.[13]

The state responded to the rise of Black Consciousness with increasingly repressive measures – banning, imprisoning and detaining its leaders. A year after the uprising, Biko was arrested for contravening his banning order and taken to Port Elizabeth for interrogation. He had been arrested before and his friend, the journalist Donald Woods, remembers that there was a general feeling that Biko was 'too important a figure in South African politics'[14] to warrant concern about his well-being, despite the fact that the Port Elizabeth precinct had a reputation for brutality under Colonel Piet Goosen.

They were wrong. About a month later, news of the thirty-year-old Biko's death reverberated around the world. Officials immediately claimed that he had died of a hunger strike, but they soon backtracked when the post-mortem revealed that he had suffered brain damage. After much public outcry, an inquest was held, but this too yielded only half-truths.

Held in an old Pretoria synagogue building over a period of two weeks, the inquest revealed the horror and loneliness of Biko's final month, during which he was kept naked in a cell for twenty days, before being manacled, interrogated and beaten. Despite the clear misconduct of several policemen and medical staff, the inquest judge, Magistrate Marthinus Prins, concluded that 'on the available evidence the death cannot be attributed to any act or omission amounting to a criminal offence on the part of any person'.[15]

Winnie Mandela
Speech at a Charge or Release Detainees meeting,
Methodist Church, Noordgesig township,
5 October 1975

In some ways, Winnie Mandela, the elegant second wife of Nelson Mandela, suffered a fate worse than life imprisonment. The pair married in 1958, but their time together was cut short when Mandela was arrested four years later. While serving a five-year sentence, he was implicated in the Rivonia Trial and convicted to life imprisonment in 1964. In their brief time together, they had two daughters, Zenani and Zindzi, aged four and one when their father was arrested in 1962.

Neither a widow nor a divorcee, Winnie once described herself as the 'most unmarried married woman'.[1] Bound to a husband whom she was initially permitted to write to and visit only twice a year,[2] the twenty-seven-year-old Winnie[3] had to raise two young girls alone. The security police severely compromised her ability to do this, and she was subjected to continual harassment, arrests, interrogations and bannings.

Although Winnie had been politically active since before she met Mandela, the government first banned her in 1962. For two years, she was confined to Johannesburg and barred from educational institutions. She was also effectively gagged, as she was forbidden to meet with more than two people at any time and the press wasn't allowed to quote her.

A year after this ban expired, she was given a new, harsher five-year banning order, which restricted her movement to her immediate neighbourhood at all hours, forcing her to leave her job as a social worker. As with Lilian Ngoyi – who was an early inspiration to Winnie[4] – the police made it difficult for her to earn a basic living, even as a clerk and shop assistant, by pressurising employers to find reasons to dismiss her. Because of the continued harassment, Winnie made the difficult decision to send her daughters, both younger than ten, to board at Waterford Kamhlaba School in Swaziland.

A defining moment in Winnie's life came in the early hours of 12 May 1969. The police raided the Mandela home just before dawn, arresting Winnie in front of her children, who were home for the holidays, under Section 6 of the Terrorism Act. After ransacking her home, they thrust her into a van, giving her no time to make arrangements for Zenani or Zindzi, and transported her to Pretoria Central Prison.

Winnie was kept in a windowless concrete cell, illuminated by a bare light bulb that burned day and night. The police withheld information about the whereabouts and well-being of her daughters and gave no indication of the charges she faced. She was provided with basic necessities: two sisal mats, a bucket and soap, a plastic water bottle, a mug and four thin blankets, which she clung to for warmth, despite their stench of urine. She remained there, with no sense of how long she would be detained and with no contact with anybody apart from her interrogators, for 200 days.

Her interrogation was led by Major Theunis Jacobus Swanepoel, a man who had a reputation for torture. The team's method involved depriving Winnie of sleep for five consecutive days and playing 'good cop, bad cop' – by, for example, offering her food, sweetened coffee, cigarettes, medical attention and improved conditions for her husband, and then quite abruptly insulting and assaulting her, claiming her comrades had testified against her, and finally, forcing her to listen to the screams of other prisoners being tortured in an adjacent room.

This last tactic succeeded in compelling Winnie to confess to everything of which she was accused. It transpired that she'd been arrested along with twenty-one others (one of whom, Caleb Mayekiso, died in detention, and three of whom went mad).[5] She finally appeared in court in October 1969, dressed in ANC colours, and was accused of promoting the aims of a banned organisation under the Suppression of Communism Act.

The four-month trial that followed was shambolic. The state's case was weakened by the lack of detail in the various confessions and by the involvement of a British national[6] whose testimony hinted at police brutality. When the defence declared its intention to call Nelson Mandela as a witness, the charges were dropped, most likely because the authorities feared international scrutiny.[7] The accused were released, only to be rearrested immediately under the Terrorism Act and placed in detention for another four months. When they were formally charged with similar offences again, the case was dismissed and Winnie was finally released in October 1970.

Her banning order had expired during her period of detention, but two weeks after her release she was served with another, even more restrictive, five-year ban and put under house arrest. This made it illegal for her to visit her husband, although she was not held to this condition.

Then, in May 1973, Winnie was arrested again – this time for meeting with *Drum* magazine photographer Peter Magubane. Magubane was a good friend of hers, but since he was also a banned person, they were both sentenced in October 1974 to twelve months' imprisonment, of which they served six months on appeal. (Incidentally, when rumours of an 'inappropriate' relationship with Magubane surfaced, the authorities saw to it that these press clippings reached Nelson Mandela.)[8] Winnie was released from Kroonstad Prison in March 1975, but she was still subject to the conditions of house arrest.

By the time her 1970 banning order expired in September 1975, the forty-one-year-old 'political widow' had effectively endured an extended period of thirteen years' 'enforced silence'[9] and the public had heard little from her for over a decade. 'She was', as Obed Musi noted, 'back from the land of the living dead'.[10] She attended a high-profile SASO trial to give encouragement to nine student leaders facing charges of terrorism,[11] was invited to speak at numerous meetings and rallies, and newspapers noted the expiration of her banning order in anticipation of her next move.[12] That she wasn't immediately banned again surprised her.[13] Perhaps the authorities thought she would back down for fear of further intimidation. They were wrong.

Wearing her signature striped headscarf, Winnie spoke to a large group for the first time in fifteen years at a meeting of a newly formed advocacy organisation called Charge or Release Detainees (CORD).[14] Held at the Methodist Church in Noordgesig, a coloured township on the northern outskirts of Soweto, the meeting was held in protest against the Terrorism Act under which Winnie had been arrested. The Act, promulgated under Prime Minister Vorster in 1967, gave the police virtually unrestricted power. They were allowed to arrest any person (including children) whom they suspected of being a threat to law and order. They needed no warrant and could detain and interrogate suspects in solitary confinement indefinitely, without giving them access to lawyers or relatives.

Winnie's beautifully composed speech, reproduced in full here, gave an intensely personal account of her experience of detention:

I feel more than honoured to speak to you on this historic occasion after more than thirteen years of mute resistance in our mass struggle for our honour, our self-respect and our human dignity. The subject on which I am asked to address you has become a familiar one in the South African scene, and such a subject could only be familiar in a country such as ours which is unique in every way. I'm here to join you in protesting against the brutal and inhuman detention of our fathers and mothers, our sons and our daughters ... men and women whose only crime perhaps is that they dared to think, to talk and to worry about the destiny of their country, men and women who were not prepared to be part of the ruthless society, a violent society in which the very meaning of life has eluded those who accept this brutality as a way of life.

Who are these men and women? According to the *Rand Daily Mail* of October 4 (1975), there are now 77 persons held under Section 6 of the Terrorism Act. From actual experience, the truth is, the exact number, or who they are, will never be known until all are charged or released. The Act under which they are held is one of the most vicious pieces of legislation to be put on the statute book of a country. It is legislation meant to destroy completely every form of opposition to this totalitarian state, a method of traumatisation so as to destroy all personal autonomy, a savage and psychological process of dehumanising men who dare to identify themselves with this struggle against the injustice perpetrated by man against man, whose only crime is the shading of the colour of their skin. This struggle has been inherited from generations before us, almost four hundred years ago, but the last 25 years have been of particular importance to the black cause.

It is when the Nationalist Party came to power on the platform of apartheid that there was a turning point in the struggle for liberation. There was an immediate onslaught on the rights of the oppressed people. Leading members of the organisation which were legal were banned, pass laws were extended to women, influx control laws were enforced, the black people were declared sojourners in the urban areas in the country of their birth; and countless other forms of repressive laws. In the 1950s the various organisations, the African National Congress, the Transvaal Indian Congress, the African People's Organisation, etc., decided to unite to fight the common enemy.

The late 1950s were characterised by a united mass struggle on an unprecedented scale. It was during this period that the historical document The Freedom Charter was adopted. It was not long before the government clamped down on all forms of opposition. The People's mouthpiece was outlawed, and banning orders were imposed on the entire leadership.

It became clear that the government was not prepared to tolerate any form of legal protest. Was this not a deliberate act of driving the people to act illegally in terms of the government laws so as to find justification for holding them incommunicado? The government then started its witch-hunt which has climaxed in these detentions that are now the order of the day.

Out of my own personal experience of seventeen months in solitary confinement, I find it hard to believe that any man with any manhood can lead a normal life in such an abnormal society. Subjecting these young men and women to this brutal experience will result in painful consequences for this country. Perhaps some of you have also accepted what they are presently going through as a way of life. Perhaps we should briefly remind ourselves, because we too, by virtue of our consciences, are ready-made prospective detainees.

Detention means that midnight knock when all about you is quiet. It means those blinding torches shone simultaneously through every window of your house before the door is kicked open. It means the exclusive right the Security Branch have to read each and every letter in the house, no matter how personal it might be. It means paging through each and every book on your shelves, lifting carpets, looking under beds, lifting sleeping children from mattresses and looking under the sheets. It means you no longer have the right to answer your telephone should a call come through, no right to speak to anyone who might come to find out if you need help. It means interrogating your employer to find out why you are employed, questioning fellow workers to find out what you discuss privately, planting informers at work, around your neighbourhood, amongst your friends, in church, in school, etc.

Ultimately it means your seizure at dawn, dragged away from little children screaming and clinging to your skirt, imploring the white man dragging mummy to leave her alone. It means leaving the comfort of your home for the bare essentials of life that hardly make life bearable in your cell. It means the haunting memories of those screams of the loved ones, the beginning of that horror story told many a time and that has become common knowledge, yet the actual experience remains petrifying.

To review but the minimum bare facts: it means, as it was for me, being held in a single cell with the light burning 24 hours so that I lost track of time and was unable to tell whether it was day or night. Every single moment of your life is strictly regulated and supervised. Complete isolation from the outside world, no privacy, no visitor, lawyer or minister. It means no one to talk to each 24 hours, no knowledge of how long you will be imprisoned and why you are imprisoned, getting medical attention from the doctor only when you are seriously ill. It means a visit from one magistrate and a retinue of prison officials against whom you may wish to lodge a complaint and at whose mercy you are held. The very manner in which you are asked for complaints in fact means 'How dare you complain'.

The frightful emptiness of those hours of solitude is unbearable. Your company is your solitude, your blanket, your mat, your sanitary bucket, your mug and yourself. You have no choice of what you are given to eat even though you have not been charged. You have only one hour exercise per day depending on whether there is enough staff to spare. To you, your very existence in prison seems to be a privilege. All this is in preparation for the inevitable hell – interrogation. It is meant to crush your individuality completely, to change you into a docile being from whom no resistance can arise, to terrorise you, to intimidate you into silence. After you have suffered the first initial shock of imprisonment for those who are inexperienced, this initial shock followed by the detainee's adaptation to prison has an effect of changing the detainee's personality and outlook in life.

In some cases it means severe moods from fervent hope to deep despair. Each day of nothingness is a struggle to survive. What sustains is the spontaneous defence mechanism, that granite desire to defend and protect at all cost [against] disintegration of personality. You ask yourself questions without answers day after day, week after week, month after month, and then you keep telling yourself – I am sane and I will remain sane.

You're subjected to countless stripping of all your clothes. You must be quite naked for the white prison wardress to search your body thoroughly, to run fingers through your hair, to look in your mouth and under your tongue. There have been alleged suicides in detention; you keep asking yourself whether you will leave the cell alive for you do not know what drove those who died to their deaths. Sometimes it is a serious effort to remember what happened, the mind becomes completely blank. Then suddenly when you have gone through all this you are whisked away from your cell to the interrogation room.

Here now you have to enter into a debate with yourself. There are only two decisions, you decide whether you will emerge a collaborator with the system or continue your identification with whatever your cause is. A prisoner writing from experience in one concentration camp states:

> By destroying man's ability to act on his own or to predict the outcome
> of his action, they destroyed the feeling that his actions had any purpose,
> so many prisoners stopped acting. But when they stopped acting they
> soon stopped living. What seemed to make the critical difference was
> whether or not the environment – extreme as it was – permitted some

minimal choices, some leeway, some positive rewards insignificant as they may seem now, when viewed objectively against the tremendous deprivation.

Prisoners who came to believe the repeated statements of the guards – that there was no hope for them, who came to feel that their environment was one over which they could exercise no influence whatsoever, these prisoners were in a literal way, walking corpses.[15]

Supposing those men and women were engaged in so-called illegal action according to those who determine our fate. Even illegal action has its own ethics. C.S. Oosthuizen writes:

Only those religious principles and moral standards which are not incompatible with the 'dignity of man' and his 'universal rights' should take precedence over allegiance to the body politic ... illegal action is justified where a body of law is not merely indifferent to the rights of men and women, but inimical to their worth and dignity. That men ought to enjoy freedom of conscience, that is to say, the right to accept or reject moral and religious beliefs which to them seem just and true, or invalid or false, does not entitle them to act in ways which would prostitute the rights of others, or impose on fellow-citizens some deplorable and unbearable indignity.

We draw hope from the people of Mozambique who after more than 500 years of colonial oppression are once again free to determine their own destiny in the land of their fathers. Samora Machel in one of his speeches on the question of efforts by the Portuguese to persuade the people not to join the struggle prior to independence says:

They do this and they will continue to do it because it is the only weapon they have – dividing the people in order to dominate them ... they cannot change their political line because they cannot stop being colonialists. They cannot stop making people do forced labour because they depend on forced labour ... They give some economic privileges to a few Mozambicans, those who have had some education and who are considered potentially active political leaders, to induce them to defend the colonial system in order to retain these privileges.

They announce 'important changes', like the new 'state' of Mozambique, to try to create the illusion – mainly among people in other countries – that the Portuguese are taking steps toward the independence of our country.

This is similar to our so-called détente.

> They also try to discredit the liberation movement by attempting to make people believe that we are terrorists … those tactics do not cause any problems for us. The people are politically aware and conscious, they have lived under Portuguese colonialism since they were born. They have experienced the oppression, exploitation and humiliation in their own flesh. They cannot be cheated. Manoeuvres will never succeed.

> I find it difficult to appeal to the powers that be to change: to charge or release detainees. I cannot call for the trial of men and women who have already been tried and found guilty by the very act of their detention. As we have seen, detention alone is a trial in itself.

Although, in later years, Winnie wrote candidly about her ordeal at the hands of the security police, and documents from the time have also been published recently,[16] this meeting was the first time she revealed details to a large contemporary audience, and the *Rand Daily Mail* gave the meeting front-page prominence, claiming that Winnie was leading a 'new protest'[17] – a headline that clashed somewhat with the demure picture of Winnie reading her speech. The event was also important because it was one of the first occasions at which Reverend Desmond Tutu, newly elected as the first black Anglican dean of Johannesburg, spoke publicly in the city. Tutu outlined the theological reasons why the Terrorism Act was abhorrent,[18] calling, even then, for reconciliation. Reconciliation without freedom, he warned the 200-strong audience, was 'cheap reconciliation'.[19]

Winnie's speech is a poignant, almost poetic account of the battle to retain sanity in the face of unspeakable brutality. The horror of the described ordeal must have been accentuated by the contrast with the venue – a church – as well as Winnie's relatively calm demeanour; she later claimed that prison had 'purified' her soul,[20] and Emma Gilbey notes that, at this stage of Winnie's life, she had a remarkably reserved and warm composure.[21]

Using repetition and metaphor, Winnie takes the audience through the disorientating lead-up to the 'hell' of interrogation, which ends with the detainee entering 'into a debate' with herself, choosing between becoming a 'collaborator with the system' or remaining loyal to their own cause. The reality of interrogation was sometimes hazier than this, however – not least because detainees were frequently too weak with exhaustion, hunger and confusion to commit to anything. Even though the interrogation team had managed to extract confessions from the 1969 arrestees, the difference between defendant and witness was, as Emma Gilbey points out, 'semantic'.[22] And although, in one sense, Winnie had 'broken' during her interrogation,[23] in no way could she be described as a collaborator. In fact, after the CORD event, she told a *Times* journalist that nothing had changed her stance against apartheid.[24] If anything, the experience strengthened her commitment to the fight for freedom and she had become more determined than before.

A week later, Winnie spoke again at a meeting in Durban that was arranged in honour of her return to public life. Yet, even though she was unbanned, the reach of her words remained limited to her immediate audience; the *Rand Daily Mail* noted that they were advised not to quote her for fear of contravening the Riotous Assemblies Act,[25] and there appears to be no record of the speech.

Winnie enjoyed ten months of relative freedom, during which time she resumed active involvement in politics, attending court cases and acquainting herself with the new generation of Black Consciousness leaders. When the Soweto riots broke out in June 1976, Winnie's involvement in politics took a new turn and she began to command respect, not only by virtue of her position as the wife of Nelson Mandela but also because she now 'reflected the mood of the masses'.[26] In the aftermath of the uprising, she sought out missing bodies, comforted parents and arranged funerals;[27] she also went on to help with the formation of the Black Parents' Association (BPA) – 'the first time she took on a leadership position in her own right'[28] – and her speech at the organisation's launch reveals the extent to which she absorbed the discourse of the Black Consciousness Movement. She called on Soweto parents to organise themselves in support of their protesting children and to fight for 'black solidarity, black unity and black respect'.[29]

Winnie's period of 'freedom' soon came to an end, however, and on 28 December 1976 she received her harshest banning order yet: she was effectively banished from her Orlando home to a dry and dreary township outside Brandfort in the Orange Free State. There she spent eight years, leaving only to visit Nelson Mandela and receiving visitors only under the watchful eyes of police officers who were appointed to ensure that she did not contravene her restrictions. She displayed remarkable strength of character by keeping herself busy with small upliftment projects for the community – starting a crèche, running an informal soup kitchen and establishing a mobile health unit.

Being banished, she explained in a 1983 interview, 'means being imprisoned at your own expense'.[30] For Winnie, Brandfort was ultimately a fate worse than exile, and the successive years of harassment, banning, imprisonment and banishment eventually took their toll. Her biographers note that she grew increasingly distrustful, even paranoid,[31] and found it more and more difficult to accept criticism, leading ultimately to the tragic events of the late 1980s, when Winnie would fall from grace.

In 1986, she finally moved back to Soweto, but both she and the place she knew as home were much changed. In the wake of Oliver Tambo's call to make the country ungovernable, the township had become chaotic and violent, as communities turned on themselves in the people's war. Winnie immediately began to mobilise and established an informal group for young radicals, the Mandela United Football Club. Her increased militancy was symbolised by her preference for a khaki uniform and by her inflammatory rhetoric. Most notably, addressing a packed hall in Munsieville in 1986, she seemingly endorsed the controversial practice of necklacing, saying, 'Together, hand in hand, with our boxes of matches and our necklaces we will liberate this country.' Necklacing – a practice that involved placing a petrol-soaked tyre around a victim's neck and setting it alight – was a particularly brutal form of execution meted out to suspected apartheid collaborators. Although it was never officially sanctioned by the ANC, the government frequently referred to instances of necklacing in the propaganda war of the 1980s to justify the need for military force in the townships. Winnie's comments were an embarrassment to the organisation.

Increasingly, Winnie's football club developed a reputation for vigilantism under their 'coach', Jerry Richardson, and in 1987 angry high school pupils burnt down the Mandela home in Orlando West after the club members allegedly assaulted a schoolgirl. When Winnie moved to an ostentatious house in Diepsloot, the situation worsened, and the group of about thirty youths continued with their reign of terror under the auspices of serving as Winnie's bodyguards. On 29 December 1988, four youths were abducted from the home of a local pastor, whom Winnie had accused of sexual molestation. When the club was linked to their disappearance, the Mandela Crisis Committee was formed to deal with the situation.

A few days later, the body of one of the boys, fourteen-year-old Stompie Moeketsi Sepei, was found in a dumping site near Winnie's home. He had been brutally beaten and his throat had been slit. At the same time, the vanishing of two more youths was linked to the club, and the doctor who'd examined Sepei days before he'd died was also murdered. The crisis committee officially distanced itself from Winnie, and spokesperson Murphy Morobe released a statement, saying, 'We are outraged at Mrs Mandela's complicity in the recent abductions of Stompie.'[32] The newspapers were full of reports on the disgraced Mother of the Nation's demise.

By all accounts, Winnie, the tortured, had become the torturer.

B.J. Vorster

Reply to a motion of no confidence in the government
by the leader of the opposition, House of Assembly,
Parliament, Cape Town, 30 January 1976

On 24 April 1974, the National Party secured its biggest ever election victory, winning 124 of the 169 parliamentary seats. Although it grew its position by only 5 seats, the opposition was divided between the waning United Party (at 47 seats) and the growing but relatively minor Progressive Reform Party (PRP) (with 7 seats). Prime Minister B.J. Vorster had led the party since 1966, meaning that it had enjoyed an extended period of stability and that the government's confidence was at an all-time high.

But events from afar were about to disrupt the NP election party. One day later, Lisbon underwent a military coup d'état, ending the reign of the deeply unpopular Estado Novo after twenty-nine years. There was very little resistance to the coup, known as the Carnation Revolution because of the blooms handed to soldiers by flower sellers, and few shots were fired. Although the revolution was relatively bloodless in Europe, it had devastating long-term consequences in southern Africa, and Vorster's government dragged South Africa into the conflict.

The new Portuguese regime had no desire to continue with the expense of maintaining power in its colonies, and it withdrew Portugal's military personnel from Guinea-Bissau, Mozambique and Angola, leaving these countries vulnerable to Soviet-aligned liberation movements. At the same time, Rhodesia's unilaterally declared independence of 1965 was under threat from guerrilla fighters. The Lisbon coup rendered the region politically unstable and put South Africa into a precarious position as one of the last remaining white-ruled countries in southern Africa.

Initially, Vorster's government didn't appear too concerned about the Portuguese withdrawal. The situation in Mozambique was contained, as the border with South Africa covered a small area, and the country was relatively stable given that the Mozambique Liberation Front (FRELIMO) was the sole political heir. In warning against private support of right-wing insurrection in Mozambique, minister of defence P.W. Botha echoed the Department of Foreign Affairs's 'religious adherence to the policy of non-interference'[1] in Parliament in September 1974: 'We do not believe it is in the interest of the republic to interfere in the affairs of other countries,' Botha said, 'because we do not want other countries to poke their noses into our affairs.'[2]

This 'live-and-let-live' attitude[3] contradicted what unfolded in Angola, however. One year later, on 14 October 1975, the South African Defence Force (SADF) launched a covert military campaign, Operation Savannah, with vague intentions, even to those leading the operation.[4] Troops had been in the Ruacana–Calueque area near the South West African border since August, and the official line was that the military was simply protecting the South African–funded hydroelectric complex after foreign-aid workers were caught up in skirmishes involving Angolan guerrilla fighters, although it is now widely thought that this served as a pretext for placing troops in the region.[5]

The government looked on the Angolan situation differently for several reasons. For one thing, an independent Angola would offer refuge to the South West Africa People's Organisation (SWAPO), which was fighting to liberate the South African-controlled protectorate. On a larger scale, Angola was no longer 'part of the buffer of white-ruled states that separated South Africa from black-ruled Africa to the north.'[6] Three groups were jostling for control in the country – the National Liberation Front of Angola (FNLA), the National Union for the Total Independence of Angola (UNITA), and the People's Movement for the Liberation of Angola (MPLA) – and when the Alvor Agreement to form a government of national unity between them failed in January 1975, Vorster, encouraged by his minister of defence,[7] became concerned about the potential rise of the Marxist MPLA. Intelligence forces had determined that the movement had a decidedly hostile view of South Africa.[8]

Because of the covert nature of Operation Savannah and because the authorities feared losing electoral votes as well as support for conscription, there was a military injunction to keep casualties to an absolute minimum.[9] However, concealing Savannah from the public was near impossible because it involved white conscripts.[10] Before long, reports of casualties – many of them young servicemen – began to surface, but there was still no official identification of an 'enemy,'[11] and the public began to wonder what exactly South African troops were doing in the area. Reports of Cuban and Soviet military involvement emerged as early as October, leading to panicked predictions of an outbreak of a full-scale war and speculation about whether South Africa's presence was fomenting the situation.

When Botha returned from the area in late November, he warned the media to 'pay attention only to authoritative and official statements on defence matters.'[12] Journalists of course took this as a signal to do exactly the opposite, casting aspersions on the government's insistence that it was simply protecting

Calueque infrastructure with contradicting reports in the latter months of 1975. The papers were full of speculation. For instance, the *Rand Daily Mail* publicised comments from a Radio Uganda interview with UNITA chief Jonas Savimbi on 17 December in which he said that South African troops were 'deep in Angola' and not simply within the so-called 'operational area'.[13]

Things got worse when, a day later, news emerged that the MPLA had captured four SADF soldiers near Quibala, some 800 kilometres north of the Angolan border with South West Africa. The MPLA released a photo of the dejected-looking soldiers (three of whom were teenage national servicemen) and proceeded to parade two of them at a special press conference in Lagos[14] and to interrogate them on Radio Luanda. In a bid to portray South Africa as an aggressor in the conflict, the MPLA released a statement condemning the Organisation of African Unity (OAU) for its 'passivity in the face of South Africa's deep penetration into Angola' and calling for recognition and 'maximum support' to 'defeat racism and imperialism in Africa'.[15]

Capitalising on the apartheid state's bungled communication, the MPLA sowed further confusion by boasting that they had in fact captured fifty SADF soldiers.[16] Botha denied this claim (it was indeed false) and explained that the captives were 400 kilometres from Luanda because they'd left the 'operational area' in order to retrieve an unserviceable vehicle and had got lost (which raised serious questions about the reach of the operational area). By now, the South African public didn't know who or what to believe, and the image of the men – handcuffed and visibly shaken – brought home the implications of South Africa's involvement in the Angolan conflict, and the leader of the PRP, Colin Eglin, called on Vorster to convene Parliament urgently.[17]

In early 1976, three more SADF soldiers were captured about 400 kilometres south-east of Luanda and similarly paraded at a press conference in Addis Ababa. On 15 January, the newly established South African television service screened footage of one of the servicemen, eighteen-year-old Lodewyk Kitshoff, being made to spell out his name by his captors[18] – most likely an attempt to drum up support for the Angolan effort.

By the time Parliament reconvened towards the end of the month, the public wanted answers. 'Tell us NOW!' a *Rand Daily Mail* editorial demanded,[19] and on 27 January the leader of the UP, Sir De Villiers Graaff, brought forward a motion of no confidence against the government. Graaff spoke about the 'deep impression' left on the nation by the photographs of South African prisoners of war and said that 'the government could not expect to enjoy the unqualified support of the people if it committed them by stealth to war'.[20]

Three days later, after months of rumour, miscommunication and speculation about the extent and benefit of South Africa's involvement, Vorster
spoke at length about the 'Angolan matter' in Parliament. Yet, despite a two-
hour-long speech, an excerpt of which is reproduced below, he succeeded in
raising more questions than he answered:

> I come now to the essence of the Angolan matter, and I want to say at
> once that hon. members will understand that it is an exceptionally
> delicate matter. Even on this occasion there are things which I simply
> dare not say. South Africa's involvement was not an isolated involvement;
> others were also involved. I am not going to mention their names. It is
> not for me to do so. Everyone must speak for himself on this matter. I am
> only prepared to say what I said at Stellenbosch, i.e. that I am prepared
> to stand up and be counted in regard to this matter. It goes without
> saying that, on the question of their involvement, those people should
> come forward themselves.
>
> Let us now approach the matter from a different point of view.
> Let us ask ourselves what would have happened if South Africa had
> not become involved. Then, firstly, the MPLA, with Russian and
> Cuban help, would have taken over the whole of Angola and would
> have subjugated the entire population. They would have had the
> harbours of Lobito, Moçâmedes and other harbours at their disposal
> right at the outset. They would have had the Benguela railway line
> at their disposal. They would have created the impression in the
> outside world that the people of Angola wanted the MPLA and were
> well-disposed to the MPLA. Initially the MPLA did not disclose the
> presence of the Russians and the Cubans. They concealed their presence;
> they did not mention them, and the Russians and the Cubans did not
> announce their own presence there either. They tried to create the
> impression that it was the MPLA that was finding favour with the
> people of Angola and had the support of all the people in Angola.
> They did this although they controlled only one-third of the population
> and less than one-third of the territory. I maintain in all seriousness that
> South Africa's involvement exposed the Russian–Cuban involvement.
> Even if South Africa did nothing else, South Africa did do the free
> world a service in Africa by causing this to emerge very clearly. But what
> would have happened further? The OAU would have recognised the
> MPLA unanimously or with few dissenting votes at its conference,

and South Africa would have been condemned in one morning at Addis Ababa. This did not happen.

[...]

Sir, when reproaches are made about Angola, I think it can best be discussed by reference to a leader in *The Cape Times* of 20 January 1976. In that leader the editor of *The Cape Times* put four questions to me:

(1) Is South Africa fighting in the Angolan Civil War?; (2) If so, why have we departed from our policy of non-intervention in the affairs of our neighbours; (3) Why was the public not kept informed; and (4) What is the extent of our present commitment and what will it be in the future? These questions more or less deal with the whole Angolan situation, also the questions that were put to members on this side of the House. When the question is put to me whether South Africa is fighting in the Angolan Civil War, I say that South Africa was never a party in this civil war. South Africa did not become involved in Angola because it wanted to take part in the civil war. There must be absolute clarity about that. What is more, it must be at all times understood, because that is the situation, and hon. members know that that is so, that our involvement in Angola was not the cause of Russian and Cuban intervention. Our involvement was the effect of Russian and Cuban intervention. If they had not entered Angola, if they had not taken part in this affair, if they had not tried to subvert the whole of Angola and to suppress its people, South Africa would never have entered Angola at all. We were not involved in the civil war. We had nothing to do with it whatsoever; it was not our affair. I therefore say that we were not a party to the civil war. My hon. colleague explained that. He went further and said that our objectives were limited and that we achieved our ends. That is so. If hon. members ask me what our objectives were, then I say:

Firstly, to chase the MPLA and the Cubans away from the borders for which we were responsible, to chase them away from the dam, because we did not go there in the first instance to occupy the dam. You will remember that my colleague explained that we went there to investigate the situation and were fired upon. That was the first time we ever went into Angola. We went in to chase Cuba and the MPLA away from the dam.

Mr R.J. Lorimer: And now?

[Vorster:] By force, naturally. We did not merely say 'Shoo, Shoo!' [Laughter.]

Mr R.J. Lorimer: My question was not 'how'. It was 'and now?'

[Vorster:] I am coming to the 'now'. You must first take your medicine before you come to the 'now'. I am busy with the 'how' at the moment. Sir, we chased them away from the borders for which we were responsible. My hon. colleague over here [Botha] told you about the build-up of arms on the borders of South West Africa and for what purpose. And then, secondly, and I want to be very candid about this, it is rather difficult, Sir, when you chase a man away to decide when to stop. That, candidly, is a difficulty. Naturally it must be left to the people who are responsible for doing the job to decide how far they are going to chase away the man, knowing that if they chase him away a short distance he may come back. I make no bones about the fact that we chased him a very long way, and I take full responsibility for that. [Interjections.] Secondly, let us look at what happened next. Again I am only talking about my involvement and my government's involvement, and not about the involvement of other countries of the free world. We became involved to prevent the MPLA and the Cubans from harassing the people in the traditionally Unita and FNLA areas, harassment to such an extent that they had to flee to Owambo and South West Africa in their tens of thousands. I make no apology for having done that either. Thirdly, we became involved in order to bring to the notice of the free world and of Africa the fact that an unwilling people was being driven into the communist fold at the point of a bayonet, or otherwise was being shot to pieces. We did exactly that. Because we did that, there are those who turn round and say, firstly, that we should not have done it. If I understood the hon. member for Yeoville[21] correctly, he is with me on this point, that there are some who do not hold it against us that we did it. There are those, however, who immediately turn round and say: 'Why did you throw overboard your policy of non-intervention? You acted in a certain way in Mozambique but took an opposite course of action in the case of Angola.' However, one cannot equate the two. They are absolutely and totally different. I was accused, first of all by Dr Albert Hertzog, closely followed by the hon. member for Sea Point,[22] though he managed to beat the hon. member for Sea Point by a short head, or a short beard.

Let us now look at the arguments of hon. members on the other side. This was thrown at my head also by the hon. member for Bezuidenhout,[23] and he was applauded by the hon. member for Rondebosch. In fact, they appeared on the same page of *The Cape Times* – Karperde! The hon. member for Rondebosch applauded him for the stand he took, unlike the stand taken by the hon. member for Durban Point and the hon. Leader of the Opposition. He congratulated the hon. member for Bezuidenhout. No wonder! They are birds of a feather. I do not often give advice to the hon. member for Bezuidenhout. However, I think it is appropriate that I do give him advice on this occasion. Let me say to him, in the popular turn of phrase: Why do you not take your seat where your mouth is? [Interjections.]

Mr Speaker: Order!
[...]

[Vorster:] Let us now consider the hon. member for Bezuidenhout. The hon. member for Bezuidenhout said more about this matter outside than he did inside this House, for it is easier to say things outside this House. After all, there is no one who can call you to order.

Mr J.D. du P. Basson: I only get a half-hour to speak. You have already been speaking for nearly two hours.

[Vorster:] What did the hon. member say in his speech at Middelburg? He made a very serious accusation, an accusation which is now being made against us at the UN. I quote:

'Speaking at a public meeting at Middelburg, Transvaal, on Monday night, Mr Basson said the two main pillars of the country's foreign policy – non-intervention in the domestic affairs of other countries and the undertaking that South West Africa would not be used as a basis for military action across the border – had been thrown overboard by South Africa's involvement.'

This is the man who had no information, who did not know what the position was! Before the parliamentary session began, however, he spoke of how 'involved' we were, and of how we had thrown our principles overboard.

Mr J.D. du P. Basson: I stated both sides of the case.

[Vorster:] Sir, I am now referring to these facts. I shall come to the hon. member again, if I consider it worthwhile. Now I come to a real jewel in this report, and I quote:

'Dr Slabbert, the PRP chief defence spokesman, was accompanied on the trip to the military zone by his United Party counterpart, Mr Vause Raw, and the chairman of the National Party's parliamentary defence group, Mr Coetsee.'

He went, and you went with him. I hope that my genial friend on the other side has thanked the hon. member for Rondebosch[24] appropriately for taking him along.

The hon. member for Bezuidenhout put a question to me in this debate about the difference between the allegation that they wish to liberate South West Africa from Angola, and the statement made by FRELIMO against South Africa this week in Lourenço Marques. My reply is that there is a tremendous difference between Mozambique and Angola. Mozambique was handed over to one government. It made no difference whether or not one likes that government. South Africa's foreign policy is still that if there is a government which it does like, it does not make war against it. As long as that government leaves South Africa in peace, South Africa will leave that government in peace. Surely we made it very clear that we were not seeking a quarrel with Mozambique, that we were not interested in who comprised that government, just as long as there was a stable government and that country was not used as a base for an attack on South Africa.

Mr J.D. du P. Basson: They say it is now going to become one.

[Vorster:] No, Sir. Many a lie is told from hearsay. After all, there are many people who say they are going to attack us. The hon. member says that his party is going to win the by-election in Alberton, but should I worry about this now? [Interjections.]

Mr J.D. du P. Basson: You yourself say in your amendment that they are going to attack us!

[Vorster:] It does not stop at talk only; after all, I want to explain this now. On the one hand it is a matter of talking, and on the other hand a matter of doing. There was no build-up of an arsenal of weapons on the border between Mozambique and South Africa. What is more – the hon. member probably does not know this – we fenced off the border between South Africa and Mozambique at a time when one would have expected feelings to be at their highest pitch. I was on that border myself; we were on the one side and FRELIMO on the other. We recruited labour among them, and we fenced off that border which we had not been able to fence off in the time of the Portuguese, without there even being an argument about where the border ran.

Mr J.D. du P. Basson: Why did you not fence off the border of South West Africa as well?

[Vorster:] Surely no attack was planned on South Africa, and if an attack on South Africa is planned and executed, we shall repel it. I told Mozambique this at the time. In the case of Angola forces were built up on our border. After all, there are no SWAPO activities in Mozambique. In the case of Angola refuge was granted to members of SWAPO, and those members were allowed to enter South West Africa to commit murder there. What is more, they occupied the dam and fired on our people. We did not intervene: we acted in self-defence, and we shall at all times continue to do so.

[...]

Mr Speaker, I have tried to argue and prove that we did not become involved because we wanted to be involved. South Africa has a record in this regard. We do not want to become involved, but we were involved because we had no alternative. I am grateful for the understanding shown by my friends, the hon. member for Durban Point,[25] the hon. the Leader of the Opposition, and others, in this regard. They themselves said that they did not agree with everything we were doing, but I appreciate the spirit in which they discussed matters with us, even when they reproached us.

I referred at the outset to the communist objectives. Those objectives have always remained the same. We have learned a lesson in Angola, a lesson which reminded us of what we already knew, for I am on record as having said a long time ago in this House that, when it comes to the worst, South Africa stands alone. People will have to realise this. I think our people have realised this for a long time, for the instincts of a people whose survival is at stake, are never wrong. That is why our people are moving closer together, and that is why there is the intensification of feeling among our people which one sees in these days, and which we saw more than ever before on the day of humiliation. One observes it in one's correspondence, and one hears it in one's conversation with people. There are difficult days for us. It is going to be a difficult year, a year of endless problems. It is a watershed year. But I believe, as I stand here before you, that it is also a year of grace. It is a year of hope and a year of faith, because we have a task which we have to accomplish. Thank God our people are prepared to accomplish that task.

By the time Vorster delivered his speech, the Defence Force had in fact made the decision to withdraw troops from Angola,[26] and the information – scanty as it was – was thus a case of 'too little, too late'. Having already had the question of 'if' South Africa was involved answered by the foreign press, Vorster could only address the issue of 'when' and 'why'. The question of 'when' is elided throughout (he mentions no dates in relation to military events) and he adroitly circumvents the question of 'why' by recasting it as 'what would have happened if South Africa had *not* become involved'.

He is rich in detail when speculating (the MPLA would have taken over Lobito's and Moçâmedes's harbours and the Benguela railway line; the OAU would have recognised the MPLA; etc.) but comically vague when it comes to presenting actual events ('We chased them away from the borders … it must be left to the people who are responsible for doing the job to decide how far they are going to chase away the man').

Throughout, he evades questions. In answer to the query of whether South Africa is involved, he first says 'no' ('I say that South Africa was never a party in this civil war') and then, immediately afterwards, 'yes' ('South Africa did not become involved in Angola because it wanted to take part in the civil war').

And in what must have been a frustrating experience for the House, Vorster constantly alludes to state secrets. 'There are things which I simply dare not say', he announces, and 'others were also involved' but it is not for him to 'mention their names'. He then goes on to condescendingly dismiss speakers' readings of events on account of their lack of information – the PRP's Japie Basson is attacked for speaking about South Africa's stance when he 'did not know what the position was!' and also 'probably does not know' that the SADF fenced off the border between South Africa and Mozambique.

Because the chicken-and-egg question of who went to Angola first dominated public debate, Vorster goes to great lengths to deny that South Africa's presence was the cause of Russian–Cuban aggression, attempting even to portray the SADF's role as positive in exposing the communists' involvement to the 'free world', of which he clearly considers South Africa to be a part. The question of 'who started it' remains unanswered. Around the time of Vorster's speech, US secretary of state Henry Kissinger was misquoted to imply that the Soviet-backed Cuban intervention was a result of South African meddling[27] – to Botha's fury, who claimed that, if correctly quoted, Kissinger, like the rest of the world, 'was not fully informed'.[28] Piero Gleijeses, the only researcher to have accessed the Cuban archives, argues that the Soviets and Cubans began to support the MPLA only after South Africa got involved,[29] but, as with many such squabbles, it's not likely that the question will ever be satisfactorily answered.

Thickset, thick-accented and thick-spectacled, Vorster is better on paper than in video recording. Here, his use of idiom adds a touch of wry humour to an otherwise serious debate – 'You must first take your medicine before you come to the "now"', he tells the PRP's Rupert Lorimer, and – in a reworking of the English 'put your money where your mouth is' – he asks the party-hopping Japie Basson rhetorically, 'Why do you not take your seat where your mouth is?'

Despite his wit, in the context of growing disapproval of Afrikaner nationalism, Vorster's physical demeanour couldn't have done much to endear him and his cause to Africa and the rest of the world. Yet the desire to do just this, according to Hermann Giliomee, is likely a large part of the reason for the Angolan bungle.[30] Vorster was at the time pursuing his own détente foreign policy with receptive African states, and when both Zambia and the CIA made clandestine requests for the SADF to help repel the spread of communism in Angola, the deeply unpopular apartheid state was too flattered to resist.[31] Vorster hoped that South Africa's attempts to 'solve' African problems, particularly those of a colonial nature, would prove its commitment to the continent, thus securing a rightful place for it, and the Afrikaner *volk*, in Africa.[32] But the attempt to realise diplomatic ambitions through military means was ultimately unsuccessful.[33] The government had totally overestimated the level of US support – both diplomatic and financial – and on 19 December, the US senate voted to cut aid to the two opposing Angolan movements, leaving South Africa high and dry.

Vorster's speech did little to satisfy the public's desire for answers, and Bernadi Wessels noted that both opposition parties were 'hamstrung by the lack of answers from the Government' even if Vorster had won the debate 'hands down'.[34] In the days that followed, the papers were full of additional speculation, pitching Kissinger's comment against Vorster's and calling for the prime minister to clear up the contradiction.[35]

What's more, on 10 February, just over a week after the address, everything that Vorster had predicted would happen had South Africa not become involved happened anyway: the OAU recognised the MPLA as the official government of Angola, and the last of the South African troops withdrew in mid-March.[36]

The suspension of the conflict was temporary, however, and what became known as the Border War – convoluted, costly and controversial – would rage on for more than a decade.

Allan Boesak

Speech at the launch of the UDF,
Rocklands Civic Centre, Mitchells Plain,
20 August 1983

The 1980s was the most turbulent decade of apartheid rule, rocked by the state's two-pronged approach to maintaining power. The government became ever-more brutal in suppressing dissent while offering a range of symbolic concessions and half-hearted reforms.

When *Rand Daily Mail* journalists exposed Prime Minister B.J. Vorster's role in the Information Scandal of 1978 – a government-backed plan to use defence-budget money to fight a propaganda war – he was replaced by his minister of defence, P.W. Botha, a long-serving and military-minded politician known for his '*kragdadigheid*' (forcefulness). In response to what he called the 'Total Onslaught' facing the country, Botha initiated a policy of 'Total Strategy', mobilising all state resources at his disposal – economic, political, psychological and military. The result was the radical militarisation of society. In 1982/3, defence spending alone took up 23.7 per cent of the national budget,[1] and in 1977, military service increased from one to two years, with camps increasing by an additional month in 1982. The South African Police (SAP) had been trained to handle mass protests, and in 1981 the Tear-Gas Act was extended to allow more prolific use of tear gas. By the start of the decade, the state had built up a sophisticated security police with an established web of informers, and the National Intelligence Service, which had replaced the Bureau of State Security in 1978, was brought under tighter control. In 1981, the Defence Act was amended to allow for troops to be deployed in the 'suppression of internal disorder',[2] and throughout the decade conscripts and soldiers were increasingly used to quell unrest.

At the same time, part of 'Total Strategy' involved a 'hearts and minds' campaign to win increased support for the state by initiating reforms – some of which were perceived as cosmetic and others of which inadvertently helped to bring about the demise of apartheid towards the end of the decade. At the end of the 1970s, limited residential rights were granted to qualifying urban blacks and, importantly, trade union rights were granted to workers. In 1980, Botha promised to abolish 'hurtful, unnecessary discriminatory measures',[3] following up with the repeal of a number of petty apartheid Acts. These gestures were met with mixed responses. On the one hand, they raised hopes that Botha's administration planned to end apartheid. On the other, they were read as 'adaptation' rather than reform strategies. In a 1980 interview, Oliver Tambo, the head of the ANC in exile, said that the people were 'no longer asking for slight shifts in the official forms of domination ... the government is still playing around with what is called petty apartheid. If Prime Minister Botha means well, he has come too late in the day.'[4] The liberation movement had its own vision of what a total strategy should entail.

It was too much for some of the NP members, however. Led by Dr Andries Treurnicht – whom the media dubbed 'Dr No' because of his refusal to accept any reforms – they broke away to form the Conservative Party on 20 March 1982.

The most controversial reform was the government's attempt to co-opt coloured and Indian support for the state. In 1982, the President's Council – at Botha's request for potential reform ideas – presented a proposal for a form of power-sharing among white, Indian and coloured communities. Botha approved the proposal and planned an all-white referendum to canvass support for a new constitutional structure, known as the Tricameral Parliament.

The plan was bound to sow dissension, both within Botha's party and among South Africans more generally. The Conservative Party called it a 'shocking' and 'dangerous innovation'.[5] At the other end of the spectrum, the Progressive Federal Party (PFP) objected to the exclusion of black South Africans from the power-sharing deal and saw the plan as 'constitutional decoration for the extremely wide powers of the president', which would make redundant the role of the official opposition.[6] For black South Africans, of course, the plan was an insult. Even the usually conciliatory Mangosuthu Buthelezi said of Botha's plan: 'The elephant has given birth to a mouse.'[7]

Within the coloured and Indian communities, the plan was divisive. The coloured Labour Party (formed in 1969 and broadly opposed to apartheid) was split down the middle over the idea.[8] When the party voted in favour of support in its January 1983 congress, there was an outcry, particularly from the outspoken liberation theologian Dr Allan Boesak, who said the decision 'reeked of opportunism'[9] and called its supporters the 'junior partners of apartheid'.[10]

Boesak, then president of the World Alliance of Reformed Churches, is usually credited as being the first to propose the idea for a mass broad-based multiracial coalition of anti-apartheid organisations.[11] In response to what he saw as the government's attempt to 'divide and conquer', he repeatedly called for unity. Speaking at a conference held to oppose the South African Indian Council's decision to accept the plan – the Anti-SAIC Conference – he said, 'there is no reason why churches, civic associations, trade unions, student organisations should not unite on this issue, pool our resources, inform people of the fraud which is about to be perpetrated in their name, and on the day of the election expose the plans for what they are'.[12] At the same time, in his annual 8 January Radio Freedom address, Tambo had named 1983 'The Year of United Action', telling listeners 'we must organise the people into strong mass democratic organisation'.[13]

These rallying calls – apparently only coincidentally connected[14] – set in motion plans for the formation of a loose alliance of anti-apartheid groups, and after a number of regional conferences, the United Democratic Front (UDF) was officially launched, just a few months before the scheduled all-white referendum. The launch was both a conference (for delegates from specific organisations) and a larger public rally. On a 'bitterly cold' winter's day,[15] between 6 000 and 15 000 people – 1 500 of whom represented organisations of some kind[16] – crammed inside the Rocklands Civic Centre in the heart of the coloured township of Mitchells Plain. The hall was packed to the rafters, and yellow-and-red UDF banners were draped across the walls. Additional tents had been erected to accommodate the crowds and ensure that nobody was arrested under the Illegal Gatherings Act,[17] and the atmosphere was chaotic, crowded and euphoric.

Boesak, whose oratory style was reminiscent of Martin Luther King Jr's,[18] was the final speaker at the public rally. Taking his place at the lectern, to cries of 'Boesak! Boesak! Boesak!',[19] the speech, excerpts of which are reproduced here, was greeted with wild applause:

> The most immediate reason for us coming together here today is the continuation of the government's apartheid policies as seen in the constitutional proposals. In recent weeks some people have asked me in the newspapers with more urgency than before (and I am sure this question has been put to you also) 'Why don't you see the positive side of apartheid?'
>
> Now, Mr Chairman, brothers and sisters, when you are white, and when your children's education is guaranteed and paid for by the state; when your job is secure and blacks are prevented from being too much competition; when your home has never been taken away and your citizenship of the country of your birth is not in danger; when your children don't have to die of hunger and malnutrition and when your over-privileged position is guaranteed by security laws and the best-equipped army on the continent – then I can understand why some people believe that apartheid has its positive side.

But for those of us who are black and who suffer under this system there is no positive side. [...]

For the time has come for white people to realise that their destiny is inextricably bound with our destiny and that they shall never be free until we are free, and I am so happy that so many of our white brothers and sisters are saying that today by their presence here.

Because it is true: people who think that their security, and peace lie in the perpetuation of intimidation, dehumanisation and violence, are NOT free. They will never be free as long as they have to lie awake at night worrying whether a black government will one day do the same to them as they are doing to us, when white power will have come to its inevitable end.

But we must also ask the question: what is positive about the Government's constitutional proposals? In order that there should be no misunderstanding, let me as clearly and briefly as possible, repeat the reasons why we reject these proposals.

Racism, so embedded in South African society, is once again written into the constitution. All over the world, people are beginning to recognise that racism is politically untenable, sociologically unsound and morally unacceptable. But in this country, the doctrine of racial supremacy, although condemned by most churches in South Africa as heresy and idolatry, is once again enshrined in the constitution as the basis upon which to build the further development of our society and the nurturing of human relationships.

All the basic laws, those laws which are the very pillars of apartheid, indeed, those laws without which the system cannot survive – mixed marriages, group areas, racial classification, separate and unequal education, to name but a few – remain untouched and unchanged.

The homelands policy, which is surely the most immoral and objectionable aspect of the apartheid policies of the government, forms the basis of the wilful exclusion of 80% of our nation from the new political deal. Indeed, in the words of the proposals by the President's Council, the homelands policy is to be regarded as 'irreversible'.

So our African brothers and sisters will be driven even further into the wilderness of homeland politics, millions will have to find their political rights in the sham independence of those bush republics; millions more will be forcibly removed from their homes into resettlement camps.

Clearly the oppression will continue, the brutal break-up of black family life will not end. The apartheid line is not all abolished, it is simply shifted so as to include those so-called coloureds and Indians who are willing to co-operate with the Government.

Not only is the present system of apartheid given more elasticity making fundamental change even harder than before, but in the new proposals the dream of democracy to which we strive is still further eroded.

So while the proposals may mean something for those middle-class blacks who think that the improvement of their own economic position is the highest good, it will not bring any significant changes to the life of those who have no rights at all, who must languish in the poverty and utter destitution of the homelands, and who are forbidden by law to live together as families in what is called 'white South Africa'.

[...]

We must turn to one other important question, namely the question of whites and blacks working together. This has been mentioned as a reason why the United Democratic Front has been so severely attacked by some and why they have refused to give their cooperation.

They are saying to us that white people cannot play a meaningful role in the struggle for justice in this country because they are always, by definition, the oppressor. Because the oppression of our people wears a white face, because the laws are made by a white government, because we are suffering so much under a system created and maintained by white people, they say there can be no cooperation between white and black until all of this is changed.

I would like to say to those who think this way I understand the way they feel. We have seen with our own eyes brutalisation of our people at the hands of whites. We have seen police brutality. We have experienced the viciousness and the violence of apartheid.

We have been trampled on for so long; we have been dehumanised for so long. But it is not true that apartheid has the support of all white people. There are those who have struggled with us, who have gone to jail, who have been tortured and banned, there are those who have died in the struggle for justice.

And we must not allow our anger for apartheid to become the basis for a blind hatred of all white people. Let us not build our struggle upon hatred and hopes for simple revenge. Let us even now seek to lay the foundations for reconciliation between white and black in this country by working together, praying together, struggling together for justice.

No, the nature and the quality of our struggle for liberation cannot be undermined by the colour of one's skin, but rather by the quality of one's commitment to justice, peace and human liberation. And in the final analysis, judgment will be given, not in terms of whiteness or blackness, whatever the ideological content of those words may be today, but in terms of the persistent faithfulness we are called to in this struggle.

Besides, the very fact that we are talking about the constitutional proposals already reveals the paradox in this argument. The government have been pushing ahead with these proposals precisely because they have been supported and accepted by some people from the black community who think that the short-term economic gains and the semblance of political power are more important than the total liberation of all South Africa's people.

So, our struggle is not only against the white government and their plans, but also against those in the black community who through their collaboration seek to give credibility to these plans.

But there is something else that we must say. South Africa belongs to all its people. That is a basic truth we must cling to tenaciously for now and for the future. This country is our country, and its future is not safe in the hands of people who despise democracy and trample on the rights of the people whether they be white or black.

Its future is not safe in the hands of people – black or white – who depend upon economic exploitation and human degradation to build their empires: its future is not safe in the hands of people – black and white – who need the flimsy and deceitful cloak of ethnic superiority to cover the nakedness of their racialism.

Its future is not safe in the hands of people – white or black – who seek to secure their unjustly acquired privileged positions by violent repression of the weak, the exploited and the needy.

Its future is not safe in the hands of people – white or black – who put their faith simply in the madness of growing militarism. So for the sake of our country and our children, whether you be white or black, resist those people, whether they be white or black.

So let us not be fearful of those who sit in the seats of power, their lips dripping with the words of interposition and nullification. Let us not be intimidated by those who so arrogantly, so frighteningly, echo their master's voice.

We are doing what we are doing not because we are white or black, we are doing what we are doing because it is right. And we shall continue to do so until justice and peace embrace and South Africa becomes the nation it is meant to be.

In the meantime, brothers and sisters, let me remind you, as I've done before, of three little words that I think we ought to hold on to as we continue the struggle, and these are three words that express so eloquently our seriousness in this struggle. You don't have to have a vast vocabulary to understand them. You do not need a philosophical bent to grasp them – they are just three little words.

And the first word is the word all! We want all of our rights. Not just some rights, not just a few token handouts here and there that the government sees fit to give – we want all our rights. And we want all of South Africa's people to have their rights. Not just a selected few, not just a few so-called 'coloureds' or 'Indians' after they had been made honorary whites. We want all of our rights for all South African people, including those whose citizenship has already been stripped away by this government.

The second word is the word here! We want all of our rights and we want them here, in a united, undivided South Africa. We do not want them in impoverished homelands, we don't want them in our separate little group areas. We want them here in this land which one day we shall once again call our own.

And the third word is the word now! We want all of our rights, and we want them here and we want them now.

And as we struggle on, let us continue to sing that wonderful hymn of freedom that has sustained us through all of these years and shall sustain us in the years to come. Let us continue to sing 'Nkosi sikelel' iAfrika!'

At this point, the hall erupted into song, and Boesak – who as a cleric in the Reformed Church was accustomed to securing audience participation – delivered the final, increasingly rousing lines of his speech alongside the crowd's singing. In the style of Martin Luther King Jr – and in keeping with the Christian tradition of witnessing and making public vows – he concluded with a call-and-response pledge, asking the audience to commit themselves to anti-apartheid ideals: 'And now therefore we pledge to come together in this United Democratic Front and fight side by side against the government's constitutional proposal and the Koornhof Bills.'

Like the success of the UDF itself, Boesak's speech is effective because of its appeal to broad ideals – to family values, unity, morality, justice and non-racialism. In response to the complexity of the constitutional proposals – which in summary sound like a step in the right direction, but whose fine print many interpreted as an attempt to hoodwink the oppressed into the illusion of self-governance – the UDF proposed a simpler message, best expressed in their slogan 'Apartheid divides, UDF unites'. Throughout, Boesak exemplifies this approach: the proposals of those sitting in power are 'dripping with the words of interposition and nullification', he says, whereas you don't need a 'vast vocabulary' or 'philosophical bent' to grasp the will of the people. This approach helped to unify the disparate religious, racial and class groups under the UDF's umbrella. As Jamie Frueh points out, the UDF 'resisted all positively defined ideology and only defined itself negatively in opposition to apartheid'.[20] The organisation also harked back to the ANC's Charterism – which Boesak echoes with the line 'South Africa belongs to all its people' – and its inclusive approach was exemplified in its choice of presidents and patrons from a range of racial and political backgrounds. Boesak's 'all', 'here' and 'now' conclusion – which he also used at the Anti-SAIC Conference – neatly encapsulated the demands of his audience and drew wide applause.

Described as a 'serious setback' to the 'government's constitutional reform',[21] the launch's significance was widely debated in the liberal media afterwards, with Anton Harber wondering if the UDF could become 'the real force of the 1980s' and adding, 'There can be no doubt that the launch signalled the beginning of a new stage in South African politics, since it symbolised a regeneration of activity among opposition groups that has taken place in recent months.'[22]

The muscle of the UDF was not immediately evident, however. Its formation (and the PFP's 'no' campaign) did little to deter white voters at the referendum for constitutional reform in November. In answer to the question 'Are you in favour of the implementation of the Constitution Act, 1983, as approved by Parliament?', 66.3 per cent of the ballots cast said yes. With a 76 per cent voter turnout, Botha must have been crowing.

But this soon changed. In 1984, in the general election for the Tricameral Parliament, voter turnout among coloureds and Indians was pathetic (at 17.6 and 16.2 per cent respectively)[23] and the entire event was marred by protests, boycotts and arrests. The Times denounced the election as an 'attempt to redraw the boundaries by bringing the coloureds (2 800 000) and Asians (900 000) onto the white (4 500 000) side of the dividing line', while the Guardian said that the coloured community had 'turned its back on the new dispensation'.[24] Clearly, Botha had won no hearts and minds – neither locally nor abroad.

Insultingly, he dismissed the implications of the low turnout, saying that the 'coloured people still show no interest in exercising their political rights'.[25] Over the next few years, this gross misreading of the situation would be proved wrong.

Oliver Tambo

'Year of the Women' address, Lusaka,
Radio Freedom, 8 January 1984

To this day, the ANC's birthday on 8 January is an important annual event. Every year, the National Executive Committee releases a statement to take stock of its position, to give thanks for past support, to pay homage to comrades who have died, to articulate its vision for the forthcoming months and, echoing Chinese tradition, to proclaim a theme for the year (1980 was declared the 'Year of the Charter', for instance, and 1985 the 'Year of the Cadre'). During the apartheid period, the statement was released through ANC leader Oliver Tambo, affectionately known as 'Comrade O.R.', and it became a galvanising yearly highlight, linking supporters in exile around the world with the people in South Africa.

Former MK intelligence officer Barry Gilder recalls the anticipation with which the statement was received:

> In the exile years, wherever we were, we would wait with great expectation
> for the words of our movement through the voice of Oliver Tambo,
> perhaps crowded around a transistor radio tuned to Radio Freedom in
> our camps in Angola, or eagerly awaiting a printed version of the speech
> in our safe flat in Moscow, or perhaps lucky enough to be in Lusaka or
> London to receive Tambo's words in person. The January 8 statement
> never disappointed. Always it captured with precision and insight our
> own intellectual and emotional recognition of the challenges we faced.[1]

While the tradition began in 1972 on the occasion of the organisation's sixtieth birthday, this was a one-off event and it suffered a six-year hiatus as the ANC reconstituted itself in exile. Then, rejuvenated by the student uprisings, the opening up of the frontline states and the beginning of MK's low-key guerrilla insurgency, the tradition was resumed in 1979, which Tambo proclaimed the 'Year of the Spear' in recognition of the 'central role played by the people's weapon, the spear'[2] (Umkhonto we Sizwe, the Spear of the Nation). As Tom Lodge points out, the sporadic MK attacks of the late 1970s acquired 'great symbolic and psychological importance' to internal and external ANC members.[3]

Tambo, who had succeeded Luthuli as ANC leader, was the perfect spokes-person for the ANC. Instructed by the ANC leadership to leave the country to seek overseas assistance after the Sharpeville massacre, he managed the ANC headquarters in London from 1961 until 1969, when he moved them to Lusaka. A lawyer by training and described as an 'adroit diplomat',[4] he handled the world's media with aplomb, collaborating effectively with the Anti-Apartheid Movement in the UK. In addition, as a founding member of the ANC Youth League, and later as head of MK, he commanded a great deal of genuine respect from those at the forefront of the struggle.

The authorship of the speeches was attributed to the ANC national exec-utive, but, increasingly, the task of writing them fell to Thabo Mbeki[5] – the forty-two-year-old son of Rivonia trialist Govan Mbeki and a young protégé of Tambo's. The articulate Sussex-educated Mbeki excelled in this role and was appointed head of the ANC's Department of Information and Publicity in 1984.

While Mbeki was the perfect scribe and Tambo the perfect speaker, Radio Freedom was the ideal platform for the ANC's address. Although the station had fizzled out after its 1963 launch and the Rivonia arrests, it began to play an integral role in the 1970s and 80s in connecting the ANC leadership in exile with its supporters back home. According to Raymond Suttner, the station was properly relaunched in Lusaka, Zambia, in 1967, and at its height it aired daily in five countries: Angola, Ethiopia, Madagascar, Zambia and Tanzania.[6] Its inimitable signature opening – the staccato sound of shots fired from an AK-47 – inspired revolutionary fervour, together with defiant slogans such as *Amandla Ngawethu!* (Power to the people!) and *Mayibuye iAfrica!* (Africa – let it return!). The shows, typically half an hour in length, consisted of a mix of news, music and commentary.[7] The freedom songs that it played were often banned in South Africa and included frequent references to struggle heroes Sisulu and Mandela. Sometimes, inspired by Tambo's 8 January address, the broadcasts set strategic tasks, such as the creation of organisations in under-represented areas in South Africa.[8]

Radio Freedom was broadcast on medium wave, which caused it to suffer problems because of the apartheid state's earlier launch of high-frequency low-wave broadcasts to eliminate, as minister of posts and telegraphs Albert Hertzog put it, the possibility of 'being influenced by overseas'.[9] As a solution, the ANC included instructions on how to tune in to the station in pamphlets and newsletters, such as *Mayibuye*, *Dawn* and *Sechaba*[10] as well as *The African Communist*.

To ensure a wider reach, these periodicals also included copies of the 8 January speech, and increasingly sophisticated underground networks were used to spread Tambo's words and raise the morale of the oppressed population. Suttner recounts how underground operatives used time-delay rockets to release showers of leaflets with ANC messages, often accompanied by recorded announcements playing from a hidden location.[11] A 1986 *Los Angeles Times* article tells the story of one Sipho, a Soweto man who described himself as a 'human radio' because of his daily habit of repeating the content of Radio Freedom broadcasts on his train journeys.[12] Mondli Makhanya remembers that illegal copies of the 8 January address would flood the streets in the days after the event each year.[13] It seems likely that some of these were recorded in South Africa from the broadcast itself. Others were smuggled in from abroad. In 1980, funded by Swedish organisations, 4 000 cassette recordings of the 8 January statement were snuck in, shortly followed by another 4 000 tapes with liberation messages.[14]

This was dangerous speech – not least because of its incendiary nature but also because possession of recordings or copies of it could land one in prison for up to eight years.[15] Despite defence attempts to argue that possessing material didn't amount to activism,[16] in 1983 Thabo Moloi was sentenced to two years' imprisonment when he was caught with a cassette recording of one of Tambo's speeches.[17] And in 1985, the twenty-one-year-old Edward Ngobeni was given four years for playing ANC tapes to friends.[18]

By the mid-1980s, the 8 January tradition was firmly established. As opposition to apartheid swelled abroad, information-deprived supporters in South Africa were hungry for guidance from those in exile. On the one hand, the results of the Tricameral Parliament referendum had been a blow to the struggle movement; on the other, hopes were bolstered by the formation of the UDF and the promise of mass action. The country was poised for battle.

In the meantime, exiled ANC leaders had formulated a strategy for a 'people's war' – their own 'total onslaught'. A high-profile ANC and SACP delegation visited Vietnam in 1978 and found inspiration in General Võ Nguyên Giáp's description of the country's struggle against the US, particularly regarding the synergy between mass struggle, the underground and the army in pursuit of revolutionary aims.[19] They were also impressed by the way in which the North Vietnamese had secured the participation of the full population in the fight against the enemy, thus collapsing the categories of combatant and non-combatant. The unity of the internal situation with international solidarity and the party's leadership role over the armed forces were additional important approaches.[20] The visit sparked a new approach to the struggle, and over the next few years the leadership developed a comprehensive new strategy termed the 'Four Pillars of the Revolution'.

Tambo's January 1984 address – in which he proclaimed 1984 the 'Year of the Women' – was the first time that he publicly laid out this new strategy. It led directly to later calls to make the country ungovernable, established the basis for cooperation with the UDF, and explained the ways in which military and political actions could be combined:

Dear Compatriots,
Brothers and Sisters in the Struggle,
Comrades

Today, the 8th January, your organisation, the African National Congress, is 72 years old. In keeping with established practice, we ask you to share with us today some thoughts on the tasks that confront us during 1984. Allow me to begin by extending to you all, the wishes of the National Executive Committee and the general leadership of the ANC for great successes in the New Year.

This time last year, when we marked the 71st anniversary of the founding of our organisation, we pointed out that our long struggle had come to a point where the revolutionary ferment had reached unprecedented heights and had plunged the ruling racist clique into deeper and deeper levels of crisis. We went on to state that within the confines of the apartheid system there was no way out of this crisis situation. Apartheid cannot be reformed. The only real solution lies in the victory of the revolutionary forces, the dismantling of the apartheid machinery and the transfer of political and economic power to the democratic majority.

Events of the past year have fully borne out the correctness of this assessment. The momentous struggles of the past year have taken us further upon the road to our cherished goal and have driven the racist rulers into further acts of desperation. For us, the future is brightening daily whilst for the Pretoria racist clique, the future is getting darker each passing day.

[...]

The Four Pillars of Our Revolution
Our revolutionary struggle rests on four pillars. These are, first, the all-round vanguard activity of the underground structures of the ANC;

second, the united mass action of the peoples; third, our armed offensive, spearheaded by Umkhonto we Sizwe; and fourth, the international drive to isolate the apartheid regime and win worldwide moral, political and material support for the struggle.

Over the last few years, the guardians of reaction in our country have devised a programme of action centred on the twin notions of so-called national security and total strategy. This programme is based on the recognition that the apartheid system is immersed in a deep and permanent general crisis. The ruling group in Pretoria has therefore been addressing itself to the question of how to manage this crisis to ensure that it does not get out of hand.

The bantustan scheme, the militarisation of society, the offensive against the ANC, the new apartheid constitution and other recent pieces of legislation, notably, those covering industrial relations, the so-called community councils, the press and the economy, all are elements in this programme of crisis management. Coupled with the criminal war against the Namibian and Angolan people, and increased aggression against the rest of southern Africa, these measures point to the desperation of the regime as it battles for its survival.

In other words, the fascists recognise that they can no longer rule in the old way. We recall how, at the height of the Soweto uprising, J.B. Vorster made bold to declare, 'there is no crisis' – no crisis for minority rule. But a few years later, P.W. Botha called on the whites to adapt to reality or perish with apartheid.

[...]

Revolutions Are About State Power

[...] We must begin to use our accumulated strength to destroy the organs of government of the apartheid regime. We have to undermine and weaken its control over us, exactly by frustrating its attempts to control us. We should direct our collective might to rendering the enemy's instruments of authority unworkable. To march forward must mean that we advance against the regime's organs of state-power, creating conditions in which the country becomes increasingly ungovernable.

We Must Hit the Enemy Where It Is Weakest

You are aware that the apartheid regime maintains an extensive administrative system through which it directs our lives. This system includes organs of central and provincial government, the army and the police, the judiciary, the bantustan administrations, the community councils, the local management and local affairs committees. It is these institutions of apartheid power that we must attack and demolish, as part of the struggle to put an end to racist minority rule in our country... We must hit the enemy where it is weakest.

[...]

Now is the Time to Choose

The intolerable hardships and sufferings; the persecutions, detentions and murders of patriots and democrats in other bantustans call for the establishment of fighting organisations to organise and lead the struggle for the destruction of these racist institutions of oppression.

This year, Botha and Malan will be busy implementing the provisions of their apartheid constitution. In this regard, our democratic movement must mobilise to ensure that the so-called coloured and Indian sections of the black population refuse to be recruited to play the role of partners in apartheid tyranny. White South Africa alone should man the apartheid constitutional posts, which it alone has created, for its exclusive benefit. Those who elect to serve in these apartheid institutions must expect to face the wrath of the people.

We must go further to say that our white compatriots, with even a modicum of anti-apartheid feeling, have to abandon the delusion that they can use Botha's constitutional institutions to bring about any change. The forces struggling for a new order in our country are outside of these structures. It is within the ranks of these extra-parliamentary forces that the anti-apartheid whites can make a significant contribution to democratic change in our country. Now is the time to choose.

[...]

At this juncture allow me to single out the creation of the UDF as a historic achievement in our people's efforts to unite in the broadest possible front for the struggle against the inhuman apartheid system. The formation of the United Democratic Front was a product of our people's determination to be their own liberators.

The Spirit of Rebellion and Politics of Revolutionary Change

The growth of the democratic trade union movement and its power to wrest recognition from both the regime and the employers, together with the determined efforts to form one national trade union federation, constitute one of the most significant advances of our struggle in recent years.

[...]

Quite clearly, we have made great strides in these areas of work. This is evident in the strength of the UDF and the pace at which it continues to grow. It is evident also from the struggles we have conducted, in some areas for months on end. We can see it in the organisational growth of the trade union movement. There have been commendable advances in the development of the youth and students' as well as civic and women's movements.

We refer here in particular to the organisation of the working class into a revolutionary trade union movement; the organisation of the rural masses, inside and outside the bantustans; the organisation of the womenfolk of our country and the religious community into struggle.

Let us now take a brief look at each of these areas of work.

The Working Class Must Lead

Millions of workers in our country, including the unemployed and those engaged in the agricultural sector, remain unorganised. We have to make determined efforts to reach these unorganised workers, bearing in mind that it is the historic responsibility of the working class to take the lead in our struggle for people's power.

The task of forming one federation to unite the democratic trade union movement has not yet been accomplished. We should pursue this goal with even more determination and speed...

[...]

The Rural Masses Say, 'Seize the Land!'

The organisation and mobilisation of the rural population is clearly lagging behind those of our people in the towns and cities. And yet it is in these rural areas that the apartheid system has its most disastrous impact on our people. We have the organisational capacity to begin to tackle the rural areas seriously and continuously.

[...]

Apartheid Threatens Peace

In the past period we have seen the increased involvement of the religious community in our struggle for liberation. In this context, you are aware that at the National Conference of the Council of Churches last year, a proposal was made to convene a conference in 1986 to decide on the issue of the contribution of the Christian church to change in our country. It was then said: 'When peace is broken or threatened by injustice, the Christian has a responsibility to work for peace, to work for righteousness, by striving to rectify what is unrighteous, unjust.'

Those words constitute a serious challenge not only to Christians, but also to people of other faiths in our country. While the evil and unjust apartheid system exists in our country, we cannot have peace, nor can the peoples of Southern Africa.

[...]

We are entitled to expect that people of all faiths in our country, including the Christian, the Jew, the Hindu and the Moslem, will in fact act, and act now, in defence of justice, peace and life, against a system that is totally evil and inhuman.

Woman's Place Is in the Battlefront

It will be our special task this year to organise and mobilise our womenfolk into a powerful, united and active force for revolutionary change. This task falls on men and women alike – all of us together as comrades in the struggle.

[...]

Our struggle will be less than powerful and our national and social emancipation can never be complete if we continue to treat the women of our country as dependent minors and objects of one form of exploitation or another. Certainly no longer should it be that a woman's place is in the kitchen. In our beleaguered country, the woman's place is in the battlefront of struggle.

People Determined to Be Free

We have come a long way from the time, as in the 50s, when we fought barehanded disarmed and unarmed – against the military might and the trigger-happy army and police force of the apartheid regime. No black hand was allowed to touch a firearm or possess any instrument more lethal than a pen-knife.

Today, the racist regime's army and police generals who occupy a central position in Pretoria's state machinery, through the State Security Council, are making frantic efforts to recruit and arm the 'Kaffirs, Coolies and Hotnots' of the 50s, to serve as cannon fodder in the defence of a system that has fallen foul of the times, a system that has enslaved and debased us these past 70 years.

It is not that the military might of the regime has declined. It is rather that the people, determined to be free, have taken up arms and, through their own army, Umkhonto we Sizwe, have moved on to the offensive.

Today, armed struggle is a vital, indispensable component of the struggle for national and social liberation in South Africa. Where the apartheid regime relies for survival on its fascist army and police, on black mercenaries, and on puppet armies and murderous puppet administrations who slaughter men as readily as they butcher children, the democratic majority in our country supports the People's Army – Umkhonto we Sizwe – whose rising sophistication will yet compound the survival problems of the apartheid system.

But the challenge confronting Umkhonto we Sizwe, in the face of current developments in southern Africa, has never been greater. Therefore, in commending its units and commanders on the sustained offensive of the past year, we charge them, and call upon our people, to carry the struggle to new heights, and sue for victory tomorrow rather than the day after tomorrow.

To this end, Umkhonto we Sizwe must deepen its roots and grow inextricably among the popular masses: among us – the workers, the peasants, the youth, the women; we, the unemployed, the landless, the homeless, and the starving millions.

[...]

We address a special message to the white youth. Your future is in issue. The apartheid regime has no future. Like Adolf Hitler and his war machine, after spreading death and destruction everywhere, the regime will be defeated and destroyed everywhere.

The Future Belongs to the Majority

The future belongs to the majority of the people of South Africa, black and white, who, in struggle, are today laying the foundations of a united, non-racial democratic South Africa in what will then, but only then, become a peaceful and rapidly advancing region of Africa.

Your proper place is among these builders of a new order in our country. Join them. Refuse to join an army whose sole function is to murder, murder, murder, African people everywhere.

It goes without saying that black youth – African, Indian and so-called coloured – must under no circumstances serve in Pretoria's army of violent repression and criminal aggression. The democratic movement should immediately take up this issue with our youth throughout the country.

Our democratic movement, our movement for national liberation, is part of a multi-million-strong world alliance of forces which fights for national independence, democracy, social progress and peace. On the other hand, the apartheid regime belongs firmly within the camp of imperialist reaction, and is active within this camp to further counter-revolutionary goals.

We therefore have an international obligation to be active in the struggle to defeat the counter-offensive that the imperialists, led by the Reagan Administration of the United States, have launched. We too must raise our voice against the war-mongers within NATO who have brought humanity closer to a nuclear holocaust by sabotaging all efforts at nuclear disarmament and who have, instead, unleashed a new arms race and heightened international tension and insecurity. We too must struggle together with the world peace forces, especially because the Pretoria regime itself possesses nuclear weapons and maintains secret military relations with the most belligerent circles on the world scene.

[...]

Policy of Military Terror and Economic Strangulation

In this regard, through a policy of military terror and economic strangulation, the racists seek to compel the independent states of our region to surrender their independence and, as an important part of that surrender, to help evict the ANC from the whole of southern Africa. Never was there a clearer illustration of the relationship between the struggle to liberate our country and the struggle to defend the independence and sovereignty of the countries of southern Africa. The peoples of our region share one common destiny. Certainly, that can never be a destiny of subservience to the criminal regime of Pretoria.

As the Maputo Frontline States Summit of March 1982 agreed, the only way forward for the peoples of our region is to support the ANC and SWAPO in our common struggle against the Pretoria regime and to repulse the offensive of this regime against independent Africa.

[...]

Of course the Botha regime is frantic about the emergence of the ANC as the alternative power on the South African political scene.

The regime is frantic also because of its inability to block the powerful and evidently dangerous thrust of the ANC and the people towards the goal of liberation. The regime is therefore blackmailing African States into an alliance targeted on the destruction of the ANC.

ANC – Integral Part of the World Revolutionary Process

But the ANC has grown among the people of Southern Africa in the past 70 years. It has always embraced and always will embrace them as allies and comrades-in-arms. It is a child of Africa's determination to achieve and enjoy human dignity, freedom and national independence; it will never betray that parentage. It is an integral part of the world revolutionary process; it will stay in the revolution until final victory. The ANC is at once the life, the national awareness and the political experience of the popular masses of South Africa. As the people cannot be liquidated, neither can the ANC.

We take this opportunity to give a stern warning to some of our people against the dangerous temptation to work as enemy agents for the liquidation of the people's struggle.

The indestructibility of the ANC should however not induce complacency on our part. In order for the ANC to pursue and accomplish its historic mission effectively, we must be unceasing in our efforts to strengthen and expand its underground structures, ensuring its active presence everywhere in this country.

We Support Independent States of Southern Africa

We hereby extend our unequivocal support to the independent states of southern Africa, including Seychelles, in the common struggle to defeat the aggressive policies of the Botha regime. The training, arming and deployment of counter-revolutionary bandits into Mozambique, Lesotho and Zimbabwe forms part of this aggression. We are greatly inspired by the heroic struggle of the people of Angola to expel the occupying South African forces from their country and to wipe out the puppet UNITA bandits. We salute the internationalist Cuban forces which have contributed so decisively to frustrate the schemes of the Pretoria regime and its ally, the Reagan Administration.

We extend our greetings to our comrades-in-arms of SWAPO, the People's Liberation Army of Namibia and the Namibian people as a whole and pledge to fight side by side with them until our continent is rid of all vestiges of colonial and white minority domination.

As we enter this New Year – we hail the firm and positive role played by the frontline states and the forward country of Lesotho, despite Pretoria's destabilisation efforts and naked aggression against them. The dream of the total liberation of Africa is in sight.

We salute the resilience of the OAU in the face of concerted imperialist manoeuvres and call upon both the OAU and the nonaligned countries to increase their material and moral support for our struggle as well as that of SWAPO and the frontline countries.

Socialist Countries – Pillar of Support

The Socialist countries remain a solid pillar of support to our national liberation struggle. We are assured of their continued internationalist solidarity till the triumph of our revolutionary struggle.

In the past year we have succeeded in widening and deepening our support in the western countries. We are particularly cognisant of the consistent support we receive from Sweden and other Nordic countries, from Holland, Italy and Austria to mention a few. We are happy to report the establishment of a new office in Australia, at the supportive invitation of the government and people of that friendly country.

Our efforts to win international support have been significantly sustained by a wide spectrum of anti-apartheid solidarity and mass organisations in almost all the western countries as well as the countries of Asia, Africa and Latin America. [...]

We pay tribute to the progressive forces in the USA for their valiant efforts to achieve wide-scale US disinvestment in South Africa. On them rests the heavy responsibility to defeat the Reagan Administration's racist 'constructive engagement' policy with Pretoria, and to curb and confine the aggressive character of American imperialism.

[...]

1984 – The Year of the Women

One of the principal tasks we have to accomplish this year is, as I have said, the organisation and mobilisation of our womenfolk into struggle. For this reason, in the name of the National Executive Committee of the African National Congress, I declare 1984 THE YEAR OF THE WOMEN, and charge the entire democratic and patriotic forces of our country with the task of joining in the effort to mobilise our women to unite in struggle for people's power!

To all true patriots of our country, we extend best wishes for success
in our common struggle during this, THE YEAR OF THE WOMEN!
MOBILISE AND MARCH FORWARD TO PEOPLE'S POWER!
Amandla ngawethu!
Matla ke a rona!
Power to the people!

Tambo characterises Botha's government as a dying beast battling for its
survival – it is a desperate, 'frantic' regime in the last days of power, while the
proffered reforms are simply a way of managing the 'deep and permanent
general crisis' into which it has fallen. The signs of weakness require urgent
action, and we must 'sue for victory tomorrow rather than the day after
tomorrow', says Tambo. The reference to Pretoria's future 'getting darker each
passing day' suggests that freedom is no longer a distant possibility but an
attainable reality just around the corner.

The four-pronged approach to crippling the government is set out. The
'people's war' would not be waged on the conventional battlefield alone. What
is rather needed, Tambo explains, is all-round vanguard underground activity, rolling mass action, MK's armed offensive and continued international
pressure to ensure South Africa's isolation – the four pillars of the revolution.
As the ANC would later state in a submission to the Truth and Reconciliation
Commission, the intention with the 'people's war' was to 'make every patriot
a combatant and every combatant a patriot'.[21] To this end, Tambo, using
first-person plural address, collapses the division between soldiers and the
masses, hailing 'all of us together as comrades in the struggle' and calling for
MK to 'deepen its roots and grow inextricably among the popular masses…
among us – the workers, the peasants, the youth, the women'.

The second pillar is given fuller expression in the call to make the country
ungovernable by attacking the administrative centres of the state. 'We should
direct our collective might to rendering the enemy's instruments of authority
unworkable,' says Tambo. 'To march forward must mean that we advance
against the regime's organs of state-power, creating conditions in which the
country becomes increasingly ungovernable.' This directive would eventually
be distilled into the popular slogans 'Make apartheid unworkable' and 'Make
the country ungovernable'.

Targets for those taking up the people's war are also identified: 'those who
elect to serve … apartheid institutions' and 'organs of central and provincial
government, the army and the police, the judiciary, the bantustan administrations, the community councils, the local management and local affairs

committees'. As the people's war escalated in the second half of the 1980s, the targeting of non-military persons would conflict with the fourth pillar: to 'win worldwide moral, political and material support for the struggle'. The corollary of this approach – civilians becoming targets of military action – proved to be controversial, as communities took matters into their own hands, identifying and killing hundreds of potential collaborators (*impimpi*) of the system.

The people's war was launched on 3 September in several Vaal townships later that year. The day was symbolic because, despite poor voter turnout, it was the date on which the new Constitution – which included provision for the Tricameral Parliament – was promulgated. At the same time, angered by Lekoa and Everton Town Councils' announcements of hefty service and permit increases, the Vaal Civic Association called for the resignation of councillors and arranged a successful stayaway, which was extended to include a school boycott. When a march to Sebokeng Council was intercepted by police, residents burnt down councillor Esau Mahlatsi's house, violence spread and thirty-three people were killed, including three councillors.[22]

The event sparked a protracted period of violence throughout the country, and the ANC continued to apply pressure. A month later, Tambo took to Radio Freedom to repeat his call to make the country ungovernable, asking listeners, 'Are we achieving our objectives of making our country ungovernable? Are we challenging in action the right of the apartheid regime to rule our country? Can we truly say that we have mounted such an offensive that the enemy finds it difficult to stop our forward march to liberation?'[23]

By the beginning of 1985, the strategy was in full swing. Tambo's 8 January speech – in which he lauded the masses for taking 'impressive strides towards rendering the country ungovernable' – is remembered as being his 'most dramatic',[24] and four days later the government banned all pamphlets titled 'Make the country ungovernable'.[25]

By the middle of May 1985, a total of 260 councillors had resigned, 150 of whom had had their homes or businesses destroyed.[26] From the beginning of the Vaal Uprising in September 1984 to the end of July 1985, the death toll mounted to 517, reaching a peak of 96 in July 1985 when Botha imposed a partial state of emergency[27] – an act that the ANC leadership saw as an aggressive reaction to an effective strategy.

The success of the people's war was mixed. On the one hand, it created diplomatic flak for Tambo and the ANC.[28] With outbreaks of disorganised violence and a rise in 'false flag' attacks, the ANC lost some of its control and some of its moral high ground – a turn that the apartheid state exploited to great effect in its propaganda war.[29]

On the other hand, the increased turmoil led to urgent calls for negotiation. In October 1985, the PFP's Frederik van Zyl Slabbert led his party's executive to Lusaka in order to meet with members of the ANC, and a month later, at a meeting of the Commonwealth Heads of Government, an Eminent Persons Group was established to encourage solutions to the South African deadlock. The group later recommended that in order for any talks to take place, the state needed first to declare its unambiguous intention to dismantle apartheid, unban the PAC and ANC, and withdraw the military from the townships. Another key requirement was the release of political prisoners, starting with Nelson Mandela, the 'living legend' without whom no future could be secured.[30]

Zindzi Mandela

'My Father Says' speech, UDF rally,
Jabulani Stadium, Soweto, 10 February 1985

After Mandela was transferred to Pollsmoor Prison in 1982, the authorities began to relax his harsh prison restrictions. In 1984, he was allowed his first contact visits with Winnie and Zindzi in twenty-two years, and his ban on receiving news material was lifted.[1] Mandela and his fellow Rivonia trialists were now permitted to read a fairly wide range of newspapers and magazines and were given access to a radio, which aired local news reports.

So it was that on the morning of 31 January 1985 Mandela, now sixty-six, tuned in to hear President P.W. Botha addressing Parliament.[2] To his surprise, the issue of his release was raised. The president had an offer for him:

> The government is not insensitive to the fact that Mr Mandela and others have spent a very long time in prison, even though they were duly convicted in open court.
>
> The government is also willing to consider Mr Mandela's release in the Republic of South Africa on condition that Mr Mandela gives a commitment that he will not make himself guilty of planning, instigating or committing acts of violence for the furtherance of political objectives, but will conduct himself in such a way that he will not again have to be arrested.
>
> [...] As I have indicated, the government is willing to consider Mr Mandela's release, but I am sure that Parliament will understand that we cannot do so if Mr Mandela himself says that the moment he leaves prison he will continue with his commitment to violence.
>
> It is therefore not the South African government which now stands in the way of Mr Mandela. It is he himself. The choice is his. All that is required of him is that he should unconditionally reject violence as a political instrument.

While Mandela had been informed that the government would be making some kind of a proposal, he didn't expect it to be quite so public.[3] The 1985 offer was in fact the sixth conditional offer of freedom from the apartheid government. The previous offers had been presented in private.

In 1974, minister of prisons Jimmy Kruger had travelled to Robben Island, offering to release Mandela if he agreed to settle in the Transkei – one of the 'independent' homelands established ten years earlier. Mandela refused the offer (both then and when Kruger repeated the proposal in 1976), explaining later that 'it was an offer only a turncoat could accept'.[4]

By the late 1970s, when the Anti-Apartheid Movement's Free Nelson Mandela campaign began to gather momentum, Mandela was starting to pose an enormous challenge for the government: 'Just as the jailing of nationalist leaders like Mahatma Gandhi and Jomo Kenyatta invested them with a unique aura', the Eminent Persons Group would later state, 'so … the imprisonment of Nelson Mandela is a self-defeating course for the South African Government to take'.[5] With each passing year, this had become more apparent.

Then, in the mid-1980s, Botha came up with what he thought was a brilliant solution to the 'Mandela problem', as it was referred to in government circles.[6] After visiting the Bavarian apartheid-apologist Franz Josef Strauss, who advised against Mandela's continuing imprisonment,[7] the president returned with news for his cabinet: he would offer to free Mandela on condition that he publicly reject the armed struggle. Botha was fully confident that Mandela would refuse the offer.[8] Here was a way, he thought, of exposing the ANC's hero as a terrorist. What kind of person wouldn't renounce violence? Finally the rest of the world would understand why the apartheid state had to keep him in prison, Botha reasoned.[9]

Some of the president's advisors weren't so sure. Both Kobie Coetsee, minister of justice, and Louis le Grange, minister of law and order, thought that the plan was risky and tried to get Botha to rephrase his proposal more positively.[10] But Botha went ahead, ensuring that the proposal was made as publicly as possible.

To begin with, everything went according to plan. Within days, word came from Lusaka that Mandela wouldn't be accepting the offer, and there was worldwide approval for Botha: Britain swiftly backed the proposal.[11] Opposition leaders were uncharacteristically supportive. Dr Frederik van Zyl Slabbert said that the offer was 'tolerant' and 'reasonable', and even Helen Suzman could see no problems with it, saying that she hoped it would be considered.[12] The local *Sunday Times* said that it demonstrated the president's 'praiseworthy willingness' to negotiate,[13] and *Rapport* said that the offer was 'sincere'.[14] *Die Volksblad*, more cynically, echoed Botha's hope that 'the world will see who is pursuing peace sincerely' and who is 'clinging to an ideology of violence, personal ambition and concern for its ANC power base'.[15]

But back at Pollsmoor, Mandela and his fellow political prisoners were not impressed, and they prepared an official response to expose the duplicity of what Mandela saw as Botha's 'public challenge'.[16] Together with Andrew Mlangeni, Raymond Mhlaba, Walter Sisulu and Ahmed Kathrada, Mandela crafted a speech of immense moral clarity. George Bizos and Arthur Chaskalson also weighed in to ensure that there were no legal glitches.

At the same time, Winnie Mandela hatched a superb plan for its delivery. According to Bizos, Winnie 'stage managed events to achieve maximum effect',[17] and she invited an entourage of journalists to accompany her to Pollsmoor to receive her husband's official response on 8 February. Despite incessant questioning from journalists, the response was withheld until 10 February when, on a swelteringly hot Sunday, it was read out to a crowd of 9 000 UDF supporters at Jabulani Stadium in Soweto. The occasion could not have been more perfect: the crowd had gathered for a welcome meeting in celebration of Archbishop Desmond Tutu's return from Oslo, where he had just been awarded the Nobel Peace Prize. The UDF created a good deal of media hype around the event by simultaneously announcing and withholding information: journalists were told that a 'special event' would precede Tutu's speech[18] and that a European parliamentarian would be attending,[19] but no further details were given.

The choice of speaker for the address was also a stroke of genius. As she was still banned, Winnie – who had apparently been keen to break her restrictions[20] – was unable to read out her husband's response. It's not clear who came up with the idea to have Mandela's youngest daughter, Zindzi, deliver the address, but the choice of speaker appears to have been part of the speech's conceptualisation.

Wearing a yellow UDF T-shirt and looking younger than her twenty-five years, Zindzi was ushered by Desmond Tutu and Allan Boesak through the jubilant crowd, which then lifted her, shoulder-high, to the platform, chanting 'Sisulu' and 'Mandela'.

Zindzi's address, reproduced in full below, was electrifying:

On Friday my mother and our attorney saw my father at Pollsmoor Prison to obtain his answer to Botha's offer of conditional release. The prison authorities attempted to stop this statement being made but he would have none of this and made it clear that he would make the statement to you, the people.
    Strangers like Bethell from England and Professor Dash from the United States have in recent weeks been authorised by Pretoria to see my father without restriction, yet Pretoria cannot allow you, the people,

to hear what he has to say directly. He should be here himself to tell you what he thinks of this statement by Botha. He is not allowed to do so. My mother, who also heard his words, is also not allowed to speak to you today.

My father and his comrades at Pollsmoor Prison send their greetings to you, the freedom-loving people of this our tragic land, in the full confidence that you will carry on the struggle for freedom. He and his comrades at Pollsmoor Prison send their very warmest greetings to Bishop Desmond Tutu. Bishop Tutu has made it clear to the world that the Nobel Peace Prize belongs to you who are the people. We salute him. *Amandla!*

My father and his comrades at Pollsmoor Prison are grateful to the United Democratic Front who without hesitation made this venue available to them so that they could speak to you today. My father and his comrades wish to make this statement to you, the people, first. They are clear that they are accountable to you and to you alone. And that you should hear their views directly and not through others. My father speaks not only for himself and for his comrades at Pollsmoor Prison, but he hopes he also speaks for all those in jail for their opposition to apartheid, for all those who are banished, for all those who are in exile, for all those who suffer under apartheid, for all those who are opponents of apartheid and for all those who are oppressed and exploited.

Throughout our struggle there have been puppets who have claimed to speak for you. They have made this claim, both here and abroad. They are of no consequence. My father and his colleagues will not be like them. My father says:

I am a member of the African National Congress. I have always been a member of the African National Congress and I will remain a member of the African National Congress until the day I die. Oliver Tambo is much more than a brother to me. He is my greatest friend and comrade for nearly fifty years. If there is any one amongst you who cherishes my freedom, Oliver Tambo cherishes it more, and I know that he would give his life to see me free. There is no difference between his views and mine.

I am surprised at the conditions that the government wants to impose on me. I am not a violent man. My colleagues and I wrote in 1952 to Malan asking for a roundtable conference to find a solution to the problems of our country, but that was ignored. When Strijdom was in power, we made the same offer. Again it was ignored. When Verwoerd was in power we asked for a national convention for all the people in South Africa to decide on their future. This, too, was in vain.

It was only then, when all other forms of resistance were no longer open to us, that we turned to armed struggle. Let Botha show that he is different to Malan, Strijdom and Verwoerd. Let him renounce violence. Let him say that he will dismantle apartheid. Let him unban the people's organisation, the African National Congress. Let him free all who have been imprisoned, banished or exiled for their opposition to apartheid. Let him guarantee free political activity so that people may decide who will govern them.

I cherish my own freedom dearly, but I care even more for your freedom. Too many have died since I went to prison. Too many have suffered for the love of freedom. I owe it to their widows, to their orphans, to their mothers and to their fathers who have grieved and wept for them. Not only I have suffered during these long, lonely, wasted years. I am not less life-loving than you are. But I cannot sell my birthright, nor am I prepared to sell the birthright of the people to be free. I am in prison as the representative of the people and of your organisation, the African National Congress, which was banned.

What freedom am I being offered while the organisation of the people remains banned? What freedom am I being offered when I may be arrested on a pass offence? What freedom am I being offered to live my life as a family with my dear wife who remains in banishment in Brandfort? What freedom am I being offered when I must ask for permission to live in an urban area? What freedom am I being offered when I need a stamp in my pass to seek work? What freedom am I being offered when my very South African citizenship is not respected?

Only free men can negotiate. Prisoners cannot enter into contracts. Herman Toivo ya Toivo, when freed, never gave any undertaking, nor was he called upon to do so.

My father says: I cannot and will not give any undertaking at a time when I and you, the people, are not free.

Your freedom and mine cannot be separated. I will return. *Amandla!*

The entire stadium erupted in applause in response to the speech, which was memorable not only because of its stirring content but also because it was the first public statement from Mandela in twenty-two years. Zindzi, and presumably the speechwriters, drew attention to the momentous significance of the words, which came after decades of Mandela being silenced, by repeating the phrase for which the speech became known: 'My father says'. The repetition also invoked Mandela's identity not only as the father denied to Zindzi for so many years but also as 'father of the nation'.

The speech referred briefly to the ANC's decision to resort to armed struggle, citing the various unsuccessful attempts to engage the government in peaceful talks. Turning the table on Botha's request, Zindzi expressed her father's view that it was in fact the president who must renounce violence, drawing loud cheers from the crowd.

Irrevocably linking Mandela's freedom with that of the people, the speech also clarified the conditions under which he would accept a release offer, thus enhancing his martyr status in the eyes of the world. Only the full abolition of apartheid would put him in a position to enter negotiations, Zindzi declared, concluding with her father's now-legendary statement: 'Only free men can negotiate. Prisoners cannot enter into contracts.'

The speech completely reversed any PR gains Botha had achieved with his offer. Against Mandela's morally authoritative response, Botha's proposal appeared as a petty challenge from a stubborn man. As Patti Waldmeir points out, instead of solving the 'Mandela problem', Botha succeeded only in giving his prisoner 'a veto over his own release'.[21]

At first, Botha gave no immediate comment on the speech, stating only that he hadn't been sent a copy of the address.[22] Later, he repeated his offer, which was less favourably represented by the media. 'Botha not budging on Mandela release', declared *The Times* of London,[23] while the *Rand Daily Mail* asked if the offer had been a 'ploy, couched in such terms that Mandela had little choice but to reject it?'[24] The *Star* called the president's offer a 'Trojan horse'.[25]

In the years that followed, pressure to free Mandela mounted, to the extent that by his seventieth birthday in 1988 even the Afrikaans-language newspaper *Beeld* was campaigning for his release. 'Do we really want to let it be inscribed in our history that we let an old man die in jail while there was still the opportunity to negotiate with him on the aspirations of his people?'[26] the newspaper asked in its editorial.

It became clear that there would be only one solution to the 'Mandela problem': unconditional release.

P.W. Botha

Address at the opening of the NP Congress ('Rubicon' speech), Durban City Hall, 15 August 1985

The speech for which P.W. Botha is best remembered was, in every sense of the word, a flop. Described by F.W. de Klerk's communications advisor as the 'worst political communication by any country at any time',[1] the 'Rubicon' speech was a profound anticlimax at a time when half-hearted reforms had raised expectations to a fever pitch.

By the mid-1980s, South Africa was burning. Heeding Oliver Tambo's call to make the country ungovernable, a number of South Africans arranged a sustained series of boycotts, riots, stayaways and protests, and an average of ten township residents were killed monthly between 1984 and 1985 in the Port Elizabeth region alone.[2] The 'black weekend' consumer boycott, held in March 1985, resulted in violent clashes with police, and on the 21st of that month (the anniversary of the Sharpeville massacre) would-be attendants of a banned funeral were shot dead. When the burnt and mutilated bodies of the popular Cradock activists Matthew Goniwe and Fort Calata were found on the roadside in early July, violence erupted in eleven townships.[3] The following day, Botha declared a partial state of emergency in thirty-six magisterial districts (mainly in the Eastern Cape). This extended the police's already gratuitous powers to include random detention, the imposition of curfews and control of the media, which was prohibited from filming, recording, publishing, disseminating and broadcasting information about public disturbances or detainees. Two days later, Tambo spoke on Radio Freedom, making his most direct appeal for continued rebellion: 'Make apartheid unworkable!' he urged. 'Make South Africa ungovernable! Prepare the conditions for the seizure of power by the people!' The unrest raged on.

To make matters worse for Botha's government, foreign media interest in events had also intensified. In March that year, Ted Koppel's *Nightline* had broadcast a series of debates between South African ministers and grass-roots leaders, in which the state had not come off well. The heightened demand for news on South Africa saw a particular rise in photojournalism.[4] Footage of police officers beating and gassing black protestors leaked out of the country, causing dismay around the world. The beleaguered apartheid state was facing a continuing border conflict, outbreaks of internal rebellion and a tattered international reputation.

To address the general crisis, the cabinet met informally on 2 August at the Ou Sterrewag building in Pretoria, and it was there that the seeds of the Rubicon speech were sown. There are several accounts of what happened at this meeting – some of which conflict – and it's unlikely that a single story will be agreed upon by those who attended. News reports from that time suggest that various potential reforms were discussed, some of which were wildly divergent. One was to expand the cabinet to include homeland leaders; another was to do away with the homelands altogether; yet another was to initiate talks with exiled leaders. Some accounts suggest that Mandela's release was also on the agenda.[5]

What happened after Sterrewag is anybody's guess. Botha was reportedly unusually quiet during the meeting, possibly because, unbeknown to his cabinet, the sixty-nine-year-old president had suffered a stroke in May and was following doctor's orders to avoid confrontations. Those who attended the meeting, Hermann Giliomee guesses, might have misread Botha's silence as support for the proposals that were presented.[6] Alternatively, at some point between Sterrewag and the delivery of the Rubicon speech, Botha might have had a change of mind.

Whatever the case, after the meeting, 'Pik' Botha, the sweet-talking minister of foreign affairs, embarked on a foreign charm offensive to try to salvage what was left of South Africa's reputation. At a series of meetings with British, West German and US representatives, he created the impression that significant reforms were on the way – possibly because he hoped that if there was an expectation of reforms, Botha might actually follow through with them.[7] For whatever reason, according to Werner Scholtz, a South African diplomat who attended the meetings, an enthusiastic Pik Botha told the ambassadors at several points: 'Gentlemen, we are crossing the Rubicon.'[8]

By the time of Botha's anticipated address to the NP Natal Congress, the stakes were high. Various advisors collaborated to draft the president's speech. At the same time, the media raised hopes by claiming that the president was on the brink of introducing historic reforms. 'A free Mandela?' asked *The Times* of London three days before the address,[9] while *Time* magazine told the world to 'expect the most important statement since Dutch settlers arrived in the Cape of Good Hope 300 years ago'.[10] International broadcast networks flocked to the country to capture the speech, the first time that live coverage had been bestowed upon a South African premier.[11] The stage was set for Botha to make history.

But instead of delivering a speech that crossed the Rubicon, on 15 August, standing on the stage of Durban City Hall, before the world's cameras and a global audience of 200 million, Botha retreated into the laager.[12] Here are several excerpts from the infamous address:

During recent months and particularly the last few weeks, I have received a great deal of advice.

Most of the persons and institutions who offered advice and still offer advice have good and well-meaning intentions. I thank them and where the advice is practical, it is considered.

[...]

Most of the media in South Africa have already informed you on what I was going to say tonight, or what I ought to say, according to their superior judgment.

Of all the tragedies in the world I think the greatest is the fact that our electorate refrained so far to elect some of these gentlemen as their government. They have all the answers to all the problems.

And these answers differ from day to day and from Sunday to Sunday!

Seldom in our past has there been a party congress of the National Party for which so many expectations were raised as this Congress in Natal. Some of the reasons for this are evident, for example the partial emergency situation in less than 14% of the magisterial districts of the RSA. Other reasons are more sinister, such as the motives of those who have put words in my mouth in advance.

During recent weeks there was an unparalleled scurry from different sources, within and outside South Africa, to predict and prescribe what is to be announced at the Congress. It was also envisaged that worldwide, people are going to be dissatisfied if certain things are not announced as were predicted.

It is of course a well-known tactic in negotiations to limit the other person's freedom of movement about possible decisions, thus forcing him in a direction where his options are increasingly restricted.

It is called the force of rising expectations.

Firstly, an expectation is raised that a particular announcement is to be made. Then an expectation is raised about what the content of the announcement should be ...

[...]

Moreover, the subject of most of the speculations, namely the constitutional future of the black peoples in South Africa, is of such a nature that it must be determined in consultation with those concerned. We cannot confront them with certain final decisions.

Over the years, that was exactly the criticism against our government – that we make decisions about people and not with them. Now, suddenly I'm expected to make the decision for them.

[...]

We must deal with our relationships and accept future challenges in a balanced way and with devotion. You will find that balance in thinking and devotion in the National Party – the only political party which is representative of the vast majority of white South Africa.

[...]

It is true that as a result of serious world recessionary circumstances, South Africa, which was also hit by recessionary conditions and overspending in some fields, could not make progress as we would have preferred.

But it is common knowledge by now that the official economic strategy applied in South Africa during the past twelve months has produced excellent results:

Overspending by the private and public sectors have been eliminated.

The money supply is under control.

Government spending is being effectively curbed and soundly financed.

The balance of payments on current account is showing a surplus of about R5 billion per year – much larger than anticipated.

[...]

The so-called 'economic fundamentals' are therefore at present very favourable in South Africa.

Many of the present perceptions of the South African situation overseas are, of course, quite erroneous. Nobody would deny that we face problems that demand solutions, but every country has. I can name you quite a number of countries who have more problems than SA.

But the perceptions of many overseas observers bear little relationship to the realities of the situation.

People are flocking to South Africa tonight, from neighbouring countries because they are looking for work and health services. Only last week I was in the north of our country and there I had the experience that people were flocking from Mozambique into South Africa in their tens of thousands. How do you explain that? Do people flee to hell?

The Republic of South Africa still remains the leading country in the sub-continent of southern Africa. If the Republic of South Africa suffers from economic setbacks, the whole of southern Africa will pay a heavy price.

[...]

I have the knowledge because I have the facts. As head of this government I am in the position to tell you tonight what the facts are. No government in this country or elsewhere in the world can solve all the problems in its country in a given time.

But despite our human weaknesses and our limited powers as human instruments, we can attempt to be on time. We can make serious attempts not to be behind time.

[...]

I now wish to deal with some other aspects of our National Life.

It is my considered opinion that any future constitutional dispensation providing for participation by all South African citizens, should be negotiated.

But let me point out at once that since South Africa freed itself from colonialism, democracy has already been broadened and millions of people who never had a say in governmental affairs under the British Colonial system, have it today.

I am pressed by some who mean it well and those who wish to destroy orderly government in this country, to make a Statement of Intent. I am not prepared to make it, not now and not tomorrow.

I say it would be wrong to be prescriptive as to structures within which participation will have to take place in the future.

It would also be wrong to place a time limit on negotiations. I am not going to walk into this trap – I am responsible for South Africa's future.

However, I believe that the majority of South Africans as well as independent states, which form our immediate neighbours, have much in common apart from our economic interests.

We believe in the same Almighty God and the redeeming grace of His Son, Jesus Christ.

And I know what I am talking about, because only a few months ago I stood before an audience of 3 million Black people, proving the truth of what I am saying now. I don't know whether one of our critics ever saw three million people together in a meeting. I did.

We believe and wish to uphold religious freedom in South Africa. This is a country of religious freedom.

[...]

We believe that our peace and prosperity is indivisible.

We believe in the protection of minorities. Is there anybody in this hall who would get up and say he is not for the protection of minorities? Let me see how such a fool looks.

We know that it is the hard fact of South African life, that it will not be possible to accommodate the political aspirations of our various population groups and communities in a known defined political system, because our problems are unique.

We have often found that our efforts to find solutions have been impeded and frustrated because of different interpretations of the terminology that we use to describe our particular form of democratic solutions.

Some years ago, with the best intentions on my part, I advocated a confederation of southern African states to cooperate with one another. The idea was belittled and prejudice was created against it and that is why I say I am not going to fall into that trap again, before I had the opportunity to discuss with the elected leaders of other communities in South Africa the structures we jointly agree on.

Now let me state explicitly that I believe in participation of all the South African communities on matters of common concern. I believe there should exist structures to reach this goal of co-responsibility and participation.

I firmly believe that the granting and acceptance of independence by various black peoples within the context of their own statehood, represent a material part of the solution. I believe in democratic neighbours, not neighbours that call out elections and then stop them in their mysterious ways.

I would, however, like to restate my government's position in this regard, namely that independence cannot be forced upon any community. Should any of the Black National States therefore prefer not to accept independence, such states or communities will remain a part of the South African nation, are South African citizens and should be accommodated within political institutions within the boundaries of the Republic of South Africa. This does not exclude that regional considerations should be taken into account and that provision be made for participation in institutions on a regional and/or group basis. We must be practical in this regard.

But I know for a fact that most leaders in their own right in South Africa and reasonable South Africans will not accept the principle of one-man-one-vote in a unitary system. That would lead to domination of one over the other and it would lead to chaos. Consequently, I reject it as a solution.

Secondly, a so-called fourth chamber of parliament is not a practical solution and I do not think responsible people will argue in favour of it.

We must rather seek our solutions in the devolution of power and in participation on common issues.

But I admit that the acceptance by my government of the permanence of black communities in urban areas outside the National States means that a solution will have to be found for their legitimate rights.

The future of these communities and their constitutional arrangements will have to be negotiated with leaders from the National States, as well as from their own ranks.

But let me be quite frank with you – you must know where you stand with me. I have no unfulfilled ambitions in political life in South Africa. I am standing where I am standing because people asked me to stand here. Let me be quite frank with you tonight, if you do not like my way of thinking, if you do not like the direction I am going in, it is the right of the Party Congresses to state whether they agree with their leader or not.

I am not prepared to lead white South Africans and other minority groups on a road to abdication and suicide.

Destroy white South Africa and our influence, and this country will drift into faction strife, chaos and poverty.

Together with my policy statements earlier this year in Parliament, I see this speech of mine as my Manifesto for a new South Africa.

In my policy statements in January and June of this year, I indicated that there would be further developments with regard to the rights and interests of the various population groups in southern Africa.

Since then we have had to contend with escalating violence within South Africa, and pressure from abroad in the form of measures designed to coerce the Government into giving in to various demands.

[…]

I have a specific question I would like to put to the media in South Africa: How do they explain the fact that they are always present, with cameras etc., at places where violence takes place? Are there people from the revolutionary elements who inform them to be ready? Or are there perhaps representatives of the reactionary groups in the ranks of certain media?

My question to you is this: Whose interests do you serve – those of

South Africa or those of the revolutionary elements? South Africa must know, our life is at stake.

From certain international as well as local quarters, appeals are being made to me to release Mr Nelson Mandela from jail.

I stated in Parliament, when put this question, that if Mr Mandela gives a commitment that he will not make himself guilty of planning, instigating or committing acts of violence for the furtherance of political objectives, I will, in principle, be prepared to consider his release.

But let me remind the public of the reasons why Mr Mandela is in jail. I think it is absolutely necessary that we deal with that first of all. When he was brought before court in the sixties, the then Attorney-General, Dr Yutar, set out the State's case inter alia as follows: 'As the indictment alleges, the accused deliberately and maliciously plotted and engineered the commission of acts of violence and destruction throughout the country...

'The planned purpose thereof was to bring about in the Republic of South Africa chaos, disorder and turmoil...

'They (Mr Mandela and his friends) planned violent insurrection and rebellion.'

The saboteurs had planned the manufacture of at least seven types of bombs: 48 000 anti-personnel mines, 210 000 hand grenades, petrol bombs, pipe bombs, syringe bombs and bottle bombs.

A document was produced during the Court case in Mandela's own handwriting in which he stated: 'We Communist Party members are the most advanced revolutionaries in modern history... The enemy must be completely crushed and wiped out from the face of the earth before a Communist world can be realised.'

In passing sentence at the time, the Judge, Mr Justice de Wet, remarked:

> The crime of which the accused have been convicted, that is the main crime, the crime of conspiracy, is in essence one of high treason. The State has decided not to charge the crime in this form...

The violence of our enemies is a warning to us. We, who are committed to peaceful negotiation, also have a warning to them. Our warning is that our readiness to negotiate should not be mistaken for weakness.

I have applied much self-discipline during the past weeks and months. I have been lenient and patient. Don't push us too far in your own interests, I tell them. Reform through a process of negotiation is not weakness. Talking, consulting, bargaining with all our peoples' leaders is not weakness. Mutual acceptance of and joint responsibility for the welfare and stability of our country is not weakness. It is our strength.

[...]

If we ignore the existence of minorities; if we ignore the individual's right to associate with others in the practice of his beliefs and the propagation of his values; if we deny this in favour of a simplistic 'winner-takes-all' political system – then we will diminish and not increase the freedoms of our peoples. Then we would deny the right of each and everyone to share in the decisions which shape his destiny.

Between the many and varied leaders in this country, in the National States and the independent states neighbouring on our borders, in our urban areas I recognise this, but I also know that their love for South Africa is intense as my own. I am therefore in no doubt that working together, we shall succeed in finding the way which will satisfy the reasonable social and political aspirations of the majority of us.

[...]

We are not going to be deterred from doing what we think best, nor will we be forced into doing what we don't want to do. The tragedy is that hostile pressure and agitation from abroad have acted as an encouragement to the militant revolutionaries in South Africa to continue with their violence and intimidation. They have derived comfort and succour from this pressure.

My Government and I are determined to press ahead with our reform programme, and to those who prefer revolution to reform, I say they will not succeed. If necessary we will use stronger measures but they will not succeed.

We prefer to resolve our problems by peaceful means: then we can build, then we can develop, then we can train people, then we can uplift people, then we can make this country of ours a better place to live in. By violence and by burning down schools and houses and murdering innocent people, you don't build a country, you destroy it.

[...]

I am encouraged by the growing number of black leaders who are coming forward to denounce violence. Any reduction of violence will be matched by action on the part of the Government to lift the State of Emergency and restore normality in the areas concerned.

Moreover, as violence diminishes, as criminal and terrorist activities cease, and as the process of dialogue and communication acquires greater momentum, there would be little need to keep those affected in detention or prison.

The implementation of the principles I have stated today can have far-reaching effects on us all. I believe that we are today crossing the Rubicon. There can be no turning back. We now have a manifesto for the future of our country, and we must embark on a programme of positive action in the months and years that lie ahead. The challenges we face call for all concerned to negotiate in a spirit of give and take. With mutual goodwill we shall reach our destination peacefully.

We undertake to do all that man can possibly do. In so saying, I pray that Almighty God would grant us the wisdom and the strength to seek to fulfil His Will.

I thank you.

Despite the high stakes, Botha made no attempt to placate black anger or court the foreign media, and the speech is a perplexing mix of pompous boast, veiled threat and defiant declaration. After praising the government for its leadership, and chastising the media for putting words in his mouth, the president, famous for didactic finger-wagging, warned the world against pressuring the South African state: 'Don't push us too far in your own interests,' Botha fumed, and 'I am not prepared to make [a statement of intent], not now and not tomorrow'. At the same time, the president's remarks suggest that he is in fact about to initiate historic changes: 'I believe that we are today crossing the Rubicon,' he says towards the end, and 'There can be no turning back.' But the more analysts examined his words, the harder it was to understand what he was talking about.

The president, dressed in a blue suit and described as being in a 'jaunty mood',[13] clung to several divisive apartheid creations, continuing to speak of the homelands as 'national states' and dismissing the idea of a fourth African chamber of Parliament, which would extend the power-sharing deal to black South Africans. Despite the backlash over the Mandela release offer, and the speculation about whether the speech would announce a new offer, he dredges up twenty-year-old court verdicts, making it clear that Mandela's release was not on the cards.

The only real suggestion of significant reform came in the vague assertion that any 'national states' (homelands) wishing to remain a part of South Africa would not be forced into accepting independence and that a solution must be found to address the permanence of blacks in urban areas. At another time, these might have seemed progressive, but couched as they were between bombast and lambast, they did not sound like anything momentous – certainly not to the Western world.

The economic and diplomatic fallout was catastrophic. The rand tumbled to a record low, and despite Botha's brags of 'favourable' 'economic fundamentals', the economy was hit hard. While Chase Manhattan had decided some time before that it would no longer roll over loans,[14] it announced its decision immediately after the speech and various banks followed suit, forcing South Africa to declare a unilateral moratorium on the repayment of foreign debt.[15]

France withdrew its ambassador from the country and banned new investment in its economy; Australia announced its intention to formally endorse sanctions; and the leader of the Labour Party in the UK quipped that 'the Bothas, like the Bourbons, forget nothing and learn nothing',[16] in reference to the long-standing French dynasty.

The media was also disenchanted. *The Times* of London said that the speech was not merely an anticlimax but 'marked a crossing of the wrong Rubicon before a perilous land'.[17] The *Natal Witness* described the speech as a 'damp squib',[18] and Port Elizabeth's *Evening Post* expressed the nation's disappointment, saying that the address 'offered little cause for hope that the South African crisis is anywhere nearer resolution'.[19] More forgivingly, the *Sunday Times* wondered whether Botha was perhaps too frightened of the conservatives and urged him to 'forget about the *verkramptes*'.[20]

How is it that the president who had, several years earlier, told NP conservatives that whites must 'adapt or die' now dug in his heels so?[21] As it turns out, Botha was supposed to have delivered a different speech that evening. According to Giliomee, who provides a comprehensive and illuminating study on events prior to the speech, the president's advisors had written a draft with a different tone after the meeting at Sterrewag. The articulate South African diplomat Carl von Hirschberg was asked to give foreign affairs input, adding a rhetorical flair acceptable for an international audience, and Pik Botha contributed the resounding conclusion about 'crossing the Rubicon'. Chris Heunis's Department of Constitutional Development and Planning then elaborated on the Sterrewag reforms as well as proposals put forward several months earlier in a way that 'tried to convey a picture of a government that had abandoned old-style white arrogance'.[22]

Bewilderingly, Botha reacted to the draft with rage, seemingly because he was vexed by the media hype over the event. Heunis claims that Botha dismissed the speech as 'Prog' (a demeaning term for Progressive) and later subjected senior cabinet ministers to a forty-five-minute reading of the new version, which had gutted much of the original draft.

Giliomee puts forward the possibility that Botha's actions were linked to his stroke in May. According to neurosurgeons, one of the psychological effects of the kind of stroke that afflicted Botha is uninhibited temper outbursts, which were subsequently widely reported in Botha's case. Certainly, if the reports of Stephen Solarz, then a US member of Congress and leading advocate of disinvestment, are anything to go by, this seems to be the case. Solarz had met with Botha just days before the Rubicon address, and in a conversation that Solarz said made a 'cold shower warm by comparison', Botha had likened the continued imprisonment of Nelson Mandela to the incarceration of Nazi war criminal Rudolf Hess.[23]

The president appeared to have lost his mind, and the country would suffer much because of it.

Frederik van Zyl Slabbert

Resignation speech, Parliament,
Cape Town, 7 February 1986

In 1974, the fortunes of the Progressive Party were improved when Frederik van Zyl Slabbert, a young Afrikaner academic, joined their ranks. Both the United Party and the Progressive Party had been wooing Slabbert in the hope of improving their standing among moderate Afrikaners, but the sociology professor chose the Progressive Party at the eleventh hour and unexpectedly won the seat of Rondebosch in the Cape.

The victory, rated in somewhat exaggerated terms by the *Rand Daily Mail* as 'one of the outstanding individual political achievements since 1948', was attributed to the thirty-four-year-old professor's 'personal appeal and charm as well as his rare political astuteness'.[1] Fiercely intelligent, handsome and charismatic, Slabbert's emergence in Parliament seemed to rejuvenate the political scene, and liberal newspapers even spoke of his becoming prime minister one day.[2] This was partly because, like Suzman before him, Slabbert, a reluctant-seeming politician, articulated the frustrations and hopes of liberal whites at a time when they were looking for a rising star. As a journalist later put it, 'Like so many other white South Africans, Slabbert has suffered acutely from the realisation that moderates have little chance of ever carrying out their ideal of a negotiated settlement between the races'[3] – a description that conflicted with the prediction of his becoming premier and which also turned out to be accurately prescient.

But Slabbert was also an Afrikaner – the *volk*'s golden boy of the 1960s,[4] a former Western Province rugby player, and a lover of Afrikaner culture and literature – making it impossible for the Nats to dismiss his arguments as those of a mere *volksvreemd* (outsider).[5] The fact that Vorster reportedly refused to greet Slabbert whenever they passed each other in the corridors was most likely born of a sense of betrayal as well as a 'feeling of sadness in the Afrikaner Nationalist movement that he was not part of the ruling party'.[6] In recognition of this very unique attribute, the Progressive Party voted for Slabbert to succeed Colin Eglin as party head in 1979, and he was widely perceived as an extremely effective opposition leader – even if this had much to do with the strength and culture of the party that he inherited from Suzman and Eglin.[7] The Progressive Party had grown incrementally over the years, acquiring additional members when it merged with the Reform Party in 1975 to become the Progressive Reform Party. With its new members, the PRP ousted the UP as the official opposition in 1977, when a number of ejected UP members defected, at which point the PRP was renamed the Progressive Federal Party.

Still, under Slabbert's leadership the PFP continued to grow, and it acquired another ten seats in 1981, taking the total number of seats to twenty-seven. Then came Botha's era of reform, and each new amendment chipped away at the party's support base, as the NP gradually acquired a more reasonable image. In 1983, after campaigning vigorously against Botha's constitutional reforms, the PFP was forced to concede defeat – and to participate in the new parliamentary set-up – when it was estimated that about one-third of its constituency had voted for a Tricameral Parliament.[8] Slabbert took the referendum as an enormous personal blow, predicting a negative impact on support for the opposition and seeing it as a ruse to reposition the NP to ensure its continued power rather than as a genuine attempt to begin the process of dismantling apartheid. Most importantly, in his own words, it also 'entrenched the generic apartheid law, the Population Registration Act, as a basis for its functioning'.[9] Of Botha's Rubicon speech, Slabbert despondently said that the only positive was that the president 'had not gone back on what he [had] stated before'.[10] He grew increasingly disillusioned with the lack of progress in Parliament, and this was compounded by a sense of betrayal when he discovered, after meeting with Mozambican president Samora Machel on 3 January 1986, that the state was actively supporting the anti-communist Mozambican National Resistance (RENAMO), in contravention of the Nkomati Accord – a non-aggression pact signed with the Mozambican government in 1984.

By the beginning of 1986, Slabbert had more or less decided to withdraw from Parliament, but he claimed that he 'had one last hope': that the 'traumatic events' of the previous year would jolt the government to abandon apartheid in the proper sense.[11] He decided to wait for Botha's opening of Parliament before making a decision, asking about the RENAMO transgression and seeking clarity on the government's proposals for handling the crisis in the country. When the response was more of the same, a disappointed Slabbert decided to resign.

There have been many attempts to understand the reasons for Slabbert's departure from Parliament. One interpretation attributes his dramatic exit to his personality, concluding that Slabbert lacked the stamina required for success in politics, particularly opposition politics. Over the years, many politicians had commented on his lack of staying power, his low boredom threshold[12] and his preference for 'leading from the front'.[13] In the mid-1970s, Prime Minister B.J. Vorster had dismissed Slabbert's political ambitions, saying, 'I get the idea that being a back-bencher in a small party with limited time for debate is steadily killing Slabbert.'[14] And in 1979, Suzman had contested his position for party leader because she suspected that he might vacate office in pursuit of academia (he had been offered the vice-chancellorship at the University of Cape Town). When he was elected as PFP leader, his colleague Dr David Welsh predicted what would happen, saying in a newspaper interview, 'If he finds he can't [do the job], he would be the first person to say "I'm off" and make way for someone else to try.'[15]

Another reason for his resignation, posited by R.W. Johnson,[16] is that Slabbert was so seduced by Thabo Mbeki at their October 1985 meeting that he had cut a deal with him: in return for Slabbert's resignation from Parliament, the ANC would reward him with a public place at the negotiating table. Although the Mbeki meeting did have an enormous influence on Slabbert – and it is true that he was hungry to begin negotiating – the disillusioned and sincere tone of his resignation speech, excerpted here,[17] suggests that his reasons were less self-seeking than this.

Parliament's reaction to 1985 in its first week of the 1986 session was, as far as I am concerned, a grotesque ritual in irrelevance. We carried on as if nothing had happened. In the year 1986, the essence of politics in South Africa revolves around point-scoring and petty debating points concerning overworked prejudices that we cherish against one another, a kind of macabre ballad of mediocrities who are too afraid to peep over the top of their trenches and see the reality outside.

Whatever the deficiencies of my introductory speech, one underlying theme in that speech was an intense and sincere appeal: Will the Government make Parliament relevant to the crisis of the country? It did not happen in 1985. What about 1986? This was one consistent theme.

[...]

The State President never said that apartheid was dead – just go and read the speech – however much the whole world wants to believe that. He said that we had outgrown the outdated concept of apartheid. Those were the exact words of the State President in that speech.

That could mean *inter alia* one of two things: That we are now looking for a new, more adaptable concept of apartheid, or that any form of apartheid has been outgrown, whether or not it has been outdated. Which of the two is it? This was the dilemma of the reaction of the hon the Minister of Foreign Affairs and of those other hon ministers to the State President's speech. The CP [Conservative Party] is 100% correct. There cannot be a first-class and a second-class apartheid. Whether one tells a man in a brutal or a nice way that he is a second-class citizen, the fact remains that he is still a second-class citizen. There is a simple text question to determine whether the Government has outgrown apartheid. It is this: Is residential separation outdated? Yes or no? Today the State President said that it was not outdated. If it is not outdated then both the concept and the practice of apartheid are alive and well for the majority of people in our country.

[...]

My other problem with the hon the Minister [Magnus Malan] is his deliberate and calculated misrepresentation of the ANC. How will that help us? I should like the State President to react to this too. According to the hon the Minister of Defence and the State President, the ANC is a group of alien terrorists under the control of communists who are financed and supported by Moscow – and that is all. However, this is a misrepresentation in stark conflict with reality.

Yes, it is true that there are communists and communistic influences in the ANC. I myself said as much to the State President, and to the Chief of the National Intelligen[ce] Service. That is true. After all, they say so themselves. It is also true that their strategy is one of armed struggle, which entails acts of terror and murder. I recognised this in my introductory speech. [...]

The question, however, is what we here in South Africa are going to do about it. According to the hon the Minister of Defence we must shoot, carry out hot pursuit operations and eliminate, because that is the problem on our borders. It is a problem on our borders. It is the neighbouring states that do not wish to help and assist, and the attitude, as the saying goes, is one of 'Let us give them a thrashing!'

I wish to convey a simple and crystal-clear truth to the hon the Minister. It is not the external ANC that is radicalising the internal situation – with all due respect to the State President. It is the internal ANC that is radicalising the external ANC. That is our dilemma. What happened in 1984 did more to exert pressure on the external ANC than anything that they themselves could have thought up. They were not involved in interactions with Casspirs. They did not begin fighting in the townships! They sit out there and are radicalised by what goes on here, in the interior. That is where our problem lies. Supporters and members of the ANC here in South Africa work in our kitchens, our gardens, our factories. We dare not mislead ourselves on that score.

[...]

I wish to conclude on a more personal note and without acrimony and bitterness. This is my twelfth year in parliament, five of which spent as an ordinary member of Parliament and I'm entering my seventh as leader of the official opposition. Particularly in my latter capacity I have often asked myself what the role of an opposition must be in a complex and conflict-ridden society such as ours. Even now, with clarity and conviction I can answer that an opposition must question the actions of Government – which we have done. It must expose the contradictions and shortcomings of Government, which we have done. It must protest against injustice and the erosion of civil liberties – which we have done. It must define alternatives to the policy dead-ends in which Government leads us – that also we have done. In all these respects I wish to pay sincere tribute to my colleagues for their efforts and to encourage them to continue to do so in the future. It is vital and it is important that this Government continue to be opposed in all these respects which I have just mentioned.

There is, however, another aspect of opposition which has a momentum and life of its own and which is independent of these very important political functions I have just mentioned. That aspect is political leadership in opposition. This too has to be judged, but on different grounds and the important judge is the person himself. He has to decide when the tension between analysis and practice is no longer bearable for himself; in other words he has to decide when the moment has arrived to go. The magic moment for any political leader is to find the right time to go. I believe it is perhaps slightly less painful to go when people want one to stay than to stay when people want one to go.

I have decided the time has come for me to go. Perhaps the issue finally clarified itself for me when I listened to the State President's Opening Speech and the commentaries which followed it, even today. My gut feeling was: 'Here is the 1983 referendum all over again' – everybody getting excited about something which I simply could not see no matter how hard I tried. One of the most painful periods in my political life was the 1983 referendum when out of deep conviction I had to be critical and negative whilst together with everybody else I would have liked to believe we were getting out of the mess. This time I thought that I must weigh my words and wait for the state president to respond to some of the issues that puzzled me.

He has done so, but some of his Ministers did so as well. All that I can say to him and his Government in all sincerity, is that what I have heard and seen from all of them, including the State President, is simply not good enough. It is a false start. I do not say this easily or without a certain degree of anguish. I have made it my business to get to know this Government and to try to understand its thinking. Given my position I think I have explored every nook and cranny for possible leverage to promote the politics of negotiation and therefore I do not make conclusions without experience or from a remote distance. I have some idea of what lies behind a speech or an advertisement. The circumstances in our country are simply too serious for us to bluff ourselves in the clubby atmosphere of Parliament, no matter how desperately a way out is needed, and we need a way out.

Another reason why it is time for me to go is that a political leader is blessed when he can realise that he is being taken for granted, either by others or by himself. It is bad enough when one's opponents start taking one for granted – either as a political punch bag, or a nice guy to have around but not to be taken seriously – but it is worse when one feels one is starting to take oneself for granted; in other words, when one feels that this is where one is going to be for the rest of one's life. That is like one of those mantelpiece musical boxes that people dust off from time to time and listen to with a certain quaint nostalgia. Political leadership is a pro-active career; not a safe route to a retirement gratuity and pension. I have done my share and I believe it is time for someone else to have a go at it.

As this is my last speech in this House, I hope Honourable members will forgive me when I end with a few general comments about the state of politics in the country.

Let me start by stating the obvious, for the benefit of the hon Minister of Defence. I am not a radical, a revolutionary, or even a violent protester. If our intelligence services are worth anything – and I think they are – they know that is so. If they want to check me in the future, they can bug my house and even my motor-car – they will find nothing. This is what I am – what Honourable members see is what there is. I believe passionately in the politics of negotiation.

[...]

I am afraid that this Government – I do not say this in any acrimonious sense – does not understand the principles of negotiation, or if they do, they do not abide by them. The dismantling of apartheid has nothing to do with negotiation. It is simply the first step towards negotiation. Apartheid is not up for negotiation. It has to go completely. What is up for negotiation is its alternative. That is where negotiation lies. One is not going to negotiate a position for Blacks, Coloureds and Asians within group areas. The Government must forget about it! They are not going to do it.

The second point is that reform or constitutional change will never be successful as long as this Government insists that it takes place on the basis of compulsory group membership. It cannot happen. I am not saying this because I am trying to be funny. The evidence points this out to us. One cannot build a new constitution on compulsory group membership.

Thirdly – this is an honest conviction of mine and I have said it to the hon the Minister of Transport Affairs many times – the tricameral Parliament is a hopelessly flawed and failed constitutional experiment. It does not begin to solve the problem of political domination; in fact it compounds it. It has nothing to do with effective power-sharing. Those who have come into it, however good their intentions may be – I believe their intentions are good – have slightly eased the harshness of their own domination by administering it themselves. If the Government extends the principle of co-optive domination to Blacks as it has done to Coloureds and Indians, violence and conflict are inevitable. The search for consensus does not lie in finding co-optive clients. It lies in genuine negotiation with those who can deliver the goods. That is why the regional services councils are going to be in difficulty from the outset. This is not because I say so, but the people in the communities will demonstrate it.

Fourthly, I remain an incurable democrat. This motives my involvement in politics and inspires my vision of the future. I do believe we can become a non-racial, united South Africa where all its people can participate voluntarily in the governmental institutions of this land. For twelve years I have tried to pursue this goal inside Parliament. I will continue to do so outside, although at this moment I have no plans, no intentions to join any organisation or movement, or to start one, whatever hon members may think. In fact, as of the moment my resignation becomes effective, I will be looking for a job. I go out as I came in, an ordinary, concerned citizen of my country. I will continue to explore the politics of negotiation as best I can.

In conclusion I wish to speak as an Afrikaner. I hope that my hon friends in the CP will accept me as such. I have no fear for the future of my language in a democratic, united South Africa based on the voluntary association of its citizens. Indeed, that is the only way in which the Afrikaner can come into his own on a co-equal basis in the cultural diversity of South Africa. However I do fear for my language if the Afrikaner insists that domination and partition will be the way in which he wants to achieve this. To me this is one of the tragic aspects of us Afrikaners. I do not say this with any venom.

The whole philosophy of Dr Verwoerd, who was not a born Afrikaner but was a naturalised Afrikaner who came here as the child of a Dutch couple, and whose Afrikanerhood was therefore so much more important to him, was in fact an effort to separate the Afrikaner from others in the country of his birth. To a certain extent the Afrikaner had to be made an extension of Europe. It is those separate structures that bedevil our negotiation politics at this moment. If Afrikaners reject their fellow Africans because they want to be apart, then we shall be rejected in future in the country of our birth.

Many of the things I have said have absolutely nothing to do with the political divisions within this House. Hon members are aware of that. Indeed, the political divisions as they stand at the moment are absolutely artificial and incapable of coping with the tremendous demands of our time. The time will come before long when we shall divide across language, colour and party lines so that those who truly believe the same thing, stand together and work together will not be trapped in obsolete political remnant from the past. We are an artificial political phenomenon in this House. There are members of the NP who differ very little with what I am saying here and with what I feel. I know who they are and I shall not 'drop' them now, as the hon the Minister of Transport Affairs always says. We have spoken together a great deal. There are also hon members there who belong with the members of the CP. We know that that is so.

An HON MEMBER: There are many of them.

The LEADER OF THE OFFICIAL OPPOSITION: However, here we stand, trapped in a ridiculous political debate, while out there our country is bleeding. I do not see how this can continue.

Finally, Mr Speaker, I just wish to convey my personal thanks to you for the courtesy and politeness with which you have always received me and for the goodwill you have displayed towards me. I appreciate that tremendously.

I also express my thanks to the parliamentary staff. They are in fact a remarkable phenomenon, Mr Speaker. They really try to keep the remains of democracy alive in South Africa. They do so against tremendous odds and they do it faithfully and sincerely. I thank them for their friendliness.

To the hon members of this House I say that I leave here without any feelings of bitterness towards any hon member of this House. We have fought a great deal across the floor of this House, but hon members are aware that I do not bear any ill feeling or suspicion towards any of them. I wish them well.

To my colleagues I wish to express my sincere appreciation for their support; my best wishes to them for the extremely difficult time that lies ahead. It is a time that is going to be very difficult for all of us.

Slabbert's speech illustrates his rare ability to 'reduce politics to a series of simple, logical arguments that progress to a single, devastating conclusion',[18] particularly in its analysis of Botha's assertion that the country had out-grown the outdated concept of apartheid. This cannot be so, Slabbert insists, if the state president also says that residential separation is not outdated. By seeking simple yes/no answers to direct questions, he consistently exposes the duplicity of the NP's position, finding common ground with the CP's assessment of the party as seeking both first- and second-class apartheid – an impossible endeavour.

His analysis of the unrest in South Africa puts the blame squarely at the feet of minister of defence Magnus Malan. While acknowledging the ANC's armed struggle and 'people's war' strategy, he inverts the popular perception of an exile organisation sowing terror from beyond the country's borders. The current crisis stems not from the ANC's radical directives, he argues, but from the radical militarisation of society.

Slabbert's speech suggests a profound search for relevance. Parliament is 'trapped in a ridiculous political debate', he says, 'while out there our country is bleeding' and parliamentarians are 'too afraid to peep over the top of their trenches and see the reality outside'. Despite his attempts to acknowledge the 'vital' and 'important' role of the opposition in Parliament, ultimately he sees this as futile and the entire institution as 'obsolete'. 'I am interested in getting rid of apartheid,' he wrote to the London *Times* a week after his resignation, 'not just protesting against it',[19] casting doubt on the South African Parliament's ability ever to effect change.

Like his entrance to politics, Slabbert's departure was described in grandi-ose terms, and it was met with a mixture of shock, praise and condemnation. His own party felt betrayed, not only by his resignation but also by the shock-ing and seemingly casual manner in which he carried it out. Informing his caucus only forty-five minutes before his speech,[20] he left the Progressives with very little time to institute any kind of damage control. Who would have faith in a party described by its own leader as irrelevant, an irritated Suzman wondered.[21] When Slabbert told her that he had devoted twelve years to Parliament, Suzman, who'd served for twice as many, including thirteen as the sole voice of opposition, was unimpressed: 'Twelve years!' she reportedly snapped,[22] and proceeded to ignore him for a further three.[23]

The liberal press, initially offering praise,[24] soon became similarly critical. 'The judgement on Dr Van Zyl Slabbert's dramatic exit from parliamentary politics must, sadly, be harsh,' a *Sunday Times* editorial declared. 'He leaves behind him a bewildered party that may well be rent asunder.'[25] Columnist Ken Owen accused him of being a *trekboer* – always seeking greener pastures.

While a *trekboer* to liberal whites, he was a 'new *Voortrekker*' to Mbeki, who released an ANC press statement on the day of Slabbert's resignation in which he lauded the move: 'Never in the history of our country has a white establishment political leader confronted the iniquity of the system of white minority domination as Dr Slabbert did today.'[26]

Botha, unhappy about the way in which he'd been portrayed in Slabbert's speech, released transcripts from a secretly taped conversation held in Novem-ber 1985 in a bid to discredit him. In his speech, Slabbert had said that the conversation had left him with a 'pervasive sense of despair and helplessness' because of his failure to convince Botha that a bold initiative was needed to solve the political deadlock.[27] The leaked exchange was fairly incriminat-ing, casting some doubt on Slabbert's version of events. On the one hand, 'Dr Stabber', as he was dubbed in some circles,[28] came off as having remarkably few political disagreements with Botha; on the other, it seems clear that some of the president's comments 'must have exasperated' Slabbert,[29] even if he appears not to have confronted the state president about them.

In the months that followed, the political landscape in South Africa shifted. Fellow parliamentarian Alex Boraine resigned soon afterwards and together with Slabbert formed IDASA (the Institute for a Democratic Alternative for South Africa), an organisation that began to play an important role in pre-paring the ground for future negotiations with the ANC. At the same time, the PFP did indeed lose support – influenced by both Slabbert's resignation and Botha's reforms.

Interestingly, Slabbert's own early prediction of the NP's fortune came true. In 1973–74, writing about apartheid, he had guessed that the Nats would become increasingly intolerant of liberal opposition, channelling dissent into state-sanctioned institutions. They would also, he anticipated, likely be weakened by mounting pressures such as economic fluctuations and black demands. Additionally, Slabbert expected that the government would eventually feel pressure in the elections only from the right.[30]

At the next election, this was indeed the case, as Treurnicht's right-wing Conservative Party overtook the PFP as the official opposition.

Desmond Tutu

'Rainbow People of God' speech,
City Hall and Grand Parade, Cape Town,
13 September 1989

In 1989, which came to be known as the year of miracles across the globe, a number of countries were engaging in major political change. Communist rule in Eastern Europe was openly challenged as thousands of protestors refused to accept the outcome of the East German election in May, and a number of peaceful 'vigils for change' were held across several cities. In China, millions of pro-democracy supporters protested against communism, erecting a ten-metre-high replica of the Statue of Liberty after a six-week-long occupation of Tiananmen Square in Beijing.

Closer to home, the decade-long conflict in Angola finally subsided when the United States and the Soviet Union brokered a peace settlement, and a UN-sanctioned process prepared the ground for South West Africa's independence.

In South Africa, the tide was also turning, as the struggle against apartheid gathered popular support. The autocratic reign of P.W. Botha appeared to be on the wane after he suffered another stroke in January. Initially planning only to take six weeks' sick leave, Botha soon resigned as NP leader and then as state president amid diminishing cabinet support.

Over the years, Botha had come to blows with one of the country's most prominent anti-apartheid leaders, Archbishop Desmond Tutu. During the 1980s, the church – led by leaders from all denominations, including Beyers Naudé, Allan Boesak, Denis Hurley and Frank Chikane – had become an increasingly uncomfortable thorn in the apartheid state's side,[1] and the outspoken Desmond Tutu, described in the *New York Times* as 'looking just a bit like a black leprechaun',[2] was a force to be reckoned with. The man 'gives more speeches than he eats breakfasts',[3] said journalist Denis Beckett in 1982; certainly, Tutu used his position as a cleric to mount a formidable attack on apartheid. As the 1984 Nobel Peace Prize winner, the leader of the Anglican Church in South Africa, and a former patron of the multiracial United Democratic Front, Tutu possessed a global credibility that surpassed even that of ANC leaders. He enjoyed a particularly warm relationship with Anglo-Western media and was widely quoted in the mainstream press. He was also the most consulted South African authority on apartheid on the influential American current-affairs television show *Nightline*,[4] and in a 1985 televised debate, he had defeated foreign affairs minister Pik Botha, declaring to the world (and to South Africa, in a specially permitted screening) that despite being a fifty-three-year-old bishop in the church of God, he was still treated like a child in the land of his birth. 'You would, I suppose, say that I'm reasonably responsible,' said Tutu on live television, yet '[i]n my own country I do not vote.'

Tutu's relationship with P.W. Botha had been abrasive, and the president's perception of the archbishop was reflected on national television, which Rian Malan remembers portraying Tutu as an agitator, doing 'its best to catch him wearing shades, which gave him a cool and predatory look, and saying something that could be construed as incendiary'.[5] When Tutu was awarded the Nobel Peace Prize in 1984, Botha claimed that he was a political preacher, undeserving of the award,[6] and the South African Broadcasting Corporation included a mere ten-minute insert towards the end of the news broadcast. In 1988, when Tutu visited Botha to plead for clemency for the Sharpeville Six – six youths condemned to death for murdering the mayor of Sharpeville when they were caught up in the people's war of 1984 – the two fought, according to Tutu, 'like little boys' and Botha accused Tutu of being arrogant.[7]

In spite of Botha's increasingly totalitarian leadership style, his departure elicited little new hope, as his replacement, Transvaal NP leader F.W. de Klerk, had a reputation for conservatism. His appointment as the acting president in August was, according to Tutu, 'just musical chairs'.[8] But De Klerk was also considered to be more pragmatic and amiable than his predecessor, and over the next few months Tutu's assessment of the man would be proved wrong.

One of De Klerk's first challenges as president came when the Mass Democratic Movement, a loose grouping of organisations that had reconvened after the UDF was banned in 1987, called for a six-week-long 'defiance campaign'. No doubt inspired by the Eastern European vigils, the movement planned to hold marches throughout city centres and in white suburbs, areas and beaches.[9] Although the first of these proceeded without incident, it was not long before violence broke out. On 2 September, police sprayed a crowd of Cape Town protestors with purple dye from a water cannon for easy identification of their targets before hunting them down, and then beating and arresting them. One protestor managed to gain control of the water cannon and ended up spraying the city headquarters of the NP. In the days that followed, the ironic slogan 'The Purple Shall Govern' – an adaptation of the Freedom Charter's 'The People Shall Govern' – appeared as graffiti on the old townhouse in Greenmarket Square. Tutu, who had not been at the event, rushed to the scene to discover terrified protestors, some of them badly beaten, hiding in the cathedral.[10] Horrified, he decided, together with Allan Boesak and others, to stage a mass protest march. Over the next week, incidents of repression increased, as police tried to break up or pre-empt smaller protest events: a church service scheduled to include an address from Beyers Naudé was banned; a university choir was prevented from performing in St George's Cathedral; and there were twenty fatalities in the city's townships on election day. Support for what became known as Tutu's 'peace march' swelled and when the newly elected Cape Town mayor Gordon Oliver joined the organising team, it was clear that this was no ordinary anti-apartheid protest.

Fearing a bloodbath, Dirk Hattingh, moderator of the Western Cape Synod of the Dutch Reformed Church (DRC), and three other DRC leaders acted as mediators between the march organisers and De Klerk. After receiving Tutu and Boesak's assurance that the march would be peaceful, but that it would be held irrespective of whether it was approved or not, they approached De Klerk to explain that it would be near impossible to stop the march. De Klerk had two choices: to deem the march illegal, which risked overreaction from a heavy-handed police force, or to allow it to proceed, despite the fact that it would technically break a dozen state-of-emergency and security laws.[11]

One day before the march, De Klerk officially sanctioned it, announcing, 'The door to a new South Africa is open; it is not necessary to batter it down',[12] and that he hoped his gesture would 'prove conclusively that a new spirit has arisen in our beautiful country'.[13]

On Wednesday 13 September, an estimated 20 000 to 35 000 people of all races, many dressed in white, gathered in the city, walking in a 'triumphant wave' from St George's Cathedral to the Grand Parade.[14] It was the first 'legal' protest in three years and one of the largest gatherings since the banning of the ANC. Posters declaring 'Peace in our city, stop the killings', UDF banners, images of Oliver Tambo and ANC flags were visible from the streets, and onlookers cheered the crowd from their offices. The apparent absence of police no doubt reduced the possibility of conflict and paved the way for future events.

Speakers addressed the crowds at various points, including general secretary of the Congress of South African Trade Unions Jay Naidoo, who claimed, 'We have liberated Cape Town today. Now our task is to make that liberation permanent',[15] and Boesak, who declared that De Klerk would be the 'last white president'.[16] Wearing his signature purple cassock and a large silver cross around his neck, Tutu gave the following short speech to the 2 000-strong audience inside the City Hall.

I'm just an old man after all these fiery speeches. I think actually we maybe ought to go home. But I want to say to you: today is the day on which we the people have scored a great victory for justice and for peace. And it is important that that is registered...

In England...Hyde Park has got...something called Speaker's Corner where you can go and say anything. A policeman stands next to you, not to arrest you, he stands there to protect you from the people who may get annoyed at what you are saying. On one occasion there was a West Indian who got up on his soapbox and said: 'There is nothing wrong with England', and he kept quiet for a bit, 'except for the English'. We can say: 'There is nothing wrong with South Africa except for the perpetrators of apartheid.' No, no, no. We believe they can change. So let us not say, 'except for the perpetrators of apartheid'.

There is nothing wrong with this beautiful country except for apartheid! There is nothing wrong with this beautiful country except for injustice! There is nothing wrong with this country except for the violence of apartheid!

And so we say to Mr de Klerk: 'Hallo!' Let's say to Mr de Klerk: 'You wanted us to show you that we can be dignified. You wanted us to show you that we are disciplined. You wanted us to show you that we are determined. You wanted us to show you that we are peaceful. Right! Mr de Klerk, please come here! We are inviting you, Mr de Klerk, we invite you Mr Vlok, we invite all the Cabinet. We say, come, come here, and can you see the people of this country? Come and see what this country is going to become.'

This country is a rainbow country! This country is technicolour. You can come and see the new South Africa!

I'm not going to speak for long. This is rather unusual for me. But before I tell you one or two things that we want to tell Mr de Klerk as well, I believe there are a few people that we really must give very, very warm ovations to. We've done a little bit of that but I think we ought to show that we recognize goodness when we see it, and I want you to give, in his absence, Lieutenant Rockman a big clap. Do you think that is a big cheer? It must be heard outside...There are very many others that I would want us to give a big cheer to. You gave Allan [Boesak] a big cheer but not very many people remember that Allan became the youngest President of the World Alliance of Reformed Churches, which was a remarkable achievement. But, as if that were not enough, Allan did something that nobody else could do. He is the first person to be re-elected to that position ... We must give Allan a loud cheer, man, a humdinger! Then I think the last persons I would like us to give a very warm cheer to: the people of Cape Town, yourselves. You have been remarkable.

We want to say to Mr de Klerk: 'We have already won. Mr de Klerk, we have already won. Mr de Klerk, if you know really what is good for you, join us! Join us! Join us! Join us in the struggle for this new South Africa ... Join us in this new South Africa ...'

I want you to do something to finish. Really. I told you I was not going to be long. I want us to stand – Capetonians, South Africans, black, white, whatever, and hold hands and know that nothing can stop us. We are unstoppable. Unstoppable!

After the City Hall address, Boesak, Tutu and others emerged onto the balcony, which was draped in an ANC flag, to speak to the larger awaiting crowd of 10 000. There, Tutu gave the final speech of the event:

Hello, hello, as an old man I should really shut up, but because I am an African I will say I have nothing to say and I take thirty minutes to say it. But I want to say to you that today is a victory for common sense. It is a victory for the people. It is a victory for peace.

I think we want to invite Mr de Klerk. We want to say, 'Mr de Klerk ... hallo! Just come here. You said you wanted to know whether we were going to be peaceful. Come here and see peaceful people.'

Just show Mr de Klerk your hands. Just lift up your hands. They are empty hands. They are the hands of peaceful people. And then we say, 'Mr de Klerk, come and have a look at disciplined people.'

Now let us just show him that we are disciplined. Let's just keep quiet. Just keep quiet.

Mr de Klerk, did you hear a pin drop? We want to invite him and say, 'Mr de Klerk, come and look at technicolour.' They tried to make us one colour: purple. We say: we are the rainbow people! We are the new people of a new South Africa! We say, 'Hey, hey, hey, hey, Mr de Klerk, you have lost. You have already lost.' We say, 'Come and see.'

Now I want you to hold hands. I want you to lift your hands. I want you to say: 'Our march to freedom ... is unstoppable. Our march to freedom, for all of us. South Africans, black and white. Mr de Klerk, please come. Thank you.

The crowd repeated Tutu's final words in unison before dispersing peacefully, and the event was deemed an enormous success, launching what was called South Africa's own 'Pretoriastroika'.[17] As with Boesak's UDF launch speech, Tutu's call for crowd participation was greeted with enthusiastic applause, and, in the case of the request for silence, impressive quiet of ten seconds. Eager to show De Klerk that supporters sought peace and that the atmosphere was ripe for negotiation, Tutu shrewdly orchestrated a demonstration of discipline – echoing the self-control displayed at the 1956 Women's March.

Tutu also brought much-needed humour to a tense atmosphere, particularly with his casual greeting to the president. Boesak's speech had concluded with the powerful chanting of the line 'Our freedom is coming! Our freedom is coming!' and the crowd was in a state of heightened emotion. But when Tutu said, 'We want to say, "Mr de Klerk...hallo!"' there was an almost palpable change in atmosphere, as laughter provided a kind of pressure valve for the pent-up audience.

The speech is structured as an invitation, a plea and a challenge, and Tutu addresses De Klerk directly throughout. 'Mr de Klerk, if you know really what is good for you, join us!' he says. 'Come and have a look at disciplined people.' In keeping with the 'peace' theme of the march, and with his own religious belief, Tutu's speech embraces reconciliation, which would become a major theme of the post-apartheid era. The perpetrators of apartheid, he claims, are not the enemy; only apartheid is the enemy, for the perpetrators can change. To illustrate this, he praises the actions of one Lieutenant Gregory Rockman, a police officer who days earlier had spoken out against the brutality of his colleagues.[18] Tutu calls on the marchers to demonstrate unity by joining hands and raising them in the air in a declaration of peace.

But what is perhaps most distinctive about Tutu's speech, both here and on several later occasions, is the way in which his discourse ushers in a 'new' South Africa. Philippe-Joseph Salazar points out that Tutu's oratory succeeded in transforming the 'fiction' of the rainbow nation into 'history'.[19] 'We are the new people of a new South Africa,' says Tutu triumphantly. And – likely influenced by his travels in America where he'd been exposed to Jesse Jackson's National Rainbow Coalition[20] – he refers to the crowd as the 'the rainbow people'. The speech is one of the first in which the metaphor of the rainbow nation is conjured, and Tutu is generally credited with coining the term.

At the same time, the march positively influenced De Klerk's profile as a statesman, and he was praised for his flexibility in managing a potentially dangerous situation.[21] De Klerk later reflected that approving the march was one of the most difficult decisions of his career but that he realised that if he'd refused permission, there might have been 'instead of thirty thousand people marching, half a million marching',[22] with all the 'attendant risks of violence and negative publicity'.[23] It is also likely that the event's success, and the praise bestowed on De Klerk, encouraged him to move forward with further reforms. Patti Waldmeir notes that it was at this point that he began to believe 'that he could manage not only protest marches but also the entire process of change'.[24]

In the wake of the event, US president George H.W. Bush announced that further sanctions against South Africa would be counterproductive, given the new atmosphere in the country,[25] and De Klerk's official inauguration took place on 20 September. South Africans awaited their new president's next move. A month later, he released all but one of the Rivonia trialists. One month after this, the Berlin Wall fell. The stage was set for the release of Nelson Mandela.

F.W. de Klerk
Opening of Parliament, Cape Town, 2 February 1990

In 1989, the departure of 'Die Groot Krokodil' (The Great Crocodile) – as P.W. Botha had come to be known – brought new hope. The seventy-three-year-old Botha first announced that he would be taking six weeks' sick leave after suffering what his aides called a 'mild' stroke.[1] Then on 2 February 1989, he resigned as leader of the NP but held on to his position as state president and the prospect of running for another term in the next parliamentary election.[2]

Frederik Willem de Klerk, the leader of the Transvaal NP, was elected as the new NP leader by the cabinet, beating Botha's preferred candidate, finance minister Barend du Plessis. In his position as acting president, De Klerk locked horns with his predecessor[3] and matters came to a head in August when Botha objected to De Klerk's 'unauthorised' meeting with President Kenneth Kaunda on the grounds that Zambia hosted the ANC in exile. Finally, on 15 August, two weeks before the parliamentary election, Botha resigned, refuting the official line that his resignation was due to ill health. On national television, he instead cited cabinet disputes, saying that he had no choice but to resign because he was being 'ignored' by his ministers.[4] De Klerk's magnanimous response indicated the differences in their leadership styles: 'We are sad that a man who has done so much for his country has to retire under these unhappy circumstances,' he said.

Fifty-three years old, De Klerk was the equivalent of royalty in Afrikaner nationalist circles and the 'ultimate party loyalist'.[5] He was the nephew of J.G. Strijdom, and his father had served under Strijdom, Verwoerd and Vorster. De Klerk, who had studied law, had a reputation for conservatism and had been an ardent supporter of the tricameral parliamentary system. In discussions around Botha's replacement, he was seldom considered to be the progressive candidate, and, on paper, he certainly didn't appear like the leader who would finally cross the Rubicon.

But De Klerk was, above all, a pragmatist, whom his finance minister described as being excellent at reading 'how the currents were running'.[6] And towards the end of 1989, they were running in a very clear direction. De Klerk's success in managing Tutu's peace march in September and the subsequent fall of the Berlin Wall in November prepared the ground for serious changes.

De Klerk was also strategic. His wife, Marike, claims that one week after the fall of the wall, he decided to end apartheid, seeing a chance to garner his cabinet's support for sweeping change.[7] 'When history opens a window of opportunity,' De Klerk later said, 'it is important to jump through it.'[8] In early December, he arranged a *bosberaad*-style meeting of ministers at D'Nyala Nature Reserve near Botswana, primarily to test his colleagues. Here, minister of constitutional development Gerrit Viljoen set out the possibilities for negotiations involving all parties, including the ANC. Then Du Plessis outlined the financial situation, putting 'the hard facts on the table': sanctions were hurting the already debt-crippled economy, and oil was in short supply.[9] There was the possibility of 'holding out', but only for another decade or so, and this would likely escalate the violence. 'We must use this golden opportunity,'[10] De Klerk reportedly urged.

Once there was general support for the idea of power-sharing, De Klerk sought advice on the 'Mandela problem'. When he had freed the remaining Rivonia trialists in October 1989, it was more or less expected that Mandela's release would follow, so this wasn't really the question. Instead, he sought opinions on how to stage-manage the affair and whether he ought to release Mandela and denounce him as a terrorist (as one securocrat faction had advised) or welcome him as an important leader. Pik Botha was strongly in favour of the latter option and advised De Klerk to arrange a photo opportunity with Mandela immediately after his release.[11] The issue of unbanning the ANC was never discussed explicitly, but debates over Mandela's release implied that this would be the case, as did the discussion about all-party negotiations. The meeting concluded with general support for Mandela's release and for power-sharing, as long as there would be some protection of minority rights.[12] In reality, however, releasing Mandela was like letting a genie out of a bottle: there was no telling what future it would herald.

A week later, on 13 December, De Klerk met with Mandela for the first time, at Mandela's request. Although Mandela was 'brought under cover of darkness' to De Klerk's Cape Town office,[13] the event was reported by the SABC, which also screened an old stills image of him. This was a departure from official protocol, which forbade publication of his likeness. Although no important decisions were taken at the meeting, and the two were simply sizing one another up, it raised expectations that Mandela's release was imminent.[14]

International media swarmed to the country to hear De Klerk's opening of Parliament speech two months later, which was exactly one year after Botha had relinquished his party leadership. De Klerk gave what is likely the most important South African speech, launching the irreversible march towards democracy. Fearing that news of his announcement would leak, De Klerk informed his ministers of the proposed reform 'package' only two days beforehand, making them promise 'not to tell even their wives',[15] and he wrote the final draft of the speech at one in the morning of 2 February. Having witnessed the disaster with the Rubicon speech, De Klerk later recalled, 'We wanted to ensure that the surprise element would not be lost.'[16]

The speech, broadcast live, announced the far-reaching changes that the majority of the country had been waiting for:

The general elections on September the 6th, 1989, placed our country irrevocably on the road of drastic change. Underlying this is the growing realisation by an increasing number of South Africans that only a negotiated understanding among the representative leaders of the entire population is able to ensure lasting peace.

The alternative is growing violence, tension and conflict. That is unacceptable and in nobody's interest. [...]

Let us put petty politics aside when we discuss the future during this Session.

Help us build a broad consensus about the fundamentals of a new, realistic and democratic dispensation.

Let us work together on a plan that will rid our country of suspicion and steer it away from domination and radicalism of any kind.

[...]

1. Foreign relations

[...] The year of 1989 will go down in history as the year in which Stalinist Communism expired.

These developments will entail unpredictable consequences for Europe, but they will also be of decisive importance to Africa. The indications are that the countries of Eastern and Central Europe will receive greater attention, while it will decline in the case of Africa.

The collapse, particularly of the economic system in Eastern Europe, also serves as a warning to those who insist on persisting with it in Africa. Those who seek to force this failure of a system on South Africa, should engage in a total revision of their point of view. [...]

The countries of Southern Africa are faced with a particular challenge: Southern Africa now has an historical opportunity to set aside its conflicts and ideological differences and draw up a joint programme of reconstruction. It should be sufficiently attractive to ensure that the

Southern African region obtains adequate investment and loan capital from the industrial countries of the world. Unless the countries of Southern Africa achieve stability and a common approach to economic development rapidly, they will be faced by further decline and ruin.

The Government is prepared to enter into discussions with other Southern African countries with the aim of formulating a realistic development plan. The Government believes that the obstacles in the way of a conference of Southern African states have now been removed sufficiently.

Hostile postures have to be replaced by co-operative ones; confrontation by contact; disengagement by engagement; slogans by deliberate debate.

The season of violence is over. The time for reconstruction and reconciliation has arrived.

[...]

At present the Government is involved in negotiations concerning our future relations with an independent Namibia and there are no reasons why good relations should not exist between the two countries. Namibia needs South Africa and we are prepared to play a constructive part.

Nearer home I paid fruitful visits to Venda, Transkei and Ciskei and intend visiting Bophuthatswana soon. In recent times there has been an interesting debate about the future relationship of the TBVC countries with South Africa and specifically about whether they should be re-incorporated into our country.

Without rejecting this idea out of hand, it should be borne in mind that it is but one of many possibilities. These countries are constitutionally independent. Any return to South Africa will have to be dealt with, not only by means of legislation in their parliaments, but also through legislation in this Parliament. Naturally this will have to be preceded by talks and agreements.

2. Human rights

[...] The whole question of protecting individual and minority rights, which includes collective rights and the rights of national groups, is still under consideration by the Law Commission. Therefore, it would be inappropriate of the Government to express a view on the details now. However, certain matters of principle have emerged fairly clearly and I wish to devote some remarks to them.

The Government accepts the principle of the recognition and

protection of the fundamental individual rights which form the
constitutional basis of most Western democracies. We acknowledge,
too, that the most practical way of protecting those rights is vested in
a declaration of rights justiciable by an independent judiciary. However,
it is clear that a system for the protection of the rights of individuals,
minorities and national entities has to form a well-rounded and
balanced whole. South Africa has its own national composition and our
constitutional dispensation has to take this into account. The formal
recognition of individual rights does not mean that the problems of a
heterogeneous population will simply disappear. Any new constitution
which disregards this reality will be inappropriate and even harmful.
[...]

3. The death penalty
The death penalty has been the subject of intensive discussion in recent
months. [...]

After the Chief Justice was consulted, and he in turn had consulted
the Bench, and after the Government had noted the opinions of
academics and other interested parties, the Government decided on
the following broad principles from a variety of available options:
• that reform in this area is indicated;
• that the death penalty should be limited as an option of sentence to
  extreme cases, and specifically through broadening judicial discretion
  in the imposition of sentence; and
• that an automatic right of appeal be granted to those under sentence
  of death.

[...] The proposals require that everybody currently awaiting execution,
be accorded the benefit of the proposed new approach. Therefore, all
executions have been suspended and no executions will take place until
Parliament has taken a final decision on the new proposals. [...]

4. Socio-economic aspects
A changed dispensation implies far more than political and constitutional
issues. It cannot be pursued successfully in isolation from problems
in other spheres of life which demand practical solutions. Poverty,
unemployment, housing shortages, inadequate education and training,
illiteracy, health needs and numerous other problems still stand in the
way of progress and prosperity and an improved quality of life.

The conservation of the physical and human environment is of cardinal importance to the quality of our existence. For this the Government is developing a strategy with the aid of an investigation by the President's Council.

[...]

From this will emanate important policy announcements in the socio-economic sphere by the responsible Ministers during the course of the session. One matter about which it is possible to make a concrete announcement, is the Separate Amenities Act, 1953. Pursuant to my speech before the President's Council late last year, I announce that this Act will be repealed during this Session of Parliament. [...]

5. The economy

A new South Africa is possible only if it is bolstered by a sound and growing economy, with particular emphasis on the creation of employment. With a view to this, the Government has taken thorough cognisance of the advice contained in numerous reports by a variety of advisory bodies. The central message is that South Africa, too, will have to make certain structural changes to its economy, just as its major trading partners had to do a decade or so ago.

[...]

In respect of Government expenditure, the budget for the current financial year will be the most accurate in many years. The financial figures will show:

- that Government expenditure is thoroughly under control;
- that our normal financing programme has not exerted any significant upward pressure on rates of interest; and
- that we will close the year with a surplus, even without taking the income from the privatisation of Iscor into account. [...]

6. Negotiation

In conclusion, I wish to focus the spotlight on the process of negotiation and related issues. At this stage I am refraining deliberately from discussing the merits of numerous political questions which undoubtedly will be debated during the next few weeks. The focus, now, has to fall on negotiation.

[...]

I wish to urge every political and community leader, in and outside Parliament, to approach the new opportunities which are being created, constructively. There is no time left for advancing all manner of new conditions that will delay the negotiating process.

The steps that have been decided, are the following:

- The prohibition of the African National Congress, the Pan Africanist Congress, the South African Communist Party and a number of subsidiary organisations is being rescinded.
- People serving prison sentences merely because they were members of one of these organisations or because they committed another offence which was merely an offence because a prohibition on one of the organisations was in force, will be identified and released. Prisoners who have been sentenced for other offences such as murder, terrorism or arson are not affected by this.
- The media emergency regulations as well as the education emergency regulations are being abolished in their entirety.
- The security emergency regulations will be amended to still make provision for effective control over visual material pertaining to scenes of unrest.
- The restrictions in terms of the emergency regulations on 33 organisations are being rescinded. The organisations include the following: National Education Crisis Committees, South African National Students Congress, United Democratic Front, Cosatu, Die Blanke Bevrydingsbeweging van Suid-Afrika.
- The conditions imposed in terms of the security emergency regulations on 374 people on their release, are being rescinded and the regulations which provide for such conditions are being abolished.
- The period of detention in terms of the security emergency regulations will be limited henceforth to six months. Detainees also acquire the right to legal representation and a medical practitioner of their own choosing.

[...] About one matter there should be no doubt. The lifting of the prohibition on the said organisations does not signify in the least the approval or condonation of terrorism or crimes of violence committed under their banner or which may be perpetrated in the future. Equally, it should not be interpreted as a deviation from the Government's principles, among other things, against their economic policy and aspects of their constitutional policy. This will be dealt with in debate and negotiation.

At the same time I wish to emphasise that the maintenance of law and order dares not be jeopardised. The Government will not forsake its duty in this connection. Violence from whichever source, will be fought with all available might. Peaceful protest may not become the springboard for lawlessness, violence and intimidation. No democratic country can tolerate that.

[...]

On the state of emergency I have been advised that an emergency situation, which justifies these special measures which have been retained, still exists. There is still conflict which is manifesting itself mainly in Natal, but as a consequence of the countrywide political power struggle. In addition, there are indications that radicals are still trying to disrupt the possibilities of negotiation by means of mass violence.

It is my intention to terminate the state of emergency completely as soon as circumstances justify it and I request the co-operation of everybody towards this end. [...]

Our country and all its people have been embroiled in conflict, tension and violent struggle for decades. It is time for us to break out of the cycle of violence and break through to peace and reconciliation. The silent majority is yearning for this. The youth deserve it.

With the steps the Government has taken it has proven its good faith and the table is laid for sensible leaders to begin talking about a new dispensation, to reach an understanding by way of dialogue and discussion.

The agenda is open and the overall aims to which we are aspiring should be acceptable to all reasonable South Africans.

Among other things, those aims include a new, democratic constitution; universal franchise; no domination; equality before an independent judiciary; the protection of minorities as well as of individual rights; freedom of religion; a sound economy based on proven economic principles and private enterprise; dynamic programmes directed at better education, health services, housing and social conditions for all.

In this connection Mr Nelson Mandela could play an important part. The Government has noted that he has declared himself to be willing to make a constructive contribution to the peaceful political process in South Africa.

I wish to put it plainly that the Government has taken a firm decision to release Mr Mandela unconditionally. I am serious about bringing this matter to finality without delay. The Government will take a decision soon on the date of his release. Unfortunately, a further short passage of time is unavoidable.

Normally there is a certain passage of time between the decision to release and the actual release because of logistical and administrative requirements. In the case of Mr Mandela there are factors in the way of his immediate release, of which his personal circumstances and safety are not the least. He has not been an ordinary prisoner for quite some time. Because of that, his case requires particular circumspection.

Today's announcements, in particular, go to the heart of what Black leaders – also Mr Mandela – have been advancing over the years as their reason for having resorted to violence. The allegation has been that the Government did not wish to talk to them and that they were deprived of their right to normal political activity by the prohibition of their organisations.

Without conceding that violence has ever been justified, I wish to say today to those who argued in this manner:

- The Government wishes to talk to all leaders who seek peace.
- The unconditional lifting of the prohibition on the said organisations places everybody in a position to pursue politics freely.
- The justification for violence which was always advanced, no longer exists.

These facts place everybody in South Africa before a fait accompli. On the basis of numerous previous statements there is no longer any reasonable excuse for the continuation of violence. The time for talking has arrived and whoever still makes excuses does not really wish to talk. Therefore, I repeat my invitation with greater conviction than ever:

Walk through the open door, take your place at the negotiating table together with the Government and other leaders who have important power bases inside and outside of Parliament.

Henceforth, everybody's political points of view will be tested against their realism, their workability and their fairness. The time for negotiation has arrived.

To those political leaders who have always resisted violence I say thank you for your principled stands. This includes all the leaders of parliamentary parties, leaders of important organisations and movements, such as Chief Minister Buthelezi, all of the other Chief Ministers and urban community leaders.

Through their participation and discussion they have made an important contribution to this moment in which the process of free political participation is able to be restored. Their places in the negotiating process are assured.

Conclusion

In my inaugural address I said the following:

All reasonable people in this country – by far the majority – anxiously await a message of hope. It is our responsibility as leaders in all spheres to provide that message realistically, with courage and conviction. If we fail in that, the ensuing chaos, the demise of stability and progress, will for ever be held against us.

History has thrust upon the leadership of this country the tremendous responsibility to turn our country away from its present direction of conflict and confrontation. Only we, the leaders of our peoples, can do it.

The eyes of responsible governments across the world are focused on us. The hopes of millions of South Africans are centred around us. The future of Southern Africa depends on us. We dare not falter or fail.

This is where we stand:

- Deeply under the impression of our responsibility.
- Humble in the face of the tremendous challenges ahead.
- Determined to move forward in faith and with conviction.

I ask of Parliament to assist me on the road ahead. There is much to be done.

I call on the international community to re-evaluate its position and to adopt a positive attitude towards the dynamic evolution which is taking place in South Africa.

I pray that the Almighty Lord will guide and sustain us on our course through unchartered waters and will bless your labours and deliberations.

Mr Speaker, Members of Parliament,

I now declare this Second Session of the Ninth Parliament of the Republic of South Africa to be duly opened.

De Klerk's speech begins like any other. Proposals such as 'Let us put petty politics aside' and 'Let us work together on a plan that will rid our country of suspicion' did not sound markedly different from some of the statements that had preceded them. After all, in the Rubicon speech, Botha had likewise said that 'any future constitutional dispensation ... should be negotiated', citing a preference for resolving problems through 'peaceful means'. In tone, however, De Klerk's overtures were markedly different from Botha's defiant declarations. He emphasises reasonableness, unity, inclusiveness. Threats, however, are not beyond him and he warns against economic ruin – 'Unless the countries of Southern Africa achieve stability ... they will be faced by further decline' – and the consequences of unrest – 'Violence ... will be fought with all available might.'

Most important, of course, is the substance of the speech, and De Klerk utters the words that many South Africans had been waiting decades to hear. He structures the address for maximum effect, leaving the most dramatic news for the conclusion. Beginning with general remarks about events in Europe and an overview of the country's economy, he ends with the news that, after thirty years, he is unbanning the ANC, PAC and SACP and intends to release the person the world had been waiting to meet: Nelson Mandela.

With this announcement, the deed was done. Although apartheid was of course not formally dismantled, these steps were interpreted as a move towards scrapping it altogether.[17] In reflection of this, Conservative Party members interjected increasingly throughout the speech's delivery, opposing De Klerk's announcement that the Separate Amenities Act would be repealed and jeering at the news that liberation parties would be unbanned. At this point, several CP members rose, bowed and walked out.

As with Desmond Tutu's 'rainbow people' speech, De Klerk refers several times to a 'new South Africa' and a 'new, realistic and democratic dispensa-tion', as if the very announcement of a new era eradicates the old version. 'The season of violence is over,' he says. 'The time for reconstruction and reconciliation has arrived.' In that one breath, he neatly establishes the dis-course of the post-apartheid era. His use of the pronoun 'we' flits between reference to the NP government ('we will close the year with a surplus') and a more inclusive reference to all leaders: 'Only we, the leaders of our peoples, can do it,' he claims, and 'We dare not falter or fail.'

He is careful to position himself and the NP government in a favourable position for negotiations, conceding to almost all of the ANC's pre-talk demands without acknowledging any fault on the part of the apartheid state. He externalises many of the former barriers to peace, suggesting that reform was crippled by the situation in eastern Europe and claiming that the events of 1989 created an 'historical opportunity' for southern Africa 'to set aside its conflicts'. Similarly, he claims that his parliamentary announcement removes any need for continued armed struggle: 'The justification for violence which was always advanced, no longer exists,' he says, as if his words, somewhat magically, have eradicated it.

Reactions to De Klerk's speech ranged from jubilation and disbelief to dis-trust and disappointment. Politicians around the world lauded the decisions taken. British prime minister Margaret Thatcher called the speech a 'major step forward', and United Nations secretary-general Javier Pérez de Cuéllar likened it to 'celestial music'.[18] UDF-aligned leaders were similarly positive, particularly Tutu, whose role in encouraging De Klerk during the 'peace' march appeared to have paid off. 'We are almost on the verge of being euphoric,' he said, 'because political life has been normalised in our country.' Allan Boesak's remarks were more cautious. 'I have a lot more faith in his [De Klerk's] ability now than I had a week ago,' he said reservedly.[19]

ANC leaders appeared to be taken aback, with some finding the news totally unbelievable – perhaps because of the various half-reform measures and near Rubicon crossings over the years. Mathews Phosa recalls being utterly flummoxed upon hearing the news in Mozambique. 'We couldn't believe it,' he remembers, 'we pinched ourselves and asked: "But what does it mean?" We've got orders to continue to shoot.'[20] Others were concerned that the reforms would delay the proper dismantling of apartheid. The issue of sanctions was key, and with so many celebrating the end of apartheid somewhat prematurely, this tactical weapon was in danger of being defused. The newly released Walter Sisulu emphasised this, saying at the time, 'The normalisation of relations with South Africa by other countries should continue to depend on a removal of apartheid.'[21]

On the other end of the political spectrum, the Conservative Party expressed deep concern about the future implications for 'minorities' in the country, despite De Klerk's insistence that their protection would be on the agenda during talks. A stony-faced Treurnicht said, with little glee, that the president was the 'only leader in the Western world who is negotiating himself, his party and his people out of power'.[22] He proceeded, unsuccessfully, to mount a vote of no confidence against De Klerk in Parliament.

The most surprising response came from the person perhaps most affected by the speech: Winnie Mandela. Her remarks suggest that she was incapable of believing the sincerity of De Klerk's promise to release her husband, despite the forcefulness of his statement of intent. 'I wish to put it plainly that the Government has taken a firm decision to release Mr Mandela unconditionally,' De Klerk had said, adding, 'I am serious about bringing this matter to finality'. Despite this insistence, Winnie said that De Klerk had offered 'a bone without any meat'.[23] Once again, De Klerk would prove his detractors wrong.

On 5 February, in anticipation of Mandela's release, the cover of *Time* magazine carried an artist's imagined impression of what the ANC leader would look like. The illustrated image of a greying, lined, smiling man last seen in public during the 1964 Rivonia Trial emphasised 'the degree to which the world's most famous political prisoner was also its most invisible'.[24] Alongside the image ran the single cover line: 'Free at last?' It was the question on everybody's mind.

Nelson Mandela

Release speech, Grand Parade, Cape Town,
11 February 1990

The date of Nelson Mandela's release was kept under wraps until the very last moment. Yet De Klerk kept his promise to expedite the matter and announced at a televised press conference on 10 February that he would be releasing Mandela the following day.[1] 'Mr Mandela,' the president reportedly said to his prisoner when Mandela asked for more time to make arrangements for the event, 'you have been in prison long enough.'[2] As magnanimous as this sounded, De Klerk's haste was also tactical. 'We were worried,' he said later, 'about the risk of an uncontrollable gathering to greet him after his release and felt that we could avoid this if we kept the time and place secret until just before it was due to take place.'[3] This proved to be a poor decision. After waiting for twenty-seven years, the ANC was given a mere twenty-four hours to prepare, and the events that unfolded the following day nearly marred the entire occasion.

During the period between Mandela's arrest and his release, his popularity soared. Anthony Sampson notes that in the wake of the Rivonia Trial international interest in Mandela waned; while he was mentioned twenty-four times in the *New York Times* in 1964, he vanished from the newspaper for the rest of the decade.[4] This changed with the success of the Anti-Apartheid Movement's Free Mandela campaign, which peaked in 1988 on the occasion of his seventieth birthday. In protest against his continued imprisonment, a mass pop concert, dubbed FreedomFest, was held at Wembley Square in London. A-list celebrities, including Elton John, Sting, Jonathan Butler, Peter Gabriel and Whitney Houston, as well as Whoopi Goldberg, Billy Connolly and Richard Attenborough, performed and delivered speeches to an audience of 74 000 people, and the event was broadcast live in seventy-two countries around the world (although not, of course, in Mandela's home country). Mandela had, in his absence, become a global icon.

By 1990, the entire world was waiting to meet him. In January, the ANC had formed the Mandela Reception Committee to make arrangements for his anticipated release, but both the committee and the apartheid government underestimated the amount of media interest in the occasion. Immediately after De Klerk's press conference, the committee asked the UDF network to arrange a welcome rally, but there was insufficient time to organise some of the necessities, such as walkie-talkies, information printouts and marshals. 'By that time,' recalled Willie Hofmeyr, one of the organisers of the event, 'we were fairly experienced rally-putters-togethers ... but this was a real last-minute thing.'[5]

On the evening of 10 February, following Pik Botha's advice, De Klerk's communications team released the first known photograph of Mandela in twenty-six years: a lean, greying, smiling man standing awkwardly alongside De Klerk. The image was splashed across the front pages of newspapers the following morning, in some cases with De Klerk deftly cropped out. The team had decided, after much deliberation, that the event should be broadcast live on national television, and South Africans huddled around their screens to catch a glimpse of the man.

The release itself was planned for 3 p.m. on Sunday afternoon, and De Klerk and Mandela had negotiated its terms; while De Klerk wanted to fly Mandela to Pretoria and release him from the Union Buildings, Mandela insisted on being released from Victor Verster Prison,[6] where he'd lived in a warder's house for the past two years. He was adamant, also, that he was to be accompanied by his wife, Winnie.

It was a swelteringly hot Sunday, and the lead-up to the event was a comedy of errors. Despite the fact that correctional services had assured the government that the event would be executed with 'military precision',[7] proceedings were delayed by well over an hour. This was mainly because Winnie Mandela and the ANC contingent from Johannesburg were late. Some accounts attribute her tardiness to an extended hair appointment;[8] others say it was because she refused to fly in the same plane as Murphy Morobe.[9] Either way, they had to take two charter planes, and these turned out to be propeller planes, 'the slowest planes in the world', according to Cyril Ramaphosa, who had his own story to tell. He was in hospital when he heard the news late on Saturday afternoon; without waiting to be discharged by his doctor, he pulled out his drips and told the hospital staff, 'I'm out of here!'[10]

Outside the prison, the awaiting crowd and journalists jostled for position in the heat. All the while, the SABC's anchor, Clarence Keyter – who'd been given the impossible task of reporting the event without glorifying it[11] – had to ramble away on live television about the beauty of the Paarl winelands. There were no interviews with the crowd, the studio had no backup footage to use as filler, and he and political editor Andre le Roux had to 'keep the thing going without talking about what was actually happening'.[12] In desperation,

Keyter at one point resorted to describing the prison as 'the most beautiful prison in the world'![13]

Meanwhile, on the Grand Parade, a crowd of 50 000 people had gathered – four times the number that had attended Tutu's peace march the year before. Tutu himself had only just managed to get there, having missed his flight after christening his first-born grandson in Soweto that morning. Luckily, he managed to get a lift with a BBC crew, and he and Allan Boesak implored the crowd to maintain calm, but the situation was volatile and the fringes of the gathering grew increasingly restless.

Finally, at 4.15 p.m. Mandela took his first steps to freedom, walking out of Victor Verster Prison while holding Winnie's hand in a victorious power salute. Surprised by the welcome and startled by the cameras, which sounded to him like a 'great herd of metallic beasts',[14] he realised how ill-prepared he was for what awaited. When he was driven out of the prison gates, the crowd swarmed around the vehicle, and the chaotic footage of the car's attempt to drive away suggests that too little consideration had been given to security.

Getting to City Hall was the next challenge. Traffic had been congested since 11 a.m. and Mandela's chauffeur made the mistake of trying to access the building directly from the front, which meant driving through the masses. The balcony was completely inaccessible, with supporters having climbed halfway up the facade of the hall. There was no direct route to the building and when the crowd threatened to engulf Mandela's car, beating upon its windows and chanting, the driver lost courage, reversed and left the city centre.

The convoy briefly sought refuge in the southern suburbs, where Mandela and his entourage had cool drinks while he tried to persuade the driver to return them to City Hall.[15] Tutu and Trevor Manuel, another of the organisers, feared the worst. The crowd was losing control, the police were getting trigger-happy, and they'd 'lost Madiba'.[16] At this point, with the sun descending and the patience of the crowd growing thin, looting broke out at a nearby shopping centre and the police opened fire. The panicked onlookers did not know 'whether it was ammunition, rubber bullets or tear gas'.[17] The whole occasion threatened to explode when a man was fatally wounded.[18]

Finally, at dusk, having accessed City Hall from behind, Mandela emerged on the balcony. The crowd roared, surged and chanted 'ANC! ANC! ANC!' Standing between Walter Sisulu and Cyril Ramaphosa, Mandela pulled out his speech to address the crowd, only to discover that he'd left his reading glasses behind and needed to borrow Winnie's. 'Viva! Viva! Viva!' the crowd shouted. Ramaphosa and Sisulu pleaded with the audience to give their leader a 'dignified hearing', and for a moment it appeared as though he wouldn't manage to address them at all. Then Mandela raised his arms in an authoritative appeal for calm and, for the first time in twenty-six years, spoke to his people:

Friends, comrades and fellow South Africans.

I greet you all in the name of peace, democracy and freedom for all.

I stand here before you not as a prophet but as a humble servant of you, the people. Your tireless and heroic sacrifices have made it possible for me to be here today. I therefore place the remaining years of my life in your hands.

On this day of my release, I extend my sincere and warmest gratitude to the millions of my compatriots and those in every corner of the globe who have campaigned tirelessly for my release.

I send special greetings to the people of Cape Town, this city which has been my home for three decades. Your mass marches and other forms of struggle have served as a constant source of strength to all political prisoners.

I salute the African National Congress. It has fulfilled our every expectation in its role as leader of the great march to freedom.

I salute our President, Comrade Oliver Tambo, for leading the ANC even under the most difficult circumstances.

I salute the rank and file members of the ANC. You have sacrificed life and limb in the pursuit of the noble cause of our struggle.

I salute combatants of Umkhonto we Sizwe, like Solomon Mahlangu and Ashley Kriel who have paid the ultimate price for the freedom of all South Africans.

I salute the South African Communist Party for its sterling contribution to the struggle for democracy. You have survived 40 years of unrelenting persecution. The memory of great communists like Moses Kotane, Yusuf Dadoo, Bram Fischer and Moses Mabhida will be cherished for generations to come.

I salute General Secretary Joe Slovo, one of our finest patriots. We are heartened by the fact that the alliance between ourselves and the Party remains as strong as it always was.

I salute the United Democratic Front, the National Education Crisis Committee, the South African Youth Congress, the Transvaal and Natal Indian Congresses and COSATU and the many other formations of the Mass Democratic Movement.

I also salute the Black Sash and the National Union of South African

Students. We note with pride that you have acted as the conscience of white South Africa. Even during the darkest days in the history of our struggle you held the flag of liberty high. The large-scale mass mobilisation of the past few years is one of the key factors which led to the opening of the final chapter of our struggle.

I extend my greetings to the working class of our country. Your organised strength is the pride of our movement. You remain the most dependable force in the struggle to end exploitation and oppression.

I pay tribute to the many religious communities who carried the campaign for justice forward when the organisations for our people were silenced.

I greet the traditional leaders of our country – many of you continue to walk in the footsteps of great heroes like Hintsa and Sekhukune.

I pay tribute to the endless heroism of youth, you, the young lions. You, the young lions, have energised our entire struggle.

I pay tribute to the mothers and wives and sisters of our nation. You are the rock-hard foundation of our struggle. Apartheid has inflicted more pain on you than on anyone else.

On this occasion, we thank the world community for their great contribution to the anti-apartheid struggle. Without your support our struggle would not have reached this advanced stage. The sacrifice of the frontline states will be remembered by South Africans forever.

My salutations would be incomplete without expressing my deep appreciation for the strength given to me during my long and lonely years in prison by my beloved wife and family. I am convinced that your pain and suffering was far greater than my own.

Before I go any further I wish to make the point that I intend making only a few preliminary comments at this stage. I will make a more complete statement only after I have had the opportunity to consult with my comrades.

Today the majority of South Africans, black and white, recognise that apartheid has no future. It has to be ended by our own decisive mass action in order to build peace and security. The mass campaign of defiance and other actions of our organisation and people can only culminate in the establishment of democracy. The destruction caused by apartheid on our sub-continent is incalculable. The fabric of family life of millions of my people has been shattered. Millions are homeless and unemployed. Our economy lies in ruins and our people are embroiled in political strife. Our resort to the armed struggle in 1960 with the

formation of the military wing of the ANC, Umkhonto we Sizwe, was
a purely defensive action against the violence of apartheid. The factors
which necessitated the armed struggle still exist today. We have no
option but to continue. We express the hope that a climate conducive to
a negotiated settlement will be created soon so that there may no longer
be the need for the armed struggle.

I am a loyal and disciplined member of the African National
Congress. I am therefore in full agreement with all of its objectives,
strategies and tactics.

The need to unite the people of our country is as important a task
now as it always has been. No individual leader is able to take on this
enormous task on his own. It is our task as leaders to place our views
before our organisation and to allow the democratic structures to
decide. On the question of democratic practice, I feel duty bound to
make the point that a leader of the movement is a person who has
been democratically elected at a national conference. This is a principle
which must be upheld without any exceptions.

Today, I wish to report to you that my talks with the government
have been aimed at normalising the political situation in the country.
We have not as yet begun discussing the basic demands of the struggle.
I wish to stress that I myself have at no time entered into negotiations
about the future of our country except to insist on a meeting between
the ANC and the government.

Mr. De Klerk has gone further than any other Nationalist president
in taking real steps to normalise the situation. However, there are
further steps as outlined in the Harare Declaration that have to be met
before negotiations on the basic demands of our people can begin.
I reiterate our call for, inter alia, the immediate ending of the State of
Emergency and the freeing of all, and not only some, political prisoners.
Only such a normalised situation, which allows for free political activity,
can allow us to consult our people in order to obtain a mandate.

The people need to be consulted on who will negotiate and on the
content of such negotiations. Negotiations cannot take place above the
heads or behind the backs of our people. It is our belief that the future
of our country can only be determined by a body which is democratically
elected on a non-racial basis. Negotiations on the dismantling of
apartheid will have to address the overwhelming demand of our people
for a democratic, non-racial and unitary South Africa. There must be
an end to white monopoly on political power and a fundamental

restructuring of our political and economic systems to ensure that the inequalities of apartheid are addressed and our society thoroughly democratised.

It must be added that Mr. De Klerk himself is a man of integrity who is acutely aware of the dangers of a public figure not honouring his undertakings. But as an organisation we base our policy and strategy on the harsh reality we are faced with. And this reality is that we are still suffering under the policy of the Nationalist government.

Our struggle has reached a decisive moment. We call on our people to seize this moment so that the process towards democracy is rapid and uninterrupted. We have waited too long for our freedom. We can no longer wait. Now is the time to intensify the struggle on all fronts. To relax our efforts now would be a mistake which generations to come will not be able to forgive. The sight of freedom looming on the horizon should encourage us to redouble our efforts.

It is only through disciplined mass action that our victory can be assured. We call on our white compatriots to join us in the shaping of a new South Africa. The freedom movement is a political home for you too. We call on the international community to continue the campaign to isolate the apartheid regime. To lift sanctions now would be to run the risk of aborting the process towards the complete eradication of apartheid.

Our march to freedom is irreversible. We must not allow fear to stand in our way. Universal suffrage on a common voters' role in a united democratic and non-racial South Africa is the only way to peace and racial harmony.

In conclusion I wish to quote my own words during my trial in 1964. They are as true today as they were then:

'I have fought against white domination and I have fought against black domination. I have cherished the ideal of a democratic and free society in which all persons live together in harmony and with equal opportunities. It is an ideal which I hope to live for and to achieve. But if needs be, it is an ideal for which I am prepared to die.'

Mandela's speech rescued an occasion that had begun to turn violent and was threatening to explode. Although he claimed to be a 'humble servant' of the crowd and not a 'prophet', he could not have appeared more prophet-like, standing on the balcony in the waning light and raising his arms in a call for calm. His release and address were subsequently spoken about in messianic terms. *Time* magazine described him as 'Hero. Unifier. Healer. Savior.'[19]

In contrast with these descriptions, Mandela and his fellow speechwriters Cyril Ramaphosa and Trevor Manuel were at pains to dispel the one-man leadership style so contrary to ANC culture and to 'assert collective leadership'.[20] Mandela describes himself first and foremost as a 'loyal and disciplined' member of the ANC, and the opening of the speech is a litany of thanks to individuals and organisations that had played their part in the fight against apartheid, ranging from the UDF and COSATU to MK and the SACP.

The speech's measured delivery – Mandela spoke in slow, deliberate sentences – suggests both his own astonishment at the massive reception and his eagerness to contain the chaos at the Parade. The speech was 'loyal and disciplined' in content too. Noting that he would give a fuller address after he had consulted with his comrades, Mandela was also careful to put paid to the rumour – circulating since he'd met with De Klerk the year before[21] – that he'd begun negotiating (or, worse, collaborating) with the government unilaterally.

Responses to the speech were likewise wary. Mandela's release was watched by more white South Africans than any other television event in history,[22] and to many of them the sight of Mandela standing on a balcony with the red SACP flag draped across it must have been alarming – an impression not helped by his tribute to the 'memory of great communists' and his praise of Joe Slovo, dubbed Public Enemy No. 1 by the apartheid state. Anthony Sampson points out that they had expected 'a grand conciliator, even a national savior', but instead, Mandela 'sounded almost as militant as he did 30 years ago'.[23]

Many were also disappointed by the 'overly formal and formulaic'[24] nature of the address; Martin Meredith described it as a 'crude, partisan speech' that consisted mainly of the 'narrow, parochial interests' of the party officials who'd had a hand in its composition.[25] But Mandela claims that he 'spoke from the heart',[26] and he is clearly moved when he speaks of his family's suffering during his period of imprisonment. Apart from this passing mention, however, there is no reference to his personal experience, and the speech is a good example of Mandela's almost extreme self-effacement and the way in which his identity fused first with that of the ANC and then with that of the nation. As Elleke Boehmer points out, in all of Mandela's oratory, 'we were not to know how Mandela the man, the human being, felt'.[27]

There was no immediate government response to the speech, but De Klerk later expressed his disappointment, saying that Mandela 'failed completely to rise to the occasion' and was less conciliatory than he had hoped.[28] Indeed, although Mandela describes De Klerk as a 'man of integrity', he is quick to add the veiled warning about 'the dangers of a public figure not honouring his undertakings'.

Mandela was in fact in no position to make grand gestures of reconciliation at this point, and the speech was a prudent balancing of various expectations. Although militant in tone, it gave an indication of the way in which Mandela's leadership would go on to address the often-conflicting needs of black and white South Africans. Its commitment to party strategy reassured the ANC leadership abroad,[29] while references to NUSAS and the Black Sash, as well as to opposition parties, acknowledged the role played by white liberals.

At the same time, Mandela was insistent that only continued pressurisation of the state could achieve the proper end to apartheid. Whereas De Klerk had spoken mainly of negotiation and a new era in his 2 February speech, Mandela assumed no change in the contemporary context, saying instead, 'Now is the time to intensify the struggle on all fronts.' The fear was that the West would drop sanctions and weaken black opposition, allowing De Klerk to co-opt selected black politicians into positions of power and dupe the world into thinking that apartheid had ended. As George Bizos put it, 'Because your opponent has said he will settle, it doesn't mean you send home the witnesses and dismiss your counsel.'[30]

Mandela might have taken his first steps to freedom, but there was still a long road ahead.

Nelson Mandela

Televised address after Chris Hani's death,
13 April 1993

As the power struggle between the ANC and the Inkatha Freedom Party (IFP) escalated between 1990 and 1994, some 14 000 South Africans died in the political violence that swept through the country – more than in any other period during apartheid rule.[1] But in April 1993, the threat of a full-scale civil war loomed over the country after the assassination of one man: Chris Hani.

Hani was the charismatic chief of staff of MK and the leader of the SACP, having succeeded Joe Slovo in 1991. He had displayed immense military prowess as a solider during the fight against apartheid, commanding the respect of both his soldiers and his adversaries. By 1990, he'd successfully evaded three assassination attempts and probably a few others of which he was unaware. In the 1980s, for instance, when military intelligence officers asked SADF chief Constand Viljoen to 'formally sanction Hani's elimination' using an air strike in Maseru, Viljoen refused because of the possibility that Hani's family were with him,[2] and Hani escaped again.

But Hani's opponents weren't limited to the South African authorities. He'd made enemies in suppressing mutinies in ANC camps[3] and in building an ANC culture of self-reflection. In 1969, he and six other MK leaders had signed what became known as the Hani Memorandum, criticising the rot that had set in the organisation. This was the catalyst for an important conference in Morogoro, Tanzania, which opened ANC membership to non-Africans.[4]

In the transition period, he was also a valuable player in the negotiation process. 'Chris Hani, more than anyone else,' said Desmond Tutu, 'had the credibility among the young to rein in the radicals.'[5] He was immensely effective as a grass-roots campaigner in the townships, sometimes delivering up to four rallies a day.[6] He was tipped to serve as Mandela's successor, having received the most votes in the 1991 ANC National Executive Committee election, but this possibility looked unlikely when he left the party's structures in 1992 to grow the SACP[7] after Slovo's departure due to cancer. Regardless of which party he led, in 1992 a survey revealed that he was the second most popular political figure in the country after Mandela.[8]

So when news broke that Hani's fifteen-year-old daughter had found her father dead in the driveway of their home in Dawn Park, Boksburg, the country reeled in anger. And when the killer's racial identity was made known a few hours later, De Klerk knew he had a crisis on his hands.

Over the 1993 Easter weekend, Hani had broken from his usual security protocol and had driven to the shops without his chauffeur-cum-bodyguard. He returned at about 10 a.m., newspaper in hand, and as he was walking to the front door of his home, he had turned in response to a man calling 'Mr Hani!' The man proceeded to shoot him at point-blank range.[9]

By some stroke of luck, a neighbour, Mrs Margaretha Harmse, was driving past the scene. She heard the shots and was alarmed to see a white man standing with a gun over a black man's body. After she witnessed him fire another two shots, she stopped her car and watched from her rear-view mirror as the killer got into a red Ford Laser hatchback.[10] Then, in what the judge would later call 'a remarkable display of self-possession',[11] she reversed in order to get a closer look at the car's number plate, asking her parents, who were travelling with her, to memorise it.

When the police received Harmse's tip-off, they took a mere ten minutes to apprehend the vehicle some six kilometres from the crime scene.[12] They found a warm gun in the rear of the vehicle and arrested the driver: a forty-year-old man named Janusz Waluś, who was a Polish immigrant and white right-winger.

Since the ANC's unbanning, there had been many politically motivated assassinations and racist killings, but this was the first high-profile execution and the first major interracial political attack. It sparked major fears of a black backlash. To make matters worse, De Klerk's leadership had been severely tested since Mandela's release. While De Klerk had managed to secure a mandate to proceed with negotiations on behalf of the white electorate with the 1992 referendum, his ability to calm the rising anger of black communities had been called into question – particularly in the aftermath of the Boipatong massacre that year. On the night of 17 June, a group of hostel dwellers from KwaMadala murdered forty-six inhabitants of Boipatong, including a pregnant woman and baby. The perpetrators were loosely aligned with the IFP and the victims with the ANC. A rumour circulated that the SAP had assisted the killers, building on the Inkathagate scandal of 1991, when the *Weekly Mail* revealed that police had covertly directed funds to Mangosuthu Buthelezi's IFP. When De Klerk tried to pay a courtesy visit to the township, his convoy met with a crowd of protesting community members so incensed by his presence that he was unable to exit his vehicle.[13] He had clearly overestimated his credibility among the South African populace.

What's more, the SAP had been criticised for its unwillingness to investigate an earlier assassination attempt on Hani's life. In July 1992, a young black man had been noticed tailing Hani in broad daylight in Marshall Street, near the SACP offices in central Johannesburg. Realising that he'd been spotted, the would-be assassin fled the scene in a Toyota Cressida with two white accomplices. Convinced that an assassination attempt had been averted, the SACP held a press conference immediately afterwards, but when the number plates of the car turned out to be false, the trail went cold and the police dropped the case.[14]

De Klerk was in no position to succeed with an appeal for calm. Indeed, when he later appeared on television to announce triumphantly that the case had been solved with Waluś's arrest, the public was sceptical,[15] and he was later proven wrong in this assessment. To his credit, he realised that more was needed and that any 'high-profile appearance' on his part – 'no matter how well intentioned – would probably have the opposite effect'.[16] He turned to Mandela for help, and over the next week the ANC leader addressed the nation in a series of radio and television broadcasts. Speaking in direct-address mode to 'all South Africans, black and white', in the first speech screened on the very night of Hani's death, Mandela called the murder a 'crime against all the people of our country' and called for the 'killing to stop'.[17]

But the following day the killing did not stop. Protests resulted in police clashes and there were at least five fatalities, including a Soweto resident, a police sergeant and two white men burnt to death in Lwandle.[18] The broadcast appeals continued and, on 13 April, Mandela spoke on television again. This time, his address was a more personalised appeal that took on an even more reconciliatory tone:

> Tonight I am reaching out to every single South African, black and white, from the very depths of my being.
>
> A white man, full of prejudice and hate, came to our country and committed a deed so foul that our whole nation now teeters on the brink of disaster.
>
> A white woman, of Afrikaner origin, risked her life so that we may know, and bring to justice, this assassin.
>
> The cold-blooded murder of Chris Hani has sent shock waves throughout the country and the world. Our grief and anger is tearing us apart.
>
> What has happened is a national tragedy that has touched millions of people, across the political and colour divide.
>
> Our shared grief and legitimate anger will find expression in nationwide commemorations that coincide with the funeral service.

Tomorrow, in many towns and villages, there will be memorial services to pay homage to one of the greatest revolutionaries this country has ever known.

Every service will open a Memorial Book for Freedom, in which all who want peace and democracy pledge their commitment.

Now is the time for all South Africans to stand together against those who, from any quarter, wish to destroy what Chris Hani gave his life for – the freedom of all of us.

Now is the time for our white compatriots, from whom messages of condolence continue to pour in, to reach out with an understanding of the grievous loss to our nation, to join in the memorial services and the funeral commemorations.

Now is the time for the police to act with sensitivity and restraint, to be real community policemen and women who serve the population as a whole. There must be no further loss of life at this tragic time.

This is a watershed moment for all of us.

Our decisions and actions will determine whether we use our pain, our grief and our outrage to move forward to what is the only lasting solution for our country – an elected government of the people, by the people and for the people.

We must not let the men who worship war, and who lust after blood, precipitate actions that will plunge our country into another Angola.

Chris Hani was a soldier. He believed in iron discipline. He carried out instructions to the letter. He practised what he preached.

Any lack of discipline is trampling on the values that Chris Hani stood for. Those who commit such acts serve only the interests of the assassins, and desecrate his memory.

When we, as one people, act together decisively, with discipline and determination, nothing can stop us.

Let us honour this soldier for peace in a fitting manner. Let us rededicate ourselves to bringing about the democracy he fought for all his life; democracy that will bring real, tangible changes in the lives of the working people, the poor, the jobless, the landless.

Chris Hani is irreplaceable in the heart of our nation and people.

When he first returned to South Africa after three decades in exile, he said: 'I have lived with death most of my life. I want to live in a free South Africa even if I have to lay down my life for it.'

The body of Chris Hani will lie in State at the FNB Stadium, Soweto, from 12 noon on Sunday 18 April until the start of the vigil at 6pm. The funeral service will commence at 9am on Monday, 19th April. The cortege will leave for Boksburg Cemetery, where the burial is scheduled for 1pm.

These funeral service and rallies must be conducted with dignity.

We will give disciplined expression to our emotions at our pickets, prayer meetings and gatherings, in our homes, our churches and our schools. We will not be provoked into any rash actions.

We are a nation in mourning.

To the youth of South Africa we have a special message: you have lost a great hero. You have repeatedly shown that your love of freedom is greater than that most precious gift, life itself. But you are the leaders of tomorrow. Your country, your people, your organisation need you to act with wisdom. A particular responsibility rests on your shoulders.

We pay tribute to all our people for the courage and restraint they have shown in the face of such extreme provocation. We are sure this same indomitable spirit will carry us through the difficult days ahead.

Chris Hani has made the supreme sacrifice. The greatest tribute we can pay to his life's work is to ensure we win that freedom for all our people.

Mandela's speech heralded the reconciliatory rhetoric that would come to characterise his presidency. He summons a national 'we', inclusive of black and white South Africans, sharing grief, equally hurt and united in the fight for freedom. 'Now is the time for all South Africans to stand together,' a bespectacled Mandela implores, looking very much like the de facto president of the country. In close-up footage, he addresses the camera directly, seated in an office with a bookcase behind him and the once-banned ANC flag to his left.

Mandela foregrounds Harmse's role in apprehending the victim and emphasises her white Afrikaner identity in an attempt to forge a more inclusive reaction to the event. At the same time, he deftly projects the right-wing insurgency behind the assassination onto one man, an outsider, who came to this country 'full of prejudice and hate'.

The best response to the implicit enemy, those who 'worship war', Mandela suggests, is 'iron discipline' and restraint. He frames this also as a response to Hani's legacy. 'Any lack of discipline is trampling on the values that Chris Hani stood for.'

The ANC called for a rolling campaign of mass action in the wake of the event, inciting De Klerk's ire and his belief that the party had 'failed to exercise control over its followers'.[19] He responded, to Mandela's equal annoyance, by deploying further security personnel, and South African police chief General Johan van der Merwe also appeared on television to announce that the Defence Force would be deploying 23 000 soldiers to 'maintain law and order'.[20] Such news, however, was only reassuring to a small sector of the population.

Thus, when Mandela repeated his plea for restraint at Hani's funeral service several days later, he also launched a scathing attack on De Klerk's perceived need for 23 000 security troops to contain the masses. Angry about the rise in police shootings, he asked, 'why deploy troops against mourners?'[21] and went on to claim that it was in fact the police who needed to exercise control. At the funeral, he framed the conflict as one involving the police and protestors but still argued for a battle of restraint. In addition, he used the opportunity to articulate political demands: 'We want an end to white minority rule now!' Mandela concluded. 'We want an election date now!'

Although the funeral speech is markedly more militant in tone, it is certainly not a call to arms. It illustrated Mandela's ability to tailor his discourse for different contexts. If the televised address served as a means of allaying white fears, then the funeral speech acted as a means of deflecting black anger.

A further thirty-four people were killed in the aftermath of the funeral,[22] though it is not known if these killings stemmed directly from Hani's assassination. Tutu went on to claim that the country would have 'gone up in flames if Mandela had not gone on television and radio'.[23] It was soon uncovered that Hani's killing was part of a larger conspiracy to achieve just this. An alleged 'hit list' was uncovered in the cubby hole of Waluś's car, with the names and addresses of a number of influential politicians and journalists, including Nelson Mandela, Joe Slovo, Mac Maharaj, Karin Brynard, Chris Hani, Pik Botha, Richard Goldstone, Ken Owen and Tim du Plessis. Then, on 17 April, Conservative Party MP Clive Derby-Lewis was arrested for masterminding the attack, providing the firearm and plotting further high-profile assassinations. Although never convicted for the latter charge, Derby-Lewis and Waluś were both sentenced to death, a charge that, in the new dispensation that they so despised, was later commuted to life imprisonment. In a bid for freedom, Derby-Lewis later confessed to the country's Truth and Reconciliation Commission that by assassinating Hani, he'd hoped to spark a race war.[24] Though it is impossible to know the extent to which Mandela's appeals curtailed further violence, the killers' aim was never achieved.

Instead, ironically, Hani's killing tipped the balance of power in the ANC's favour. De Klerk's decision to defer to Mandela suggested how much he had come to rely on the ANC leader's authority in managing crises and, because direct televised addresses are usually reserved for government leaders and royals,[25] the speech helped white South Africans to perceive Mandela as presidential,[26] changing his image from liberator to politician.

Negotiations pushed ahead with a renewed sense of urgency, and two months later an election date was set for 27 April 1994. In recognition of their dual role in managing the volatile situation, De Klerk and Mandela were jointly awarded the Nobel Peace Prize at the end of 1993, though neither was particularly complimentary about their partner's eligibility. When asked why he thought De Klerk had received the award alongside him, Mandela quipped, 'Just ask the Nobel Peace Prize Committee', while, a bit more magnanimously, De Klerk said that the award was bestowed on the process and not on individuals.[27]

Nelson Mandela

Inauguration speech, Union Buildings, Pretoria,
10 May 1994

The lead-up to South Africa's first democratic election on 27 April 1994 was bloody. Violence increased in the latter half of 1993, as the Azanian People's Liberation Army (APLA) targeted white establishments in terror attacks in East London and Cape Town, and the American Fulbright scholar Amy Biehl was stoned to death in August by youths who'd been attending a PAC rally. Groups that felt threatened by the idea of a new South Africa rallied together in their attempts to resist change, and it appeared a civil war was brewing.

Homelands, both old and new, proved to be a major stumbling block, as well as the catalyst for unlikely alliances. The white right-wing wanted their own independent homeland – or *Volkstaat* – and they unified under the Afrikaner Volksfront (AVF), a military-minded umbrella organisation led by Constand Viljoen, former chief of the SADF. The AVF included numerous disparate and disaffected groups, including far-right organisations such as Eugène Terre'Blanche's Afrikaner Weerstandsbeweging (AWB), which had made its feelings about negotiations clear in June 1993 when its members stormed through the glass doors of the World Trade Centre in Kempton Park to disrupt talks.

At the same time, some of the puppet governments in the apartheid-created Bantustans clung to their homelands, seeing no political future for themselves in the emerging dispensation. In 1992, roughly 80 000 demonstrators protested against the continuing leadership of Brigadier Oupa Gqozo at a stadium near the Ciskeian capital of Bisho. When a group led by Ronnie Kasrils defied the march orders and entered Bisho, Gqozo's army opened fire, killing twenty-three protestors. The blame for the event ultimately fell at the feet of the NP, since the so-called 'independent' states were, after all, Frankenstein creations of the party's own making.

Then, in early 1994, events in Bophuthatswana turned violent. When President Lucas Mangope announced that he wouldn't be participating in the election, a civil-service strike broke out. By 9 March, the situation was out of control, and Mangope turned to Viljoen's AVF for military assistance, stipulating that he shouldn't send the racist AWB, because it would likely provoke anger. Viljoen agreed to help defend key locations, but Terre'Blanche got wind of the plan and sent AWB commandos blundering into Mmabatho, only to find that their presence was unwanted. As the AWB men departed, they reportedly drove through the streets, shouting out racial abuse and shooting randomly at civilians.[1] The Bophuthatswana soldiers retaliated, and three AWB members driving a pale-blue Mercedes-Benz were gunned down in broad daylight under the gaze of television cameras. When photographs of the dying men's last moments were splashed across the newspapers the following day, the hard reality of continued resistance struck home, and within twenty-four hours both Mangope and Viljoen agreed to take part in the election. As Allister Sparks pointed out, Bophuthatswana was the 'ultimate irony' since 'it was the very worst of white racists who finally cleared the way for South Africa's one-person, one-vote election'.[2]

But there was in fact more to come. On 28 March 1994, in what became known as the 'Shell House massacre', ANC snipers shot at Zulu marchers in downtown Johannesburg. The protestors were marching for the continued independence of the soon-to-be-former homeland of KwaZulu. Anticipating the ANC's victory, Buthelezi's IFP wanted nothing to do with a new South Africa.

Still, the country lurched towards the election, with the death toll mounting. Between 6 and 13 April, 103 people died in countrywide violence.[3] Three days before citizens were due to vote, right-wingers detonated a bomb outside ANC offices in Johannesburg, killing nine people. In Natal, election campaigners were murdered while encouraging communities to vote.

Then, to everybody's surprise, Buthelezi gave in, adopting an 'if you can't beat them, join them' approach. His decision, described by Cyril Ramaphosa as a 'miracle',[4] came so late in the day that the Independent Electoral Commission had to print special stickers to add to the election ballots. 'Saved by the sticker!' Sky News declared triumphantly, while CNN described it as 'the moment that an anxious South Africa had been waiting for'.[5] The IFP's participation in the election allayed some of the fears of post-election violence and brought fresh excitement to the event.

Finally, on 27 April, South Africans prepared to cast their ballots, most of them for the first time in their lives. The voting process was fairly chaotic, with long queues, shortages of ballots and a last-minute extension of voting hours. But, given the sacrifices made to reach this day at all, these inconveniences were minor, and after years of protracted violence, the media reported no fatalities. 'For once, there was peace across the land', the *Mail & Guardian* exulted, and 'the unflagging human spirit made it a day to be proud of'.[6]

To top it off, the election results were, according to the *Weekend Star*, a

'Dream Outcome'.[7] As expected, the ANC led with nearly 63 per cent of the vote, but its rivals were happy too: the NP managed to win the majority in the Western Cape and succeeded in preventing the ANC from achieving the much-feared two-thirds majority, whereas the IFP, despite a late entrance, won KwaZulu-Natal and over 10 per cent of the vote.

The subsequent inauguration of Mandela was a massive celebration. Not since John F. Kennedy's funeral had an event attracted so many heads of state,[8] and the extensive parade of foreign dignitaries – after so many years of global isolation – inspired a new sense of national pride. A multiracial crowd of 50 000 people came to watch a big-screen televised version of the ceremony on the lawns outside the venue, waving their new South African flags in the wind.

The peaceful transfer of power – both judicial and military – was illustrated by the visual symbolism of the event. Held at the Union Buildings in Pretoria, the official heart of political power in the country, the occasion embraced diverse cultural displays and traditions. Mandela, by now estranged from Winnie, attended the event with his daughter Zenani. Backed by white military generals and flanked by his two deputies, F.W. de Klerk and Thabo Mbeki, he was sworn in by Chief Justice Michael Corbett, who was dressed in traditional judicial robes. An array of religious leaders spoke, concluding with Desmond Tutu, who bestowed blessings upon the new president in both English and Xhosa. He was followed by the deep-voiced praise poet Mzwakhe Mbuli, whose 'rap-like riffs and roars ... drew open-mouthed stares'[9] and ululations from the crowd, adding an African aesthetic to the Western democratic tradition. To great applause, Mandela launched the new 'rainbow nation', delivering his first speech as the country's first democratically elected president:

Your Majesties, Your Highnesses, Distinguished Guests, Comrades and Friends:

Today, all of us do, by our presence here, and by our celebrations in other parts of our country and the world, confer glory and hope to newborn liberty.

Out of the experience of an extraordinary human disaster that lasted too long, must be born a society of which all humanity will be proud.

Our daily deeds as ordinary South Africans must produce an actual South African reality that will reinforce humanity's belief in justice, strengthen its confidence in the nobility of the human soul and sustain all our hopes for a glorious life for all.

All this we owe both to ourselves and to the peoples of the world who are so well represented here today.

To my compatriots, I have no hesitation in saying that each one of us is as intimately attached to the soil of this beautiful country as are the famous jacaranda trees of Pretoria and the mimosa trees of the bushveld.

Each time one of us touches the soil of this land, we feel a sense of personal renewal. The national mood changes as the seasons change.

We are moved by a sense of joy and exhilaration when the grass turns green and the flowers bloom.

That spiritual and physical oneness we all share with this common homeland explains the depth of the pain we all carried in our hearts as we saw our country tear itself apart in a terrible conflict, and as we saw it spurned, outlawed and isolated by the peoples of the world, precisely because it has become the universal base of the pernicious ideology and practice of racism and racial oppression.

We, the people of South Africa, feel fulfilled that humanity has taken us back into its bosom, that we, who were outlaws not so long ago, have today been given the rare privilege to be host to the nations of the world on our own soil.

We thank all our distinguished international guests for having come to take possession with the people of our country of what is, after all, a common victory for justice, for peace, for human dignity.

We trust that you will continue to stand by us as we tackle the challenges of building peace, prosperity, non-sexism, non-racialism and democracy.

We deeply appreciate the role that the masses of our people and their political mass democratic, religious, women, youth, business, traditional and other leaders have played to bring about this conclusion. Not least among them is my Second Deputy President, the Honourable F.W. de Klerk.

We would also like to pay tribute to our security forces, in all their ranks, for the distinguished role they have played in securing our first democratic elections and the transition to democracy, from blood-thirsty forces which still refuse to see the light.

The time for the healing of the wounds has come.

The moment to bridge the chasms that divide us has come.

The time to build is upon us.

We have, at last, achieved our political emancipation. We pledge ourselves to liberate all our people from the continuing bondage of poverty, deprivation, suffering, gender and other discrimination.

We succeeded to take our last steps to freedom in conditions of relative peace. We commit ourselves to the construction of a complete, just and lasting peace.

We have triumphed in the effort to implant hope in the breasts of the millions of our people. We enter into a covenant that we shall build the society in which all South Africans, both black and white, will be able to walk tall, without any fear in their hearts, assured of their inalienable right to human dignity – a rainbow nation at peace with itself and the world.

As a token of its commitment to the renewal of our country, the new Interim Government of National Unity will, as a matter of urgency, address the issue of amnesty for various categories of our people who are currently serving terms of imprisonment.

We dedicate this day to all the heroes and heroines in this country and the rest of the world who sacrificed in many ways and surrendered their lives so that we could be free.

Their dreams have become reality. Freedom is their reward.

We are both humbled and elevated by the honour and privilege that you, the people of South Africa, have bestowed on us, as the first President of a united, democratic, non-racial and non-sexist South Africa, to lead our country out of the valley of darkness.

We understand it still that there is no easy road to freedom.

We know it well that none of us acting alone can achieve success.

We must therefore act together as a united people, for national reconciliation, for nation building, for the birth of a new world.

Let there be justice for all.

Let there be peace for all.

Let there be work, bread, water and salt for all.

Let each know that for each the body, the mind and the soul have been freed to fulfil themselves.

Never, never and never again shall it be that this beautiful land will again experience the oppression of one by another and suffer the indignity of being the skunk of the world.

Let freedom reign.

The sun shall never set on so glorious a human achievement!

God bless Africa!

Thank you.

Mandela finally allows himself to speak of the 'new world' or nation in the speech, echoing De Klerk's 2 February lines 'the season of violence is over' as well as the Bible's Ecclesiastes 3:1–8 'There is a time for everything': 'The time for the healing of the wounds has come,' says Mandela. 'The moment to bridge the chasms that divide us has come.' It is only now, after a successful election, that 'political emancipation' has been achieved.

Contributing to the perception of a seemingly peaceful transfer of power, the speech transcends all possible divisions and makes only the vaguest mention of the internal clashes of the past. Instead of depicting South Africa as 'a country at war with itself', as the UDF had said of it in the 1980s,[10] he speaks of a country 'spurned, outlawed and isolated by the peoples of the world' because of racial oppression. There is no identification of the actual oppressors. Mandela's rhetoric unites South Africans against the abstract and unidentified 'blood-thirsty forces', but again, there is no reference to who they may be. What's more, despite their mutual dislike, he singles out De Klerk as one of the leaders in South Africa's 'glorious' achievement. (Mandela was later even more lavish in his praise. When he visited the crowd on the Union Buildings lawn, he raised De Klerk's hand aloft and hailed him as 'one of the greatest reformers, one of the greatest sons of our soil'.[11])

Surprisingly, the speech posits the divisive issue of land as the force that connects all South Africans. '[E]ach one of us is ... intimately attached to the soil of this beautiful country,' says Mandela, using the word 'soil' several times and infusing the speech with references to jacaranda and mimosa trees, grass turning green and flowers blooming. The overall suggestion is that, after a tumultuous storm, South Africa's return to humanity's 'bosom' has restored the natural order of things.

'These were Mandela's finest words since his speech from the dock at the Rivonia Trial in 1964,' Mark Gevisser later said of the speech, before pointing out that they were actually written by Thabo Mbeki.[12] Increasingly, in his role as deputy president, Mbeki would script some of Mandela's 'greatest "performances" of reconciliation'.[13] Memorably, and echoing Mandela's praise of the Afrikaner woman in his Hani address, it was Mbeki who suggested that Mandela open his first State of the Nation Address two weeks later with the Afrikaans poem 'Die Kind' by Ingrid Jonker. In describing Jonker as 'an Afrikaner woman who transcended a particular experience and became a South African, an African and a citizen of the world',[14] Mandela opened his arms to Afrikaners who might have felt alienated by the new government.

Nothing symbolised the forgiveness and harmony of his presidency more powerfully than the metaphor of the rainbow. Drawing on Tutu's prior utterances, the inauguration speech is the first in which he uses this central metaphor: we are 'a rainbow nation at peace with itself and the world',

Mandela declares. The rainbow perfectly symbolises both reconciliation and the ideal of 'unity in diversity', another trope of the post-apartheid nation. The metaphor harks back to the biblical story of Noah, in which the rainbow symbolised God's rainbow covenant never to wreak vengeance on the world again. The lines 'Never again will all life be destroyed by the waters of a flood; never again will there be a flood to destroy the earth'[15] are echoed in Mandela's own covenant: 'Never, never and never again shall it be that this beautiful land will again experience the oppression of one by another'.

The speech concluded with a navy-band rendition of the national anthem, 'Die Stem van Suid-Afrika', followed by the anthem-in-waiting, 'Nkosi Sikelel' iAfrika', the once-banned song of the ANC. For Mandela, the day was symbolised by the vision of black and white South Africans singing these anthems. 'Although that day neither group knew the lyrics of the anthem they once despised, they would soon know the words by heart,'[16] he reflected hopefully in his autobiography. As the audience sang, South African Air Force planes soared overhead, trailing rainbow-hued smoke in a visual celebration of the new president's words.

South Africans enjoyed a new and shared sense of national pride, with newspapers declaring, after years of isolation: 'We're on top of the world'[17] and 'The World [is] at Mandela's Feet'.[18] Similarly, the international media revelled in the miracles of the day, noting the many ironies of the occasion: the Muslim and Hindu prayers in the formerly Calvinist Christian country, the navy band playing Zulu migrant-worker songs, the appearance of Fidel Castro as a guest,[19] and, not least, the sight of Mandela, former prisoner, now president.

Nomonde Calata and Nyameka Goniwe
Testimony at the Truth and Reconciliation Commission,
East London, 16–17 April 1996

While Mandela's inauguration speech wished away the conflict of the past, in reality the past was not so easily transcended. There were two issues that haunted the fledgling government. One was the question of amnesty, for perpetrators from both sides of the political spectrum. On the one hand, there were still many political prisoners whose freedom had not been negotiated, and there were also new convictions in the violent run-up to the election; on the other, the foot soldiers of apartheid, many of whom had committed brutal acts, feared prosecution under the new dispensation. To resolve this problem, at the eleventh hour, the Interim Constitution of 1993 included a controversial amnesty clause, promising that 'amnesty shall be granted in respect of acts, omissions, offences associated with political objectives'.[1]

At the same time, there were also calls for a truth commission to uncover the full details of the past. What had really happened to those who died in detention? Where were the missing sons, brothers and fathers who hadn't returned from ANC camps after 1990? And who gave the orders for the many acts of torture and oppression? There were many unanswered questions.

In 1989, when a death-row prisoner and former security policeman, Almond Nofomela, told journalists that he'd worked as a hit man for the state, Max du Preez and Jacques Pauw's anti-apartheid publication *Vrye Weekblad* went on to expose the existence of a covert death squad called Vlakplaas. To investigate, De Klerk set up the one-man Harms Commission, and the judge's report quashed the claims, concluding that the journalists' sources were untrustworthy, but the public was dissatisfied with this outcome, rightly suspecting that other policemen had lied during the inquiry.

The ANC's self-appointed inquiry into the treatment of former ANC prisoners and detainees, the Skweyiya Commission, was similarly deemed inadequate, since it relied on witnesses' willingness to come forward, it had poorly conceived terms of reference and its work wasn't public. It ended up being perceived by some as an 'official fudge'.[2]

A fuller investigation was needed, leading to the establishment of the Truth and Reconciliation Commission (TRC), which was mandated to uncover 'as complete a picture as possible of the nature, causes and extent of gross violations of human rights'[3] that had occurred between 1960 and 1993. In addition, the Commission had to make a call on individual amnesty applications, granting it in cases of politically motivated acts on condition that the applicant told the full truth and that the act was not disproportional to the political aim. The hope was that perpetrators, fearing prosecution, would come forward and offer hitherto unknown information about the past. Lastly, the TRC was asked to recommend suitable reparations for victims. It was a mammoth task, which turned out to be larger than anybody expected, and it took several years for the Commission to complete its work.

Mandela appointed Desmond Tutu as chairperson and Alex Boraine as his deputy, and the rest of the Commission was made up of publicly nominated individuals from a variety of language, gender and racial groups. Despite the attempt to ensure non-partisan leadership, the Commission was hugely controversial. Many Afrikaners feared that it would devolve into a witch-hunt; the IFP, still seething after recent clashes with the ANC, actively discouraged its members from participating; and others, such as the family of Steve Biko, rejected the whole basis of amnesty, taking the Commission to court to test its constitutionality. The day before the first hearing, a bomb scare threatened to derail proceedings.

The Commission began with the work of the Human Rights Violations Committee, which gathered accounts from victims of gross human rights violations. In a departure from the work of previous truth commissions, the South African hearings were open to the public, and willing and representative participants were asked to come forward to tell their stories. Given broad media attention, with extensive coverage and live radio broadcasting for a full year, the work of the TRC pervaded South African public life for two years.

The first week of hearings in East London in April 1996 was deeply painful, as the country heard heart-rending stories from the widows of the PEBCO Three and Cradock Four, whose husbands had been abducted and murdered in the 1980s. Nohle Mohape, whose husband had died in detention in 1976, also spoke, as did the widower of Jeanette Schoon, who had lost his wife and six-year-old daughter to a letter bomb in Angola. When Singqokwana Ernest Malgas recounted the excruciating torture that he had experienced at the hands of the security police, Tutu held his head in his hands and wept.

The moment that would symbolise the Commission's work came from Nomonde Calata, the widow of Fort Calata, one of the Cradock Four. The four men – the others were Sparrow Mkhonto, Sicelo Mhlauli and Matthew Goniwe – had disappeared in 1985 while travelling between Port Elizabeth and Cradock, and their burnt and mutilated bodies were found a week later.

Although the story of their deaths was well known, there was still much interest in the case. The apartheid authorities had blamed the killings on an 'internecine power struggle between opposing radical organizations'[4] – a claim that was rubbished in 1992 when the newspaper *New Nation* published a top-secret message from military intelligence calling for their 'permanent removal from society'. Despite this, and two inquests into the deaths, nobody had ever been arrested.

On the second day of hearings, the East London City Hall was packed – with an audience of around 1000 people. Calata faced the commissioners, who were seated on stage, framed by the South African flag and a massive banner declaring 'Truth and Reconciliation Commission: Healing Our Past'. Speaking in Xhosa, Calata recalled the confusion of her husband's disappearance.

> We started to feel very unhappy and uneasy, we were really in the dark.
> We slept uneasily on Friday as we did not know what happened to our
> husbands. Usually the *Herald* was delivered at home because I was
> distributing it. During the time that it was delivered I looked at the
> headlines and one of the children said that he could see that his father's
> car was shown in the paper as being burnt. At that moment I was
> trembling because I was afraid of what might have happened to my
> husband, because I wondered: if his car was burned like this, what might
> have happened to him? I started distributing the papers as usual, but I was
> very unhappy. After a few hours some friends came in and took me and
> said I must go to Nyami [Nyameka Goniwe], who was always supportive.
> I was still twenty at the time and couldn't handle this. When I got to
> Nyami's place, Nyami was crying terribly and this affected me also.

At this point, Calata released an anguished wail of pain, described later by Antjie Krog in *Country of My Skull*, her powerful account of the hearings, as the real 'beginning of the Truth Commission – the signature tune, the definitive moment, the ultimate sound of what the process is about ... that sound ... it will haunt me for ever and ever'.[5] Proceedings were briefly paused, giving Calata a chance to compose herself. In the interim, Tutu led the audience in a rendition of the struggle dirge '*Senzeni na?*' ('What have we done?')

The following day, Calata's testimony was followed up with that of Nyameka Goniwe, the widow of Matthew Goniwe. He was the most prominent of the four Cradock men. Loved by his community as a popular school principal, who 'churned out matric pupils with As and Bs in science and mathematics',[6] he was hated by the authorities for leading one of the most potent resistance campaigns. His funeral in 1985, attended by UDF patrons Allan Boesak, Beyers Naudé and Steve Tshwete, was a galvanising moment in the struggle and was followed by a partial state of emergency.

Although the convention was for commissioners to guide witnesses through their testimony with questions, Nyameka Goniwe had waited ten years to have her say and had prepared a full statement in advance. She asked to read it without interruption and went on to describe her relationship with her husband, his gradual politicisation and subsequent harassment, and, finally, the events leading up to his death.

On a Monday the 24th of June 1985, Matthew telephoned the secretary of the UDF of the Eastern Cape Region, Derek Swarts, informing him that he won't be coming to the usual Wednesday meeting due to other commitments, but will be coming for a briefing on the 27th of June 1985 instead. He made a second telephone on the 27th of June 1985 to confirm that he was coming. Both conversations were taped by the security police and a transcript of these telephones was produced as evidence during the second inquest. This confirms what we long suspected, that Matthew's movements were closely monitored for 24 hours, in fact on the day he left for Port Elizabeth, with his friends and colleagues, his movements were monitored.

On the 27th of June 1985 he left for Port Elizabeth in the company of his friends, Fort Calata, Sicelo Mhlawuli, and Sparrow Mkhonto and that was the last time we saw them. They were due back on the same night and when they did not come back, we knew that something serious had happened. Early in the morning of the next day, I telephoned the UDF offices in Port Elizabeth, I also phoned Derek Swart and Molly Blackburn, to establish their whereabouts. Derek Swart informed me that Matthew left with his friends for Cradock the previous night of the 27th of June 1985 at about 9 p.m. You can imagine the shock, and I shivered to think what might have happened to these comrades.

I kept the news secret for a while from all the families, excepting my brother-in-law who was planning what to do next. The brother-in-law, Alex and I, we picked up a few activists and went and looked for them. We decided to drive towards Port Elizabeth, and on our way we stopped over at Cookhouse and Bedford police stations, to check whether they have seen them, but we drew a blank.

I just want to say something mysterious happened then, well not mysterious but very interesting. As we approached the police station, of course they didn't know who we were up and till my brother-in-law identified himself. Immediately their whole mood changed and all the young police officers stood on guard, just in front of the door and we asked them whether they had seen them. And they said that the last time they saw them was at 12 o'clock the previous day. And that also made us to wonder, because the police station in Cookhouse is far from the National Road. Something clicked, it could be through their monitoring network that they picked up that Matthew was passing by at about that time.

A similar search party looked for them in the Port Elizabeth area with no result. We drove [to] Patterson and returned back home. On arrival at home we were informed that the police had phoned, they left a message with a child, my brother-in-law's son, to inform the family that Matthew's burnt car had been found near the Scribante Racing Course outside Port Elizabeth. Immediately we knew that something serious had happened.

Of course we had pointers because in May, you know, the PEBCO Three had disappeared without a trace. Relatives and the Community were informed and some members of the family had to go to Port Elizabeth to establish what had happened. It was this group that also assisted the families to identify the bodies later on. So I alerted the press, the national media, international media and everybody of influence to try and put pressure onto the police authorities, or the government to produce them. Of course, during those days anything could have happened, I mean we thought of detentions, whatever.

The community immediately embarked on a school and a shop boycott to add more pressure on to the government. On Saturday the 29th June 1985, the bodies of Sparrow Mkhonto and Sicelo Mhlauli were found first and those of Matthew and Fort were found on the 2nd of July 1985. All the bodies had multiple stab wounds and were badly burned.

Our lawyers during the second inquest argued that Matthew was monitored for 24 hours, a factor that was confirmed by Winter and Snyman, who was regional head of the security branch of the Eastern Cape at the town station in Port Elizabeth during cross-examination. He couldn't have slipped the police monitoring networks. Whatever befell him on that night of the 27th was known to the police and they killed him.

We have stated why we believe that Matthew had to die. We think that it was because he was seen as a person who was responsible for the collapse of the community councils discipline in Lingalishle. We also think that he was also held responsible for disrupting the schools by instigating the students to engage in school boycotts and for the resignation of all school communities in Cradock. He was also accused for mobilising the people of Cradock and the neighbouring towns under the banner of the then banned ANC. They hated him for raising the level of political awareness of people in the rural areas. He was seen as a communist, a terrorist and therefore a dangerous man, who was a threat to the state.

Goniwe's testimony concluded with questions from commissioners and committee members:

Mr Smith: Now you realise of course that it's quite possible for persons to come forward and to actually admit to the killing of your husband and to apply for amnesty to one of the committees of this Commission. What would be your attitude to that? How would you feel towards these people if they were in fact identified and that you were to know that these are the people who are responsible for the brutal slaying of your husband?

Mrs Goniwe: Well, I look forward to that. I mean I know it's difficult after suffering such pain and trauma. But we need to know what happened and who they are, and also, I mean they have to ... need to show some remorse.

Mr Smith: Are you saying that just coming forward and applying for amnesty would not be sufficient, that you would also maybe require a person to show remorse for what they have done?

Mrs Goniwe: Yes. They have to show us remorse, that they're sorry for what they did. I don't say that I mean it would immediately make us happy; it's a challenge, we're going to be challenged in that kind of way, and grapple with that, inside and it will take a long time. Healing takes a long time.

Goniwe's testimony, in contrast with Calata's, is remarkably composed. Speaking in English, her factual and lucid statement illustrated the extent to which she had stored up and pieced together the details of her husband's story, preparing for its eventual investigation. If given the chance, she would have made an excellent witness in court. One of the Commission's greatest achievements was its provision of a platform for narratives that had previously been silenced. Inviting victims to come forward to tell their stories to the world served as an acknowledgement of their pain, and it differed markedly from the treatment meted out to them in police stations and courtrooms under apartheid. At the TRC hearings, new legitimacy was bestowed upon them: they could choose their language for testimony, a professional counsellor was on hand to comfort them in the process, and their stories were considered important enough to be included in the evening news.

Like many TRC participants, Goniwe wanted the perpetrators to express some form of remorse – the sincerity of which is of course impossible to judge. For this reason, 'saying sorry' was not a condition for amnesty, although it was widely perceived as one because, under Tutu's guidance, victims and perpetrators were encouraged to reconcile. The family of the Cradock Four were all asked about their preparedness to forgive the perpetrators, which was a case of putting the cart before the horse – as the daughter of Sicelo Mhlauli pointed out: 'I mean we don't know who to forgive, we don't know the killers, you know ...'[7]

Embracing the TRC's focus on restorative justice, Goniwe appeared to want answers more than retribution. The desire for information was a heartfelt request in most victims' testimonies. Sindiswa Mkhonto, widow of Sparrow Mkhonto, implored the Commission to 'establish who did this to my husband',[8] while Nomonde Calata hoped, in the spirit of the proceedings, that information would bring closure: 'If I can know the individuals who are responsible for this,' she said, 'I will be able to understand why they did it.'[9] Most distressingly, Nombuyiselo Mhlauli's main concern seemed to be her husband's missing hand. His body had been found with the right hand hacked off, and there were rumours that it was kept in a bottle in Major Graham Lombard's office to terrorise detainees. 'Even if I say these people should be given amnesty, it won't return my husband,' the widow testified, 'but that hand, we still want it. We know we have buried them, but really to have the hand which is said to be in a bottle in Port Elizabeth, we would like to get the hand.'[10]

Yet, although the Commission's truth-for-amnesty model was partially successful in uncovering new information, many cases remained unsolved. Over 22 000 victim statements were recorded, which was poorly matched by the 7 116 amnesty applications for some 14 000 incidents. What's more, many of these came from prisoners who were already serving sentences.

The case of the Cradock Four was an exception, and in January 1997 the details of several applications were leaked to the media. The applicants were all white Afrikaner security policemen,[11] who confessed to abducting and murdering the Cradock leaders at St George's Beach in Port Elizabeth under instruction. Some claimed responsibility for giving orders; others confessed to carrying them out. Eugene de Kock, the notorious former commander of

Vlakplaas, applied for his role in helping with the cover-up of the killings. Their case was heard in February 1998, two years after the victims' testimony, and the men, looking fearful rather than remorseful, did not, according to the Commission, make a 'good impression as witnesses'.[12] In comparison with Nyameka Goniwe's statement, their testimony was hazy, full of uncertainty. They couldn't recall details and spoke, as one applicant continually put it, 'under correction'.[13]

Claiming to be influenced by the situation in the townships in 1984 and 1985, when there was 'absolutely no law and order' in the so-called 'liberated zones … where alternative structures had been established to supplant the legal governmental structures',[14] General Nic Janse van Rensburg confessed to planning the operation, under instruction from Colonel Harold Snyman (who was ill with cancer and therefore absent from the hearing). The general said he believed that assassination was the only solution to the unrest in the area and that 'it was in the interests of the country and the state'.[15]

It fell to twenty-four-year-old Warrant Officer Gerhard Lotz to fulfil the order to kill Goniwe, and he claimed partial responsibility, testifying that he *might* have been responsible for killing him. 'I took one of the persons out of the vehicle while he was still cuffed and made him walk ahead of me,' Lotz confessed. 'I had a steel spring with me which I brought along. While the person walked ahead of me, I hit him on the back of the head with the spring, after which he appeared to be unconscious or dead, he wasn't moving …' Lotz went on to claim that 'the black members then stabbed the person with knives', referring to three black sergeants whose assistance in the case led to their own murder in the 1989 Motherwell bombing. Goniwe's murder, the commissioners pointed out in their cross-examination, sounded far more 'humane' and 'civilised' than some of the evidence suggested.[16]

Lotz's apology, unsurprisingly, was woefully inadequate: 'After the facts, the only thing that remains to be said is: I am sorry about what happened,' he stated, and 'I believe that today the family will surely hate me for what I have done.'[17] The Commission was not satisfied and deemed the testimony of all but one of the applicants insufficient. Only De Kock, who participated in the cover-up, was granted amnesty, leaving the others open to prosecution. It seemed justice would be served.

But by 2008, there had still been no arrests in respect of the murders, and the case continued to fester. The National Prosecuting Authority (NPA) had simply failed to follow up on the incidents, so, in frustration, the Cradock Four widows, together with similarly disillusioned parties, took them and the perpetrators to the High Court. The afterlife of the Commission has been disappointing, to say the least, both because of the state's failure to prosecute perpetrators and because of the belated and meagre reparations that were handed out to victims after the conclusion of the hearings.

When, in March 2016, the fifty-six-year-old Gerhard Lotz shot himself in his Framesby home in Port Elizabeth, the case was resurrected again. Lukhanyo Calata, son of Fort Calata, came forward with a plea to the remaining killers: 'Come and tell us the truth. We don't want you prosecuted, we don't harbour ill feelings towards you, all we want is you to come forward and tell us what happened, that you're sorry. Even if you're not sorry, just come forward and tell us what happened.'[18]

Thabo Mbeki

'I am an African', statement on the occasion
of the Constitution's adoption,
Parliament, 8 May 1996

During his presidency, Nelson Mandela left much of the day-to-day running
of the country to his right-hand man, Thabo Mbeki – Oliver Tambo's former
protégé, who had so impressed Slabbert in 1986. Mbeki, perhaps more than
any other ANC leader, understood how to position the organisation favourably in the eyes of the West, which counted in the country's favour when it
came to attracting investment in the post-apartheid period. He had completed
a master's degree in economics at the University of Sussex in 1968 and became
Tambo's political secretary a decade later. This was a position more powerful
than its official title suggested[1] and, in Jacob Zuma's perhaps envious view, it
was given to Mbeki because of his superior 'drafting skills'.[2] Within the ANC,
Mbeki was quietly powerful, always acting on the mandate of the president,
which drew both respect and envy from his comrades.[3]

Mbeki was also one of the first ANC leaders to be introduced to white
South Africans. The year after his first meeting with Slabbert, he led a delegation of sixteen ANC members to Dakar, Senegal, to meet with a group of
progressives from IDASA, many of whom were Afrikaners. The Dakar talks
were widely reported as a groundbreaking success, and the mutually affection-
ate relationship between Slabbert and Mbeki held promise for South Africa's
future. In 1989, Mbeki was appointed as head of the ANC's Department of
International Affairs. After he returned from exile in 1990, he helped to set
up meetings between the ANC and white captains of industry, and, given his
political lineage, he was frequently described as the ANC's 'crown prince' and
the presidential 'heir apparent'.

On a one-on-one basis, and to smaller audiences, Mbeki's charm was
legendary. Journalist Max du Preez remembers him from Dakar as 'charming,
smiling, generous, warm, straightforward',[4] and in the years to come he would
frequently long for the Mbeki he had encountered there.[5] But to the general
public, the urbane, pipe-smoking Mbeki appeared distant and aloof. As an
exile, he would always strain to transcend the image of the outsider 'black
Englishman',[6] and he lacked the mass appeal of leaders who'd borne the brunt
of the struggle under apartheid – rivals such as Cyril Ramaphosa, the powerful trade unionist (whom Mandela had initially favoured for the position of

deputy president),[7] and Chris Hani, the brave MK soldier. As William Gumede points out, no struggle songs were ever written in Mbeki's honour.[8] In the lead-up to 1994, when he'd squared off against Pik Botha as part of a series of pre-election debates, his constituency felt that his gentlemanly performance had been 'too nice'.[9]

Unlike Mandela, the celebrity politician, Mbeki was also media shy and lacked the common touch. So while Mandela took on a figurehead leadership role, focusing on nation-building and reconciliation, Mbeki increasingly played 'prime minister', writing many of Mandela's speeches, undertaking committee work and often chairing cabinet meetings when the president was abroad.[10] By 1997, Mandela told a London audience that 'the ruler of South Africa, the de facto ruler, is Thabo Mbeki. I am shifting everything to him.'[11]

Perhaps the moment when Mbeki first stepped out of Madiba's long shadow came with the ratification of the Constitution two years into Mandela's presidency. The event was considered the pinnacle of an extraordinary achievement. After years of negotiation and unprecedented public participation, the 140-page document established a federal system with a strong presidency and a two-chamber legislature. The Bill of Rights, considered to be among the most progressive in the world, was particularly applauded because of its inclusion of additional human rights that were seldom wholly fulfilled: the right to housing, health care, water, food and education.

Mbeki, who'd crafted so many speeches for others, wrote and delivered the ANC's official statement for the occasion. His 'I am an African' speech captured the imagination of the nation and prepared the ground for his vision of an African Renaissance. Some even believed that the speech would come to have the 'same force for contemporary South Africans as Nelson Mandela's Rivonia Trial speech had for his generation'.[12] Delivered to a joint sitting of Parliament on 8 May 1996, the speech's opening declaration drew much applause.

Chairperson,
Esteemed President of the democratic Republic,
Honourable Members of the Constitutional Assembly,
Our distinguished domestic and foreign guests,
Friends,

On an occasion such as this, we should, perhaps, start from the beginning.
So, let me begin.

I am an African.

I owe my being to the hills and the valleys, the mountains and the glades, the rivers, the deserts, the trees, the flowers, the seas and the ever-changing seasons that define the face of our native land.

My body has frozen in our frosts and in our latter day snows. It has thawed in the warmth of our sunshine and melted in the heat of the midday sun. The crack and the rumble of the summer thunders, lashed by startling lightning, have been a cause both of trembling and of hope.

The fragrances of nature have been as pleasant to us as the sight of the wild blooms of the citizens of the veld.

The dramatic shapes of the Drakensberg, the soil-coloured waters of the Lekoa, iGqili noThukela, and the sands of the Kgalagadi, have all been panels of the set on the natural stage on which we act out the foolish deeds of the theatre of our day.

At times, and in fear, I have wondered whether I should concede equal citizenship of our country to the leopard and the lion, the elephant and the springbok, the hyena, the black mamba and the pestilential mosquito.

A human presence among all these, a feature on the face of our native land thus defined, I know that none dare challenge me when I say – I am an African!

I owe my being to the Khoi and the San whose desolate souls haunt the great expanses of the beautiful Cape – they who fell victim to the most merciless genocide our native land has ever seen, they who were the first to lose their lives in the struggle to defend our freedom and dependence and they who, as a people, perished in the result.

Today, as a country, we keep an audible silence about these ancestors of the generations that live, fearful to admit the horror of a former deed, seeking to obliterate from our memories a cruel occurrence which, in its remembering, should teach us not and never to be inhuman again.

I am formed of the migrants who left Europe to find a new home on our native land. Whatever their own actions, they remain still, part of me.

In my veins courses the blood of the Malay slaves who came from the East. Their proud dignity informs my bearing, their culture a part of my essence. The stripes they bore on their bodies from the lash of the slave master are a reminder embossed on my consciousness of what should not be done.

I am the grandchild of the warrior men and women that Hintsa and Sekhukhune led, the patriots that Cetshwayo and Mphephu took to battle, the soldiers Moshoeshoe and Ngungunyane taught never to dishonour the cause of freedom.

My mind and my knowledge of myself is formed by the victories that are the jewels in our African crown, the victories we earned from Isandhlwana to Khartoum, as Ethiopians and as the Ashanti of Ghana, as the Berbers of the desert.

I am the grandchild who lays fresh flowers on the Boer graves at St Helena and the Bahamas, who sees in the mind's eye and suffers the suffering of a simple peasant folk, death, concentration camps, destroyed homesteads, a dream in ruins.

I am the child of Nongqause. I am he who made it possible to trade in the world markets in diamonds, in gold, in the same food for which my stomach yearns.

I come of those who were transported from India and China, whose being resided in the fact, solely, that they were able to provide physical labour, who taught me that we could both be at home and be foreign, who taught me that human existence itself demanded that freedom was a necessary condition for that human existence.

Being part of all these people, and in the knowledge that none dare contest that assertion, I shall claim that – I am an African.

I have seen our country torn asunder as these, all of whom are my people, engaged one another in a titanic battle, the one redress a wrong that had been caused by one to another and the other, to defend the indefensible.

I have seen what happens when one person has superiority of force over another, when the stronger appropriate to themselves the prerogative even to annul the injunction that God created all men and women in His image.

I know what it signifies when race and colour are used to determine who is human and who, subhuman.

I have seen the destruction of all sense of self-esteem, the consequent striving to be what one is not, simply to acquire some of the benefits which those who had improved themselves as masters had ensured that they enjoy.

I have experience of the situation in which race and colour is used to enrich some and impoverish the rest.

I have seen the corruption of minds and souls in the pursuit of an ignoble effort to perpetrate a veritable crime against humanity.

I have seen concrete expression of the denial of the dignity of a human being emanating from the conscious, systemic and systematic oppressive and repressive activities of other human beings.

There the victims parade with no mask to hide the brutish reality – the beggars, the prostitutes, the street children, those who seek solace in substance abuse, those who have to steal to assuage hunger, those who have to lose their sanity because to be sane is to invite pain.

Perhaps the worst among these, who are my people, are those who have learnt to kill for a wage. To these the extent of death is directly proportional to their personal welfare.

And so, like pawns in the service of demented souls, they kill in furtherance of the political violence in KwaZulu-Natal. They murder the innocent in the taxi wars.

They kill slowly or quickly in order to make profits from the illegal trade in narcotics. They are available for hire when husband wants to murder wife and wife, husband.

Among us prowl the products of our immoral and amoral past – killers who have no sense of the worth of human life, rapists who have absolute disdain for the women of our country, animals who would seek to benefit from the vulnerability of the children, the disabled and the old, the rapacious who brook no obstacle in their quest for self-enrichment.

All this I know and know to be true because I am an African!

Because of that, I am also able to state this fundamental truth that I am born of a people who are heroes and heroines.

I am born of a people who would not tolerate oppression.

I am of a nation that would not allow that fear of death, torture, imprisonment, exile or persecution should result in the perpetuation of injustice.

The great masses who are our mother and father will not permit that the behaviour of the few results in the description of our country and people as barbaric.

Patient because history is on their side, these masses do not despair because today the weather is bad.

Nor do they turn triumphalist when, tomorrow, the sun shines.

Whatever the circumstances they have lived through and because of that experience, they are determined to define for themselves who they are and who they should be.

We are assembled here today to mark their victory in acquiring and exercising their right to formulate their own definition of what it means to be African.

The constitution whose adoption we celebrate constitutes an unequivocal statement that we refuse to accept that our Africanness shall be defined by our race, colour, gender or historical origins.

It is a firm assertion made by ourselves that South Africa belongs to all who live in it, black and white.

It gives concrete expression to the sentiment we share as Africans, and will defend to the death, that the people shall govern.

It recognises the fact that the dignity of the individual is both an objective which society must pursue, and is a goal which cannot be separated from the material well-being of that individual.

It seeks to create the situation in which all our people shall be free from fear, including the fear of the oppression of one national group by another, the fear of the disempowerment of one social echelon by another, the fear of the use of state power to deny anybody their fundamental human rights and the fear of tyranny.

It aims to open the doors so that those who were disadvantaged can assume their place in society as equals with their fellow human beings without regard to colour, race, gender, age or geographic dispersal.

It provides the opportunity to enable each one and all to state their views, promote them, strive for their implementation in the process of governance without fear that a contrary view will be met with repression.

It creates a law-governed society which shall be inimical to arbitrary rule.

It enables the resolution of conflicts by peaceful means rather than resort to force.

It rejoices in the diversity of our people and creates the space for all of us voluntarily to define ourselves as one people.

As an African, this is an achievement of which I am proud, proud without reservation and proud without any feeling of conceit.

Our sense of elevation at this moment also derives from the fact that this magnificent product is the unique creation of African hands and African minds.

But it also constitutes a tribute to our loss of vanity that we could, despite the temptation to treat ourselves as an exceptional fragment of humanity, draw on the accumulated experience and wisdom of all humankind, to define for ourselves what we want to be.

Together with the best in the world, we too are prone to pettiness, petulance, selfishness and shortsightedness.

But it seems to have happened that we looked at ourselves and said the time had come that we make a super-human effort to be other than human, to respond to the call to create for ourselves a glorious future, to remind ourselves of the Latin saying: Gloria est consequenda – Glory must be sought after!

Today it feels good to be an African.

It feels good that I can stand here as a South African and as a foot soldier of a titanic African army, the African National Congress, to say to all the parties represented here, to the millions who made an input into the processes we are concluding, to our outstanding compatriots who have presided over the birth of our founding document, to the negotiators who pitted their wits one against the other, to the unseen stars who shone unseen as the management and administration of the Constitutional Assembly, the advisers, experts and publicists, to the mass communication media, to our friends across the globe – congratulations and well done!

I am an African.

I am born of the peoples of the continent of Africa.

The pain of the violent conflict that the peoples of Liberia, Somalia, the Sudan, Burundi and Algeria is a pain I also bear.

The dismal shame of poverty, suffering and human degradation of my continent is a blight that we share.

The blight on our happiness that derives from this and from our drift to the periphery of the ordering of human affairs leaves us in a persistent shadow of despair.

This is a savage road to which nobody should be condemned.

This thing that we have done today, in this small corner of a great continent that has contributed so decisively to the evolution of humanity says that Africa reaffirms that she is continuing her rise from the ashes.

Whatever the setbacks of the moment, nothing can stop us now!

Whatever the difficulties, Africa shall be at peace!

However improbable it may sound to the sceptics, Africa will prosper!

Whoever we may be, whatever our immediate interest, however much we carry baggage from our past, however much we have been caught by the fashion of cynicism and loss of faith in the capacity of the people, let us err today and say – nothing can stop us now!

Thank you.

Mbeki's landmark speech is often mistakenly referred to as a poem, most likely because, as Stephen Grootes points out, 'it was a speech made by the writing'.[13]

Indeed, the words of 'I am an African' are surely among the most lyrical ever delivered in Parliament. While Mbeki spoke, Mandela, seated to his right, appeared visibly entranced, and the audience, unsure of how to respond to such unusually literary language, eventually gave up on applauding and allowed Mbeki to speak virtually uninterrupted until the end of the speech. Gumede points out that Mbeki was 'an intellectual at heart' and 'never an inspiring public speaker',[14] but this instance stands as a rare exception. Although perhaps ineffective in the rough-and-tumble environment of the mass political rally, he appears perfectly at home in the hallowed halls of Parliament, and his perfectly timed delivery did justice to the poetic words.

In seeking to answer the question of what it means to be African, Mbeki sets the scene with a quasi-biblical reference: 'On an occasion such as this, we should, perhaps, start from the beginning. So, let me begin.' He goes on to invoke Genesis through recounting the elements, followed by the animal life and, finally, the various histories of southern Africa,[15] thus establishing an epic resonance for the address.

This mythic mode is emphasised by the speech's broad geographical and historical scope. It roves from the 'dramatic shapes of the Drakensberg' to the 'Berbers of the desert' in North Africa, and it dives back in time to the Basotho and Xhosa kingdoms of Moshoeshoe and Hintsa. Love for the land courses through the address – as in Mandela's inauguration speech, this is what unites Africans – but here it is expressed in decidedly Romantic intonations. The speaker's wonderment at nature is evident in the 'trembling' and 'hope' evoked by the 'crack and the rumble of the summer thunders' and nature provides the ever-present backdrop, the 'natural stage on which we act out the foolish deeds of the theatre of our day'.

The speech, like the Constitution it launches, offers a visually rich illustration of the Freedom Charter's assertion that 'South Africa belongs to all who live in it, black and white', but Mbeki embraces an inclusive form of African nationalism by extending the borders of South Africa to incorporate the entire continent, and the racial identities of black and white to include Khoi and San, Malay, Chinese, Indian, European migrant and Boer, as well as the flora and fauna of the African environment – listing even the 'pestilential mosquito', which drew tittered amusement from the audience.

As he was when penning Mandela's inauguration speech, Mbeki is careful to subsume the potentially divisive past in metaphor and allusion. There are no direct references to past aggressors, and descriptions of the natural world stand in for human conflict. The 'frosts' and 'snows' refer to the old South Africa, while the current context is 'thawed in the warmth of our sunshine'.[16]

Contrastingly, the conflicts of the present are more accurately identified, and for this reason they jar somewhat with the use of understatement and metaphor that otherwise fill the speech. Here, Mbeki singles out the 'taxi wars', the continuing (although abating) political violence in KwaZulu-Natal and the drug trade that characterised the early 1990s.

With reference to past aggressions, the most damning assertion comes with his reconciliatory allusion to the deeds of former European colonialists. Described as 'migrants who left Europe' rather than as colonialists, Mbeki says of them: 'Whatever their own actions, they remain still, part of me.' He goes on to inscribe his own personhood into the identities of all those connected to the African continent. As Thiven Reddy points out, 'Mbeki does not say the past experiences merely "influence", or that he "recognises" or "embraces" these: he is emphatic that he is a *product* of these experiences.'[17] 'I am formed of the migrants who left Europe,' says Mbeki, and 'I am the grandchild who lays fresh flowers on the Boer graves'. This is a profound avowal of the African concept of ubuntu: the African humanist philosophy popularised by Desmond Tutu and distilled in the expression 'I am what I am because of who we all are.'[18] Part of what constitutes being African, Mbeki suggests, is ubuntu. 'I owe my being to the Khoi and the San,' he intones, and 'In my veins courses the blood of the Malay slaves'. With this philosophy, the histories of slavery, colonialism and Boer suffering, as well as the 'conflict [of] the peoples of Liberia, Somalia, the Sudan, Burundi and Algeria', become shared pains. These collective histories have all contributed to the historic formation of the 'magnificent product', the Constitution, crafted by 'African hands and African minds' as defined in the speech.

The line 'I am an African', repeated as a lilting leitmotif throughout the speech, draws power from a host of earlier utterances. Most notably perhaps, Mbeki echoes John F. Kennedy's famous speech '*Ich bin ein Berliner*' ('I am a Berliner'),[19] delivered in 1963 as an expression of solidarity to West Berliners after the erection of the Berlin Wall. Some in the audience might also recognise Mbeki's self-reference to an address made in Dakar nearly ten years earlier. In an introduction to the group of progressive but reportedly nervous whites, he disarmed his (mainly) Afrikaner audience with a similar declaration of shared identity: 'My name is Thabo Mbeki,' he said. 'I am an Afrikaner.' 'Afrikaner' is of course the Dutch derivative of 'African',[20] and Mbeki merged his own identity into that of his audience – as if to say, 'We are one and the same.' It was, as Richard Calland points out, 'a brilliant piece of diplomacy and by most accounts it not so much cut the ice as melted the iceberg'.[21]

Some would also be familiar with the reference to an earlier speech given by lawyer Pixley ka Isaka Seme, the founder of the ANC.[22] Speaking at Columbia University in the United States in 1906, Seme won the George William Curtis Medal for oratory. Titled 'The Regeneration of Africa', Seme's speech, which opens with the line 'I am an African, and I set my pride in my race over against a hostile public opinion', appears to have influenced both Mbeki's 1996 address and the African Renaissance project that would come to define his presidency, which began when Mandela stepped down in 1999.

Mbeki's ambitious vision for the African Renaissance differed from Mandela's popular 'scattershot'[23] rainbow nationalism in that the ANC formally and enthusiastically adopted it as a strategic task in 1997. Influenced by the liberation slogan *'Mayibuye iAfrica'* ('Let Africa return'),[24] it entered public discourse via a series of workshops and conferences across the continent[25] and was realised in political initiatives such as NEPAD (New Partnership for Africa's Development). Mbeki sought to accelerate socio-political, economic, moral and cultural renewal in Africa, with a particular focus on eradicating debt and reincorporating the continent into the global economy. Inspired by Africanists such as Anton Lembede, as well as by the Black Consciousness Movement, his vision emphasised self-reliance: he wanted 'to persuade Africa to set up its own institutions and mechanisms for solving its problems, thus ending the constant, humiliating requests for aid to the West's former colonial powers'.[26] Upon his return from exile, he'd reportedly been shocked by the 'pathological self-hate of black South Africans' and wanted the continent to free itself from the shackles of this 'slave mentality'.[27]

It was a hope-filled and glorious vision. After decades of colonial oppression, the post-colonial era had not delivered on the promises made by liberation movements, and the prospect of an era of blossoming growth across the continent was as seductive as Mbeki himself. It was also, however, a flawed vision, which poorly affected his subsequent handling of two issues: the political situation in Zimbabwe and the HIV/AIDS pandemic, which was spreading through southern Africa faster than any renaissance.

Nkosi Johnson

Speech at the opening ceremony of
the 13th International AIDS Conference,
Durban, 9 July 2000

The optimism of the Mandela era and Mbeki's grand vision for an African Renaissance were both gradually eroded by political instability in southern Africa, slow economic growth and increasing unemployment, as well as the growing HIV pandemic. Many of these problems were of course emerging in the heady days of Mandela's presidency, but the country was so pleased to have shed its pariah past and so charmed by the globally beloved Mandela figure of its present that it forgot to look forward to the challenges of the future.

The situation was exacerbated by Mbeki's responses to these problems. Hoping for similar successes as he'd achieved in the Congo, he adopted a policy of 'quiet diplomacy' in regard to Zimbabwe, where Robert Mugabe's ZANU-PF was trampling over human rights and suffocating voices of dissent. Mbeki's 'softly, softly' approach – to attempt a brokered compromise – conflicted with some of his other Africa-wide projects that were aimed at deepening democracy on the continent. NEPAD, for example, sought to promote good governance through an African peer-review mechanism, and the defunct Organisation of African Unity was resurrected in a new incarnation, the African Union. The international media was particularly critical of his response to Mugabe, claiming that Mbeki's Africanist solidarity, and old loyalties, trumped the ambitions of these projects. 'Indeed, it looks as if South Africa has already exhausted the means of quiet diplomacy,' *The Economist* reported in 2006, 'yet Mr Mbeki proudly refuses to say anything louder.'[1]

But most tragic was Mbeki's handling of the HIV/AIDS pandemic in his own country. South Africa swiftly acquired the dubious honour of being the country with the highest number of infections in the world, with only Botswana having a higher prevalence rate. In 2000, one year into Mbeki's presidency, estimations for the overall number of adults with the virus sat at 4.2 million.[2] Meanwhile, in the West, where medical treatment was being made available, numbers were declining. Most notably, the antiretroviral (ARV) drug Nevirapine had been included in the World Health Organization Model List of Essential Medicines because of its potential to decrease mother-to-child transmission of the virus.[3] There were some side effects, yes, but it was saving lives.

Despite this, Mbeki stalled, claiming that South Africa lacked the infra-structure to oversee the proper dispensation of ARVs and cautioning against their potential toxicities.[4] In addition to this, he treated the emergence of the virus like a kind of science experiment instead of the pandemic it was, querying the orthodox scientific understanding of the disease, especially the link between the HI virus and AIDS symptoms. He was widely criticised when in May 2000 he set up a Presidential Advisory Panel on AIDS, which included several scientists known to be sceptical of the disease's aetiology.

Mbeki's meddling interest in the science of the disease was already evident in 1997. As deputy president, he'd come to blows with the Medicines Control Council over a cabinet hearing that he'd arranged for two quack doctors ped-dling a 'homegrown' drug called Virodene, which turned out to be properly toxic. Deeply suspicious of Big Pharma, and slow to act on supplying ARV drugs, Mbeki gambled with the lives of his people, seeking, in line with his African Renaissance vision, an African approach to the pandemic.[5] The matter wasn't helped by his 1999 appointment of Manto Tshabalala-Msimang as his health minister, who later attracted exasperated ridicule when she placed emphasis on the curative properties of vegetables such as garlic and beetroot rather than on Western ARV medicines.

When criticised for his actions, Mbeki dug in his heels. He accused some of his critics of racism,[6] and, in a telling letter leaked to the press, which equated science with religion,[7] he likened the treatment of AIDS denialists to that of heretics during the Inquisition: 'In an earlier period in human history,' Mbeki claimed, 'these [dissidents] would be heretics that would be burnt at the stake!'[8] The country could ill afford this kind of approach. The disease was spreading at an alarming rate, and, to make matters worse, it was shrouded in stigma, leading to a reluctance to test or acknowledge one's status. UNAIDS reported that, in 2000, the word 'AIDS' was totally absent in a care programme run at a city hospital with a high prevalence rate.[9] The message from public-health experts was clear: people need to get tested and know their status, and HIV-positive persons need to take ARVs. The president, in contrast, spouted mumbo-jumbo.

Meanwhile, the death toll rose. In 1999, an estimated quarter of a million South Africans died of the disease.[10] Outraged by Mbeki's AIDS denialism, the scientific community made its disagreement with him explicit in the form of the Durban Declaration, a petition signed in the early months of 2000 expressing widespread support for the mainstream scientific view on HIV and AIDS. Calling the causal link between HIV and AIDS 'clear-cut, exhaustive and unambiguous',[11] the petition was published in the journal *Nature*. It was signed by over 5 000 scientists, eleven of them Nobel Prize winners.

In July of that year, a week after the publication of the declaration, Mbeki was scheduled to deliver a speech at the opening of the 13th International AIDS Conference held at a cricket stadium in Durban, and the world waited to hear the president's response. The conference, the largest of its kind, is an annual meeting of top researchers and scientists from around the world, and it was being hosted for the first time in Africa, in the country with the highest HIV infection rate. Many hoped that Mbeki's address, broadcast live on national television, would clarify his position, break with AIDS denialism and show leadership in a time of crisis. They were disappointed.

Mbeki began his speech with a 'story' told by the World Health Organization in 1995. 'The world's biggest killer,' he quoted, 'and the greatest cause of ill health and suffering across the globe is listed almost at the end of the national Classification of Diseases. It is given the code Z59.5 – extreme poverty.'[12] He went on to mention a host of diseases linked to poverty, and, in what sounded like a direct retort to his critics, he exclaimed, 'What I hear being said repeatedly, stridently, angrily, is – do not ask questions!'

While holistic and developmental approaches would go on to become an important part of AIDS management, Mbeki's failure to acknowledge the fundamental scientific cause of the disease provoked jeers from the audience, and hundreds of delegates walked out.[13]

The next speaker was a wide-eyed HIV-positive boy, Nkosi Johnson. The child, who looked even younger than his eleven years, stepped on to the stage and delivered a short speech that reflected more damningly on Mbeki's comments than any of the jeering or walkouts. An undersized figure in an oversized suit and sneakers, Nkosi captivated an audience of 10 000 delegates and appeared as living proof of the science that Mbeki had denied.

Hi, my name is Nkosi Johnson. I live in Melville, Johannesburg, South Africa. I am 11 years old and I have full-blown AIDS. I was born HIV-positive.

When I was two years old, I was living in a care centre for HIV/AIDS-infected people. My mommy was obviously also infected and could not afford to keep me because she was very scared that the community she lived in would find out that we were both infected and chase us away.

I know she loved me very much and would visit me when she could. And then the care centre had to close down because they didn't have any funds. So my foster mother, Gail Johnson, who was a director of the care centre and had taken me home for weekends, said at a board meeting she would take me home. She took me home with her and I have been living with her for eight years now.

She has taught me all about being infected and how I must be careful with my blood. If I fall and cut myself and bleed, then I must make sure that I cover my own wound and go to an adult to help me clean it and put a plaster on it.

I know that my blood is only dangerous to other people if they also have an open wound and my blood goes into it. That is the only time people need to be careful when touching me.

In 1997, Mommy Gail went to the school, Melpark Primary, and she had to fill in a form for my admission. It said, 'Does your child suffer from anything?' So she said yes: AIDS.

Mommy Gail and I have always been open about me having AIDS. And then my Mommy Gail was waiting to hear if I was admitted to school. She phoned the school, who said we will call you and then they had a meeting about me.

Of the parents and the teachers at the meeting, 50 percent said yes and 50 percent said no. And then on the day of my big brother's wedding, the media found out that there was a problem about me going to school. No one seemed to know what to do with me because I am infected. The AIDS workshops were done at the school for parents and teachers to teach them not to be scared of a child with AIDS. I am very proud to say that there is now a policy for all HIV-infected children to be allowed to go into schools and not be discriminated against.

In the same year, just before I started school, my Mommy Daphne died. She went on holiday to Newcastle and she died in her sleep. Mommy Gail got a phone call and I answered. My aunty said, 'Please can I speak to Gail?' Mommy Gail told me almost immediately my mommy had died and I burst into tears. My Mommy Gail took me to my mommy's funeral. I saw my mommy in the coffin and I saw her eyes were closed and then I saw them lowering it into the ground and then they covered her up. My granny was very sad that her daughter had died.

Then I saw my father for the first time and I never knew I had a father. He was very upset but I thought to myself, why did he leave my mother and me? And then the other people asked Mommy Gail about my sister and who would look after her. Mommy Gail said to ask the father.

Ever since the funeral, I have been missing my mommy lots and I wish she was with me. But I know she is in heaven. And she is on my shoulder watching over me and in my heart.

I hate having AIDS because I get very sick and I get very sad when I think of all the other children and babies that are sick with AIDS. I just wish that the government can start giving AZT to pregnant HIV mothers to help stop the virus being passed on to their babies. Babies are dying very quickly. I know one little abandoned baby who came to stay with us and his name was Micky. He couldn't breathe, he couldn't eat and he was so sick and Mommy Gail had to phone welfare to have him admitted to a hospital [where] he died. But he was such a cute little baby. I think the government must start doing it because I don't want babies to die.

Because I was separated from my mother at an early age, and because we were both HIV positive, my Mommy Gail and I have always wanted to start a care centre for HIV/AIDS mothers and their children. I am very happy and proud to say that the first Nkosi's Haven was opened last year. And we look after 10 mommies and 15 children. My Mommy Gail and I want to open five Nkosi's Havens by the end of next year because I want more infected mothers to stay together with their children. They mustn't be separated from their children, so [here] they can be together and live longer with the love that they need.

When I grow up, I want to lecture to more and more people about AIDS. And if Mommy Gail will let me, [I want to lecture] around the whole country. I want people to understand about AIDS, to be careful and respect AIDS. You can't get AIDS if you touch, hug, kiss, or hold hands with someone who is infected.

Care for us and accept us – we are all human beings.

We are normal. We have hands. We have feet. We can walk, we can talk, we have needs just like everyone else. Don't be afraid of us. We are all the same!

Born Xolani Nkosi to an HIV-positive woman, Nonthlanthla Nkosi, Nkosi was one of an unknown number of children born with the disease in 1989. By the year 1999, the number had risen to 40 000,[14] and there could be no more powerful message to a government withholding life-saving ARVs than a speech delivered by a dying indictment of its policy. Since Nkosi was born when there were no mother-to-child ARV provision programmes anywhere in the world, his illness couldn't have been prevented.[15] Yet by speaking about the virus, he became a powerful symbol of the tragedy and innocence of all children, many of them future orphans, born with HIV. His message was simple, as well as simply written and delivered. 'I just wish that the government can start giving AZT to pregnant HIV mothers to help stop the virus being passed on to their babies,' a visibly nervous Nkosi said in 'halting tones'.[16] Alongside the defiant complexity of Mbeki's speech, Nkosi's unassuming delivery was damning, and he received a standing ovation. One of the signatories of the Durban Declaration, Dr Charles van der Horst, afterwards summed up the effect of the speech. 'It is amazing to me that an 11-year-old boy can hit all the nails on the head, but his president couldn't.'[17]

Nkosi's speech, published in the press the following day, was written by his foster mother, Gail Johnson, the volunteer worker who'd become his guardian when Nkosi's biological mother became too weak to care for him. Together, Johnson and Nkosi became a formidable activist duo. A well-resourced and media-savvy white woman, Johnson – who'd specialised in public relations – used Nkosi's personal case of being refused a place in school to draw attention to the problems of HIV stigmatisation and fear. After the issue was taken to court and won by Johnson, schools were required to change their policies, and media coverage of the case most likely clarified some misconceptions about how the disease is spread – a point that Nkosi emphasised at the conference, saying, 'I know that my blood is only dangerous to other people if they also have an open wound and my blood goes into it.' The problem of stigmatisation and misinformation was a large part of the reason why activists sought clear and unambiguous statements from their president.

Gail Johnson received a certain amount of flak for what some saw as her exploitation of Nkosi, and, judging from Mbeki's fondness for quoting from a text called the 'Castro Hlongwane' document,[18] he likely would have perceived the speech as a cheap publicity stunt. In the controversial text, which was distributed at an ANC National Executive Committee meeting in 2002, Johnson is taken to task for denying Nkosi his name and removing him from his culture. He became, according to the author (who Gevisser suggests might be Mbeki himself[19]), 'the property and the hapless dependant of a world to which he did not belong. He was reborn as a creature of the imagination and the resources of white South Africa.'[20] Mbeki left the conference halfway through Nkosi's speech, reportedly because he had to catch a plane, but to the audience it looked like a deliberate walkout.

Rightly or wrongly, Nkosi's speech made him a public figure in the drive to destigmatise the disease and compel government to provide adequate treatment. The Treatment Action Campaign (TAC) printed posters of him alongside Hector Pieterson[21] and he was frequently referred to as the 'Hector Pieterson of the HIV generation'.[22] He became, as Didier Fassin points out, 'an iconic figure in spite of himself, but even so, he did give children a face at a time when the extent of their plight was not fully reckoned in the toll of the epidemic'.[23]

Later that year, Nkosi attended another AIDS event in Atlanta, Georgia, delivering a similar message about the disease. But he never realised his dream of growing up to 'lecture to more and more people about AIDS'. That Christmas, he collapsed and was diagnosed with brain damage. Although Mbeki's wife, Zanele, visited the child,[24] Mbeki himself never met him, a point that the media drove home in the 'obscene media watch'[25] on the deterioration of Nkosi's health in the early months of 2001. During this time, various politicians visited Nkosi, and the press published a host of letters addressed to Mbeki, begging for government to change its policies. These were attributed to the dying child, but it later transpired that Gail Johnson must have written them, since Nkosi had been in a coma since the end of 2000.[26] Though probably one of the longest-surviving children with AIDS in South Africa at the time, he died, aged twelve, on 1 June 2001, International Children's Day.

Nkosi's death, however, was not in vain. Soon afterwards, the TAC filed a claim against the government, arguing that the denial of treatment is unconstitutional. It won the case in December but had to fight a government appeal against the ruling, which the TAC won in the Constitutional Court in August 2002. The following year, cabinet sidelined the views of the president and the health minister, and plans for a national treatment programme were drawn up. Unfortunately, implementation was slow, as well as geographically uneven and sometimes impeded by a lack of political will.[27] It would take many years until the programme was effectively rolled out and people began living with, rather than dying from, HIV. By 2008, it was estimated that over 300 000 South Africans had died because of AIDS denialism.[28]

Thabo Mbeki

Resignation speech, 21 September 2008

In some ways Mbeki's presidency came to an end several months before he resigned in September 2008. His ignominious defeat at the 52nd National Conference of the ANC in his bid for another term as ANC president greatly diminished the power he'd established over the years through centralised control of government. The conference, held that year in Polokwane, Limpopo, is where the party's electoral candidates are chosen. Unlike the presidency, the ANC leadership isn't limited to two terms, but, in seeking a third, Mbeki confirmed the widespread suspicion that he was clinging to power.

This perception, and Mbeki's autocratic leadership style, had more to do with his eventual departure than his inept handling of the HIV pandemic. Under other circumstances, the health crisis might have resulted in a vote of no confidence, but over the years Mbeki had surrounded himself with 'yes' men, creating what Desmond Tutu described in 2004 as a culture of 'syco-phantic, obsequious conformity'.[1] One of the problems with such cultures is that they seldom allow for the emergence of a viable successor – a catastrophe entirely of Mbeki's own making. Additionally, 'yes' men are never as uniform as they appear; there are always a number of alienated persons seething in the shadows, and Jacob Zuma became the figure around whom they rallied.

Zuma was a traditionalist with a large and loyal following from KwaZulu-Natal. He'd served as an MK solider and also spent ten years on Robben Island, giving him all of the credentials that Mbeki lacked. He was, in many ways, the opposite of the president. If, according to the *New York Times*, Mbeki was 'skillful but lack[ing] a common touch',[2] the uneducated Zuma had the common touch in abundance – an attribute that, for a time, helped to com-plement Mbeki's aloof leadership style[3] until he realised that the man destined to succeed him had 'a dangerous combination of unhealthy ambition and poor judgment'.[4]

Mbeki's suspicions about Zuma were first aroused in the early 2000s when the Directorate of Special Operations (the Scorpions), a unit in the National Prosecuting Authority, began investigating the possibility of corruption in a R30-billion arms deal concluded by the government in 1999. In 2002, a press leak revealed that Zuma's shady financial advisor Schabir Shaik appeared to have sought bribes from arms dealer Thomson-CSF on Zuma's behalf. In 2003, NPA head Bulelani Ngcuka brought a case against Shaik, saying, with Mbeki's express permission,[5] that 'whilst there is a *prima facie* case of corruption against the deputy president, our prospects of success are not strong enough'.[6] Zuma's supporters interpreted this as a deliberate smear campaign, and they counteracted it with a charge that Ngcuka was trying to exact revenge because Zuma had accused him of being an apartheid spy, agent RS452 – a charge that was eventually disproven but which led to Ngcuka's departure from the position anyway.

A year later, on 31 May 2005, Judge Hilary Squires found Shaik guilty of corruption and fraud and sentenced him to fifteen years' imprisonment, saying that he'd found evidence of a 'mutually beneficial symbiosis'[7] between Shaik and Zuma. Shaik's payments to Zuma suggested the deputy president's willingness to use his position to favourably direct his advisor's business interests. Soon after the judgment, the new NPA head Vusi Pikoli charged Zuma with two counts of corruption.

Mbeki reacted by firing Zuma two weeks later and, in what appeared like a deliberate snub, replacing him with Bulelani Ngcuka's wife, Phumzile Mlambo-Ngcuka. The president missed a major opportunity to appoint a strong successor at this point. Had he appointed a viable compromise candidate for the party's leadership, he might have countered Zuma's ascendancy, but he had sidelined many members of the senior leadership and believed, somewhat arrogantly, that only he could stand against Zuma.[8]

Then, in the midst of the debacle, a young HIV-positive woman, the daughter of a close comrade of Zuma's, laid a charge of rape against him, making the possibility of a political comeback seem wholly unlikely. But with each successive court appearance in the highly publicised rape trial that followed, Zuma's crowd of supporters swelled, and the Mbeki–Zuma conflict began to take on a frightening ethnic dimension. Many supporters wore T-shirts claiming to be '100% Zuluboy'[9] – in approval of both Zuma's Zulu and 'homeboy' status – while others burnt images of Zuma's accuser in response to whispers that the rape charges were part of a sophisticated plot being masterminded by the president to topple his rival. Bizarrely, Zuma's most ardent supporters came from the ANC Women's League, and his accuser, known to the public only as Khwezi, so feared for her life that she was forced to leave the country. Zuma was eventually acquitted of the charge on 8 May 2006, with the judge agreeing with the defence that Khwezi had consented to sleep with Zuma. Despite Zuma's self-incriminating testimony that he'd not worn a condom and that he believed a quick post-coital shower would protect him against HIV, the crowd outside the courtroom erupted in celebration.

Yet this victory did not see the end of Zuma's courtroom dramas. As part of its investigation, the Scorpions had seized documents from Zuma's homes and the offices of Thint (formerly Thomson-CSF), and Zuma's lawyers questioned the lawfulness of these raids in separate court cases throughout 2006. Without the documents, however, there was no case, and the High Court's Herbert Msimang threw the case out of court on 20 September 2006; he didn't, however, dismiss the charges, which meant that there was still a possibility of prosecution. Almost a year later, the NPA appealed to the Supreme Court of Appeal against the rulings on the legality of the raids, winning the case in November 2007.

Despite now needing to answer these charges in court, and despite confessing to having had extramarital sex with an HIV-positive woman young enough to be his daughter, the mounting scandals appeared to redound to Zuma's credit. With no real opponent for the ANC presidency, various factions formed a 'coalition of the wounded'[10] and rallied around him in their opposition to Mbeki. These included the ANC Youth League, headed by the young hothead Julius Malema (who famously declared that he'd 'kill for Zuma'[11]), as well as COSATU and the SACP. The latter two support bases opposed Mbeki's neo-liberal economic policies and the unilateral way in which he'd implemented them. Zwelinzima Vavi and Blade Nzimande, the respective leaders of the two organisations, believed that Zuma, the self-described 'herdboy from Nkandla',[12] would be more sympathetic to their pro-poor policies – at least, this was the official line. In reality, Mbeki's policies of fiscal austerity had eventually borne fruit, resulting in an unprecedented period of economic growth, which he'd followed up with a significant shift to the left in 2004.[13] The 'coalition of the wounded' had more to do with Mbeki's centralised deployments, which alienated the party's grass roots from power.

Nowhere was this more evident than at Polokwane, where Mbeki's speech was interrupted with accusatory jeers and calls for him to 'Go! Go!' When he finished speaking, the crowd sang Zuma's appropriated anthem 'Umshini Wam!' ('Bring Me My Machine Gun!') to drive the message home. Zuma defeated Mbeki by 2 329 votes to 1 505, putting him back in line for the presidency.

During the last 'lame-duck lap'[14] of Mbeki's term, the court battle between the Scorpions and Zuma raged on. Zuma was served with papers to stand trial in the High Court on 783 counts of corruption, fraud, racketeering and money laundering – this time supported by the documents seized in the searches. Zuma and Thint's last appeal to have the raids declared illegal was rejected by the Constitutional Court on 31 July 2008. Only the courts could stop Zuma now.

Instead, they vindicated him. When the corruption case was heard in the Pietermaritzburg High Court, Zuma's lawyers argued that the charges were born of a political conspiracy against him and that they were invalid because Zuma hadn't been given the opportunity to make representations to the NPA before being charged. On 12 September 2008, Judge Chris Nicholson ruled in Zuma's favour, saying that he was 'not convinced that the applicant [Zuma] was incorrect in averring political meddling in his prosecution'.[15]

This statement, vague as it was, gave Mbeki's opponents the ammunition they needed to finally eject him from office and they didn't wait for Mbeki to appeal it. Eight days after Nicholson's judgment, the ANC National Executive Committee (now made up of a hard core of anti-Mbeki advocates elected at Polokwane) announced in the wake of a fourteen-hour meeting that they were recalling Mbeki as president, even though Zuma himself reportedly favoured Mbeki completing his term in order to facilitate a smooth transition.[16]

Mbeki's reaction was swift. On 21 September, it was announced that he would be making a national address on television that evening, and South Africans tuned in to hear him address them as president for the last time.

Fellow South Africans,

I have no doubt that you are aware of the announcement made yesterday by the National Executive Committee of the ANC with regard to the position of the President of the Republic.

Accordingly, I would like to take this opportunity to inform the nation that today I handed a letter to the Speaker of the National Assembly, the Honourable Baleka Mbete, to tender my resignation from the high position of President of the Republic of South Africa, effective from the day that will be determined by the National Assembly.

I have been a loyal member of the African National Congress for 52 years. I remain a member of the ANC and therefore respect its decisions. It is for this reason that I have taken the decision to resign as President of the Republic, following the decision of the National Executive Committee of the ANC.

I would like sincerely to thank the nation and the ANC for having given me the opportunity to serve in public office during the last 14 years as the Deputy President and President of South Africa.

This service has at all times been based on the vision, the principles and values that have guided the ANC as it prosecuted a difficult and dangerous struggle in the decades before the attainment of our freedom in 1994.

Among other things, the vision, principles and values of the ANC teach the cadres of this movement life-long lessons that inform us that wherever we are and whatever we do we should ensure that our actions contribute to the attainment of a free and just society, the upliftment of all our people, and the development of a South Africa that belongs to all who live in it.

This is the vision of a South Africa that is democratic, non-racial, non-sexist and prosperous; a country in which all the people enjoy a better life.

Indeed the work we have done in pursuit of the vision and principles of our liberation movement has at all times been based on the age-old values of Ubuntu, of selflessness, sacrifice and service in a manner that ensures that the interests of the people take precedence over our desires as individuals.

I truly believe that the governments in which I have been privileged to serve have acted and worked in the true spirit of these important values.

Based on the values of Ubuntu, the significance of which we learnt at the feet of such giants of our struggle as Chief Albert Luthuli, OR Tambo, Nelson Mandela and others, we as government, embarked, from 1994, on policies and programmes directed at pulling the people of South Africa out of the morass of poverty and ensuring that we build a stable, developed and prosperous country.

Accordingly, among many things we did, we transformed our economy, resulting in the longest sustained period of economic growth in the history of our country; we introduced an indigent policy that reaches large numbers of those in need; we made the necessary advances so as to bring about a developmental state, the better to respond to the many and varied challenges of the transformation of our country.

This is, of course, not the occasion to record the achievements of government. An additional critical few are however worth mentioning. They include our achievements with regard to many of the Millennium Development Goals, the empowerment of women, the decision to allow us to host the 2010 FIFA Soccer World Cup and our election as a non-permanent member of the UN Security Council two years ago.

Despite the economic advances we have made, I would be the first to say that even as we ensured consistent economic growth, the fruits of these positive results are still to be fully and equitably shared among our people, hence the abject poverty we still find coexisting side by side with extraordinary opulence.

Importantly, we had an obligation to ensure that democracy becomes the permanent feature of our lives and that all our citizens respect the rule of law and human rights. This is one of the cornerstones of our democracy, which we have consistently striven to protect and never to compromise.

We have also worked continuously to combat the twin challenges of crime and corruption, to ensure that all our people live in conditions of safety and security. We must admit that we are still faced with many challenges in this regard.

Work will therefore have to continue to strengthen and improve the functioning of our criminal justice system, to provide the necessary resources for this purpose, to activate the masses of our people to join the fight against crime and corruption, and to achieve new victories in the struggle for moral regeneration.

With regard to the latter, our successive governments from 1994 to date have worked consistently to encourage the entrenchment in our country of a value system whose observance would make all of us Proudly South African, a value system informed by the precept of Ubuntu – umuntu ngumuntu ngabanye. Among other things this means that we must all act in a manner that respects the dignity of every human being.

We have sought to advance this vision precisely because we understood that we would fail in the struggle to achieve the national and social cohesion that our country needs, as well as the national unity we require to enable us to act together to address the major challenges we face.

Fellow South Africans,

Since the attainment of our freedom in 1994, we have acted consistently to respect and defend the independence of the judiciary. For this reason our successive governments have honoured all judicial decisions, including those that went against the Executive. This did not mean that the Executive did not at times have strong views which we would have publicly pronounced upon. The central approach we adopted has always been to defend the judiciary rather than act in a manner that would have had a negative impact on its work.

Indeed, on the infrequent instances when we have publicly expressed views contrary to those of the judiciary, we have done so mindful of the need to protect its integrity.

Consistent with this practice, I would like to restate the position of Cabinet on the inferences made by the Honourable Judge Chris Nicholson that the President and Cabinet have interfered in the work of the National Prosecuting Authority (NPA). Again I would like to state this categorically that we have never done this, and therefore never compromised the right of the National Prosecuting Authority to decide whom it wished to prosecute or not to prosecute.

This applies equally to the painful matter relating to the court proceedings against the President of the ANC, Comrade Jacob Zuma.

More generally, I would like to assure the nation that our successive governments since 1994 have never acted in any manner intended wilfully to violate the Constitution and the law. We have always sought to respect the solemn Oath of Office each one of us made in front of the Chief Justice and other judges, and have always been conscious of the fact that the legal order that governs our country was achieved through the sacrifices made by countless numbers of our people, which included death.

In this context it is most unfortunate that gratuitous suggestions have been made seeking to impugn the integrity of those of us who have been privileged to serve in our country's National Executive.

Compatriots,

Again, as you know, we have often pointed to the fact that our liberation movement has always been pan-African in its outlook and therefore that we have an obligation to contribute to the renaissance of the African continent.

All of us are aware of the huge and daunting challenges that face our continent. In the short years since our freedom, as South Africans we have done what we could to make our humble contribution to the regeneration of our continent.

We have devoted time and resources to the task of achieving the Renaissance of Africa because this is what has informed generations of our liberators, even before the ANC was formed in 1912. We have done this fully understanding that our country shares a common destiny with the rest of our Continent.

I therefore thank the many dedicated compatriots – men and women – who have made it possible for us to contribute to the resolution of conflicts and the strengthening of democracy in a number of countries including the Kingdom of Lesotho, the Democratic Republic of Congo, Burundi, Côte d'Ivoire, Comoros, Zimbabwe, Sudan and elsewhere.

We have also done this work conscious of our responsibilities as a State Member of both SADC and the African Union.

I would like to thank my colleagues, the many Heads of State and Government on the African continent whose abiding vision is that Africa must be free; that all our countries, individually and collectively should become democratic, developed and prosperous, and that Africa must unite. These African patriots know as I do that Africa and Africans will not and must not be the wretched of the earth in perpetuity.

Similarly we have worked to contribute to the achievement of the aspirations of the countries and peoples of the South, conscious of the need for us to act in solidarity and in unity with the billions with whom we share the common challenge to defeat poverty and underdevelopment.

Accordingly, I depart the Office of President of South Africa knowing that this country has many men and women who have dedicated their lives to ensure that South Africa, Africa and the countries of the South will, in time, manage to ensure a better world for all of humanity.

I depart this Office conscious that the sterling work done by the Presidency, the Ministries and departments, the provinces and local government structures will continue, driven by the determination to achieve the goal of a better life for all.

I am convinced that the incoming administration will better the work done during the past 14-and-half years so that poverty, underdevelopment, unemployment, illiteracy, challenges of health, crime and corruption will cease to define the lives of many of our people.

I have received many messages from South Africans, from all walks of life, through e-mails, telephonically and through cell phone text messages as well as those conveyed through my colleagues. I thank all of you, fellow South Africans, for these messages.

To everyone, and responding to these messages, I would like to say that gloom and despondency have never defeated adversity. Trying times need courage and resilience. Our strength as a people is not tested during the best of times. As we said before, we should never become despondent because the weather is bad nor should we turn triumphalist because the sun shines.

For South Africa to succeed there is more work to be done and I trust that we will continue to strive to act in unity to accelerate the advance towards the achievement of our shared national goals.

In this regard, it may be worth repeating what I said during the inauguration of the President of the Republic in 1999. Using the metaphor of the Comrades Marathon, I said then that:

'Those who complete the course will do so only because they do not, as fatigue sets in, convince themselves that the road ahead is still too long, the inclines too steep, the loneliness impossible to bear and the prize itself of doubtful value.'

Once more, I thank you most sincerely for affording me the opportunity to serve you and to serve the people of Africa.

Thank you, Ngiyathokoza, Ke ya Lebogang, Ndo livhuwa, Ndiyabulela, Ndza khensa, Baie dankie, Ngiyabonga.

Speaking slightly faster than usual, but still presenting a dignified front, Mbeki's first aim appears to have been to maintain calm and unity in the face of a potentially divisive situation. He acceded to his party's demands and resigned himself to his fate, reiterating his loyalty to the ANC and emphasising its Charterist values. Described as 'unusually humble' by the *Guardian*,[17] Mbeki's speech situates him as a servant of the people: the government is one in which he has 'been privileged to serve' and he thanks people 'from all walks of life' for their messages of support. In what some most likely read as a dig at his rival's corrupt greed, he refers to 'the age-old values of Ubuntu, of selflessness, sacrifice and service', which should 'take precedence over our desires as individuals'. The speaker's humility – so at odds with the supposed arrogance frequently attributed to Mbeki – gathers momentum with his repeated address of his audience using somewhat old-fashioned terms: 'fellow South Africans', a stoic Mbeki says directly to the camera and, later, 'compatriots'.

Mindful of the need for a dramatic climax, Mbeki, ever the rhetorician, builds up to the real matter at hand: the accusation of political meddling, which he 'categorically' denies. By emphasising his respect for the Constitution and the law, as well as the solemn oath of office taken before the chief justice, he skilfully manages to refute the 'Honourable' Judge Nicholson's 'inferences' while displaying the utmost respect for the judiciary. He further characterises the Zuma court proceedings as a 'painful' event, dispelling the view that his actions were motivated by political jealousy of any kind. The display of dignity, discipline and humility is vintage Mbeki.

Suggesting that a dark time lies ahead for South Africa, Mbeki says 'we should never become despondent because the weather is bad nor should we turn triumphalist because the sun shines'. This is in fact a direct echo from his glorious 'I am an African' speech, in which he'd said the 'masses do not despair because today the weather is bad. Nor do they turn triumphalist when, tomorrow, the sun shines.'

Zuma's ascendancy did indeed herald a dark time, and his presidency would continue to fracture the ANC for years to come. The National Executive Committee installed Kgalema Motlanthe as acting president the day after Mbeki's resignation. Most likely seeking to avoid accusations of appointing Zuma without a proper mandate, the committee decided that he should wait until the election the following year before he assumed office. About a third of Mbeki's cabinet resigned along with him, leading later to the formation of a new political party, the Congress of the People (COPE), which chipped away at the ANC's power base.

Then, on 12 January 2009, the Supreme Court of Appeal overturned Nicholson's judgment, claiming that 'for reasons that are impossible to fathom' he'd ruled on issues extraneous to the matter at hand and made 'gratuitous findings against persons who were not called upon to defend themselves'.[18] The motives for the charges against Zuma were irrelevant, the court said, claiming: 'A prosecution is not wrongful merely because it is brought for an improper purpose ... the best motive does not cure an otherwise illegal arrest and the worst motive does not render an otherwise legal arrest illegal.' Mbeki immediately claimed that the judgment 'vindicated' him,[19] but it was, of course, too late. He may have reclaimed his integrity but his political career was over.

The judgment meant, however, that Zuma was back in the firing line, and the NPA reinstated the charges against him. Even a sentence of just one year would have made him ineligible to occupy the position of president. It was a blow to the ANC's election campaign, casting a cloud of doubt over their already compromised candidate.

The allegations remained unanswered, however. Eight years into the case and just two weeks before the election, the NPA announced that it was dropping the charges against Zuma, citing political motivation on the part of the Scorpions' head. Although the ANC lost support to COPE and other opposition parties, the organisation went on to win at the polls, holding 65.9 per cent of the vote. In what Adam Habib described as the 'greatest political comeback ever',[20] Zuma was inaugurated on 9 May 2009. When his former rival arrived at the swearing-in ceremony, sections of the crowd greeted him with boos.

Julius Malema
Speech at Marikana, 18 August 2012

When South African police gunned down thirty-four mineworkers near Rustenburg on a late-winter afternoon in 2012, the country's political landscape shifted. The deaths, and the government's subsequent attempt to distort what had happened, undermined many South Africans' belief in the ANC as the party of the people. Not since Sharpeville had the state used such deadly force against civilians, and the media soon began to refer to the tragedy as the Marikana massacre.

The shootings were an inevitable result of growing disillusionment in a country where conditions for workers have changed very little since apartheid. Mining in South Africa has long been a political issue; since colonial times, the intertwined interests of government and mining magnates have fuelled everything from pass laws to the migrant labour system. When reforms allowed for the establishment of trade unions in the early 1980s, the National Union of Mineworkers (NUM) began to flex its muscle, making immense sacrifices to help put the ANC in power. In the post-apartheid era, this trend continues in the form of the Tripartite Alliance. The ruling party draws heavily on the allegiance of COSATU and the SACP to maintain dominance.[1]

Despite this support, there have been meagre payoffs for workers. The situation at Marikana in 2012 is a stark illustration of the aphorism that the more things change, the more they stay the same. Although legislation requires mining companies to have a 24 per cent black shareholding,[2] the Lonmin mine is otherwise UK owned. And although black workers are now able to move up the ranks and can, for instance, acquire blasting certificates, the lives of the majority of mineworkers remain nasty, brutish and short. Migrant labour continues, accommodation is dismal, workers' wages are still low and are often the only form of income for entire extended families, and the miners' working lives are frequently cut short because of unhealthy employment conditions.

While new legislation ushered in an era in which unions helped to improve the lot of workers, they, too, have become compromised. Increasingly, the unions are led by better-educated black workers, the so-called *clevas*, who are out of touch with 'the lesser-educated miners who [make] up the majority of the workforce'.[3] The fact that only unions with high memberships are recognised by companies creates bitter competition for union membership as well as dissatisfaction among workers who feel that their needs aren't satisfactorily represented by the larger organisations. At Lonmin, workers in the Karee mine had grown dissatisfied with NUM's ability to negotiate in their interests, and as Greg Marinovich points out, 'Lonmin had for a long time practically outsourced employee relations to the unions.'[4] The perception of collusion with management was not helped by the fact that union trail-blazers from the apartheid era, such as Gwede Mantashe, Kgalema Motlanthe and Cyril Ramaphosa, were now top party leaders,[5] or by Ramaphosa's position as both a major beneficiary of Lonmin's required black economic empowerment policy and a non-executive director of the company.

The rock-drill operators throughout the sector were especially dissatisfied with their lot. Their jobs, physically gruelling and dangerous but integral to the whole operation, were comparatively poorly paid. In early 2012, led by rock-drill operators, miners at Impala Platinum mine (or Implats), a neighbouring operation, had held a drawn-out but ultimately successful wildcat strike. Bypassing the unions, the strikers had managed to achieve a significant salary increase – from R6 540 to R9 991. The miners at Lonmin, where drillers were paid even less than at Implats, were emboldened by their neighbour's success and set a figure of their own: R12 500, the amount they determined would provide a living wage. Throughout the winter, various negotiations between non-union representatives and mine managers led to the expectation on the part of the workers that they could negotiate with their employers directly. In reality, the miners were locked into a wage agreement for another year and a half, and there was little chance that Lonmin would meet their ambitious request. 'Both sides were gambling from high-risk positions,' says Marinovich, 'with a confrontational approach that resembled a zero-sum game.'[6]

The strike began on 9 August, and the situation was immediately exacer-bated by ensuing conflict between two unions: NUM and the Association of Mineworkers and Construction Union (AMCU), founded by former NUM official Joseph Mathunjwa in 2001. AMCU, which had operated mainly in the coal-mining sector, sought to increase membership across the platinum belt by taking up the cause of the aggrieved drill operators and used the Implats strike to embark on a successful membership drive.[7] AMCU had ousted NUM in Lonmin's Karee mine, but since the union wasn't yet formally recognised, the strike was unprotected. When reports of intimidation in the hostels at the hands of NUM representatives emerged, more workers joined the strike in sympathy and anger.

Over the next few days, there were clashes between various groups. NUM men attacked some of the strikers with pangas, two strikers sustained bullet injuries, two Lonmin security guards were hacked to death, and two non-striking workers were slain on their way to work on the night of 11 August. The growing group of strikers, now carrying sticks, began to gather on a koppie near one of the surrounding settlements, receiving rites from a sangoma in the belief that it would protect them from harm.

Meanwhile, Lonmin human capital manager and executive member Barnard Mokwena met with the provincial police chief, Lieutenant General Mirriam Mbombo, to discuss suppressing the strike. Later, transcripts of these discussions would reflect poorly on them: neither showed any interest in negotiating, and they overstepped their roles as law enforcers and employers. Most damning was Mbombo's concern for the political implications of the strike. The Implats strike earlier that year had shown how miners' grievances could be exploited by both the rival union AMCU and the former leader of the ANC Youth League, the rebellious Julius Malema, who had for years been advocating for the mines to be nationalised.

Malema, who'd famously declared that he would 'kill for Zuma' during the Mbeki–Zuma power struggle, had by 2012 fallen out of favour with the ANC. His unsuccessful appeal of his five-year expulsion from the party for bringing it into disrepute was handled by none other than Cyril Ramaphosa at the beginning of the year. Malema had visited the striking Implats workers, succeeding where heavyweights such as COSATU's Zwelinzima Vavi had failed,[8] and the six-week strike ended on 29 February, a day after Malema's visit. In a contradictory but nevertheless appeasing speech, Malema told the workers in one breath to return to work, and in another that 'you must fight until you benefit'.[9]

The Lonmin strike needed to be quelled, Mbombo argued, because it 'has a serious political connotation that we need to take into account'.[10] If the strike continued and Malema arrived on the scene as he had at Implats, she explained, he could exploit the situation for political gain. National police commissioner Riah Phiyega, a Zuma loyalist, had given Mbombo a strong sense that she'd been pressurised by Lonmin representatives, particularly Ramaphosa.[11] At the meeting's conclusion, the Lonmin executive and police chief had agreed on one central point. In Mbombo's words: 'We need to act such that we kill this thing.'[12]

Back at the koppie, however, there were high hopes for some kind of negotiation. The crowd of 4 000 strikers heard from an optimistic Mathunjwa that if they agreed to go back to work, the company would address their grievances, a message they took as an agreement to negotiate. They decided to reassemble at nine o'clock the following morning to discuss the proposal. Despite news of this potentially peaceful end to the strike reaching police authorities, that evening, in a covert meeting, they agreed on an altogether different plan, deploying over 550 police officers, 4000 rounds of live R5 ammunition and four mortuary vans with berths for four bodies each.

Mathunjwa had been mistaken: the company had no intention of dealing with the strikers' grievances or engaging him as their representative. The next day, 16 August, he found that nobody was prepared to talk to him, and he was excluded from a press conference that was attended by NUM officials. Mbombo announced simply, 'We are ending the strike today', with no mention of Mathunjwa's offers. When the union leader returned to the increasingly unsettled strikers at the koppie, he found that the police had begun to roll out barbed wire in front of them, and helicopters were circling in the sky.

Mathunjwa tried one last time to meet with Mbombo and Lonmin representatives, but all the communication channels had been shut down. At 3.30 p.m. he returned to the strikers again, telling them disappointedly to drop the strike: 'Comrades, the life of a black person in Africa is so cheap ... They will kill us, they will finish us and then they will replace us and continue to pay wages that cannot change black people's lives.'[13]

After he'd left, some of the miners began to walk down from the koppie. Led by the charismatic leader of the strike, Mgcineni 'Mambush' Noki, who would later become known as 'the man in the green blanket', a group hoped to make their way past a cattle kraal to the Nkaneng settlement. Police officers and vans moved in to block their path, releasing tear gas and firing a water cannon. After a stun grenade was thrown, one of the miners shot a pistol and, shortly afterwards, several police officers opened fire, killing seventeen men, including Noki. In the ensuing chaos, the rest of the miners scattered back towards the koppie. After a ceasefire of about fifteen minutes, two groups of officers then sought out the dispersed strikers with a second explosion of fire – an act that they later tried to cover up. A total of 295 bullets were fired and another seventeen men died huddling behind rocks on the hill. The 276 uninjured survivors were arrested and taken to Lonmin's Number One shaft, where they were held, without access to toilets, until one in the morning.[14]

It was a national disaster and images of the first, confusing set of killings played out across the nation's television screens that evening. Zuma, who'd been attending a SADC meeting in Maputo at the time, was slow in returning to the country, and the first high-profile politician to visit the scene was none other than Malema.

Arriving two days after the massacre, in the midst of the miners' grief and

confusion, Malema was greeted with thunderous applause. No longer a
representative of the ANC, he was dressed in a red-and-black tracksuit and
sneakers, and he 'affected a common touch'.[15] Before addressing the crowd,
he asked the police presence on the scene to leave, a gesture that at once
established his authority and indicated his sympathy with his audience.

Malema: Amandla!

Crowd: Awethu!

Malema: Long live the fighting spirit of Peter Mokaba, long live!

Crowd: Long live!

Malema: Long live the fighting spirit of O.R Tambo, long live!

Crowd: Long live! [...]

Malema: The government made of short people will fall, it will fall!

Crowd: It will fall! [...]

Malema: Down with Jacob Zuma, down!

Crowd: Down! [...]

Malema: To the lawyers, mineworkers and leaders of the youth league,
comrade secretary general and comrade Floyd Shivambu. We have come
here to support you because most people are afraid to come to you,
especially those you voted into power. Today they have turned their
backs against you. They treat you as though you are the enemy. They
don't want to hear anything from you, and we took a decision that we
are going to come here and listen to you one by one. [...]

This mine that you work in is owned by Britain. [...] The British are
making money out of this mine, but these people who work in television and radio do not mention that Cyril Ramaphosa is one of the
shareholders of this mine. [...] The reason the workers were killed is
because there is a highly connected political figure in that mine. [...]

We were all watching as workers when you were on strike. The way
you strike, holding sticks and weapons, you are not the first to do so.
That thing is always done, including President Zuma. When he marries
every December, he holds a spear. [...] So why would police [...] be
intimidated by sticks and pangas? When the IFP marches every year,
Inkatha, they do so carrying weapons, but they were never shot. Never!

But today they come here and kill workers. [...] And when you
question why, they justify it by saying you were threatening the police.
It's not true. Even if you were threatening the police, they have no right

to use live ammunition against civilians. They were supposed to shoot at you with rubber bullets, or use tear gas and alternatively spray you with water. [...] They also say that there was an employee amongst you who had a gun, and that worker, they are saying he was the first one to shoot.

Even if that was the case, they had no right to shoot! If they are well-trained police, they were supposed to isolate that individual and take him on, and leave the rest of the masses. [...] So comrades, the minister of police must step down, because this massacre occurred under his supervision. The same thing with President Zuma: he must step down. [...]

Last night President Zuma was here, but he went to meet up with the big shots. He never came to check up on you, the employees. [...] He will only come back to you when we go for elections. Exactly! When they want your votes, they will all be here telling you how they are going to change your lives, how you are going to get water and electricity, how you are all going to get jobs. Once you put your vote down, they disappear.

Even when people are dead, our president lacks the courage to come here. I was not escorted by the police; I told them not to come with me, because we don't need their protection. [...] They could kill us, these murderers. President Zuma presided over the massacre of our people, President Zuma's gunmen murdered our people, President Zuma's government will continue murdering our people. That is why, even today, they don't regret; that is why they go around this township, not showing any remorse.

Their aim is to kill more and more, because the president, the commissioner and the minister have given them permission, and explain it as self-defence. President Zuma advised the police to use maximum force. [...] A responsible president should tell them to have order and act with restraint, but he says to them, 'Use maximum force.' [...]

Not even the apartheid government killed so many people. The government of the boere people has never killed so many people. They never killed twenty people in under fifteen minutes. [...] After shooting at them, the comrades were spread across the ground, but not even one AK47 was found. You only use an R5 when you respond to a fire-with-fire situation. [...] You cannot use an automatic machine to control the crowd. Once you use an automatic machine, you come with the intention to kill. [...]

They are killing you for your own minerals; you are not stealing anything. But I want to tell you that you must never retreat, even in the face of death, never retreat. Do not go back! The only thing you must listen to is anybody who suggests that they are going to pay you the R12 500.

Because the people who lost their lives cannot die in vain [...] we need to show our lost ones that what they died for is achieved: we now have R12 500. The president should just step down, and tell the mining bosses that they have messed up. The only way we can correct this is to give the workers what they want. [...]

Comrade, you are not alone, you are fighting a right course. Not even for a moment should you think that there is any wrong that you are doing, there's nothing wrong you are doing. Demand your rights. Those are your rights. We are with you and will continue doing so. We did not come here to take advantage of you, being in a crisis. We have always been with you, the people in Impala can tell you, even from the squatter camps can tell you that we are the few leaders who can still go to the poorest. [...] The president comes to say, 'We are mourning the death of those who died.' How do you kill people and then mourn them? It is not possible; they are here to kill you. But we have not come here to kill you; we are here to support you. And we even told the police, 'Why are you all here, when people are gathered so peacefully? They are not even singing; they are sitting down.' [...]

From today when asked who is your president, you must answer, saying, 'I don't have a president.' We do not have a president in South Africa, because the role of the president is to defend civilians. He fails to defend ordinary people. We don't have police. We have lost confidence in SAPS, because instead of defending you, they kill you!

Comrades, we must make sure that you take care of each other. Look after one another and don't sell each other out, because the white people that own this mine do not like you. For if you run off to them to give them information, they still won't like you – you spy! You go around spying around on the workers, knowing fully well that you also want that R12 500. Workers stop selling out! The NUM is not a union. It's a company; from today it should be named NUM Pty. Ltd. It has white people, it has shares in mines, and that is why every time there is a problem, NUM is the first to sell out. [...]

Comrades, you are not alone. I extend my condolences to the begrieved family members, and just know that we will always remember them. I am sending a message to the Mpondo families, because I was advised that some of the people were Pondos, and those are our brothers. We are saying to the families in Eastern Cape, in Lesotho, Swaziland, we are with you. Comrades, those who died should know that we will continue with a struggle, and their fight will remain our fight. And the only way to honour them is to continue with the struggle to defend the rights of the workers. I extend condolences on behalf of Mama Winnie Madikizela-Mandela, who says I must tell you she is with you, and identifies with your problems and supports your cause.

Comrades, many people will die as we continue with the struggle for economic freedom. Never retreat, never surrender. We are not turning back. We will control the enemy, until the enemy delivers our demands.

Malema concluded his speech by breaking out into the poignant struggle dirge 'Senzeni na?' ('What have we done?') – a particularly apt anthem, which illustrated his keen reading of the situation. While the speech may not be an example of elegant rhetoric, Malema, described as an 'inspirational orator',[16] delivered words the crowd must have been hungry to hear. Speaking in a mixture of Setswana and English, he identifies all of the workers' grievances. He voices their distrust of NUM – no longer a union fighting for workers' rights, but rather 'sell-outs', 'NUM Pty. Ltd', a company that colludes with whites and seeks its own economic gain. He articulates the workers' loss of confidence in the police – 'Police must stop provoking our people,' he says, pointing to the helicopters circling overhead during his delivery of the speech and asking why a police presence is needed for a crowd of mourners. And, most importantly, he identifies the sense of betrayal that many in the crowd must have felt. 'Comrades, you are not alone,' he tells them, and 'we are with you'.

Malema, together with other Youth Leaguers Floyd Shivambu, Sindiso Magaqa and Anda Bici, continued to meet with mineworkers over the next few days and organised legal representation led by Dali Mpofu. The expelled leader later claimed that at the time of Marikana, he'd had no ambitions for a new political movement and that he'd been hoping for a change in ANC leadership that would see the reversal of his expulsion.[17] But given the 'us-them' dichotomy he sets up in the speech, this seems unlikely. At the very least, he must have been spoiling for an internal coup. Throughout, he repeatedly invokes an unattributed 'we' – unaffiliated to any political party. 'We are with you and will continue doing so,' he says, and then, in a statement that suggests his full appreciation of the political implications of the visit, 'We did not come here to take advantage of you, being in a crisis. We have always been with you, the people in Impala can tell you, even from squatter camps can tell you that we are the few leaders who can still go to the poorest.' At the same time, he calls for the president to step down, for he 'fails to defend ordinary people'.

Malema's singling out of Winnie Madikizela-Mandela is strategic. Not only was she the only high-profile ANC politician who had defended him during his disciplinary hearing, but she had also always been perceived as a champion of the poor. Malema's name-dropping thus had the desired effect of establishing his own continued political relevance while appealing to the values of his audience.

When Malema had visited Implats at the beginning of the year, he'd worn a T-shirt bearing an image of leftist hero Chris Hani underscored with the slogan 'Economic Freedom Fighters'. Even before he was properly expelled from the ANC, it seems that Malema was 'preparing to beat his own path, independent of the party at whose breast he had been nursed'.[18] In the Marikana speech, he launches a new struggle: the 'struggle for economic freedom'. While the previous struggle might have resulted in the achievement of political rights, Malema's focus was economic emancipation.

If, as Marinovich suggests, the 'ruling party's fear of Malema taking advantage of the strike pushed them to act more rashly than they might otherwise have done',[19] the strategy backfired spectacularly. The events that unfolded after Marikana were a further shameful indictment on the intertwined structures of power in the country. While the media at first fell for the story that the police had acted in self-defence, exposés of attempted cover-ups and the findings of the subsequently established commission of inquiry cast a dark shadow over Lonmin, the police officials and top figures such as Ramaphosa – who, the day before the massacre, had written an incriminating email to his fellow directors on the Lonmin board. Showing remarkably poor insight, Ramaphosa wrote, 'The terrible events that have unfolded cannot be described as a labour dispute. They are plainly dastardly criminal and must be characterised as such ... There needs to be concomitant action to address this situation.'[20] The correspondence, said Adam Habib, 'was a symbolic example of the degeneration of a cadre and civil activist and how he has become entrapped by his newfound wealth. It resonates so powerfully because it's typical of many in the ANC.'[21]

For Malema, however, the event served as a springboard back into politics, and just under a year later he launched a new opposition party, the Economic Freedom Fighters (EFF), in Orlando West, Soweto. Results in the 2014 elections showed the extent to which Malema's following cut into the ANC's support base. The young party did well, achieving more than 6 per cent of the vote. Nowhere was the diminished perception of the ANC more obvious than at Marikana. In the days before the election, an informal ANC office at Nkaneng settlement was burnt to the ground, and residents threw stones at ANC election canvassers.[22] The EFF beat the ANC in both of Marikana's local voting districts, a victory that was repeated in many mining communities across the platinum belt.[23]

Ahmed Kathrada

Speech at Nelson Mandela's funeral service,
15 December 2013

Fifteen minutes before midnight on 5 December 2013, a sombre-looking President Jacob Zuma appeared on national television to announce the inevitable: Nelson Mandela, the nation's beloved Madiba, had died at ninety-five years of age. 'Although we knew this day would come,' Zuma said, 'nothing can diminish our sense of a profound and enduring loss.'[1]

Mandela had retired from public life in 2004, after spending his post-presidency years helping to broker peace in conflict-ridden areas such as Burundi, campaigning tirelessly for his Nelson Mandela Children's Fund, and participating in the 46664 HIV/AIDS charity pop concerts alongside global celebrities. Two months before 'retiring from retirement',[2] as he put it, he had accepted the FIFA World Cup trophy on behalf of South Africa when the country won the bid to host the 2010 event, an honour that many reports attributed to his 'Madiba magic'.

After jokingly telling journalists 'Don't call me, I'll call you',[3] Mandela only occasionally appeared in public after 2004. At ninety, he made a surprise appearance at Ellis Park as part of the ANC's 2009 election campaign, and, apparently under immense pressure from FIFA,[4] he went on to attend the 2010 World Cup closing ceremony. He smiled and waved at the crowd as he was driven around the stadium in a golf cart with his wife Graça Machel, whom he'd married in 1998. Apart from media updates on his ailing health, there was little news of him after 2010, although many missed his moral intervention in the political tensions of the post-Mbeki period.

Then, in 2013, the media updates on his health began to increase as it became clear that, however immortal he might seem, Mandela could not live forever. By April, he had been admitted to hospital three times during the preceding five months. When he was admitted again in June, his condition was deemed 'stable' and then 'critical', and then, confusingly, 'critical but stable'. After spending three months at Pretoria's Mediclinic Heart Hospital, he was finally discharged on 1 September, ostensibly to live out his last days in the care of a team of twenty-two doctors in the comfort of his home.

In the months that followed, the media was full of conjecture. Fake news reports announcing his death sprung up all over the internet, obituaries were prematurely published and broadcast, and conspiracy theories abounded. One posited that Mandela had actually died in June but that the South African authorities weren't prepared for his death and so hid the news from the public. In reality, the Mandela Funeral Committee had been established several years before, and when the time came, it was clear that the logistics were in place, even if the nation wasn't ready. The government immediately declared an official ten-day period of mourning, during which time South Africa was utterly transformed in its shared grief over the loss of the man who had united them.

In celebration of his life, each city distributed programmes announcing an itinerary of commemorative events and religious services, and various spontaneous gatherings took shape at sites of historic importance. In Houghton, flowers piled up outside Mandela's final home, and the road became the site of an ongoing vigil, as Johannesburgers, 'draped in flags, South African football shirts, and even their pyjamas and dressing gowns',[5] came to light candles in his memory. Similar scenes of mourning played out in Vilakazi Street, Soweto, where Mandela had lived before he was arrested. In Cape Town, a stage was set up at the Grand Parade, the site of his famous release speech. For several days, musicians performed and ordinary members of the public came forward to deliver personal testimonies about the role that Madiba had played in their lives. Flowers and wreaths lined the base of the stage, together with cards, teddy bears, replicas of the South African flag, and farewell messages. In KwaZulu-Natal, crowds wanting to undertake some kind of pilgrimage even made their way to the site of Mandela's 1962 arrest in Howick in the Midlands to sign condolence books.

City spaces were transformed as hawkers lined the streets to sell Madiba memorabilia, and shop-window displays were redesigned to pay homage to the country's first democratic president. Flash mobs, singing songs in his honour, surprised shoppers in supermarkets; electric road signs were lit up, declaring 'Goodbye, Tata'; and advertisers erected billboards bearing inspirational Mandela quotes and images. The stadiums built for the 2010 World Cup held a number of free celebratory concerts featuring many of the celebrities who'd participated in Mandela's 46664 initiatives, including Annie Lennox and Johnny Clegg, whose 'Asimbonanga' ('We have not seen him'), released in 1987 during Mandela's imprisonment, took on a poignant secondary meaning in the wake of the icon's now-permanent vanishing from the world.

The official memorial service was held on 10 December at the FNB Stadium in Johannesburg, and it was attended by the world's political elite. The global guest list included no fewer than ninety-one heads of state, ten former heads of state, seventy-five dignitaries and eighty-six delegations from various organisations. In addition to Bill and Hillary Clinton, Robert Mugabe and David Cameron, as well as royals from the United Kingdom, Saudi Arabia and Japan, the event was attended by celebrities known for their philanthropy, such as Oprah Winfrey, Richard Branson and Bono. In fact, with so many elites, it became easier to identify notable *non*-attendants – the Dalai Lama, who'd struggled to acquire a visa from the South African authorities on two previous occasions; Fidel Castro, who was presumably too frail to travel; and the Pope, who, perhaps not wanting to be out-sainted, never responded to his invitation.

With South Africa firmly in the world's spotlight, a mixture of sheer magnitude, poor planning and political tensions resulted in a cumbersome and bungled affair. Transport logistics, Zuma's failure to declare a national holiday and rainy weather meant that the 95 000-seater stadium was only two-thirds full, and the state's hoped-for display of national unity was marred by the Mbeki–Zuma fallout. At an event intended to be a celebration of Mandela's life, the audience took the opportunity to express its dissatisfaction with the country's leader to the rest of the world. 'Speech after speech was drowned out by rival political factions high in the covered stands that taunted and jeered at each other but reserved their loudest, angriest boos and cries for when Zuma's face appeared on the giant screens.'[6] The audience had more time for US president Barack Obama, who seized the chance to 'position himself as Mandela's heir',[7] giving what some called the 'best speech of his presidency'.[8] Winning the loudest roar of approval from the crowd, Obama thanked South Africans for sharing their icon with the world, before identifying some of the traits that made Mandela great. 'It took a man like Madiba to free not just the prisoner, but the jailer as well,' the US president said.

The rain-sodden event was ultimately too long and there were too many formal addresses, giving mourners little chance to participate and express their grief. When the crowd grew restless, Desmond Tutu scolded them, calling for them to 'show the world that we are disciplined'. Most humiliating, however, was the discovery that the event's official signer, appointed to interpret speeches for the deaf community, was a fake who had communicated gibberish on global television.

Mandela's body lay in state from 11 to 13 December, and over 100 000 members of the public made the pilgrimage to the Union Buildings in Pretoria to view his casket. This process, too, faced logistical challenges, and large numbers of disappointed mourners, many of whom had travelled long distances and queued for hours, were turned away without being given a chance to pay their last respects. The casket was then transferred to the Water-kloof airbase for an official farewell from the ANC before being transported to Mthatha. From there, a motorcade drove the body to Qunu, Mandela's remote boyhood village and the site of his burial, and the thirty-kilometre road was lined with residents and well-wishers wanting to say goodbye.

Finally, on 15 December, the period of mourning came to an end with the official state funeral. Held in an enormous white marquee erected in Qunu, the funeral was intended to be a smaller, more intimate affair, but it was still attended by over 4000 people and included high-profile speakers – Jacob Zuma and Cyril Ramaphosa, African heavyweights such as Kenneth Kaunda and Joyce Banda, and representatives from Mandela's family.

Of the hundreds of speeches given during the pomp and ceremony of the mourning period, perhaps the most heartfelt came from an unassuming individual, Mandela's former comrade Ahmed Kathrada. Known for his humility, Kathrada brought a more personal note to the proceedings, capturing the very sincere grief felt by many South Africans.

The last time I saw Madiba alive was when I visited him in hospital.

I was filled with an overwhelming mixture of sadness, emotion and pride.

He tightly held my hand until the end of my brief visit. It was profoundly heartbreaking.

It brought me to the verge of tears when my thoughts automatically flashed back to the picture of the man I grew up under. How I wished I'd never had to confront the reality of what I saw.

I first met Madiba in 1946; that's 67 years ago. I recall the tall, healthy and strong man, the boxer, the prisoner who easily wielded the pick and shovel at the lime quarry on Robben Island.

I visualised the prisoner that vigorously exercised every morning before we were unlocked.

What I saw at his home after his spell in hospital was this giant of a man, helpless and reduced to a shadow of his former self.

And now the inevitable has happened.

He has left us and is now with the 'A Team' of the ANC – the ANC in which he cut his political teeth and the ANC for whose policy of a non-racial, non-sexist, democratic and prosperous South Africa he was prepared to die.

He has joined the 'A Team' of his close comrades: Chief Luthuli, Walter Sisulu, Oliver Tambo, Dr Yusuf Dadoo, Jack Simons, Moses

Kotane, Bram Fischer, Dr Monty Naicker, J.B. Marks, Helen Joseph, Ruth First, Professor Z.K. Matthews, Beyers Naudé, Joe Slovo, Lilian Ngoyi, Ma Sisulu and Michael Harmel.

In addition to the ANC's 'A Team', Madiba has also joined men and women outside the ANC – Helen Suzman, Steve Biko, Alan Paton, Robert Sobukwe, Cissie Gool, Bennie Kies, Neville Alexander, Zeph Mothopeng and many other leaders.

We are a country that has been blessed by many great and remarkable men and women, all of whom played a critical part in this grand struggle for freedom and dignity. We have been blessed by the contributions of many different movements and formations, both inside and outside the country, each making an indelible imprint on our history.

We have been blessed by a struggle that actively involved the masses of the people in their own liberation.

We have been blessed that under the collective leadership of the ANC, we can proudly proclaim that 'South Africa belongs to all who live in it, black and white'.

We were mightily, and unexpectedly, blessed when the old, oppressive, undemocratic order succumbed and bowed to the inevitable.

And then finally, we were truly blessed by the far-sighted wisdom of our collective leadership, with Madiba at the helm, that took us into a democratic future.

For all of this and much more, we are deeply grateful.

We are fortunate that today we live in a noisy and lively democracy.

We are eternally grateful that dignity has been restored to all South Africans.

We are forever grateful that the lives of many are improving, although not enough yet.

We are deeply grateful for a Constitution that encompasses all that is good in us and a constitutional order that protects our hard-won freedom.

Finally, we are infinitely grateful that each and every one of us, whether we are African, white, coloured, or Indian, can proudly call ourselves South Africans.

Mindful of our gains, we nevertheless know that a long, long road lies ahead, with many twists and turns, sometimes through difficult and trying times. Poverty, ill-health and hunger still stalk our land. Greed and avarice show their ugly faces.

Xenophobia and intolerance play their mischief in our beautiful land.

Parts of the world out there find themselves in unhappy situations; economies falter and stagger; extremism and fundamentalism of all kinds are rampant; the earth reels from climate change, and the poor battle to survive.

Ferocious struggles for democracy unfold daily before our very eyes and the numbers of political prisoners grow in step with rising intolerance.

For instance, we think of the Palestinian Marwan Barghouti, who is languishing in an Israeli prison.

All of these people and prisoners throughout the world will continue to draw inspiration from the life and legacy of Mandela.

And finally, Mr President, I wish to address myself directly to Madala, as we called each other.

What do we say to you in these, the last final moments together, before you exit the public stage forever?

Madala, your abundant reserves of love, simplicity, honesty, service, humility, care, courage, foresight, patience, tolerance, equality and justice, continually served as a source of enormous strength to many millions of people in South Africa and the world.

You symbolise today, and always will, qualities of collective leadership, reconciliation, unity and forgiveness.

You strove daily to build a united, non-racial, non-sexist and democratic South Africa.

In this spirit, so exemplified in your life, it is up to the present and next generations to take up the cudgels where you have left off.

It is up to them, through service to deepen our democracy, entrench and defend our Constitution, eradicate poverty, eliminate inequality, fight corruption, and serve always with compassion, respect, integrity and tolerance. Above all, they must build our nation and break down the barriers that still divide us.

Xenophobia, racism and sexism must be fought with tenacity, wisdom and enlightenment. Anything that defines someone else as 'the other' has to go. Tolerance and understanding must flourish and grow.

In all these actions we are and will be guided by your wisdom and deeds.

Today, mingled with our grief is the enormous pride that one of our own has during your life, and now in your death, united the people of South Africa and the entire world on a scale never experienced before in history.

Remarkably, in these last few days, the masses of our people, from whatever walk of life, have demonstrated how very connected they feel to you, how the story of your life is their story and how their story is your story.

Madala, you captured this relationship beautifully on the occasion of Walter Sisulu's death, when you said,

'We shared the joy of living, and the pain. Together we shared ideas, forged common commitments. We walked side by side through the valley of death, nursing each other's bruises, holding each other up when our steps faltered. Together we savoured the taste of freedom!'

To Mrs Graça Machel and the Mandela family, our love, respect and support go out to you. We wish there was a way that we could ease your grief and pain.

These last few months, have been particularly hard, and we trust that in the ensuing weeks you will be able to find the rest and peace you need so much. We mourn with you and wish you strength in this time of need.

Madala, while we may be drowned in sorrow and grief, we salute you as a fighter for freedom to the end. Farewell, my dear brother, my mentor, my leader. With all the energy and determination at our command, we pledge to join the people of South Africa and the world to perpetuate your ideals.

When Walter died, I lost a father and now I have lost a brother. My life is in a void and I don't know who to turn to.

Illuminated by a bank of ninety-five candles – one representing each year of Mandela's life – a frail-looking Kathrada gave a speech from which the 'language of personal grief emerged for the first time'.[9] One of the last three remaining Rivonia trialists,[10] 'Uncle Kathy', as he was known to his fellow prisoners, shared Mandela's struggle credentials and had himself been imprisoned for twenty-six years, many of them alongside Mandela. He had, however, known Mandela for much longer than this, longer perhaps than any of the other attendees at the event. The two met in 1946 when Kathrada was a seventeen-year-old schoolboy, slightly in awe of the older Mandela and flattered that a university student deigned to interact with him.[11] The age gap of eleven years meant that he continued to see Mandela as an 'older brother' and mentor.

While many of the eulogies focused on Mandela's legacy, Kathrada's was one of the few to conjure an image of him as a younger man, 'the tall, healthy and strong man, the boxer, the prisoner who easily wielded the pick and shovel at the lime quarry on Robben Island'. Something of their boyish fondness for one another shines through in the speech, particularly in his use of their mutual nickname 'Madala'. Through this address, Kathrada humanises the saintly icon to whom, ironically, so many ordinary people felt an unusual closeness. For South Africans, this was likely a result of the extent to which Mandela's narrative had become intermingled with the national narrative – 'how the story of your life', as Kathrada says in direct address to Mandela, 'is their story and how their story is your story'.

Just as Mandela had cited a long list of struggle activists in his release speech, so Kathrada lists the names of 'A-team' ANC members whom Mandela is presumably going to meet in heaven.[12] But Kathrada goes further. While Mandela was careful to include only affiliates of the ANC, Kathrada's list is more generous, and he allows for the inclusion of individuals often marginalised in official ANC versions of history, including Helen Suzman, Robert Sobukwe, Alan Paton and Steve Biko.

The speech espouses non-racialism, both in its treatment of the heroes of the struggle and in its reminder of the Freedom Charter's injunction that 'South Africa belongs to all who live in it, black and white'. Having influenced Mandela, Kathrada's commitment to non-racialism found expression in the establishment of the Ahmed Kathrada Foundation, founded in 2008 with the aim of deepening non-racialism.

The poignant sincerity of the speech's opening and conclusion echoed the profound sense of loss that gripped the nation. Kathrada is candid in his account of the pain he felt at seeing Mandela as a former shadow of himself, and his parting line, delivered in a wavering voice, 'My life is in a void and I don't know who to turn to', struck a chord. In the contemporary climate, compromised by political infighting and a lack of moral leadership, this seemed true for many South Africans.

For the most part, Kathrada had shied away from the limelight in the post-apartheid era, and he was often described as modest. 'Money was of no interest to him,' David Everatt noted, 'nor honours or headlines.'[13] Having served as an ANC MP and advisor to Mandela in the first five years of democracy, he declined nomination to the ANC's National Executive Committee in 1997 and resigned from politics along with Mandela in 1999. His tender and principled funeral speech reminded South Africa of his presence, positioning him and his newly established Ahmed Kathrada Foundation as a new moral voice in the political landscape.

Jacob Zuma

State of the Nation Address, Parliament,
12 February 2015

A mere seven months after Jacob Zuma's election in 2009, investigative journalists from the *Mail & Guardian* revealed that taxpayers' money was being used to foot the bill for massive extensions at the president's Nkandla homestead in rural KwaZulu-Natal.[1] While Mandela had refuted the stereotype of the African 'big man' by stepping down after one term, Zuma's leadership began showing all the opposite signs. In addition to acquiring two new wives and fathering a child out of wedlock within three years of becoming president, he appeared to have approved exorbitant upgrades to his personal homestead. In 2009, it was estimated that they involved improvements to the tune of R65 million and included a police station, helicopter pad, military clinic, visitors' centre, parking lot and at least three smaller houses to serve as staff quarters. How, asked reporter Mandy Rossouw, could such developments possibly benefit future presidents?

The government's response was a confused mixture of denial, deferral, backtracking, self-justification and blame-shifting. At first, the presidency's office accused the newspaper of setting out to embarrass Zuma and denied that there was any such work occurring. Then it said that renovations were happening but that these had been planned before Zuma took office and were being paid for by the family. Then the Department of Public Works tried to justify the expansions as part of a routine security upgrade. When *City Press* newspaper obtained documents revealing that a whopping 203 million rands' worth of public funds had in fact been budgeted for the upgrade, public works minister Thulas Nxesi claimed that the renovations had been approved and were 'in line with the Ministerial Handbook as far as it relates to security arrangements for private residences of the president'.[2]

There was one problem: the Ministerial Handbook caps the budget for such upgrades at R100 000. Nxesi then claimed that the president's home was also a National Key Point, as defined by an archaic piece of legislation, the National Key Points Act of 1980, which approves funds for locations deemed to be at risk of sabotage. But such expenses, Pierre de Vos then pointed out, can be approved only by the minister of defence, and there was no evidence to suggest that this had been done with Nkandla.[3] Clearly something was amiss.

Government announced its intention of investigating itself in November 2012, just after Lindiwe Mazibuko, the parliamentary leader of the Democratic Alliance (DA), as well as concerned members of the public, lodged complaints with the Public Protector.

Established as an independent Chapter Nine institution in 1994, the South African Public Protector is tasked with investigating corruption, maladministration and abuses of power by government and other public officials. But the success of its investigations depends both on public trust and on the will of the incumbent.[4] And occupying the position in 2012 was a former ANC member, Advocate Thuli Madonsela, appointed by Zuma just before the Nkandla scandal broke. It did not look like a promising path for recourse. Yet Madonsela would test the powers of her office far more than any of her predecessors.

In December 2013, the Department of Public Works submitted its report, reiterating the defence that the upgrades were essential, because 'safeguarding the president had become a security nightmare'. 'The violent history of this area of KwaZulu-Natal, the fact that the Zuma homestead and family members had previously been attacked on three occasions, and the fact that the president has to conduct government functions, such as receiving official delegations, necessitated major security upgrades',[5] the report concluded, adding that there may have been some misuse of funds but that this had nothing to do with Zuma. The president proceeded to instruct the Special Investigating Unit (SIU) to look into possible corruption in the building process.

Madonsela's investigation took two years and was hampered by delays in accessing information (including the Public Works report), as well as legal interference and threats of interdicts. The findings of her eagerly awaited report, published on 19 March 2014, are suggested in its title, *Secure in Comfort*. She confirmed much of what journalists had alleged: the president had 'tacitly accepted' and 'unduly benefited' from non-security upgrades to his homestead, which was 'conservatively estimated' to cost R246 million. These included a cattle kraal and chicken run, a visitors' centre, an amphitheatre, a swimming pool and extensive paving from personally appointed contractors. Many of the contractors, in turn, received payments for goods and services far exceeding their value. Unlike journalists, however, Madonsela had the power to make recommendations. Zuma should pay back any misused public funds, she said, with an amount to be determined by Treasury and the South African Revenue Service (SARS).[6]

When the electorate went to the polls a month later, it was clear that Madonsela's report, together with the Marikana massacre and the emergence of the EFF, increased support for opposition parties. The ANC lost nearly

4 per cent of the vote, whereas the DA made considerable gains, increasing its share of the electorate by more than 5 per cent. COPE, much like Mbeki, was forgotten in the fast-changing political landscape and lost twenty-seven seats, whereas the EFF acquired twenty-five. When its members appeared in Parliament on 21 May wearing red overalls and domestic-worker uniforms, it was clear that they planned to use their presence to maximum effect.

The next attempt to explain Nkandla away came from police minister Nkosinathi Nhleko who overruled the Public Protector's report on 28 May, concluding that the extensions were all in fact security related. As part of his explanation, he produced an elaborate video – complete with operatic score – of firefighters demonstrating how the R3.9 million Nkandla 'firepool', which looked remarkably like an ordinary swimming pool to right-thinking South Africans, was 'first to be used for fire fighting' and 'second, recreation in the homestead'.[7] In reaction, an ad hoc parliamentary committee was reassembled (the first committee's establishment had been disrupted by the election), which later produced the astonishingly titled 'Report of the Ad Hoc Committee to consider the report of the Minister of Police in reply to recommendations in the report of the Ad Hoc Committee to consider the report by the President regarding security upgrades at the Nkandla Private Residence of the President'.[8]

Meanwhile, it emerged that, in what appeared like an attempt to shift the blame from government institutions onto an independent businessperson, the SIU was suing the architect who'd overseen Nkandla's security upgrade for R155.3 million. The public was incredulous; even if Nkandla's overspending was as a result of the architect's inflated quotation, it suggested that Zuma's procurement procedures were wholly lacking.

By 21 August, the opposition was starting to get impatient. Towards the end of a parliamentary question-and-answer session, Julius Malema asked Zuma when he planned to respond to the legitimate findings of Madonsela's report, informing the president that the EFF would not leave until it got an answer. In response, Zuma gave his trademark chuckle and then brushed the question aside, saying that 'the people who did the upgrades at Nkandla … they are the ones who determine who pays, when to pay'. Dissatisfied, EFF MPs began chanting, 'Pay back the money! Pay back the money!' Unable to move on to the next question, the Speaker, Baleka Mbete, ordered the members to leave the House. When they refused, she called in security to have them thrown out.

A similarly heated scene played out on 13 November,[9] when Parliament voted on the ad hoc committee's report. Unsurprisingly, the report absolved Zuma of any responsibility, and the stakes were high. If adopted, it would set a dangerous precedent, opening the door to allow the state to bypass future recommendations of the Public Protector or other Chapter Nine institutions. For seven hours, in an impressive display of joint filibustering, the DA and EFF took turns to propose future debates on Zuma and Nkandla, with MPs recommending a variety of absurd topics: why Zuma is too busy to attend Parliament, the use of amphitheatres as security features, and whether Nkandla should be turned into a tourist attraction. The EFF's Godrich Gardee even suggested that the House congratulate Zuma on being exonerated on Nkandla. After what was later confirmed to be the longest session of members' motions in the history of the National Assembly, the matter went to a vote, and the report was adopted 210 to 103.

And then the EFF's Reneiloe Mashabela called Zuma a thief. When the House chair Cedric Frolick ordered her to withdraw her statements, she went on to declare, 'The president of the ANC is the greatest thief in the world!' and then, warming to her subject, repeated, 'Zuma is a thief' and 'Zuma is a criminal.' When she refused to cease, members of the Public Order Policing Unit were called in to remove her, in contravention of the rules of the National Assembly. MPs from opposition benches then jumped to Mashabela's defence, telling the police that they had no jurisdiction in the National Assembly. Police proceeded to push and shove them and the inter-action descended into a brawl. 'Something broke tonight,' DA parliamentary leader Mmusi Maimane later said about the decision to call in riot police. 'If they can call in the police today, it could be the army tomorrow.'[10]

Despite demands from the DA for Zuma to reappear in Parliament as required by the obligations of his office, he was again missing in action when the House met on 27 November for the last time that year. While MPs debated the course of action for EFF members who had disrupted Parliament, Zuma was telling an eNCA journalist that he didn't wish to 'waste his time' in Parliament with those who displayed a low 'level of maturity' and 'wished to satisfy their egos'.[11]

Thus, by February 2015 when the president was scheduled to give his annual State of the Nation Address (SONA), he hadn't appeared in Parliament for six months. In addition to Nkandla, there were a number of pressing issues that his address needed to tackle: electricity load-shedding had cost the economy millions, the country's unemployment situation had worsened, and service-delivery strikes were becoming an everyday occurrence.

In keeping with Zuma's 'big man' approach to leadership, the glamorous SONA had become an increasingly securitised affair. The city of Cape Town practically shuts down for the day, with the military enforcing road closures and helicopters circling overhead. The day of the 2015 address was no different, and there was a heavy security contingent outside the parliamentary buildings.

The opposition members presented a formidable sight. Unlike the glamorously dressed ANC members, the EFF MPs were having none of it and stuck to their workers' overalls, whereas the DA caucus arrived dressed in black – a reference to the recent electricity blackouts as well as the gloomy political climate. The proceedings, presided over by Speaker Baleka Mbete and chairperson of the National Council of Provinces (NCOP) Thandi Modise, got off to a very poor start indeed. Maimane pointed out that there was a blackout of a different kind: cellphone signals had been jammed.

This was a serious and suspicious breach; Parliament should be open to the public and to the media. It meant that members and journalists inside Parliament would be unable to communicate with the world outside. The Freedom Front Plus's Corné Mulder announced what many suspected: 'I am under the impression that maybe the executive may have something to do with this.'

To make matters worse, there was a problem with the water supply. 'I am terribly thirsty and I think a lot of people are,' the EFF's Mbuyiseni Ndlozi moaned. 'Can we get the water service up and running? … There is a service delivery crisis here in Parliament!'

It was not an auspicious start. After MPs jokingly chanted 'Bring back the signal! Bring back the signal!' it was efficiently, and equally suspiciously, unscrambled and the solemnity of the occasion was restored. The president took his position at the lectern to address the nation, beginning his speech with a self-deprecatory chuckle over his pronunciation of the Khoi greeting.

The PRESIDENT OF THE REPUBLIC: […] good evening, sanibonani, molweni, riperile, dumelang, lotshani, goeie naand, ndi madekwana, !gai//goes. [Applause.] It is not Chinese; it is a South African language. [Laughter.]

Madam Speaker and Madam Chairperson of the NCOP, I would like to thank yourselves, the presiding officers for the opportunity to address the nation this evening. The year 2015 marks 60 years of a historic moment in our history when South Africans from all walks of life adopted the Freedom Charter in 1955 in Kliptown, Soweto.

No sooner had the president begun than EFF general secretary Godrich Gardee raised a point of privilege. Zuma continued to speak for some time, seemingly hoping that Gardee would eventually pipe down, until a visibly irritated Mbete, her spectacles perched upon her nose, stopped the president:

The SPEAKER: Hon President, hon President, I am sorry to interrupt your speech; if the President would not mind just taking a seat so we can listen to this member's point of order.

Mr G A GARDEE: Thank you, Madam Speaker, I rise in terms of Rule 14(c) of the Joint Rules of Parliament 6th edition, the Parliament of the Republic of South Africa on a question of privilege. May I proceed?

Hon MEMBERS: Yes!

Mr G A GARDEE: May we ask the President as to when he is going to pay back the money in terms of what the Public Protector has said? That is the question of privilege we would like to ask, and accordingly, since he has not been answering questions, we hope that today he shall answer that question. I thank you.

The SPEAKER: I would like to remind you, hon member, that a point of order must relate to a point of procedure concerning the current proceedings. As you know, today's sitting is convened for a specific purpose; that purpose is for the President to deliver his annual address to Parliament. Members will have an opportunity to debate and respond to the address by the President at the sittings scheduled for next week, including raising any related matters. So, this is not a question session. The hon President may resume.

Mr G A GARDEE: Madam Speaker, I rose on a question of privilege, not a point of order. So, you have addressed the issue of a point of order, Madam Speaker. But on the issue of the question of privilege, can that question be answered or can we be told that it is in the speech; is he still going to tell us when the money is going to be paid? Is it going to be paid by EFT, cash or eWallet? Thank you.

Gardee knew the rules and had deliberately planned to interrupt the president on a point of privilege (a matter linked to the rights of parliamentary members), which Mbete brushed aside as a point of order (a matter linked to the rules of the House). Mbete seethingly repeated that the joint sitting was not a question-and-answer session and that they needed to return to the 'business of the day': the president's address. But before Zuma could proceed, one EFF member after another raised additional points. The EFF's Nthako Matiase claimed that the House well knew that Zuma had not met his obligation to answer questions at previous sittings, while an earnest Younus Vawda said that the nation deserved answers, to which Mbete replied, 'The people of

South Africa are waiting to hear what he has to say.' She was promptly interrupted again, this time by Julius Malema.

Mr J S MALEMA: Hon Speaker.

The SPEAKER: Hon Malema, I don't think you are going to raise anything that has not been covered by what I have said.

Mr J S MALEMA: You are making a mistake because you are reading my mind. [Laughter.] Allow me to speak.

The SPEAKER: Hon Malema. Hon Malema.

Mr J S MALEMA: Please Speaker, can I speak? Because—

The SPEAKER: On what, hon—?

Mr J S MALEMA: On the same point that the members are raising. [Interjections.] You are not doing me any favours and none of these people who are howling are doing me any favours; it is within my right to speak as a member of this House, and remind you that it is incorrect of you to want to suggest that when the president speaks, you suspend the rules. The rules are not suspended and the rules must apply even when the president speaks, and you have not answered Dr Vawda's question. Stop treating as a group; treat them as individual members of this House and respond to them as individual members. The individual member who spoke, you explained, he sat down; the other one spoke, you explained and he sat down; when Vawda's turn came, you said 'I have responded to you', and you insisted, even though he was speaking for the first time. Stop treating people as a group; we are speaking here as individual members. We want the President to answer a simple question: When is he paying the money as directed by the Public Protector? That is all we are asking.

The SPEAKER: Hon Malema, you are not raising anything new; and what you are saying is still the same thing I have responded to and explained, and I have patiently been asking you hon members to allow this House to proceed with the business of the day, and the business of the day is that the President will deliver the state of the nation address. I am not allowing any other member to raise any other point of order. [Interjections.] I am not allowing you hon members because I have explained to you that you are actually abusing—

Mr J S MALEMA: Which Rule are you using, my hon Speaker? Which Rule are you using to deny members to raise a point of order? They are protected by the Rules. You cannot be emotional about it. Point us to the Rule which gives you the power to deny us points of order.

The SPEAKER: Hon Julius Malema, I now have to ask that you leave the Chamber. [Applause.] I now ask, hon Malema, you leave the Chamber because it's clear that you are not prepared to co-operate with us.

Mr N F SHIVAMBU: Hon Speaker, can you please assist us in terms of the Rules of the Joint Sitting ... what Rule are you applying to ...?

The SPEAKER: Hon Shivambu, I now have to ask you also to leave the Chamber. [Interjections.] [Applause.]

Mr N F SHIVAMBU: I am still asking a question!

The SPEAKER: Hon Shivambu, I have now ... [Interjections.]

Mr N F SHIVAMBU: What Rule are you applying ... [Interjections.]

The SPEAKER: ... to ask you also to leave the Chamber! [Interjections.]

Mr N F SHIVAMBU: Oh! I am still asking a question.

Mr M Q NDLOZI: Order! On a point of order! [Interjections.]

Mr N F SHIVAMBU: I am still asking a question. [Interjections.]

The SPEAKER: Hon members! Hon members of the EFF ... [Interjections.]

Chaos broke out, with Malema insisting that they *were* in fact 'doing the business of the day', and several members started shouting over one another, pointing fingers and jostling. Mbete called on the serjeant-at-arms and Usher of the Black Rod – official parliamentary staff with the unenviable task of maintaining order in the House – to remove the troublemakers, and when their efforts proved inadequate, a stream of efficient white-shirted men entered the chamber to do the job.

The parliamentary newsfeed remained fixed on Mbete and Modise, with Mbete looking very much like a queen bee in a towering black-and-yellow Dr Seuss–style hat, so television audiences could not see the pandemonium that erupted. The EFF didn't surrender easily and there was a good deal of shoving, dragging and punching before they were ejected. All the while, the president sat expressionless, waiting for the chaos to die down. Mbete and Modise called for order and shouted at MPs to take their seats and, when the EFF benches were emptied, ANC members applauded and ululated.

But there was more. A visibly concerned Maimane, suspecting that the EFF members had actually been removed by police officials, asked for clarity on the identity of the plain-clothed security men.

The LEADER OF THE OPPOSITION: [...] I want to understand whether the members who were sent in here to remove the members of the EFF were members of the SA Police Service; and if that is the case, may I request that in fact this ... We simply cannot allow for police to be allowed to enter this Chamber. It is a grave constitutional violation. We want to be here to get the state of the nation address, but we cannot violate this Constitution of the people of this country by allowing the police in this Chamber. We can't accept that. I would like clarity on that, Madam Chair.

The CHAIRPERSON OF THE NCOP: Hon Maimane, we have heard your point of privilege raised under Joint Rules 14. We have indeed repeatedly called members during this Joint Sitting to heed the call to take their seats and to withdraw. We sent in the Usher of the Black Rod and the Serjeant-at-arms, but they were all defied.

We then moved on in terms of the Powers, Privileges and Immunities Act to call on the security services of Parliament to come in. We are also empowered by the same Act to ensure that we can escalate to ask for security, whichever security, to act in support of public order policing, POP. I think, hon members, we should allow this House to do its business.

I think that we have called for a Joint Sitting of Parliament – it was not even convened by the Speaker and the Chairperson of the NCOP. It is convened in terms of a request raised by the President for a specific reason to come and give the nation, ourselves and the international community the state of the nation address. I think we should be allowed, hon members, to proceed with the business of the day.

Modise's answer was typically vague, and the DA's chief whip, John Steenhuisen, intervened to read out sections of the Constitution, which limits the power of the security services from prejudicing any political party interest. Clearly horrified at the prospect that SAPS members had been doing the dirty work of the ANC, Steenhuisen instructed Modise, 'We don't meet bad behaviour with bad behaviour. Now, I submit to you that the section that you have invoked is unconstitutional and incorrect. I would ask you to make a ruling on it.'

Before Modise could answer, minister of science and technology Naledi Pandor came to her aid, justifying the use of force as a necessary response to what had been itself a 'direct violation of the Constitution'. 'We should not, therefore, be selective as to when it's constitutional and when it's not,' she argued.

This comment stirred Mangosuthu Buthelezi to rise. At eighty-six, the long-time IFP leader had seen his fair share of parliamentary sittings and likely tolerated no speech interruptions in his time. (He in fact holds the world record for the longest ever legislative speech, speaking for nearly thirty hours interspersed over a period of eleven days in 1993.) He took the opportunity to tell his colleagues exactly what he thought of the EFF's behaviour:

Prince M G BUTHELEZI: Madam Chairperson of the NCOP, I think what we have seen today is disgusting. I think our country is really being torn to pieces and I think that the struggle for liberation didn't take place for people to play the fool like this with our country. [Applause.] I think that what is happening is not really what the majority of the people in this House want to see in this House. [Applause.] If there is any opportunity, if the Constitution allows us to vote, why can't we put this matter to the vote? We can't have a few people indulging in these theatrics, tearing our country apart and using all kinds of poppycock, what I regard as utter nonsense. [Applause.]

Modise pleaded with Maimane for the House to continue with 'the business of the day', but Maimane was adamant. After both he and Steenhuisen attempted and failed to get a clear answer on whether police officials had entered the House, the DA members rose, and Maimane led his members outside.

There, Malema, whose overalls had been torn in the scuffle, was holding court amid a crowd of journalists. 'We have seen that we are part of a police state,'[12] he announced somewhat jubilantly. He congratulated the DA members for their bravery, but an unimpressed Helen Zille clarified that the party's walkout was not an expression of solidarity with the EFF so much as a rejection of the use of police force to deal with the EFF members.[13]

Back inside, with the chamber devoid of the bulk of the opposition, Mbete asked for the door to be closed and then apologised to Zuma for the outbreak.

After over an hour of disruptions, Zuma finally proceeded to deliver his address to the nation.

'Let me start where I was interrupted from,' a jovial Zuma said before breaking into a hearty chuckle. He went on to give a speech 'clearly prepared by a visionless committee, telling the nation that (almost everything) was on track'.[14] He made vague promises to end the energy crisis; spoke about how many people were employed, without mentioning the 8.1 million unemployed; and blamed many of the country's economic problems on the global slowdown. He praised the government's efforts to fight corruption, citing new legislation and successful convictions. 'This demonstrates a concerted effort by government to break the back of this scourge in the country,' the president told his nation.

There was no mention of Nkandla.

Mmusi Maimane

'Broken Man' speech at the State of the Nation debate,
Parliament, 17 February 2015

In the wake of the disastrous 2015 SONA, expectations for the next parliamentary session were high. The arrival of the EFF had enlivened the House
to such an extent that 'for the first time in years South Africans [were] paying attention to Parliament'.[1] The State of the Nation debate, held a week
after the SONA, gives opposition leaders a chance to respond to the president's
assessment of the national landscape and is traditionally a space where
they can strut their stuff. The nation was full of speculation about what
the EFF would do next and how the ANC would respond. All eyes were
on Julius Malema. But in the end, it was the DA's Mmusi Maimane who
stole the show, delivering a twenty-minute speech that was both a blistering
indictment of Zuma's leadership and an eloquent vision of South Africa's
possible future.

Maimane had succeeded Lindiwe Mazibuko as the DA's parliamentary
leader in May 2014, just as the EFF arrived on the scene. But many South
Africans came to know him a few months earlier when he starred in the DA
election advert 'Ayisafani'. In the advert, a suave Maimane, whom a former
colleague once described as 'made for TV',[2] has an imaginary conversation
with himself in a mirror, questioning the moral regression of the ANC under
Jacob Zuma's leadership. At one point, he addresses the camera directly and
asks, 'Where are the jobs, President Zuma?' before the advert concludes with
the slogan 'iANC Ayisafani' ('The ANC is not the same'). The advert would
likely have remained fairly low-key had the SABC not banned it for supposedly inciting political violence because of the inclusion of an image of police
brutality. Viewers would be forgiven for thinking that Maimane, who had an
early television career as a Christian programme presenter for SABC1, was a
professional actor, whereas at the time he was the DA's national spokesperson and their candidate for Gauteng premier.

Maimane moved up the ranks of the DA with remarkable speed, most likely
because of the party's eagerness to widen its appeal by appointing black
leaders. The DA was a slow- but sure-moving tortoise in the race for political
power, having grown incrementally over the years to take its place as the official

opposition. It had effectively developed out of the various incarnations of Helen Suzman's Progressive Party, which, as the Democratic Party, did very poorly in the 1994 election, winning only 1.7 per cent of the vote. Although by 2014 it had increased its support to 22.2 per cent, the DA was struggling to shed the perception that it served white interests, and it was clear that leaders such as Helen Zille, despite having impeccable struggle credentials, were off-putting to many black voters. The thirty-four-year-old Maimane, who hailed from Dobsonville and was dubbed the 'Obama of Soweto' because of his impressive oratory skills,[3] presented an obvious choice for parliamentary leader when his predecessor Mazibuko resigned. The flip side of appointing such leaders, however, was that it opened them to charges of tokenism, and Maimane was frequently accused of being a puppet with no political vision of his own. In reaction to his first parliamentary speech in June 2014, the ANC's Lindiwe Sisulu made it clear that Maimane would face the same kinds of attack as Mazibuko (whom Malema, while he was still ANC Youth League president, had famously called Zille's 'tea girl'). Sisulu dismissed Maimane, saying, 'Madam has found another hired native in the form of honourable Maimane … a black commodity to run their election'.[4]

In addition to these kinds of charges, Maimane also had to contend with the rising power of the EFF. While the two parties complemented one another in some ways, and the EFF added brawn to the DA's brain, Malema's party tended to dominate headlines, and some pundits were starting to call it the 'first real opposition to the ANC'.[5] Despite the fact that it was the DA's Mazibuko who had initiated the Public Protector's investigation into Nkandla, this was forgotten in the aftermath of the EFF's parliamentary removals, and the party's '"Pay back the money" slogan now drove the campaign'.[6]

The need to distinguish itself as the voice of the opposition was never more apparent than in the wake of the 2015 SONA. Malema exploited his members' bruising to maximum effect, and when ANC national chairperson and Speaker of Parliament Baleka Mbete added insult to injury by calling Malema a 'cockroach' at an address shortly after the SONA fiasco,[7] the persecuted party again dominated headlines. Increasingly, the impression was that the DA was playing second fiddle.

When the National Assembly reconvened on 17 February, proceedings got off to a shaky start. Mbete was suspiciously absent, and NCOP chairperson Thandi Modise had the unenviable task of presiding over the debate. Immediately, there were complaints. The Freedom Front Plus's Corné Mulder was dissatisfied with the SONA minutes, and disgruntled EFF members raised various points of order over Mbete's 'cockroach' comment. Yet, perhaps because of sheer exhaustion, or perhaps because the State of the Nation debate was not Zuma's parade, the rest of the session was comparatively civil.

As per tradition, an ANC MP kicked off the debate, and this task fell to arts and culture minister Nathi Mthethwa, who got through his speech with no interruptions by avoiding any mention of the controversial events of the previous sitting and by trotting out platitudes, calling for South Africans to find the 'Mandela within' and 'if you want to go far, go together'. As the parliamentary leader of the official opposition, Maimane spoke next, and the contrast between Mthethwa's staid address and Maimane's speech was startling.

Madame Speaker,
Honourable President and Deputy President
Honourable Members
Fellow South Africans
Bagaetsho
Dumelang,

Eleven days ago we lost one of South Africa's literary giants, Professor André Brink. Our sadness at his passing is tempered only by his great literature he bequeathed us.

Professor Brink taught us a powerful lesson. He taught us that you cannot blame a faceless system for the evils in society. It is human beings that perpetrate wrongs against others. And it is human beings that have the power to correct these wrongs.

We would do well, honourable members, to heed these lessons as we debate the State of the Nation today.

Because, if we are to succeed as a nation, we need to start believing in the power of human agency. We need to resurrect the idea that the choices we make, the actions we take, matter.

It is true that the uneven legacy of the apartheid system weighs heavy on us. It is a fact that black children still do not have the same opportunities as white children. This is a human tragedy that nobody in this House should ever accept.

Much has been done to redress the past, make no mistake. Life in South Africa today is certainly better than it was during apartheid. But we need to hold ourselves to a much higher standard than that.

We need to become the nation that President Nelson Mandela helped us believe we could become: a place of hope, prosperity, selfless leadership and mutual respect.

And so, I think honourable members, South Africans, the question we must ask ourselves today is: what is holding us back from achieving Madiba's vision?

We can blame apartheid. We can blame the global financial system. We can even blame Jan van Riebeeck, if you like.

But in our hearts, we know what the problem is. We have allowed those in power to become bigger than our institutions, breaking them down bit by bit.

We have indeed allowed one powerful man to get away with too much for too long. Members, this honourable man is in our presence here today.

Honourable President, in these very chambers, just five days ago, you broke Parliament.

Please understand, Honourable President, when I use the term 'honourable', I do it out of respect for the traditions and conventions of this august House.

But please don't take it literally. For you, Honourable President, are not an honourable man.

You are a broken man, presiding over a broken society.

See, you are willing to break every democratic institution to try and fix the legal predicament you find yourself in.

You are willing to break this Parliament if it means escaping accountability for the wrongs you have done.

You see, on Thursday afternoon, outside this very House, Members of Parliament were being arrested and assaulted by your riot police.

A few hours later, inside this House, our freedom to communicate was violated by an order to jam the telecommunications network.

Not long after, armed police officers in plain shirts stormed into this sacred chamber and physically attacked members of this House.

This was more than an assault on Members of Parliament; it was an assault on the very foundations of our democracy, honourable members.

Parliament's constitutional obligation to fearlessly scrutinise and oversee the Executive lost all meaning on Thursday night.

In fact, the brute force of the state won. And the hearts of our nation was broken.

We knew, at that very moment, that our democratic order was in grave danger.

But here's the question: what did you do, Mr President?

You laughed. You laughed while the people of South Africa cried for their beloved country.

You laughed while trampling Madiba's legacy – in the very week that we celebrated 25 years of his release.

Honourable President, we will never ever forgive you for what you did on that day.

Madam Speaker, I led my party out of these chambers on Thursday night because we could not sit by and watch while our Constitution was being destroyed right in front of us. We could not.

In fact, the justices walked out. They walked out with the defenders of the Constitution. When we emerged from this chamber, we heard the President reading from the cold and empty words from his prepared text.

They were the words of a broken man, presiding over a broken society.

For six years, he has run from 783 counts of corruption, fraud and racketeering that have haunted him from before the day he was elected.

For six years, this broken man has spent his waking hours plotting and planning to avoid his day in court.

In this broken man's path of destruction lies a litany of broken institutions. Each one of them targeted because of their constitutional power to hold him to account.

A broken SARS, that should have investigated the fringe tax benefits from Nkandla, the palace of corruption that was built by the people's money.

A broken NPA, that should have continued with its prosecution of the President, without fear or favour.

A broken SIU, a broken Hawks, a broken SAPS. And so we can go on with the list of institutions President Zuma is willing to break to protect himself and his friends.

This is why we are a broken society. Because the abuses do not stop at the door of the Union Buildings. The power abusing is happening at every level. We have seen mini President Zumas in government and municipalities, all over South Africa in fact.

Honourable members, I went to Mogalakwena, I met a woman there who had not been able to bath for days.

The lack of water in Mogalakwena was not a system's failure. It was a failure of your local comrades, to use that term, who in that community have started to fight amongst each other and have long forgotten the people of Mogalakwena. That's whose fault it was. It was in fact that

ANC councillors waged a factional war, simply fighting over power and not for the rights of the people of this country.

Local police officers with a duty to serve the community have been co-opted by factions to intimidate residents and suppress protest. As the war rages on, rubbish piles up in the streets, sewage pipes continue to leak, and the taps in fact run dry.

This is all because of broken men, presiding over broken towns and cities. But they learned from the best.

In Atteridgeville, I met a good man running a hospice that is struggling more and more each day to care for the sick because all their money goes to fuelling a generator. This is their last line of defence against an electricity crisis that plagues them on a daily basis.

The daily struggle of this community-funded organisation is just one example of the devastating impact this electricity crisis is having on households, businesses, schools, hospitals, and countless other facets of society.

Where is the accountability from this broken man who claims to be our President, when all he can offer is more of the same? All he does is promise to bail out Eskom and secure its monopoly over our power supply.

Load-shedding is a crisis that will take our economy to the brink of an economic shutdown. Our economy has lost R300 billion since 2008 because, without a stable electricity supply, manufacturers cannot produce, investors are driven away and ultimately jobs are lost.

That is why, Mr President, when you stand here and promise more of the same, jobs every year that never materialise, we simply cannot believe you. On Thursday, the President said that the NDP's ambition to grow at 5% by 2019 is at risk as a result of slow global growth and domestic constraints. How is it then that other SADC countries are growing at a rate of 5.6%, facing the same external pressures? The answer is our real constraints are because of the policy failures of this particular government.

In his nine-point plan he failed to address the need for solid economic infrastructure. He left the electricity monopoly with Eskom. He gave the broadband monopoly to Telkom. And then left SANRAL to toll our roads in Gauteng. The legacy of this will mean more government bailouts and failing infrastructure, leading us to more job losses, more debt and a broken society.

This broken man has indeed broken our economy.

Despite all his past promises, what President Zuma failed to tell us last week was that, today, there are 1.6 million more South Africans living without jobs than when he took office in 2009. Living and breathing human beings being robbed of their feeling of self-worth, and their ability to provide for their families.

From Ikageng, to Nelson Mandela Bay, to Soweto, I met unemployed youth who have lost hope in finding a job. They are the victims of an unequal education that serves the interests of a powerful teacher union over learners, and where poorer schools go without textbooks, desks and proper classrooms.

The consequence, as parents in Riverlea told me, is that crime and drugs continue to enslave our young people, and druglords and criminals operate freely within our communities.

This is the state of our broken society, battling under the burdens of unemployment, crime, power cuts, and an unequal education system.

South Africa may be a broken society under a broken President, but, honourable members, the spirit of our people is a lot harder to break.

We are standing as a people today because South Africans were able to free ourselves from the worst forms of oppression under apartheid.

Today, we have a Constitution and a Bill of Rights that is admired across the world.

We have an obligation to future generations of South Africans to make sure we continue to fight for a fairer society, where there is a greater opportunity for all to live a better life, and where the rights and freedoms granted to us by the Constitution are protected.

But on Thursday we received a weak account of the State of the Nation from a broken President.

We can have a stable electricity supply in South Africa, but a war-room isn't certainly going to solve it.

The President knows what needs to be done to keep the lights on, and this is it: You've got to break the Eskom monopoly. As long as they are in charge of the national grid they will act to prevent any meaningful contributions by independent power producers to our electricity supply.

And, more seriously, Mr President, you must abandon the R1 trillion nuclear deal – future generations will pay for this in electricity price hikes while we wait over a decade to see any power. And of course the secrecy behind this deal means there is scope for corruption on a mega–arms deal level, as we've seen.

We can and we must have an equal education system, where schools are properly resourced, teachers are well-trained, and there is a commitment from school principals.

There are many hard-working educators out there, but the President ignores the need to hold principals and teachers accountable when they fail our children.

We believe it is possible for entrepreneurs to flourish, with an economy that grows at 8% and creates millions of jobs if we make the right choices.

But the government's ideas are stale. We need economic infrastructure that is reliable. We need a tax incentive for established businesses, business people to participate in mentorship programmes. We need a National Venture Capital Fund to [fund] start-ups. We need to roll out Opportunity Centres where advice and support is readily available. We need a real Youth Wage Subsidy that benefits even the smallest of businesses.

Our country for our country. We believe it is possible for our country to be a place where the streets are safe and communities are healthy places to raise families, where the police are properly managed and trained.

But while our communities are being over-run by druglords, and the President said nothing about crime on Thursday! Where are the anti-drug units? Drug crime has doubled since they were taken away.

People don't trust the police. If the SAPS is going to have its integrity restored, it needs to start right at the top with the national police commissioner.

Our crime-fighting institutions such as the Hawks, the NPA, and the SIU must be led by people committed to fairness and justice, and free from interference by powerful political interests.

We believe it's possible to realise a vision of South Africa where every effort is made to redress the legacy of apartheid through a land reform programme that truly benefits those who were denied access to land.

All the President has offered is a populist proposal to ban foreign land ownership. This will only kill investment and jobs.

The 17.5 million hectares of fertile soil in communal land areas must be unlocked for reform purposes. State-owned land must be fully audited and used to fast-track the redistribution to deserving beneficiaries. And farmworkers must become farm-owners in partnership with commercial farmers, through the NDP's system of identifying and purchasing available land on the market. Mr President, where is that document, the NDP, the one that the ministers don't read? That one. But we all know,

Mr President, that half the people sitting behind you don't support the NDP and will not implement it.

Only through bold reforms that go to the heart of the problem will we meaningfully redress the legacy of restricted access to land.

National Council Chairperson, the tide is turning in our country. And as Professor Brink wrote in his most celebrated work, *A Dry White Season*:

'The image that presents itself is one of water. A drop held back by its own inertia for one last moment, though swollen of its own weight, before it irrevocably falls ... as if the water, already sensing its own imminent fall, continues to cling, against the pull of gravity, to its precarious stability, trying to prolong it as much as possible.'

Madam Speaker, let me help you: change may seem slow, but it is coming. There is a swell starting to build and, when the wave crashes, it will sweep away this broken man out of power. When that happens, we will be there to start fixing our broken society, and unleash the potential of every South African.

That is why the party I lead in this Parliament will not join other parties in breaking down our institution. Because one day, when we are in government, we will want the very same institutions and this Parliament to hold us to account.

And so we will work within the institutions of democracy to hold this government to account, and we will continue creating opportunities for all where we govern. We will work tirelessly to build a truly democratic alternative in South Africa. Indeed, I stand before you pronouncing that for my children and your children, their future can only be bright under the DA when we come into power. That change is coming and I propose you get ready for it. We will restore power to the people.

Nkosi Sikelel' iAfrika. Let us live and strive for freedom in South Africa our land.

I thank you very much!

Maimane was able to speak uninterrupted, and parts of the audience murmured approval and applauded at various points, specifically when he referred to the events of the SONA and the possibility of Zuma being swept 'out of power'. The opening of the speech gives little sign of the scathing attack that will follow. He begins with a somewhat vague allusion to André Brink's lesson about the power of human agency and moves on to dispute the accusation that the DA is a 'white' party by acknowledging the 'tragedy' that 'black children still do not have the same opportunities as white children'. This is followed by Maimane's central question: 'What is holding us back from achieving Madiba's vision?' Using delay tactics, he lists a variety of possible causes: apartheid, Jan van Riebeeck, the global financial system. Then, employing the trope of the 'enemy in our midst', he claims that the audience knows 'in [their] hearts' that the real cause of the problem 'is in [their] presence here today'. It is, of course, the president.

Thereafter, Maimane is careful not to engage in any kind of slander. He doesn't directly accuse Zuma of being a liar, thief or criminal. Instead, his attack goes deeper. In the politest terms, he accuses the president of lacking moral backbone, saying, 'you, Honourable President, are not an honourable man'.

To drive the message home, Maimane repeats that Zuma is a 'broken man, presiding over a broken society' several times. The 'broken' metaphor threads through the speech: Zuma broke Parliament at the 2015 SONA; he has wrecked government institutions 'bit by bit'; Zuma's ANC is broken; and the president has broken municipalities, SARS and the economy – but not, importantly, the South African people.

Maimane is arguably most sincere when speaking about his first-hand experience of visiting people in Mogalakwena, where service delivery had ground to a halt. Going off script slightly, and breaking into his mother tongue, Setswana, his contempt for the ANC councillors – the so-called 'comrades' who have 'long forgotten the people of Mogalakwena' – is evident.

While the speech, written together with the DA's well-resourced PR team, is strong on paper, it is no masterpiece. Its real power lies in Maimane's delivery. Having developed his oratory skills as a preacher in Soweto, he dances through the words, breathing life into the phrases 'bit by bit', 'and your friends' and 'out of power'. In a political climate that appears to value the art of both speechwriting and delivery as secondary, Maimane worked hard to achieve this effect, telling journalist Sam Mkokeli, 'Gosh, I must have read that speech well over 10 times.'[8]

The effort paid off, and Maimane dominated reportage on the debate. Malema's subsequent address, a jargon-riddled speech in which he takes a break from telling Zuma to 'pay back the money', could not compete. What's more, Maimane's metaphor of Zuma as a 'broken man' found its way into public discourse and took on a life of its own.

Throughout what the media referred to as a 'roasting',[9] Zuma remained expressionless, except when Maimane attacked his response to the events of the SONA. When Maimane damningly pointed out that Zuma had laughed while the country was crying, Zuma again chuckled. There was much speculation over whether Maimane's speech would prick the president's conscience, with Ranjeni Munusamy, a former supporter, claiming that 'stinging rebukes by Julius Malema but, particularly Mmusi Maimane, will definitely have an impact on him'.[10] Yet Zuma did not deign to mention Maimane in his official response to the SONA debate the following day. Over the years, the president's few reactions to Maimane have been dismissive, suggesting that he does not take him seriously. He has occasionally referred to Maimane as a 'boy' in Parliament and has attacked his 'English from London'.[11]

Minister of local government Pravin Gordhan appeared to have been more stung by the young politician's accusations – judging by the extent to which he engaged Maimane in his response speech. Gordhan accused him of creating rather than solving problems, and said that the ANC does not have the 'luxury of merely preaching, complaining, and moaning and analysing'. Maimane 'has got to join this side', suggested Gordhan, 'if he wants to be in government' – a proposal that did not appear to draw much enthusiasm from anybody in the House.

After espousing the Charterist virtues of non-sexism and non-racialism, Gordhan went on to attack Maimane for being Zille's lackey. Ridiculing his confusion over whether to lead a walkout during the SONA debate days before, he challenged: 'Who is the real leader, Mr Maimane, and who do you really listen to?' At this stage, Zille still occupied the position of party leader, while Maimane was parliamentary leader, but this would soon change. Zille resigned a few months later, and Maimane was elected as the DA's first black leader on 10 May, receiving 90 per cent of his party's support.

Interestingly, Gordhan, like the other ANC speakers at the debate, didn't come to Zuma's defence in his response speech, perhaps because, as Munusamy points out, Zuma was 'extremely difficult to defend'.[12] Instead Gordhan focuses on restoring the reputation of the ANC. 'We are not a broken country,' he insisted. 'We are not a broken organisation.' In the years to come, he would be proved wrong in this assessment.

Barbara Hogan

Speech at Ahmed Kathrada's memorial service,
1 April 2017

At eight in the evening on 9 December 2015, Zuma released a statement to
say he had decided to replace finance minister Nhlanhla Nene with David
van Rooyen, a little-known and inexperienced MP. There was an immediate
outcry. In addition to asking the question 'Who is David van Rooyen?', newspapers speculated that Nene's axing had to do with his reluctance to fork out
funds for an expensive and unnecessary nuclear deal as well as his reining in of
excessive spending by the South African Airways (SAA) board. The finance
minister, some said, had been doing his job too well.

One of the first high-profile voices to criticise the move came from ANC
veteran Barbara Hogan, the wife of Ahmed Kathrada. Claiming that Zuma had
'become a law unto himself',[1] she called on the party to hold him to account.
Four days later, after the rand had taken a spectacular nosedive, Zuma was
persuaded to replace Van Rooyen with Pravin Gordhan, a respected former
finance minister. The rand slowly recovered, but Nenegate, as the blunder was
dubbed, had cost the country billions.

Then, in March 2016, deputy finance minister Mcebisi Jonas made the
shocking revelation that he had in fact been offered the post of finance minister prior to Van Rooyen's appointment. The offer, however, had not come from
Zuma: it had come from a trio of Indian brothers, the Guptas.[2] The Guptas
had achieved notoriety in 2013 when it was revealed that, against military protocol, they had used Air Force Base Waterkloof to land a chartered aeroplane
transporting guests from India for a family wedding at Sun City. In mid-
December 2015, the Guptas were back in the news when it emerged that their
company Tegeta Exploration and Resources had bought Glencore's Optimum
Coal Mine, which supplied Eskom with coal. The deal aroused suspicion when
it was alleged that minister of mineral resources Mosebenzi Zwane, appointed
by Zuma two months before Nenegate, had helped the Guptas to acquire the
Optimum mine under unusually favourable conditions, and that Zuma's
son Duduzane had scored a share in the deal.[3] To top it off, the Guptas were
also involved in uranium mining (again with Duduzane), and it was clear
that they stood to benefit enormously from the R1-trillion nuclear deal – if
Zuma could get approval for it. These revelations made their ownership of

the pro-government news outlets ANN7 and *The New Age* – which benefited
from disproportionate government advertising – look like small fry. In
the wake of these revelations, three complainants – the Dominican Order's
Father S. Mayebe, the DA's Mmusi Maimane and a concerned anonymous
member of the public – asked Thuli Madonsela to investigate. The Public
Protector had more work to do and, with her term coming to an end in
October that year, a mere six months to do it in.

Soon after Jonas's shock revelation, another MP, Vytjie Mentor, came forward to say that she too had been offered a government post by the Guptas.
She claimed that she met the family at their mansion in Saxonwold in 2010,
with Zuma in an adjoining room. They told her that she could have the post
of minister of public enterprises if she agreed to an important condition: she
must drop SAA's flight route to India and give it to Jet Airways, an Indian
international airline.[4] Mentor refused. If she'd accepted the proposal, the
minister she would have replaced was none other than Barbara Hogan. Hogan
was soon axed in a cabinet reshuffle and replaced by one Malusi Gigaba, whose
closeness to the Guptas had already been noted in a (soon-to-be-quashed)
investigation by the State Security Agency.[5]

Immediately after Mentor's revelations in March 2016, Hogan came forward to corroborate them. 'I cannot tell you the pressure I had from Jet Airways
to meet with them around commercial business,' Hogan told Talk Radio 702's
John Robbie. 'And I said, if you want to talk commercial airlines, speak to SAA,
I am not here to broker deals on behalf of SAA, that is their job.'[6] It was later
revealed that the Guptas were Jet Airways shareholders who stood to make
an enormous profit if SAA were to drop its India flights. Journalists began to
whisper about state capture.

At the same time, the DA and EFF finally succeeded in forcing Zuma to
take responsibility for Nkandla. When the president continued to ignore the
Public Protector's report, they took him to court and, after various rulings and
appeals, the case was heard in the Constitutional Court in early 2016. Since a
recent court ruling involving controversial SABC boss Hlaudi Motsoeneng
had clarified the binding nature of the Public Protector's powers, Zuma's
lawyer now claimed that the president had had an 'evolution of thinking' and
accepted that Madonsela's report was binding but argued that Zuma hadn't
breached the Constitution. The court disagreed, and its ruling, handed down
on 31 March, opened the grounds for impeachment. When Zuma announced
that he would be making a televised address to the nation on 1 April, many
people were expecting his resignation. But the president downplayed the
gravity of the Constitutional Court ruling. He apologised for Nkandla but

claimed that 'it all happened in good faith' and that he'd always intended to pay the money back.

A day later, the media published an open letter to Zuma, penned by Ahmed Kathrada. The struggle veteran had been quiet about political issues over the years, and so his decision to make a public comment about Zuma's presidency illustrated the extent to which Zuma had divided the organisation. Kathrada said that he had 'agonised' over writing the letter but that the recent judgment had placed him in an 'introspective' mode: 'I am not a political analyst,' he wrote with candour, 'but I am now driven to ask: "Dear Comrade President, don't you think your continued stay as president will only serve to deepen the crisis of confidence in the government of the country?" ... I know that if I were in the president's shoes, I would step down with immediate effect ... Today I appeal to our president to submit to the will of the people and resign.'[7]

The combined effect of these events hit the ANC hard in the local government elections. In August 2016, the party suffered its worst-ever electoral performance, losing three big metros: Nelson Mandela Bay, Tshwane and Johannesburg. Yet, despite his evident negative impact on the ANC's power base, Zuma showed no signs of letting up. Dudu Myeni was reappointed as the SAA board chair, even though the airline had showed a R5.6 billion loss the previous financial year, and on 7 September energy minister Tina Joemat-Pettersson announced that the government planned to go ahead with the controversial nuclear deal.

There could be no deal, however, without Treasury's approval, and when the Hawks – the police unit tasked with combating corruption – called on Gordhan to answer questions about a so-called 'rogue unit' established during his tenure at SARS, it led to expectations that he would be arrested to make way for a new finance minister. These grew when, on 11 October, the NPA brought charges against him and two former SARS officials for the supposedly irregular approval of an early retirement deal. The markets reacted negatively to what appeared like political interference on a grand scale – a suspicion fed by Gordhan's dismissal of the attack: 'This is a moment where all South Africans need to ask whose interests these people in the Hawks, the NPA and the NDPP are advancing,' the finance minister said when the news broke. 'Where do they get their political instructions from and for what purpose?'[8]

There were hopes that Madonsela's report would clarify the extent to which the state had been captured, and on 14 October, the last day of her term as Public Protector, she signed off on her widely anticipated investigation. A day before its release, Zuma, looking very much like a guilty man, applied for an interdict to stop the publication of her report.

The public was given a sense of the report's content when an affidavit signed by Mcebisi Jonas was leaked to the press on 23 October. Jonas told the Public Protector that when he'd been offered the finance minister post by the Guptas, Ajay Gupta had promised him a whopping R600 million if he agreed to 'work with us'. As a down payment, he showed Jonas a black garbage bag allegedly containing R600 000 in hard cash. Ajay swore under oath that he'd never met Jonas.

On 31 October, giving little explanation and having cost the economy millions of rands, the NPA announced that it was dropping the charges against Gordhan and his colleagues. By now, a groundswell of anti-Zuma sentiment had rallied in support of the finance minister, and opposition parties and Save South Africa – a UDF-style coalition of organisations, business leaders and civil-society bodies – went ahead with a series of mass national demonstrations on 2 November, when Gordhan had been scheduled to appear in the North Gauteng High Court.

This happened to be the same day that Zuma's application to interdict Madonsela's report was heard at the same court. Zuma withdrew the case, and the new Public Protector, Busisiwe Mkhwebane, was ordered to release her predecessor's report by 5 p.m. that day. The report, titled *State of Capture*, was damning. In addition to the leaked Jonas affidavit, Madonsela alleged that Zuma had violated the Executive Ethics Code by involving the Guptas and his son Duduzane in the removal and appointment of the finance minister in 2015. Van Rooyen was placed in the Saxonwold area, including on the day that his brief appointment was announced. Additional questions were raised around Eskom. The appointment of its board had been improper, and Madonsela had found a record of over forty phone calls from Eskom CEO Brian Molefe to Ajay Gupta over a six-month period.

Hogan's allegations added fuel to the fire. 'President Zuma made it very difficult for her to perform her job',[9] Madonsela found, and he took an inappropriately close interest in the appointment of board members for parastatals, such as Eskom and Transnet. 'This claim was particularly concerning', writes journalist Pieter-Louis Myburgh, 'given the fact that Eskom and Transnet are the two state-owned entities from which Gupta-linked companies have scored some of their most lucrative government contracts.'[10] Madonsela recommended that a commission of inquiry be tasked with investigating further, and she gave the president thirty days to put one in place.

In what was now becoming a familiar pattern, Zuma challenged this recommendation in court.

In his 2017 SONA – a replay of 2015 with the forcible removal of the EFF and a DA protest walkout – Zuma reintroduced the catchphrase 'radical economic transformation'. While lauded by some as a necessary state intervention to reduce poverty and inequality, his critics saw it as a licence to loot. Maimane claimed that by using 'the pretext of prioritising "radical socio-economic transformation" [Zuma] justifies increased state control in order to push through policies that are designed solely to enrich his political and business cronies. His real project is to facilitate and accelerate large-scale massive intensified corruption.'[11] 'Radical economic transformation' created a convenient perceived conflict between Gordhan's adherence to a market-friendly economic approach and the need to redistribute wealth in the country, whereas the real conflict appeared to be between the finance minister's fiscal discipline and Zuma's desire to spend. As Mark Swilling and his colleagues point out, 'Instead of becoming a new economic policy consensus, radical economic transformation has been turned into an ideological football kicked around by factional political players within the ANC and the Alliance in general who use the term to mean very different things.'[12]

Amid growing expectations that Gordhan would be axed, on 27 March 2017 he was abruptly ordered to return to South Africa from London, where he had just arrived for a week-long investment road show that could help to restore confidence in the battered South African economy, which was now facing a possible downgrade. Mcebisi Jonas, who had planned to join Gordhan overseas, was ordered to stay put, and, in anticipation of their dismissals, the rand weakened by almost 3 per cent.

And then, the very next day, as if in protest, Ahmed Kathrada passed away. The eighty-seven-year-old could not have chosen a more opportune time to depart, and the tributes poured in for a man who appeared to embody the very opposite values to Zuma. In a suggestive statement, the Thabo Mbeki Foundation said, 'We cannot but reflect on the valuable counsel of Comrade Kathy including and in particular the importance of promoting the understanding that leaders exist to serve the people rather than to cultivate their personal interests.'[13]

Kathrada's funeral and memorial services were transformed into political mega-events, reminiscent of activists' funerals during the 1980s. Zuma initially reacted to Kathrada's passing by declaring that there would be an official memorial service, and he instructed that the flag fly at half-mast until the memorial. But he soon found that the family wanted nothing to do with him and that he wasn't invited to the funeral, which was held on 29 March at West Park Cemetery in Johannesburg. The event was open to the public, and speaker after speaker criticised the moral decay of Zuma's presidency, with some praising Gordhan as he waited to hear his fate. Keynote speaker

Kgalema Motlanthe nailed his colours to the mast by reading out Kathrada's letter to Zuma and adding his own indictment: 'Comrade Kathy took exception to the current culture of feeding frenzy, moral corruption, societal depravity, political dissolution, the grossness and sleaze enveloping the human mind that would put to shame even some of the vilest political orders known to human history.'[14]

The next day, in what was also becoming a familiar pattern, Zuma made another night-time announcement. Citing radical socio-economic transformation as a motivating factor, he announced a cabinet reshuffle, saying, 'I have directed the new ministers and deputy ministers to work tirelessly with their colleagues to bring about radical socio-economic transformation.'[15] While many expected the president to replace Gordhan with Brian Molefe, who had recently been redeployed from Eskom to Parliament, in the end the post was given to Malusi Gigaba. Both Gordhan and Jonas were axed from the cabinet, whereas poorly performing ministers Bathabile Dlamini (who had recently created a social-grants crisis) and Faith Muthambi (under whose leadership the SABC was floundering) were kept on.

Despite being newly widowed, Hogan gave a blistering statement at a press conference the following day: 'Last night, when the news began to filter through, about the dastardly deeds that were being done in dark corners, many of us in the family began to have second doubts whether we would want a commemoration under the auspices of a president who has clearly gone rogue.'[16] It was clear, in the wake of these events, that an official memorial service would result in an awkward situation for the president, and the memorial was swiftly cancelled.

If ever there was an event that laid bare the fault lines within the ANC government, it was the independent 'people's' memorial that followed, organised by the Nelson Mandela and Ahmed Kathrada Foundations as well as by the South African Communist Party. South Africans found themselves watching an 'unofficial' tribute to a treasured icon on national television on 1 April, a year after Zuma's televised Nkandla apology. Held at Johannesburg City Hall, the memorial emphasised Kathrada's principles in a defiant protest against the president. Many held up posters declaring 'Zuma must go', and the president's absence was made all the more glaring because of the high-profile guest list, which included Graça Machel and the entire Mandela family, Eddie Daniels, Mac Maharaj, Denis Goldberg, Ronnie Kasrils, Frank Chikane and Cheryl Carolus.

Hogan was the first to speak, and her words cut to the heart of the matter.

Good afternoon,

I greet you in the name, firstly, of the wonderful Kathrada family, in whose midst Kathy grew up, who supported him in prison, who took pride in him when he came out, nurtured and sustained him, and when he was in his darkest hours loved, cared and supported him. A huge thank you to the Kathrada family for what they have done for our country.

Lots of people are very curious; they always say, 'How did you and Kathy get together?' Well, you know, you release two old jailbirds, who don't know how this world operates, and so we were like shelter from the storm for each other. I always remember Kathy, myself and Naledi Ntsiki trying to cross Sauer Street in the midst of the traffic and we'd, like, venture across and then scurry back, and go across … and we couldn't do it! And you know what? Although Kathy, Madiba and all of our great leaders performed like political professionals, let us not forget how much it took from themselves, from their personal lives – the adjustments they had to make to a great and vastly changed world.

Kathy was a fighter to the last. In hospital we had to battle with him. He didn't like … he was put in a chair, for a couple of hours every morning, to prevent pneumonia. And his carer would tell me that he'd swing his legs over the side of the chair and try to get back on the bed before she caught him. There was a moment when they were trying to put a drip for nutrition purposes into a central vein here. He fought them off, and he said to them, 'I know my rights!' And it just so happened that it was Human Rights Day, and the wonderful Dr Butler said, 'I couldn't go further. Not Ahmed Kathrada, not on Human Rights Day.' And such was the stature of Kathy. We love him and he's a man of the people. And we love him because of that.

In his last year, a man of eighty-six/eighty-seven performed 186 public engagements. And this wasn't the high-and-mighty engagements at Sandton Convention Centres and those places. They were schools, they were colleges, they were universities, they were trade union meetings. It was business meetings; it was in people's homes. Kathy never ceased to love engaging with ordinary people. We used to fight with him and say, 'Kathy, this is too much', and he just loved it.

I and all of us who have been close to him, are so exceptionally privileged to have spent the last twenty-seven years of his life with this man who was so engaged, so busy, so witty, so funny, so wise and so incredibly principled. And in all the pain that I've been suffering and all the grief that I feel, I just say: 'Thank you, thank you for those wonderful years with you.'

Kathy. For me what was so special about Kathy were two aspects of him. Firstly, he was a great soul. Kathy reached – during those Robben Island years and even before then – he had to reach deep down into his soul and himself together with his fellow prisoners, to grasp and understand a fate that said, 'You are going to be imprisoned and are going to die in prison.' A young man of thirty-four, who went to prison and who knew he would die there. Under those circumstances and how perilous the struggle was, Kathy and his fellow comrades reached deep down into themselves and they came out with universal truths. They came out with a huge, generous understanding of the human condition, its frailty and its strengths, and that is why we are here today. We are here to support and endorse and celebrate the values of an extraordinary generation who led us out of the wilderness into democracy.

Let me quote one of the most-quoted pieces that Kathy wrote. It is his writing and it characterises Kathy's approach. And I quote: 'While we will not forget the brutality of apartheid, we will not want Robben Island to be a monument of our hardship and suffering. We would want it to be a triumph of the human spirit ... a triumph of the human spirit against the forces of evil. A triumph of wisdom and largeness of spirit against small minds and pettiness. A triumph of courage and determination over human frailty and weakness. A triumph of the new South Africa over the old.' And that is our anthem now; we are going to triumph. The triumph of our democracy, the triumph of the very human spirit. Its deeply embedded non-racialism are the values on which we all here are founded and which we will die for.

I want to quote Madiba's reflections on Kathy. He writes, 'Walter Sisulu and Kathy share one common feature which forms an essential part of our friendship and which I value very much. They never hesitate to criticise me, they never hesitate to criticise me for my mistakes and throughout my political career have served as a mirror from which I can see myself.'

Would it be that our current generation of leaders held Kathy's wisdom and advice in the same esteem as the leadership of Robben Island and our leadership which brought us to victory?

Instead, they are so fearful of even his voice that they saw fit to cancel his commemoration because they were afraid it was going to become ...

[applause]. Today we stand here … today we stand here and say we will not be silenced, nor will we ever.

Mr President, Mr President, do you have ears to hear and eyes to see? When you drive past in those cavalcades which have multiplied because you have become so paranoid. Do you see those people pulling a wooden wagon behind them and scraping dustbins to eke out a living? Do you hear them? Do you see them? Mr President, do you hear, do you see all the millions of social grantees who live in absolute anxiety and fear that they might not have an income next month? Did you hear? Did you see? No, you didn't! Do you feel? Do you hear? Do you see the pain of everyone who has been flung into unemployment as our economy hits rock bottom? One unemployed person has at least five people dependent on them. Do you not understand that millions and millions of people need jobs? But instead you have sacrificed everything we have stood for on the altar of corruption, greed and more greed.

If you had ears to hear and eyes to see, you would have not appointed four finance ministers in less than three years. You would have not recalled our finance minister, one of our finest finance ministers, from an international road show. You would not be pursuing … you would not be pursuing a nuclear deal that will be the destruction of all of us. And you would have fired Faith Muthambi and Bathabile Dlamini. And, finally, Mr President, if you had ears to hear and eyes to see, you would step down as Kathy would have.

Mr President … Mr President, this country is not for sale and a people united will never be defeated.

I thank you.

Both a moving tribute to her husband and a fierce avowal of his values, Hogan's speech set the tone for what turned into a 'raucous' event.[17] Her tribute begins tenderly, as she recounts the details of her time with Kathrada. The two met upon her release in 1990 after the unbanning of the ANC. Kathrada's interest in Hogan preceded this meeting, however, and in his memoirs he remembers, 'for reasons I could not explain', taking a 'special interest' in her trial.[18] Arrested in 1982 for 'furthering the aims of a banned organisation', Hogan became the first woman in South Africa to be found guilty of high treason, and she was sentenced to ten years' imprisonment after being held in solitary confinement for a year. Her speech recalls the mutual disorientation that drew the two newly released 'jailbirds' to one another.

Taking the audience by surprise, the second half of her speech abruptly changes tone and she addresses Zuma directly, asking repeatedly, 'Mr President, do you hear?' 'Do you see?' The crowd appeared both unsettled and delighted by the shift. Former finance minister Trevor Manuel, for instance, looked at his fellow mourners in apparent astonishment, while other members of the audience shifted in their seats. By the end of the address, however, the crowd was erupting in applause and responding with chants of 'Zuma must go! Zuma must go!'

Hogan's moral denunciation of the president is striking because of her ability to describe the experience of poverty in jargon-free terms. By not using vague concepts such as 'the previously disadvantaged', 'marginalised communities' and 'radical economic transformation', Hogan's empathetic descriptions of the struggles of poorer South Africans resonate powerfully, as does her strong condemnation of Zuma's perceived worship of money: 'But instead you have sacrificed everything we have stood for on the altar of corruption, greed and more greed,' she says.

A series of speakers followed, including business leaders and SACP and COSATU representatives. The memorial concluded with keynote speaker Gordhan, who, in a speech that Richard Poplak said 'may define his future as a consensus builder',[19] was careful to preserve the reputation of his party, as well as the bond of the Tripartite Alliance. 'This ANC is still our ANC,' Gordhan said, while at the same time 'unashamedly' calling for 'mass mobilisation'.

Over the next few weeks and months, this call was heeded in various ways. There were smaller mobilising memorial events for Kathrada in Cape Town, and, as the rand continued to tumble and the country was unsurprisingly downgraded, a number of marches were held nationwide.

Despite these events, Zuma did not reverse any of his cabinet decisions, nor did the ANC recall him, as some hoped it might. The president appeared unperturbed by the marches, dismissing them as 'demonstrating that racism is real'.[20] In August 2017, Parliament voted on a motion of no confidence in Zuma; but even though MPs were permitted to use a secret ballot, the president survived – with 198 votes against 177.

The events around Ahmed Kathrada's death, however, were a clear indication that the tide was slowly turning.

Acknowledgements

There are a number of people to whom I owe a debt of thanks and who helped in various ways throughout the writing and production process of this collection. To Ian Rijsdijk and the anonymous reviewers of the book, thank you for assisting with the selection of speeches and for leading me to discover addresses I had not thought to include, even if they didn't all make it into the current book. And a special thanks to the reviewers for clarifying information about Oliver Tambo's 8 January address.

Thank you also to Dr Melissa Wallace for assisting with information around South Africa's HIV/AIDS programmes and to Lance Greyling for explaining some of the conventions of parliamentary address.

Many thanks to Gabriele Mohale from the Wits Historical Papers Research Archive and Professor Sheila Meintjes, who together helped me to locate the 'missing' Winnie Madikizela-Mandela speech included in the collection. Thanks also to Frances Jowell, who gave me permission to access her mother Helen Suzman's archival collection at the University of the Witwatersrand.

I also owe thanks to Rehad Desai and Jabulani Mzozo for providing me with the full video version of Julius Malema's speech at Marikana, without which the book would have seemed incomplete.

Lastly, I am grateful to the efficient and professional team at Penguin: to Marlene Fryer, for agreeing to publish the book in the first place. To Ryan Africa, for the inspired and classy cover design. To Rashieda Saliem, for helping with the transcription and typing up of speeches. To Bronwen Maynier, for her meticulous proofreading. To Sanet le Roux, for indexing a history that spans seventy years. And especially to Dane Wallace, for his insightful edit and remarkable error-detection skills. Thank you for your patience in the last stages of production.

Finally, thank you to Robert Plummer for undertaking the journey with me. You are the best travelling partner.

MARTHA EVANS
CAPE TOWN, OCTOBER 2017

List of abbreviations

AMCU: Association of Mineworkers and Construction Union
ANC: African National Congress
ARV: antiretroviral
AVF: Afrikaner Volksfront
AWB: Afrikaner Weerstandsbeweging
COPE: Congress of the People
CORD: Charge or Release Detainees
COSATU: Congress of South African Trade Unions
CP: Conservative Party
DA: Democratic Alliance
EFF: Economic Freedom Fighters
FNLA: National Liberation Front of Angola
FRELIMO: Mozambique Liberation Front
IDASA: Institute for a Democratic Alternative for South Africa
IFP: Inkatha Freedom Party
MK: Umkhonto we Sizwe
MPLA: Marxist People's Movement for the Liberation of Angola
NCOP: National Council of Provinces
NDP: National Development Plan
NDPP: National Director of Public Prosecutions
NEPAD: New Partnership for Africa's Development
NP: National Party
NPA: National Prosecuting Authority
NUM: National Union of Mineworkers
NUSAS: National Union of South African Students
OAU: Organisation of African Unity
PAC: Pan Africanist Congress
PEBCO: Port Elizabeth Black Civic Organisation
PFP: Progressive Federal Party
PRP: Progressive Reform Party
RENAMO: Mozambican National Resistance
SAA: South African Airways

SABC: South African Broadcasting Corporation
SACP: South African Communist Party
SADC: Southern African Development Community
SADF: South African Defence Force
SAIC: South African Indian Council
SANRAL: South African National Roads Agency Limited
SAP: South African Police
SAPS: South African Police Service
SARS: South African Revenue Service
SASO: South African Students' Organisation
SIU: Special Investigating Unit
SONA: State of the Nation Address
SWAPO: South West Africa People's Organisation
TAC: Treatment Action Campaign
TBVC: Transkei, Bophuthatswana, Venda and Ciskei
TRC: Truth and Reconciliation Commission
UDF: United Democratic Front
UNITA: National Union for the Total Independence of Angola
UP: United Party
ZANU-PF: Zimbabwe African National Union – Patriotic Front

Notes

PREFACE

1. A unique and valuable exception is Philippe-Joseph Salazar's *An African Athens: Rhetoric and the Shaping of Democracy in South Africa* (Mahwah, New Jersey; London: Lawrence Erlbaum Associates, 2002).
2. Own correspondent, '25 years of fighting against apartheid', *The Times*, London, 15 July 1977, p. 8.
3. Isabel Hofmeyr, 'Building a nation from words: Afrikaans language, literature and ethnic identity, 1902–1924', in Shula Marks and Stanley Trapido (eds), *The Politics of Race, Class and Nationalism in Twentieth Century South Africa* (London: Longman Group UK Limited, 1987).
4. Cathy LaVerne Freeman, 'Relays in rebellion: The power in Lilian Ngoyi and Fannie Lou Hamer', MA thesis, Georgia State University, 2009, (available at: http://scholarworks.gsu .edu/history_theses/39; viewed 23 April 2017).
5. Michael Lobban, *White Man's Justice: South African Political Trials in the Black Consciousness Era* (Oxford: Clarendon Press, 1996).
6. Salazar, *An African Athens.*
7. Cited in 'Those things they said', *Independent*, 31 November 1999.
8. Stephen Grootes, 'Missing: The sublime art of speech-writing and oratory', *Daily Maverick*, 14 February 2011.
9. S'thembiso Msomi, *Mmusi Maimane: Prophet or Puppet?* (Johannesburg and Cape Town: Jonathan Ball, 2016), p. 61.

D.F. MALAN, NATIONAL PARTY CAMPAIGN SPEECH

1. Nicholas L. Waddy, 'The fork in the road? British reactions to the election of an apartheid government in South Africa, May 1948', *Historia* 55 (1), May 2010 (available at: http:// www.scielo.org.za/scielo.php?script=sci_arttext&pid=S0018-229X2010000100005#not12a; viewed 27 February 2017).
2. David Welsh, *The Rise and Fall of Apartheid* (Johannesburg and Cape Town: Jonathan Ball, 2009), p. 18.
3. Jan Smuts, *The Basis of Trusteeship* (Johannesburg: South African Institute of Race Relations, 1942).
4. Sir Evelyn Baring, The National Archive, Colonial Office 936/2/4, 'The political situation in South Africa: Prospects at the coming general elections', 22 March 1948, pp. 1–2 (available at: http://www.scielo.org.za/scielo.php?script=sci_arttext&pid=S0018-229X201 0000100005; viewed 7 February 2017).
5. Lindie Koorts, *D.F. Malan and the Rise of Afrikaner Nationalism* (Cape Town: Tafelberg, 2014), p. 376.
6. Lindie Koorts, 'An unlikely charismatic leader: D.F. Malan in a Weberian light', in Jan Willem Stutje (ed.), *Charismatic Leadership and Social Movements: The Revolutionary Power of Ordinary Men and Women* (Oxford and New York: Berghahn Books, 2012), pp. 44–65.

7. Ibid.
8. J.A. Gray, 'South Africa's new voice', 23 April 1949, US Library, DFM 1/1/2472.
9. Ibid.
10. 'The shock from South Africa', *The Times* (London, England), City Notes, Saturday 29 May 1948, p. 7.
11. Cited in 'These things happen', *Time* magazine, 7 June 1948.
12. R. Ovendale, 'The South African policy of the British Labour Government, 1947–51', *International Affairs* 59 (1), 1982/83, pp. 41–58.
13. Sir Evelyn Baring, The National Archive, Colonial Office 936/2/4, 'The political situation in South Africa: Prospects at the coming general elections', 22 March 1948, pp. 1–2.

YUSUF DADOO, 'APARTHEID OVER OUR DEAD BODIES'
1. Oliver Tambo, 'Black reaction to apartheid, 1948–1973', Statement made at the annual meeting of the African Studies Association, Syracuse, 1 March 1973.
2. E.S. Reddy, 'Introduction', in E.S. Reddy (ed.), *Yusuf Mohamed Dadoo: South Africa's Freedom Struggle: Statements, Speeches and Articles, Including Correspondence with Mahatma Gandhi* (New Delhi: Sterling, 1990).
3. Chris van Wyk, *Yusuf Dadoo: Learning African History: Freedom Fighters, Series 2* (Kelvin: Awareness Publishing, 2006), p. 19; see also Tom Lodge, 'Paper monuments: Political biography in the new South Africa', *South African Historical Journal* 28 (1), 1993, pp. 249–269.
4. Yusuf Dadoo, 'Reply to Smuts' statement on inequality of races: press statement', 13 February 1948.
5. Christopher Sarma, 'Marx, the Mahatma, and multiracialism: South African Indian political resistance, 1939–1955', Honours thesis, College of Social Studies, Wesleyan University, Connecticut, 2009, p. 13.
6. No author, Entry for Yusuf Dadoo on website 'South Africa: Overcoming apartheid and building democracy', Michigan State University (available at: http://overcomingapartheid.msu.edu/people.php?id=65-251-88; viewed 3 March 2017).
7. See Farook Khan, *The Goodwill Lounge* (Durban, 2014).
8. Ellen Otzen, 'The town destroyed to stop black and white people mixing', BBC World Service, 11 February 2015 (available at: http://www.bbc.com/news/magazine-31379211; viewed 3 March 2017).

LILIAN NGOYI, PRESIDENTIAL ADDRESS TO THE TRANSVAAL ANC WOMEN'S LEAGUE
1. Cherryl Walker, *Women and Resistance in South Africa* (Cape Town: David Philip, 1991), p. 196.
2. Hilda Bernstein, 'Lilian Ngoyi', in Marie Human, Mothobi Mutloatse and Jacqui Masiza (eds), *The Women's Freedom March of 1956*, Golden Jubilee Anniversary Edition (Houghton: Mutloatse Arts Heritage Trust, 2006), p. 61.
3. Pamela E. Brooks, *Boycotts, Buses, and Passes: Black Women's Resistance in the U.S. South and South Africa* (Amherst: University of Massachusetts Press, 2008), p. 223.
4. Ibid., p. 225.
5. Staff reporter, 'Strijdom, you have struck a rock', *New Age* 2 (42), Thursday 16 August 1956, p. 1.
6. LaVerne Freeman, 'Relays in rebellion', p. 14.
7. Cited in Brooks, *Boycotts, Buses, and Passes*, p. 227.

8. LaVerne Freeman, 'Relays in Rebellion', p. 7.
9. Ezekiel Mphahlele, 'Guts and granite – Masterpiece in bronze', *Drum*, March 1956.
10. Ngoyi did not coin the phrase 'badge of slavery'. It refers back to the 13th Amendment's abolition of slavery in the United States and had been used by other South African orators in reference to the pass laws.
11. Mphahlele, 'Guts and granite'.
12. Elizabeth S. Schmidt, 'Now you have touched the women: African women's resistance to the pass laws', South African History Online (available at: http://www.sahistory.org.za/archive/now-you-have-touched-women-african-womens-resistance-pass-laws-south-africa-1950-1960; viewed 23 April 2017).
13. Bernstein, 'Lilian Ngoyi', p. 62.

ROBERT SOBUKWE, OPENING ADDRESS AT THE AFRICANIST INAUGURAL CONVENTION

1. Grahame Hayes, 'In search of the missing Robert Mangaliso Sobukwe', Book review of Benjamin Pogrund's *How Can Man Die Better: The Life of Robert Sobukwe* (2015; new edition). *Psychology in Society* 50, 2016, pp. 99–104.
2. This is fellow student Nthato Motlana's description of him, cited in Benjamin Pogrund, *How Can Man Die Better: The Life of Robert Sobukwe* (Cape Town: Jonathan Ball, 2015), p. 32.
3. Cited in ibid.
4. Cited in Donovan Williams, *A History of the University College of Fort Hare, the 1950s: The Waiting Years* (New York: Edwin Mellen Press, 2001), p. 37.
5. No author, 'Robert Sobukwe', South African History Online (available at: http://www.sahistory.org.za/people/robert-mangaliso-sobukwe; viewed 23 June 2017).
6. Pogrund, *How Can Man Die Better*, p. 91.
7. Ibid.
8. Own correspondent, 'Africa for the African', *The Times*, London, 7 April 1959, p. 7.
9. Pogrund, *How Can Man Die Better*, p. 91.

HAROLD MACMILLAN, 'WIND OF CHANGE' SPEECH

1. Much of the research for this speech comes from Saul Dubow's 'Macmillan, Verwoerd and the 1960 Wind of Change speech', in L.J. Butler and Sarah Stockwell (eds), *The Wind of Change: Harold Macmillan and British Decolonization* (Basingstoke and New York: Palgrave Macmillan, 2013).
2. C.E. Carrington, 'Mr Macmillan in Africa', *The World Today* 16 (3), March 1960, p. 119.
3. Cited in Dubow, 'Macmillan, Verwoerd and the 1960 Wind of Change speech', p. 26.
4. Ibid., p. 25.
5. Anonymous, 'Cape Town cheers Mr. Macmillan', *Rand Daily Mail*, 2 February 1960, p. 9.
6. Dubow, 'Macmillan, Verwoerd and the 1960 Wind of Change Speech', p. 25.
7. Anonymous, 'A "great" speech', *Rand Daily Mail*, 4 February 1960, p. 8.
8. This description came from Anthony Sampson, who was reporting for the *Observer* at the time (see Dubow, 'Macmillan, Verwoerd and the 1960 Wind of Change speech', p. 28).
9. Anonymous, 'Macmillan's biggest test', *Rand Daily Mail*, 6 January 1960, p. 9.
10. Philippe-Joseph Salazar, 'Harold Macmillan: The wind of change', *African Yearbook of Rhetoric* 2 (3), 2011, p. 28.
11. Leonard Ingalls, 'Macmillan, in South Africa, censures apartheid policy; MACMILLAN GIVES APARTHEID STAND', *New York Times*, 4 February 1960, p. 1.

12. Anonymous, 'A "great" speech', *Rand Daily Mail*, 4 February 1960, p. 8.
13. Dubow, 'Macmillan, Verwoerd and the 1960 Wind of Change speech', p. 33.
14. Albert Luthuli, 'What I think of Macmillan's speech', Public statement, 1 March 1960 (available at: http://www.sahistory.org.za/archive/what-i-think-macmillans-speech -article-albert-luthuli-1-march-1960; viewed 11 August 2017).
15. Anthony Sampson, *Macmillan: A Study in Ambiguity* (London: Allen Lane, 1967), p. 186.
16. Carrington, 'Mr Macmillan in Africa', p. 124.

H.F. VERWOERD, SPEECH OF THANKS TO HAROLD MACMILLAN

1. A.N. Pelzer (ed.), *Verwoerd Speaks: Speeches, 1948–1966* (Johannesburg: APB Publishers, 1966), p. 336.
2. Hermann Giliomee, *The Last Afrikaner Leaders: A Supreme Test of Power* (Cape Town: Tafelberg and University of Virginia Press, 2012), p. 27.
3. D.R. Thorpe, *Supermac: The Life of Harold Macmillan* (London: Chatto & Windus, 2010), p. 459.
4. Anthony Sampson, 'His cherubic smile seemed to say, "It's all so simple"', *Life* magazine, 16 September 1966, p. 42.
5. Cited in Alex Hepple, *Verwoerd* (Harmondsworth: Penguin, 1967), p. 136.
6. Interview with Rykie van Reenen, *Die Burger*, Byvoegsel, 14 June 1957.
7. Anonymous, 'The speech that made Verwoerd pale and tense', *Rand Daily Mail*, 4 February 1960, p. 9.
8. 'Plain words to South Africa', *Guardian*, 4 February 1960.
9. Dawie column: 'Uit my politieke pen', *Die Burger*, 6 February 1960, p. 8.
10. Anonymous, 'Wildly pro-British welcome at Cape', *Star*, 2 February 1960, p. 1.
11. Ibid.
12. TNA PREM 11/3073, Maud to Macmillan, 3 February 1960.
13. Cited in Ahmed Kathrada, *Memoirs* (Cape Town: Zebra Press, 2004), p. 136.

ALBERT LUTHULI, NOBEL PEACE PRIZE LECTURE

1. Scott Couper, *Albert Luthuli: Bound by Faith* (Scottsville: University of KwaZulu-Natal Press, 2010), p. 130.
2. Tore Linné Eriksen, 'The origins of a special relationship', in Tore Linné Eriksen (ed.), *Norway and National Liberation in Southern Africa* (Stockholm: Nordiska Afrikainstitutet, 2000), p. 18.
3. Cited in Kader Asmal, Adrian Hadland and Moira Levy, *Kader Asmal: Politics in My Blood: A Memoir* (Johannesburg: Jacana Media, 2011), p. 141.
4. Couper, *Albert Luthuli*, p. 133.
5. Ibid., p. 136.
6. Staff reporter, 'Luthuli, dressed as Zulu chief, gets his prize', *Star*, 11 December 1962, p. 1.
7. Henry Wadsworth Longfellow, extract from the poem 'A Psalm of Life', 1838.
8. Nelson Mandela, *Long Walk to Freedom* (London: Macdonald Purnell, 1994), pp. 323–324.
9. Couper, *Albert Luthuli*, p. 107.
10. Ezekiel Mphahlele, 'Albert Luthuli: The end of non-violence', *Africa Today* 14, August 1967, pp. 1–3.
11. Cited in Michael Lloyd, 'Luthuli – The impact of personality', *Sunday Tribune*, 29 October 1961.
12. Mphahlele, 'Albert Luthuli: The end of non-violence', pp. 1–3.
13. 'A continent in revolution against oppression', *The Times*, London, 12 December 1961, p. 9.

14. 'Excerpts from Nobel lecture by Luthuli in Oslo', *New York Times*, 12 December 1961.
15. Cited in Asmal, Hadland and Levy, *Kader Asmal: Politics in My Blood*, p. 142.
16. '"Incitement" by Mr. Luthuli', *The Times*, London, 14 December 1961, p. 11.
17. 'Mr Luthuli's reply', *The Times*, London, 15 December 1961, p. 10.

WALTER SISULU, FIRST RADIO FREEDOM BROADCAST

1. Stephen R. Davis, 'The African National Congress, its radio, its allies and exile', *Journal of Southern African Studies* 35 (2), 2009, pp. 349–373.
2. Own correspondent, 'Freedom Radio broadcast in South Africa', *The Times*, London, 28 June 1963, p. 14.
3. Elinor Sisulu, *Walter and Albertina Sisulu: In Our Lifetime* (Cape Town: David Philip, 2006), p. 226.
4. Ibid., p. 227.
5. Details given here come from Denis Goldberg's *A Life for Freedom: The Mission to End Racial Injustice in South Africa* (Kentucky: University Press of Kentucky, 2016), pp. 78–80.
6. Davis, 'The African National Congress, its radio, its allies and exile', p. 352.
7. Goldberg, *A Life for Freedom*, p. 79.
8. '"Freedom Radio" in Africa', *New York Times*, 2 July 1963.
9. Own correspondent, 'Freedom Radio broadcast in South Africa', *The Times*, London, 28 June 1963, p. 14.
10. Goldberg, *A Life for Freedom*, p. 79.
11. Ibid.

NELSON MANDELA, STATEMENT FROM THE DOCK

1. Amina Cachalia, interviewed by John Carlin, Frontline, PBS.org (available at: http://www.pbs.org/wgbh/pages/frontline/shows/mandela/interviews/stengel.html; viewed 21 March 2017).
2. Anthony Sampson, cited in John Carlin's *The Long Walk of Nelson Mandela: An Intimate Portrait of One of the 20th Century's Greatest Leaders* (PBS Home Video, 1999).
3. Cited in Mac Maharaj (ed.), *Mandela: The Authorized Portrait* (Kansas City: Andrews McMeel Publishing), p. 299.
4. Walter Sisulu, interviewed by John Carlin, Frontline, PBS.org (available at: http://www.pbs.org/wgbh/pages/frontline/shows/mandela/interviews/stengel.html; viewed 21 March 2017).
5. Cited in Bill Keller, 'The South African vote: The man for South Africa's future', *New York Times*, 1 May 1994.
6. Richard Stengel, interviewed by John Carlin, Frontline, PBS.org (available at: http://www.pbs.org/wgbh/pages/frontline/shows/mandela/interviews/stengel.html; viewed 21 March 2017).
7. BBC News, 'Nelson Mandela: CIA tip-off led to 1962 arrest', 15 May 2016 (available at: http://www.bbc.com/news/world-africa-36296551; viewed 2 February 2017).
8. George Bizos, cited in 'Statue marks Nelson Mandela's arrest 50 years ago', News.com.au, 5 August 2012 (available at: http://www.news.com.au/world/s-africa-marks-mandela-arrest/news-story/5e10170d20df2b8fbc98459ac0393c96; viewed 2 February 2017).
9. Thula Simpson, *Umkhonto we Sizwe: The ANC's Armed Struggle* (Cape Town: Penguin, 2016), p. 90.
10. Lauritz Stryjdom, *Rivonia Unmasked!* (Britons, 1965).

11. Penwell Dlamini, 'Liliesleaf farm snitch "was an ANC member"', *The Times*, South Africa, 18 January 2016, p. 2.
12. Stryjdom, *Rivonia Unmasked!*, p. 19.
13. Anthony Sampson, interviewed by John Carlin, Frontline, PBS.org (available at: http://www.pbs.org/wgbh/pages/frontline/shows/mandela/interviews/sampson.html; viewed 10 April 2017).
14. Joel Joffe, cited in Catherine M. Cole, 'Justice in transition: South Africa political trials, 1956–1964', in Awol Allo (ed.), *The Courtroom as a Space of Resistance: Reflections on the Legacy of the Rivonia Trial* (London and New York: Routledge, 2015), p. 112.
15. Kenneth S. Broun, *Saving Nelson Mandela: The Rivonia Trial and the Fate of South Africa* (Oxford: Oxford University Press, 2012), p. 74.
16. Denis Goldberg, interviewed by Michele Norris for NPR news, 'All things considered' (available at: http://www.npr.org/templates/transcript/transcript.php?storyId=92677815; viewed 2 February 2017).
17. Editorial, *New York Times*, 14 June 1964.
18. Cited (and translated) in 'How press reacted to Rivonia sentence', *South African Digest*, 19 June 1964 (Pretoria: Government Communications).
19. Cited in Douglas O. Linder, 'The trial of Nelson Mandela (Rivonia Trial): Testimony of Alan Paton', www.famous-trials.com (available at: http://www.famous-trials.com/nelsonmandela/706-alantestimony; viewed 5 August 2017).
20. *Post* reporter, 'After 88 days, suddenly the 8 men are gone', *The Post*, 12 June 1964, p. 2.
21. Two of the ten accused, Kantor and Bernstein, escaped this sentence. Kantor had been discharged by the judge at an earlier point in the trial, whereas Bernstein received an acquittal (he was immediately rearrested while still in the courtroom, however, and then later released on bail).
22. *Post* reporter, 'This was history', *The Post*, 12 June 1964, p. 1.

BRAM FISCHER, 'WHAT I DID WAS RIGHT'

1. Much of the biographical detail in this chapter comes from Stephen Clingman, *Bram Fischer: Afrikaner Revolutionary* (Cape Town; Amherst: David Philip, Mayibuye Books and University of Massachusetts Press, 1998).
2. Nadine Gordimer, 'Why did Bram Fischer choose jail?', in *The Essential Gesture: Writing, Politics and Places* (London: Penguin, 1988), p. 70.
3. Gordimer, 'Why did Bram Fischer choose jail?', p. 70.
4. Clingman, *Bram Fischer*, pp. 208–209.
5. Ibid., p. 338.
6. Ibid., p. 390.
7. Ibid., p. 365.
8. Thula Simpson, *Umkhonto we Size: The ANC's Armed Struggle*, pp. 113–114.
9. Clingman, *Bram Fischer*, p. 409.
10. 'Fischer – alone in big dock – impassive', *Rand Daily Mail*, 5 May 1966, p. 1.
11. Clingman, *Bram Fischer*, p. 410.
12. Ibid., p. 416.
13. Cited in 'Family must give up Bram Fischer ashes', *Cape Times*, 9 May 1975.
14. Carolyn Dempster, 'Anti-apartheid lawyer finally recognised', *BBC News*, 17 October 2003.

ROBERT F. KENNEDY, 'RIPPLE OF HOPE' SPEECH

1. Martin Legassick and Christopher Saunders, 'Aboveground activity in the 1960s', in *Road to Democracy*, vol. 1 (Houghton: Mutloatse Arts Heritage Trust, 2008), p. 680.
2. Harriet Jane Rudolph, 'A rhetorical analysis of Robert F. Kennedy's university addresses in South Africa, June 1966', PhD dissertation, Ohio State University, 1973, p. 1.
3. Cited in *RFK in the Land of Apartheid: A Ripple of Hope*, produced by Larry Shore, directed by Larry Shore and Tami Gold (Journeyman TV, 2009).
4. No author, 'The student leader and Kennedy', *The Mercury*, 8 June 2016, p. 6.
5. Rudolph, 'A rhetorical analysis of Robert F. Kennedy's university addresses', p. 7.
6. Cited in ibid.
7. Cited in ibid.
8. Own correspondent, 'News ban on Kennedy visit', *The Times*, London, 26 May 1966, p. 10.
9. 'Tactical error', *Cape Times*, 8 June 1966, no page number.
10. Jill Chisholm, 'Man alive! The human dynamo', *Rand Daily Mail* souvenir booklet 'Robert Kennedy in South Africa', 1966, pp. 2–3.
11. Reuter, 'Senator Kennedy rebuffed', *The Times*, London, 6 June 1966, p. 8.
12. Cited in *RFK in the Land of Apartheid*.
13. David Halberstam, *The Unfinished Odyssey of Robert Kennedy: A Biography* (New York: Open Road Media, 2013), no page number.
14. Cited in *RFK in the Land of Apartheid*.
15. Reuter, 'Mr. Kennedy denounces apartheid', *The Times*, London, 7 June 1966, p. 6.
16. Ian Robertson, NUSAS President, Banning Order Under Suppression of Communism Act, Cape Town, 3 May 1966.
17. Cited in 'Kennedy has a 70-minute meeting with Luthuli', *Cape Argus*, 8 June 1996.
18. Editorial, 'Kennedy, come back!', *Rand Daily Mail*, 9 June 1966.

HELEN SUZMAN, SPEECH IN PARLIAMENT ON THE NP'S RACE POLICY

1. Bernard Levin, 'Listening for the voice of freedom in S Africa', *The Times*, London, 22 March 1974, p. 16.
2. Francis Antonia, 'Bright star in a dark chamber', *Mail & Guardian*, 3 May 2013.
3. J.M. Coetzee, 'Alan Paton/Helen Suzman', in *Stranger Shores: Essays 1986–1999* (London: Vintage, 2001), p. 327.
4. Phyllis Lewsen, 'Introduction' in *Helen Suzman's Solo Years* (Johannesburg: Jonathan Ball and Ad Donker, 1991), p. 1.
5. Cited in Lewsen, *Helen Suzman's Solo Years*, p. 193.
6. Bob Hepple, 'Black man in the white man's court', Nelson Mandela Foundation, 31 October 2012 (available at: https://www.nelsonmandela.org/uploads/files/Hepple_extract.pdf; viewed 9 August 2017).
7. Coetzee, 'Alan Paton/Helen Suzman', p. 327.
8. Helen Suzman, *In No Uncertain Terms: Memoirs* (London: Sinclair-Stevenson, 1993), p. 72.
9. Ibid., p. 73.
10. Deon Geldenhuys, *The Diplomacy of Isolation: South African Foreign Policy Making* (Johannesburg: Macmillan, 1984), p. 73.
11. Jill Chisholm, 'Govt will be tougher with Urban Africans', *Rand Daily Mail*, 23 July 1970, p. 1.
12. Speech edited and reproduced in Lewsen, *Helen Suzman's Solo Years*, pp. 149–154. (Originally: Hansard Volume 29, columns 201–212.)
13. Suzman, *In No Uncertain Terms*, p. 73.

14. Coetzee, 'Alan Paton/Helen Suzman', p. 330.
15. Own correspondent, '25 years of fighting against apartheid', *The Times*, London, 15 July 1977, p. 8.

STEVE BIKO, 'WHITE RACISM, BLACK CONSCIOUSNESS'

1. Cited in Xolela Mangcu, *Biko: A Biography* (Cape Town: Tafelberg, 2012), p. 108.
2. Cited in Donald Woods, *Biko* (London: Penguin, 1987), p. 39.
3. Ian Macqueen, 'Resonances of youth and tensions of race: Liberal student politics, white radicals and black consciousness, 1968–1973', *South African Historical Journal* 65 (3), 2013, pp. 365–382.
4. H.W. van der Merwe, 'Black and white student ideals', in 'SASO Press Digest: Various reports on papers presented at Abe Bailey Institute workshop on student activism in South Africa at the University of Cape Town, 1971', 'SASO, 1969–1973' collection, AD2189, E13, Wits Historical Papers.
5. Ibid.
6. Cited in Woods, *Biko*, p. 62.
7. Macqueen, 'Resonances of youth and tensions of race', p. 368.
8. Van der Merwe, 'Black and white student ideals'.
9. Cited in Lindy Wilson, 'Biko: A life', in Barney Pityana, Mamphela Ramphele, Malusi Mpumlwana and Lindy Wilson (eds), *Bounds of Possibility: The Legacy of Steve Biko and Black Consciousness* (Cape Town: David Philip, 1991; London: Zed Books, 1992), pp. 26–27.
10. *Cape Times* political reporter, 'Whites on path of no return', *Cape Times*, 22 January 1971.
11. Staff reporter, 'Black power pleas rock Cape', Newspaper unknown (included in 'SASO Press Digest: Various reports on papers presented at Abe Bailey Institute workshop on student activism in South Africa at the University of Cape Town, 1971', 'SASO, 1969–1973' collection, AD2189, E13, Wits Historical Papers).
12. 'The young blacks' views', *Financial Mail*, 12 February 1971.
13. Jeremy Seekings, 'The "lost generation": South Africa's "youth problem" in the early 1990s', *Transformation* 29, 1995, pp. 103–125.
14. Woods, *Biko*, p. 206.
15. Cited in ibid., p. 354.

WINNIE MANDELA, SPEECH AT CHARGE OR RELEASE DETAINEES MEETING

1. Winnie Mandela, *Part of My Soul Went With Him*, edited by Anne Benjamin and adapted by Mary Benson (London: Penguin, 1985), p. 85.
2. Emma Gilbey, *The Lady: The Life and Times of Winnie Mandela* (London: Vintage, 1994), p. 66.
3. To avoid confusion with Nelson Mandela, and in keeping with newspaper conventions at the time, I've used Winnie Mandela's first name in reference to her.
4. Anné Marié du Preez Bezdrob, *Winnie Mandela: A Life* (Cape Town: Zebra Press, 2003), p. 83.
5. Gilbey, *The Lady*, p. 80.
6. Ibid., p. 84.
7. Ibid., p. 89–90.
8. Du Preez Bezdrob, *Winnie Mandela*, p. 165.
9. Nicholas Ashford, 'Mrs Mandela attacks terror law', *The Times*, London, 5 October 1975, p. 5.
10. Obed Musi, 'Back from the land of the living dead', *Rand Daily Mail*, 6 October 1975, p. 10.

11. Staff reporter, 'Winnie speaks to accused at SASO trial', *Rand Daily Mail*, 3 October 1975, p. 3.
12. Staff reporter, 'Winnie Mandela to speak', *Rand Daily Mail*, 3 October 1975, p. 3.
13. Ashford, 'Mrs Mandela attacks terror law'.
14. Du Preez Bezdrob claims that Winnie Mandela's first public address after her extended banning period was on 12 October (p. 168). This is incorrect; although the Durban FEDSAW meeting was perhaps a more high-profile welcome event, newspaper reports from the time indicate that the CORD speech preceded this. See Staff reporter, 'Winnie Mandela to speak' and Ashford, 'Mrs Mandela attacks terror law'.
15. The quote comes from psychoanalyst Bruno Bettelheim's book *The Informed Heart* (1960), which examines the effects of Nazi brutality upon the personality of victims in concentration camps.
16. Winnie Madikizela-Mandela, *491 Days: Prisoner Number 1323/69* (Athens: Ohio University Press, 2014).
17. Staff reporter, 'Winnie Mandela leads new protest', *Rand Daily Mail*, 6 October 1975, p. 1.
18. John Allen, *Rabble-Rouser for Peace: The Authorized Biography of Desmond Tutu* (London: Random House, 2012), p. 150.
19. Cited in Staff reporter, 'Winnie Mandela leads new protest', p. 1.
20. Mandela, *Part of My Soul Went With Him*.
21. Gilbey, *The Lady*, pp. 101–102.
22. Ibid., p. 80.
23. Ibid., p. 91.
24. Ashford, 'Mrs Mandela attacks terror law', p. 5.
25. Own correspondent, 'Big Durban welcome for Winnie Mandela', *Rand Daily Mail*, 13 October 1975, p. 4.
26. Gilbey, *The Lady*, p. 108.
27. Du Preez Bezdrob, *Winnie Mandela*, p. 176–177.
28. Gilbey, *The Lady*, p. 108.
29. Winnie Mandela, 'Speech given at launch of Black Parents' Association', Soweto, Reproduced in UN Centre Against Apartheid, 'Mrs Winnie Mandela: Profile in courage and defiance', p. 7–8.
30. Cited in Kevin Harris, *No Middle Road to Freedom*, documentary, 1983.
31. Du Preez Bezdrob, *Winnie Mandela*, p. 226; Gilbey, *The Lady*, p. 96.
32. Cited in Christopher S. Wren, 'Anti-apartheid groups cast out Winnie Mandela, citing terror', *New York Times*, 17 February 1989.

B.J. VORSTER, REPLY TO MOTION OF NO CONFIDENCE

1. Deon Geldenhuys, *The Diplomacy of Isolation: South African Foreign Policy Making* (Braamfontein: Macmillan, 1984), p. 79.
2. Republic of South Africa, House of Assembly Debates, no. 6, 9 September 1974, column 2537.
3. John Seiler, 'South Africa's regional role', pp. 99–113, in John Seiler (ed.), *Southern Africa Since the Portuguese Coup* (Boulder, Colorado: Westview Press, 1980), p. 103.
4. See General Constand Viljoen's comments in Hermann Giliomee, *The Last Afrikaner Leaders*, p. 124–131.
5. Rodney Warwick, 'Operation Savannah: A measure of SADF decline, resourcefulness and modernisation', *Scientia Militaria* 40 (3), 2012, p. 356; Giliomee, *The Last Afrikaner Leaders*, p. 125.

6. Christopher Saunders, 'The South Africa–Angola Talks, 1976–1984: A little known Cold War thread', *Kronos* 37 (1), 2011, p. 105.
7. Giliomee, *The Last Afrikaner Leaders*, p. 125.
8. Geldenhuys, *The Diplomacy of Isolation*, p. 78.
9. Giliomee, *The Last Afrikaner Leaders*, p. 128.
10. Warwick, 'Operation Savannah', p. 358.
11. Bob Hitchcock, 'Army kills 61, loses 3', *Rand Daily Mail*, 16 December 1975, p. 1.
12. Cited in Hitchcock, 'Army kills 61, loses 3', p. 1.
13. Larry Heinzerling, 'South African men "deep in Angola" – Unita', *Rand Daily Mail*, 17 December 1975, p. 1.
14. 'SA prisoners on show', *Rand Daily Mail*, 18 December 1975, p. 1.
15. 'MPLA delegation brings two captured South Africans to Lagos', Telegram from Lagos to various countries, 18 December 1975, published on Warinangola.com (available at: http://www.warinangola.com/default.aspx?tabid=590&forumid=2&postid=5239&view=topic; viewed 9 August 2017).
16. Own correspondent, 'SADF acts to free captives', *Rand Daily Mail*, 18 December 1975, p. 1.
17. 'Call the house, says Eglin', *Rand Daily Mail*, 20 December 1975, p. 1.
18. 'SA men flown to Khartoum', *Rand Daily Mail*, 16 January 1976, p. 1. (For the AP footage of the men, see: https://www.youtube.com/watch?v=doDsyog2sng; viewed 9 August 2017.)
19. Editorial, 'Tell us NOW', *Rand Daily Mail*, 24 January 1976, p. 1.
20. Cited and paraphrased in Political correspondent, 'Give us the facts – Vorster told', *Rand Daily Mail*, 27 January 1976, p. 4.
21. PRP member Harry Schwarz.
22. Colin Eglin, leader of the PRP.
23. PRP member Japie Basson.
24. PRP member Frederik van Zyl Slabbert.
25. PFP member W.V. Raw.
26. Hilton Hamman, *Days of the Generals: The Untold Story of South Africa's Apartheid-Era Military Generals* (Cape Town: Zebra Press, 2001), p. 26–27.
27. Richard Walker, 'SA joined the fight in September – Dr K', *Rand Daily Mail*, 31 January 1976, p. 1.
28. Political correspondent, 'Dr K not fully informed – Botha', *Rand Daily Mail*, 3 February 1976, p. 4.
29. Piero Gleijeses, *Conflicting Missions: Havana, Washington, and Africa, 1959–1976* (Chapel Hill: University of North Carolina Press, 2003).
30. Giliomee, *The Last Afrikaner Leaders*; Jamie Miller, *An African Volk: The Apartheid Regime and Its Search for Survival* (New York: Oxford University Press, 2016).
31. See Giliomee, *The Last Afrikaner Leaders*, p. 372.
32. Miller, *An African Volk*, p. 329; Warwick, 'Operation Savannah', p. 357.
33. Giliomee, *The Last Afrikaner Leaders*, p. 133.
34. Bernadi Wessels, 'Puzzles remain as PM wins', *Rand Daily Mail*, 2 February 1976, p. 5.
35. 'Who's right, PM or Kissinger? asks PRP', *Rand Daily Mail*, 3 February 1976, p. 1.
36. Warwick, 'Operation Savannah', p. 357.

ALLAN BOESAK, SPEECH AT THE LAUNCH OF THE UDF

1. John Siko, *Inside South Africa's Foreign Policy: Diplomacy in South Africa from Smuts to Mbeki* (London: I.B. Tauris, 2014), p. 25.
2. Janine Rauch, 'War and resistance', in Gavin Cawthra, Gerald Kraak and Gerald

O'Sullivan (eds), *War and Resistance: Southern African Reports* (London: Macmillan Press, 1994), no page number.

3. Cited in Gary Thatcher, '"Petty apartheid" thrives despite Botha's reform promises', *Christian Science Monitor*, 5 May 1980.

4. Oliver Tambo, interview with E.S. Reddy, 1 August 1980, South African History Online (available at: http://www.sahistory.org.za/archive/interview-oliver-tambo-newsweek-01-august-1980; viewed 12 August 2017).

5. Cited in John Battersby, 'PW's plan leaves Labour Party divided', *Rand Daily Mail*, 2 August 1982, p. 1.

6. Frederik van Zyl Slabbert, cited in ibid.

7. Cited in ibid.

8. Cited in ibid.

9. Cited in Mail correspondent, 'LP's decision is disgusting, says Boesak', *Rand Daily Mail*, 7 January 1983, p. 3.

10. John Battersby, 'Boesak hits at the spirit of Mammon', *Rand Daily Mail*, 24 January 1983, p. 7.

11. Anton Harber, 'Can the UDF become the real force of the 1980s?', *Rand Daily Mail*, 24 August 1983, p. 9.

12. For an edited version of the speech, see Battersby, 'Boesak hits at the spirit of Mammon', p. 7.

13. ANC National Executive Committee statement on the occasion of the 71st anniversary of the ANC, 8 January 1983.

14. Luli Callinicos, *Oliver Tambo: Beyond the Engeli Mountains* (Cape Town: David Philip, 2004), p. 540.

15. Chris Freimond, 'UDF backed by 400 organisations', *Rand Daily Mail*, 22 August 1983, p. 1.

16. Jamie Frueh, *Political Identity and Social Change: The Remaking of the South African Social Order* (Albany: State University of New York Press, 2003), p. 401.

17. Freimond, 'UDF backed by 400 organisations', p. 1.

18. Ryland Fisher, 'Boesak at 70', *Weekend Argus*, 20 February 2016.

19. For video footage of the event, see Afrascope's footage 'United Democratic Front (UDF) National Launch 1983' (available at: https://www.youtube.com/watch?v=bZLOk_jQnn4; viewed 14 August 2017).

20. Frueh, *Political Identity and Social Change*, p. 104.

21. Freimond, 'UDF backed by 400 organisations', p. 1.

22. Harber, 'Can the UDF become the real force of the 1980s?', p. 9.

23. Gail M. Gerhart and Clive L. Glaser, *From Protest to Challenge: A Documentary History of African Politics in South Africa, 1882–1990, Volume 6: Challenge and Victory, 1980–1990* (Bloomington: Indian University Press, 2010), p. 12.

24. Quoted in London Bureau, 'A clear rejection, say UK papers', *Rand Daily Mail*, 25 August 1984, p. 2.

25. Mail correspondent, 'It's an insult, says UDF', *Rand Daily Mail*, 25 August 1984, p. 2.

OLIVER TAMBO, 'YEAR OF THE WOMEN' ADDRESS

1. Barry Gilder, *Songs and Secrets: South Africa from Liberation to Governance* (Auckland Park: Jacana, 2012), p. 422.

2. Oliver Tambo, 'The Year of the Spear', statement of the National Executive Committee on the occasion of the 67th birthday of the ANC, 8 January 1979.

3. Tom Lodge, 'Reform, recession and resistance', in Tom Lodge and Bill Nasson (eds), *All*,

Here, and Now: Black Politics in South Africa in the 1980s (Cape Town: David Philip, 1991), p. 24.

4. Callinicos, *Oliver Tambo*, p. 357.
5. Mark Gevisser, *Thabo Mbeki: The Dream Deferred* (Johannesburg: Jonathan Ball, 2009), p. 420.
6. Raymond Suttner, *The ANC Underground in South Africa: A Social and Historical Study* (Auckland Park: Jacana, 2008), p. 68.
7. Lebona Mosia, Don Pinnock and Charles Riddle, 'Warring in the ether', *For the Record*, July 1992, p. 43.
8. Ibid., p. 69.
9. Cited in ibid., p. 41.
10. Ibid.
11. Suttner, *The ANC Underground*, p. 70.
12. Michael Parks, 'Outlawed black S. group gains impetus', *Los Angeles Times*, 1 June 1986.
13. Cited in Sekibakiba Peter Lekgoathi, 'The African National Congress's Radio Freedom and its audiences in apartheid South Africa, 1963–1991', *Journal of African Media Studies* 2 (2), 2010, p. 143.
14. Tor Sellström, *Sweden and National Liberation in Southern Africa, Volume II: Solidarity and Assistance, 1970–1974* (Stockholm: Nordiska Afrikainstitutet, 2002), p. 475.
15. Lekgoathi, 'The African National Congress's Radio Freedom', p. 144.
16. Mail reporter, 'ANC tape does not mean man is guilty – Defence', *Rand Daily Mail*, 28 July 1983, p. 3.
17. Shana L. Redmond, *Social Movements and the Sound of Solidarity in the African Diaspora* (New York and London: New York University Press, 2014), p. 323.
18. Gavin Evans, 'Four years jail for playing ANC tapes', *Rand Daily Mail*, 20 March 1985, p. 5.
19. Callinicos, *Oliver Tambo*, pp. 525–526.
20. Hilton Hamann, *Days of the Generals*, p. 123.
21. ANC, 'Submission to the Truth and Reconciliation Commission', August 1996.
22. Callinicos, *Oliver Tambo*, pp. 545–546.
23. Oliver Tambo, 'Make South Africa Ungovernable', Radio Freedom broadcast, 10 October 1984.
24. Callinicos, *Oliver Tambo*, p. 548.
25. South African Press Association (SAPA), 'ANC work is banned by censors', *Rand Daily Mail*, 12 January 1985, p. 2.
26. Pierre du Toit, Charl Swart and Salomé Teuteberg, *South Africa and the Case for Renegotiating the Peace* (Stellenbosch: Sun Press, 2016), p. 19.
27. Tom Lodge, 'The Vaal uprising', in Tom Lodge and Bill Nasson (eds), *All, Here, and Now*, p. 75.
28. Callinicos, *Oliver Tambo*, p. 531.
29. ANC, 'Submission to the Truth and Reconciliation Commission', August 1996.
30. Eminent Persons Group, cited in Malcolm Fraser and Margaret Simons, *Malcolm Fraser: The Political Memoirs* (Victoria, Australia: Miegunyah Press, 2010), p. 651.

ZINDZI MANDELA, 'MY FATHER SAYS' SPEECH

1. Mail reporter, 'Relaxing the rules of prison life', *Rand Daily Mail*, 1 February 1985, p. 7.
2. Mandela, *Long Walk to Freedom*, p. 509.
3. Ibid.
4. Ibid., p. 420.

5. Eminent Persons Group, cited in Malcolm Fraser and Margaret Simons, *Malcolm Fraser*, p. 651.
6. Martin Meredith, *Mandela: A Biography* (Michigan: Hamish Hamilton, 1997), p. 355.
7. Sisulu, *Walter and Albertina Sisulu*, p. 457.
8. Graham Leach, *South Africa: No Easy Path to Peace* (London: Methuen, 1987), p. 132.
9. Allister Sparks, *Tomorrow Is Another Country: The Inside Story of South Africa's Negotiated Transition* (Sandton: Struik, 1994), p. 49.
10. Ibid.
11. Chris Freimond, 'Govt. urged to lift ban on Winnie', *Rand Daily Mail*, 1 February 1985, p. 1.
12. Ibid., p. 7.
13. *Sunday Times*, editorial, 'An offer Mandela shouldn't refuse', 3 February 1985, reprinted in *South African Digest* (week ended 8 February 1985), p. 112.
14. *Rapport*, editorial, 'Mandela', 3 February 1985, reprinted and translated in *South African Digest* (week ended 8 February 1985), p. 112.
15. *Volksblad*, editorial, 'Mandela's choice', 3 February 1986, reprinted and translated in *South African Digest* (week ended 8 February 1985), p. 115.
16. Sisulu, *Walter and Albertina Sisulu*, p. 457.
17. George Bizos, *Odyssey to Freedom* (Cape Town: Umuzi, 2007), p. 369.
18. Anton Harber, 'Mandela's reply this weekend', *Rand Daily Mail*, 9 February 1985, p. 1.
19. Anton Harber, 'All is set for Tutu rally', *Rand Daily Mail*, 9 February 1985, p. 2.
20. Bizos, *Odyssey to Freedom*, p. 369.
21. Patti Waldmeir, *Anatomy of a Miracle: The End of Apartheid and the Birth of the New South Africa* (New Brunswick, New Jersey, London: Rutgers University Press, 1997), p. 93.
22. Anton Harber, 'Mandela rejects PW offer', *Rand Daily Mail*, 11 February 1985, p. 1.
23. 'Botha not budging on Mandela release', *The Times*, London, 15 February 1985, p. 6.
24. Editorial, 'Hoping for negotiation', *Rand Daily Mail*, 12 February 1985, p. 10.
25. *Star*, editorial, 'ANC: the dialogue must continue', 8 February 1985, reprinted and translated in *South African Digest* (week ended 15 February 1985), p. 138.
26. Cited and translated in John D. Battersby, 'Big Afrikaner newspaper calls for Mandela's release', *New York Times*, 19 July 1988.

P.W. BOTHA, 'RUBICON' SPEECH

1. Dave Steward, 'From the Rubicon to February 2nd 1990', *Politicsweb*, 11 February 2010 (available at: http://www.politicsweb.co.za/politicsweb/view/politicsweb/en/page72308?o id¼160215&sn¼Detail&pid¼472308; viewed 30 January 2011), no page number.
2. Henry E. Isaacs, 'The dynamics of conflict in South Africa: The route to peace?', in Harvey Glickman (ed.), *Toward Peace and Security in Southern Africa* (New York: Gordon and Breach Science Publishers, 1990), p. 47.
3. Associated Press, 'Two missing blacks are found stabbed to death in South Africa', *New York Times*, 2 July 1985.
4. Martha Evans, *Broadcasting the End of Apartheid: Live Television and the Birth of a New South Africa* (London: I.B. Tauris, 2014), p. 121.
5. Hermann Giliomee, 'A crossing suspended: P.W. Botha's Rubicon', in *The Last Afrikaner Leaders*, pp. 188–189.
6. Hermann Giliomee, 'The day apartheid started dying', *Mail & Guardian*, 26 October 2012.
7. Hermann Giliomee, 'Great expectations: Pres. PW Botha's Rubicon speech of 1985', *New Contree* 55, 2008, p. 1.
8. Giliomee, 'Great expectations', p. 28.

9. Nicholas Ashford, 'A free Mandela?', *The Times*, London, 12 August 1985, p. 10.
10. Cited in Giliomee 'Great expectations', p. 32.
11. Raymond Ackerman and Denise Pritchard, *Hearing Grasshoppers Jump* (Cape Town: New Africa Books, 2004), p. 196.
12. Sisulu, *Walter & Albertina Sisulu*, p. 471.
13. Ray Kennedy and Nicholas Ashford, diplomatic correspondent, 'Botha offers blacks citizenship but dashes reform hope', *The Times*, London, 16 August 1985, p. 1.
14. Giliomee, *The Last Afrikaner Leaders*, p. 202.
15. Waldmeir, *Anatomy of a Miracle*, p. 56.
16. Nicholas Ashford, diplomatic correspondent, and Christopher Thomas, 'Reaction to Botha speech', *The Times*, London, 17 August 1985, p. 4.
17. Editorial, 'Across the wrong Rubicon', *The Times*, London, 17 August 1985, p. 9.
18. *Natal Mercury*, editorial, 'Damp squib, but …', 17 August 1985, reprinted in *South African Digest* (week ended 23 August 1985), p. 773.
19. *Evening Post*, editorial, 'The talking must start', 16 August 1985, reprinted in *South African Digest* (week ended 23 August 1985), p. 771.
20. *Sunday Times*, editorial, 'It's time PW had courage to forget about the verkramptes', 8 August 1985, reprinted in *South African Digest* (week ended 23 August 1985), p. 772.
21. The events narrated here are from Hermann Giliomee's 'A crossing suspended: P.W. Botha's Rubicon', in *The Last Afrikaner Leaders*, pp. 175–206.
22. Giliomee, 'A crossing suspended: P.W. Botha's Rubicon', p. 195.
23. Ray Kennedy, 'Pretoria dampens hope of reforms', *The Times*, London, 14 August 1985, p. 1.

FREDERIK VAN ZYL SLABBERT, RESIGNATION SPEECH

1. Own correspondent, 'Slabbert victory is a sensation', *Rand Daily Mail*, 25 April 1974, p. 2.
2. Giliomee, *The Last Afrikaner Leaders*, p. 214.
3. Martin Schneider, 'Can the ivory tower star take spit and saw dust?', *Rand Daily Mail*, 9 August 1979, p. 11.
4. Giliomee, *The Last Afrikaner Leaders*, p. 213.
5. Ibid., p. 214.
6. Ibid.
7. F.A. Mouton, '"Had it too easy?" Frederik van Zyl Slabbert's resignation as leader of the official parliamentary opposition, 7 February 1986', *Historia* 60 (20), November 2015, pp. 68–86.
8. Own correspondent, 'Pretoria opposition changes tune', *The Times*, London, 21 November 1983, p. 6.
9. Frederik van Zyl Slabbert, 'Letter to London *Times*', 13 February 1986 (available at: https://digital.lib.sun.ac.za/bitstream/handle/10019.2/9407/430-e2-15-1.pdf?sequence=1; viewed 21 August 2017).
10. Kennedy and Ashford, 'Botha offers blacks citizenship but dashes reform hope'.
11. Slabbert, 'Letter to London *Times*'.
12. Ray Swart, *Progressive Odyssey* (Cape Town: Human & Rousseau, 1991), p. 157. See also Giliomee, *The Last Afrikaner Leaders*, pp. 212–213.
13. A. Le Maitre and M. Savage (eds), *The Passion for Reason: Essays in Honour of an Afrikaner African* (Johannesburg: Jonathan Ball, 2009), p. 33.
14. Cited in Giliomee, *The Last Afrikaner Leaders*, p. 214.
15. Schneider, 'Can the ivory tower star take spit and saw dust?', p. 11.
16. R.W. Johnson, 'Van Zyl Slabbert: What went wrong?' *Politicsweb*, 21 June 2010.

17. Hansard, House of Assembly Debates, 7 February 1986, column 414.
18. Ivor Wilkins, 'This man who guides ordinary people', *Sunday Times*, 19 April 1981 (cited in Giliomee, *The Last Afrikaner Leaders*, p. 213).
19. Slabbert, 'Letter to London *Times*', p. 6.
20. Mouton, '"Had it too easy?"', p. 84.
21. Suzman, *In No Uncertain Terms*, p. 255.
22. Cited in Giliomee, *The Last Afrikaner Leaders*, p. 229.
23. Patrick Laurence, 'Van Zyl Slabbert: A critical assessment', *Politicsweb*, 20 May 2010.
24. 'Apdusa Views' newsletter 11, March 1986.
25. *Sunday Times* editorial cited in Laurence, 'Van Zyl Slabbert: A critical assessment'.
26. Republished in Gerhart and Glaser, *From Protest to Challenge: A Documentary History of African Politics in South Africa, 1882–1990; Volume 6: Challenge and Victory, 1980–1990*, p. 594.
27. Cited in Mouton, '"Had it too easy?"', p. 82.
28. 'Apdusa Views' newsletter 11, March 1986.
29. Giliomee, *The Last Afrikaner Leaders*, p. 224.
30. Republished in Frederik van Zyl Slabbert, *The System and the Struggle* (Johannesburg: Jonathan Ball, 1989), pp. 21–22.

DESMOND TUTU, 'RAINBOW PEOPLE OF GOD' SPEECH
1. Alan Cowell, 'Churches on cutting edge of apartheid battle', *New York Times*, 15 March 1985.
2. Joseph Lelyveld, 'South Africa's Bishop Tutu', *New York Times*, 14 March 1982.
3. Cited in ibid.
4. David Croteau and William Hoynes, *By Invitation Only: How the Media Limit Political Debate* (California: Common Courage, 1994), p. 87.
5. Rian Malan, *My Traitor's Heart: Blood and Bad Dreams: A South African Explores the Madness in His Country, His Tribe and Himself* (London: Vintage, 1990), p. 159.
6. 'Archbishop Desmond Tutu is awarded the Nobel Peace Prize', South African History Online, 16 March 2011.
7. Allen, *Rabble-Rouser for Peace*, p. 6.
8. Ibid., p. 310.
9. Giliomee, *The Last Afrikaner Leaders*, p. 298.
10. Allen, *Rabble-Rouser for Peace*, p. 307.
11. Scott Kraft, 'Tutu leads 20,000 in peaceful S. Africa march; no police intervention', *Los Angeles Times*, 14 September 1989.
12. Cited in Allen, *Rabble-Rouser for Peace*, p. 310.
13. Cited in Kraft, 'Tutu leads 20,000 in peaceful S. Africa march'.
14. Kraft, 'Tutu leads 20,000 in peaceful S. Africa march'; J.A. du Pisani, M. Broodryk and P.W. Coetzer, 'Protest marches in South Africa', *The Journal of Modern African Studies* 28 (4), 1990, pp. 573–602; Allen, *Rabble-Rouser for Peace*, p. 311.
15. Cited in Kraft, 'Tutu leads 20,000 in peaceful S. African march'.
16. For video footage of the event, see Afravision's 'History Uncut – Cape Town Peace March' (available at: https://www.youtube.com/watch?v=ygpWizpLKSc; viewed 3 September 2017).
17. William Claiborne, '"Pretoriastroika" blossoming in South Africa', *Washington Post*, 18 September 1989.
18. John Allen (ed.), *Desmond Tutu: The Rainbow People of God: A Spiritual Journey from Apartheid to Freedom* (Cape Town: Double Storey, 2006), p. 180.
19. Salazar, *An African Athens*, pp. 1–17.

20. J.M. Coetzee, 'The 1995 Rugby World Cup', in *Stranger Shores: Essays, 1986–1999*, p. 352.
21. Du Pisani, Broodryk and Coetzer, 'Protest marches in South Africa', p. 588.
22. Interview with F.W. de Klerk by Patti Waldmeir, 23 November 1994 (cited in Giliomee, *The Last Afrikaner Leaders*, p. 299).
23. F.W. de Klerk, *The Last Trek – A New Beginning: The Autobiography* (London: Pan Macmillan, 1999), p. 159.
24. Patti Waldmeir, *Anatomy of a Miracle*, p. 139.
25. Ibid.

F.W. DE KLERK, OPENING OF PARLIAMENT
1. Christopher S. Wren, 'Botha, rebuffed by his party, quits South Africa presidency', *New York Times*, 15 August 1989.
2. Christopher S. Wren, 'Botha faces rival in new party chief', *New York Times*, 7 March 1989.
3. Ibid.
4. Wren, 'Botha, rebuffed by his party, quits South African presidency'.
5. Giliomee, *The Last Afrikaner Leaders*, p. 283.
6. Cited in ibid., p. 283.
7. Interview with Marike de Klerk by Patti Waldmeir, 2 March 1995 (cited in Giliomee, *The Last Afrikaner Leaders*, p. 302).
8. F.W. de Klerk, 'Speech to commemorate 20th anniversary of speech to parliament, 2 February 1990', 2 February 2010.
9. Giliomee, *The Last Afrikaner Leaders*, p. 302.
10. As remembered by Andre Fourie, in an interview with Hermann Giliomee, 12 December 2010 (cited in Giliomee, *The Last Afrikaner Leaders*, p. 303).
11. Giliomee, *The Last Afrikaner Leaders*, p. 104.
12. De Klerk, *The Last Trek*, p. 162.
13. De Klerk cited in Nicolas Rossier, *The Other Man: F.W. de Klerk and the End of Apartheid*, documentary, Naashon Zalk Media and DCTV, 16 February 2016.
14. Christopher S. Wren, 'De Klerk and Mandela discuss future', *New York Times*, 14 December 1989.
15. De Klerk, *The Last Trek*, p. 163.
16. Cited in Rossier, *The Other Man*.
17. Christopher S. Wren, 'South Africa moves to scrap apartheid', *New York Times*, 2 February 1990.
18. Both cited in Angie Kapelianis, 'De Klerk's historic February 2, 1990 speech changed SA', *SABC News*, 2 February 2012.
19. Both Tutu and Boesak cited in Joe Kerwin and Andrew Meldrum, 'Anti-apartheid activists divided on President de Klerk concessions', *Guardian*, 3 February 1990.
20. Cited in Rossier, *The Other Man*.
21. Cited in Kerwin and Meldrum, 'Anti-apartheid activists divided on President de Klerk concessions'.
22. Cited in Wren, 'South Africa moves to scrap apartheid'.
23. Cited in Kerwin and Meldrum, 'Anti-apartheid activists divided on President de Klerk concessions'.
24. Elleke Boehmer, *Nelson Mandela: A Very Short Introduction* (Oxford and New York: Oxford University Press, 2008), p. 72.

NELSON MANDELA, RELEASE SPEECH

1. F.W. de Klerk, 'Press conference statement', 10 February 1990 (available at: https://www
.youtube.com/watch?v=8DdNV6nbByM; viewed 7 September 2017).
2. Craig Matthew, *Welcome Nelson* (Doxa Productions, 2012).
3. De Klerk, *The Last Trek,* p. 168.
4. Anthony Sampson, *Mandela: The Authorised Biography* (Johannesburg, Jonathan Ball,
1999), p. 259.
5. Pippa Green, 'Waiting for Mandela', *Mail & Guardian,* 12 February 2010.
6. Interview with Dave Steward, 31 March 2011.
7. Evans, *Broadcasting the End of Apartheid,* p. 110.
8. John Carlin, *Playing the Enemy: Nelson Mandela and the Game that Made a Nation*
(New York: Penguin, 2008.) p. 77.
9. Green, 'Waiting for Mandela'.
10. Cyril Ramaphosa, cited in ibid.
11. Evans, *Broadcasting the End of Apartheid,* p. 107.
12. Andre le Roux, cited in 'Top TV moments: Nelson Mandela's long walk to freedom',
Observer, 12 September 1999.
13. Rob Nixon, 'Mandela, messianism and the media', *Transition* 51, 1991, pp. 42–51.
14. Mandela, *Long Walk to Freedom,* p. 553.
15. Ibid. There are various accounts of what happened during this period. According to
Mandela's autobiography, he directed the driver to Dullah Omar's house; another
account (Green, 2010) claims that the convoy stopped outside the house of a stranger,
Vanessa Watson, before having tea at the home of a local activist in Rondebosch East.
Trevor Manuel, directed via walkie-talkie by a security police colonel who had
managed to locate Mandela, eventually led the convoy back to the city via De Waal
Drive.
16. Trevor Manuel, cited in Green, 'Waiting for Mandela'.
17. Green, 'Waiting for Mandela'.
18. John P. Burns, 'South Africa's new era: Has De Klerk devised his own fall?', *New York
Times,* 12 February 1990.
19. Jill Smolowe and Scott MacLeod, 'A hero's triumphant homecoming', *Time,* 26 February
1990.
20. Elleke Boehmer, *Nelson Mandela: The Black Pimpernel* (London: Zed Book, 2013).
21. Arlene Getz, 'Mandela meets black labor leaders', United Press International, 19
December 1989.
22. Evans, *Broadcasting the End of Apartheid,* p. 110.
23. Anthony Sampson, '18 days: A South African Journal', *New York Times,* 18 March 1990.
24. Boehmer, *Mandela: The Black Pimpernel.*
25. Meredith, *Mandela,* p. 405.
26. Mandela, *Long Walk to Freedom,* p. 555.
27. Boehmer, *Mandela: The Black Pimpernel.*
28. De Klerk, *The Last Trek,* p. 169; Matthew, *Welcome Nelson.*
29. Boehmer, *Mandela: The Black Pimpernel.*
30. Cited in Sampson, '18 days'.

NELSON MANDELA, TELEVISED ADDRESS AFTER CHRIS HANI'S DEATH

1. Truth and Reconciliation Commission, Chapter 7, 'Political violence in the era of
negotiations and transition, 1990–1994', in *Final Report,* Vol. 2, 2003.

2. Dennis Cruywagen, *Brothers in War and Peace: Constand and Abraham Viljoen and the Birth of the New South Africa* (Cape Town: Zebra Press, 2014), pp. 91–93.
3. Paul Trewhela, *Inside Quatro: Uncovering the Exile History of the ANC and SWAPO* (Auckland Park: Jacana, 2009), p. 26.
4. Arianna Lissoni, 'Remembering South African struggle hero Chris Hani: Lessons for today', *The Conversation*, 9 April 2017.
5. Cited in Bill Keller, 'A black leader in South Africa is slain and a white is arrested', *New York Times*, 11 April 1993.
6. Charmain Naidoo, Charles Leonard and Charlene Smith, 'How Hani died', *Sunday Times*, 11 April 1993.
7. Ibid.
8. Ibid.
9. Ibid.
10. Simpson, *Umkhonto we Sizwe*, p. 496.
11. *State v. Walus and Another* (585/93,586/93) [1994] ZASCA 189 (30 November 1994).
12. Ibid.
13. Evans, *Broadcasting the End of Apartheid*, pp. 135–140.
14. South African Communist Party, 'Disinformation Campaign: Just the ultra-right: Who killed Hani?' *Journal of the South African Communist Party* 132, first quarter of 1993.
15. John Carlin, 'Storm warnings in South Africa: "Big war" feared after killing of ANC activist – Police guard was refused – two whites burnt to death in township', *Independent*, 11 April 1993.
16. De Klerk, *The Last Trek*, p. 276.
17. Nelson Mandela, 'Televised address to the nation, on the assassination of Martin Thembisile (Chris) Hani', 10 April 1993.
18. Carlin, 'Storm warnings in South Africa'.
19. De Klerk, *The Last Trek*, p. 276.
20. Cited in 'Remembering Chris Hani – 21 Years later, *SABC Digital News* (available at: https://www.youtube.com/watch?v=Ebf-11K9uLc; viewed 2 September 2017).
21. Address by Nelson Mandela at the funeral of Chris Hani, Soweto, 19 April 1993.
22. '10 days that shook our country', *Sowetan Live*, 24 February 2011 (available at: http://www.sowetanlive.co.za/goodlife/2011/02/24/10-days-that-shook-ourcountry; viewed 11 September 2011), no page number.
23. Cited in Kenneth S. Zagacki, 'Rhetoric, dialogue, and performance in Nelson Mandela's televised address on the assassination of Chris Hani', *Rhetoric and Public Affairs* 6 (4), 2003, p. 710.
24. SAPA, 'Derby-Lewis and Walus tried to induce a race war, TRC told', 19 March 1998.
25. Evans, *Broadcasting the End of Apartheid*, p. 148.
26. Meredith, *Mandela*, p. 484.
27. Both cited in Bill Keller, 'Mandela shares Nobel accolade with De Klerk', *New York Times*, 16 October 1993.

NELSON MANDELA, INAUGURATION SPEECH

1. Evans, *Broadcasting the End of Apartheid*, p. 160.
2. Sparks, *Tomorrow Is Another Country*, p. 214.
3. SAPA, 'Violence – HRC', 13 April 1994.
4. Cited in Sky News, 'SA relieved as IFP joins election', 19/20 April 1994 (available at: http://www.youtube.com/watch?v¼SM0CwNJYask; viewed 26 October 2011).

5. CNN, 'Inkatha joins election', 19 April 1994 (available at: http://www.youtube.com/watch ?v¼BvX59RoxSqo; viewed 26 October 2011).
6. No author, 'I have waited all my life for this day. No long queue is going to stop me', *Mail & Guardian*, 29 April 1994.
7. 'It's a dream outcome', *Weekend Star*, 7 May 1994, p. 1.
8. Kristin Skare Orgeret, 'His master's voice and back again? Presidential inaugurations and South African television – the post-apartheid experience', *African Affairs* 107 (429), 2008, p. 614.
9. Bob Drogin, 'New South Africa embraces rich traditions', *Los Angeles Times*, 25 June 1994.
10. South African Institute of Race Relations, 'Race Relations Survey, 1985' (Johannesburg: South African Institute of Race Relations, 1986).
11. Cited in Bill Keller, 'South Africa's new era: The overview', *New York Times*, 10 May 1994.
12. Gevisser, *Thabo Mbeki*, p. 656.
13. Ibid.
14. Nelson Mandela, 'State of the Nation Address', 24 May 1994.
15. Genesis 9:11.
16. Mandela, *Long Walk to Freedom*, p. 614.
17. Staff reporter, 'We're on top of the world', *Star*, 10 May 1994, p. 1.
18. Staff reporter, 'The world at Mandela's feet', *Sowetan*, 10 May 1994, p. 1.
19. Keller, 'South Africa's new era'.

NOMONDE CALATA AND NYAMEKA GONIWE, TRC TESTIMONY
1. Constitution of Republic of South Africa, Act 200 of 1993.
2. Trewhela, *Inside Quatro*, p. 71.
3. Promotion of National Unity and Reconciliation Act (Act no. 34 of 1995).
4. Cited in Alan Cowell, 'Death squads attacking blacks, South Africa opposition charges', *New York Times*, 4 July 1985.
5. Antjie Krog, *Country of My Skull* (London: Vintage, 1998), p. 62.
6. Jonathan Ancer, 'Ten years on: Who killed Matthew Goniwe?', *Mail & Guardian*, 2 June 1995.
7. Testimony of Bawuli Mhlauli at Truth and Reconciliation Commission, Human Rights Violations hearing, Nombuyiselo Mhlauli, 16 April 1996, Case: EC0079/96.
8. Truth and Reconciliation Commission, Human Rights Violations hearing, Sindiswa Mkhonto, 16 April 1996, Case: EC0029/96.
9. Truth and Reconciliation Commission, Human Rights Violations hearing, Nomonde Calata, 16 April 1996, Case: EC0028/96.
10. Truth and Reconciliation Commission, Human Rights Violations hearing, Nombuyiselo Mhlauli, 16 April 1996, Case: EC0079/96.
11. They were Eric Alexander Taylor, Gerhard Lotz, Nicholas Janse van Rensburg, Harold Snyman, Johan Martin van Zyl, Hermanus Barend du Plessis and Eugene de Kock.
12. AC/99/0350, Truth and Reconciliation Commission Amnesty Committee, application in terms of Section 18 of the Promotion of National Unity and Reconciliation Act, No. 34 Of 1995.
13. Truth and Reconciliation Commission Amnesty hearing, Gerhard Lotz, 4 March 1998.
14. Truth and Reconciliation Commission Amnesty hearing, N.J. Janse van Rensburg, 25 February 1998.
15. Ibid.
16. Truth and Reconciliation Commission Amnesty hearing, Gerhard Lotz, 4 March 1998.
17. Ibid.

18. Cited in 'Son of Cradock Four's Calata appeals to assassins to explain', eNCA, 28 March 2016 (available at: https://www.enca.com/south-africa/son-cradock-fours-calata-appeals-assassins-explain; viewed 18 September 2017).

THABO MBEKI, 'I AM AN AFRICAN'

1. Joe Nhlanhla in Gevisser, *Thabo Mbeki*, p. 413.
2. Cited in ibid., p. 415.
3. Ibid., p. 414.
4. Max du Preez, *Pale Native: Memories of a Renegade Reporter* (Cape Town: Zebra Press, 2004), p. 164.
5. Gevisser, *Thabo Mbeki*, p. 520.
6. Ibid., p. 574; p. 683.
7. Ibid., p. 639.
8. William Gumede, *Thabo Mbeki and the Battle for the Soul of the ANC* (Cape Town: Zebra Press, 2005), p. 40.
9. Noor Nieftagodien, 'Coloureds and South Africa's first democratic elections', History Workshop presented at the University of the Witwatersrand for the 'Democracy Popular Precedents Practice Culture' series, 13–15 July 1994, p. 18.
10. Richard Calland, 'Democratic government, South African style: 1994–1999', in Andrew Reynolds (ed.), *Election '99 South Africa: From Mandela to Mbeki* (Oxford, Cape Town, New York: James Currey, David Philip, St. Martin's Press, 1999), p. 5.
11. 'From Mandela to Mbeki', *Houston Chronicle*, 8 July 1996 [sic] (originally cited in Gumede, *Thabo Mbeki and the Battle for the Soul of the ANC*, p. 62).
12. Rosalind C. Morris, 'Crowds and powerlessness: Reading //kabbo and Canetti with Derrida in (South) Africa', in Myriam Diocaretz (ed.), *Demenageries: Thinking (of) Animals After Derrida* (London & New York: Brill, 2011), p. 174.
13. Stephen Grootes, 'Missing: The sublime art of speech writing and oratory', *Daily Maverick*, 14 February 2011.
14. Gumede, *Thabo Mbeki and the Battle for the South of the ANC*, p. 34.
15. Theodore F. Sheckels, 'The rhetorical success of Thabo Mbeki's 1996 "I am an African" address', in *Political Communication in the Anglophone World: Case Studies* (Maryland: Lexington Books, 2012), pp. 96–97.
16. Ibid., p. 97.
17. Thiven Reddy, *South Africa, Settler Colonialism and the Failures of Liberal Democracy* (Johannesburg: Wits University Press, 2016), no page number.
18. This interpretation of ubuntu is usually attributed to Leymah Gbowee, the Liberian Nobel Peace Prize winner.
19. Sheckels, 'The rhetorical success of Thabo Mbeki's 1996 "I am an African" address', p. 97.
20. Mark Gevisser, *A Legacy of Liberation: Thabo Mbeki and the Future of the South African Dream* (Basingstoke: Palgrave Macmillan, 2009), p. 194.
21. Richard Calland, 'Sustaining the spirit of Dakar', *Mail & Guardian*, 1 October 2007.
22. Gevisser, *A Legacy of Liberation*, p. 29.
23. Gevisser, *Thabo Mbeki*, p. 699.
24. Salazar, *An African Athens*, p. 44.
25. Eric van Grasdorff, *The African Renaissance and Discourse Ownership in the Age of Information* (Münster: LIT Verlag, 2005), p. 70.
26. 'Africa's hegemon', *The Economist*, 6 April 2006.
27. Gevisser, *A Legacy of Liberation*, p. 222.

NKOSI JOHNSON, SPEECH AT THE 13TH INTERNATIONAL AIDS CONFERENCE

1. 'Africa's hegemon', *The Economist*, 6 April 2006.
2. UNAIDS, 'Report on the global HIV/AIDS pandemic', June 2000, p. 9.
3. Ibid., p. 82.
4. See 'Edited highlights of a conversation between BBC News Online users and President Thabo Mbeki', in Thabo Mbeki, *Africa, Define Yourself* (Cape Town: Tafelberg, 2002), pp. 194–195.
5. Gumede, *Thabo Mbeki and the Battle for the Soul of the ANC*, p. 192.
6. Ibid., p. 193.
7. Seth C. Kalichman, *Denying AIDS, Conspiracy Theories, Pseudoscience and Human Tragedy* (New York: Copernicus Books, 2009), p. 101.
8. Cited in Pat Sidley, 'Mbeki appoints team to look at cause of Aids', *British Medical Journal* 320 (7 245), 13 May 2000, p. 1 291.
9. UNAIDS, 'Report on the global HIV/AIDS pandemic', p. 40.
10. Ibid., p. 124.
11. Cited in Rachel L. Swarns, 'Focus on AIDS epidemic, Mandela says', *New York Times*, 15 July 2000.
12. Thabo Mbeki, 'Extreme poverty is the world's biggest killer', address at the opening session of the 13th International AIDS Conference, Durban, 9 July 2000.
13. David Brown and Jon Jeter, 'Hundreds walk out on Mbeki', *Washington Post*, 10 July 2000.
14. Gumede, *Thabo Mbeki and the Battle for the Soul of the ANC*, p. 195.
15. Didier Fassin, 'When children become victims: The moral economy of childhood in the times of AIDS', in João Biehl and Adriana Petryna (eds), *When People Come First: Critical Studies in Global Health* (Princeton and Oxford: Princeton University Press, 2013), p. 116.
16. Brown and Jeter, 'Hundreds walk out on Mbeki'.
17. Cited in ibid.
18. Gevisser, *Thabo Mbeki*, p. 736.
19. Ibid., p. 750.
20. Cited in ibid., p. 750.
21. Fassin, 'When children become victims', p. 115.
22. Anso Thom, 'Nkosi Johnson, you were the Hector Pieterson of the Aids generation', *Daily Maverick*, 10 July 2016.
23. Fassin, 'When children become victims', p. 116.
24. Donald G. McNeil Jr, 'South Africa's small warrior against AIDS dies quietly', *New York Times*, 1 June 2001.
25. Fassin, 'When children become victims', p. 114.
26. Ibid., p. 115.
27. Rosie Burton, Janet Giddy and Kathryn Stinson, 'Prevention of mother-to-child transmission in South Africa: An ever-changing landscape', *Obstetric Medicine* 8 (1), 2015, pp. 7–8.
28. Sarah Boseley, 'Mbeki Aids denial caused 300 000 deaths', *Guardian*, 26 November 2008.

THABO MBEKI, RESIGNATION SPEECH

1. Cited in 'A man of two faces', *The Economist*, 20 January 2005.
2. Suzanne Daley, 'Mandela's successor skillful but lacks a common touch', *New York Times*, 23 July 1996.

3. Gevisser, *A Legacy of Liberation*, p. 322.
4. Ibid.
5. Ibid., p. 321.
6. 'Zuma won't be prosecuted,' *Media24*, 23 August 2003.
7. Staff reporter, 'Shaik, Zuma relationship "corrupt"', *Mail & Guardian*, 1 June 2005.
8. Gevisser, *A Legacy of Liberation*, p. 328.
9. Elizabeth Skeen, 'The rape of a trial: Jacob Zuma, AIDS, conspiracy, and tribalism in neo-liberal post-apartheid South Africa', MA thesis, Princeton University, 18 April 2007.
10. Richard Calland, *The Zuma Years: South Africa's Changing Face of Power* (Cape Town: Zebra Press, 2014).
11. Cited in 'We will kill for Zuma', *IOL*, 17 June 2008.
12. Gevisser, *A Legacy of Liberation*, p. 323.
13. Ibid., p. 325.
14. Ibid., p. 332.
15. Cited in Staff reporter, 'Zuma to oppose Mbeki's court challenge', *Mail & Guardian*, 25 September 2008.
16. 'Mbeki regime a "dead snake"', *Star*, 15 September 2008.
17. Chris McGreal, '"I have been a loyal member of the ANC for 52 years" – Mbeki resigns in TV address', *Guardian*, 22 September 2008.
18. *National Director of Public Prosecutions v. Zuma* (573/08) [2009] ZASCA 1 (12 Jan 2009).
19. Thabo Mbeki, 'Thabo Mbeki welcomes SCA judgment', *Politicsweb*, 13 January 2009.
20. Robyn Dixon, 'Jacob Zuma inaugurated as South Africa's president', *Los Angeles Times*, 10 May 2009.

JULIUS MALEMA, SPEECH AT MARIKANA
1. Greg Marinovich, *Murder at Small Koppie: The Real Story of the Marikana Massacre* (Cape Town: Penguin, 2016), p. 28.
2. In 2012, it was 18 per cent.
3. Marinovich, *Murder at Small Koppie*, pp. 29–30.
4. Ibid., p. 56.
5. Ibid., p. 28.
6. Ibid., p. 42.
7. Greg Nicolson, 'Impala strike: Welcome to the age of retail unionism', *Daily Maverick*, 22 February 2012.
8. Ibid.
9. Cited in Staff reporter, '"True leader" Malema addresses Implats strikers', *Mail & Guardian*, 28 February 2012.
10. Cited in Nick Davies, 'Marikana massacre: The untold story of the strike leader who died for workers' rights', *Guardian*, 19 May 2015.
11. Marinovich, *Murder at Small Koppie*, pp. 149; Davies, 'Marikana massacre'; Marinovich, *Murder at Small Koppie*, p. 126.
12. Cited in Davies, 'Marikana massacre'.
13. Ibid.
14. Marinovich, *Murder at Small Koppie*, p. 194.
15. Ibid., p. 192.
16. 'Julius Malema of South Africa's Economic Freedom Fighters – a profile', BBC News, 30 September 2014.

17. Vhahangwele Nemakonde, 'How the Marikana massacre gave birth to the EFF', *The Citizen*, 16 August 2017.
18. Marinovich, *Murder at Small Koppie*, p. 33.
19. Ibid., p. 192.
20. Cited in David Smith, 'Lonmin emails paint ANC elder as a born-again robber baron', *Guardian*, 24 October 2012.
21. Cited in ibid.
22. Karl Gernetzky, 'Violence, arson, ignite platinum belt tension', *Business Day*, 29 April 2014.
23. Jack Shenker, *Marikana: A Report from South Africa* (London: Zed Books, 2015).

AHMED KATHRADA, SPEECH AT NELSON MANDELA'S FUNERAL SERVICE

1. Jacob Zuma, Televised address to the nation, 5 February 2013.
2. Cited in Sandra Smith, 'What they said about Mandela's retirement', *Guardian*, 3 June 2004.
3. Ibid.
4. David Smith, 'Nelson Mandela gives World Cup a dream finale with a wave and a smile', *Guardian*, 11 July 2010.
5. Steve Nolan and Harriet Arkell, 'Dancing in pyjamas and dressing gowns to the sounds of the vuvuzela, South Africans' extraordinary celebration of the man who won their freedom', *Mail Online*, 6 December 2013.
6. Cole Moreton, 'My chance to say a personal goodbye to Nelson Mandela', *Telegraph*, 14 December 2013.
7. Ibid.
8. Jessica Elgot, 'Nelson Mandela's memorial: The 8 most unexpectedly amazing photos', *Huffington Post*, 10 December 2013.
9. Rita Barnard, 'Afterword', in Rita Barnard (ed.), *The Cambridge Companion to Nelson Mandela* (New York: Cambridge University Press, 2014), p. 293.
10. In 2013, the others were Andrew Mlangeni and Denis Goldberg.
11. Ryland Fisher, 'The life and times of Uncle Kathy', *News24*, 2 April 2017.
12. Barnard, 'Afterword', p. 293.
13. David Everatt, 'Ahmed Kathrada: Exhibit A of the values imbued in South Africa's Freedom Charter', *Independent*, 29 March 2017.

JACOB ZUMA, STATE OF THE NATION ADDRESS

1. Mandy Rossouw, 'Zuma's R65m Nkandla splurge', *Mail & Guardian*, 4 December 2009.
2. Cited in Rebecca Davis, 'Nkandlagate: DA vs. the Ministerial Handbook', *Daily Maverick*, 30 October 2012.
3. Pierre de Vos, 'Home is where the taxpayers' money is', *Daily Maverick*, 2 October 2012.
4. Mafaro Kasipo and Olwethu Majola-Kinyunyu, 'Lesser-known stories of how ordinary South Africans felt the effect of an active public protector', *The Conversation*, 30 December 2016.
5. Department of Public Works, 'Investigation Report: Prestige Project A: Security Measures President Private Residence: Nkandla', undated.
6. Public Protector of South Africa, 'Secure in Comfort: Report on an investigation into allegations of impropriety and unethical conduct relating to the installation and implementation of security measures by the Department of Public Works at and in respect of the private residence of President Jacob Zuma at Nkandla in the KwaZulu-Natal province', Report no. 25, 2013/14.

7. Cited in Jenni Evans, 'Minister gives demonstration on how to use a firepool', *News24*, 28 May 2014.
8. This insight belongs to Rebecca Davis, who calls the report title 'bleakly hilarious' in 'Parliamentary diary: Toothless ad hoc parliamentary committee won't bite', *Daily Maverick*, 6 August 2015.
9. The account described here is based on Rebecca Davis's 'Parliamentary diary: Scenes of shame', *Daily Maverick*, 14 November 2014.
10. Cited in ibid.
11. eNCA, 'Zuma: I won't waste my time with egos in Parliament', 27 November 2014.
12. Cited in Wendell Roelf, 'S. African parliament descends into chaos as Zuma gets hostile reception', *Reuters*, 13 February 2015.
13. Rebecca Davis, 'SONA: Shame of the Nation 2015', *Daily Maverick*, 13 February 2015.
14. Nel Marais, 'SONA2015: Lost in thunder, Zuma's actual speech', *Daily Maverick*, 13 February 2015.

MMUSI MAIMANE, 'BROKEN MAN' SPEECH
1. 'Red-letter day: South Africa and its Parliament', *The Economist*, 30 August 2014.
2. David Seletisha, cited in S'thembiso Msomi, *Mmusi Maimane*, p. 63.
3. Morgan Winsor, 'Who is Mmusi Maimane? Meet the first black leader of South Africa's Democratic Alliance opposition party', *International Business Times*, 5 November 2015.
4. 'Lindiwe Sisulu's attack on Mmusi Maimane: Full transcript', *Politicsweb*, 27 June 2014.
5. 'Red-letter day: South Africa and its Parliament'.
6. Msomi, *Mmusi Maimane*, p. 60.
7. SAPA, 'Maimane to Zuma: You are not an honourable man', *Mail & Guardian*, 17 February 2015.
8. Cited in Sam Mkokeli, 'The Soweto nice guy who would be DA king: Mmusi Maimane', *Sunday Times*, 4 May 2015.
9. Ranjeni Munusamy, 'From invincible man to "broken man": Zuma under pressure', *Daily Maverick*, 18 February 2015.
10. Cited in Kabous le Roux, 'He's laughing, but what does Jacob Zuma really feel when people tear into him?', Radio 702, 19 February 2015.
11. Gosebo Mathope, 'Don't feed me your English from London, Zuma tells Maimane', *The Citizen*, 22 June 2017.
12. Munusamy, 'From invincible man to "broken man"'.

BARBARA HOGAN, SPEECH AT AHMED KATHRADA'S MEMORIAL SERVICE
1. Cited Genevieve Quintal, 'Barbara Hogan calls on ANC to speak out on Zuma', *Mail & Guardian*, 12 December 2015.
2. Pieter-Louis Myburgh, *The Republic of Gupta: A Story of State Capture* (Cape Town: Penguin, 2017), pp. 185–186.
3. Ibid., p. 181.
4. Ibid., pp. 187–188.
5. Ibid, p. 88.
6. Cited in Amanda Watson, 'Hogan slams Guptas over airline', *The Citizen*, 17 March 2016.
7. Ahmed Kathrada, 'Letter to Zuma', 31 March 2016.
8. Cited in Siyabonga Mkhwanazi, 'Pravin: where do they get their instructions?', *IOL*, 11 October 2016.
9. Public Protector, 'State of Capture: Report on an investigation into alleged improper and

unethical conduct by the President and other state functionaries relating to alleged improper relationships and involvement of the Gupta family in the removal and appointment of Ministers and Directors in State-Owned Enterprises resulting in improper and possibly corrupt award of state contracts and benefits to the Gupta family's businesses', Report no. 6 of 2016/17.

10. Myburgh, *The Republic of Gupta*, p. 251.
11. Mmusi Maimane, 'SONA: The State against the Nation', *Bokamoso* newsletter, 16 February 2017.
12. Mark Swilling et al., 'Betrayal of the promise: How South Africa is being stolen', State Capacity Research Project, May 2017, p. 3.
13. Cited in 'Tributes pour in for the "giant of the struggle" Ahmed Kathrada', *Mail & Guardian*, 28 March 2017.
14. Kgalema Motlanthe, 'Tsamaya sentle mogale wa bagale: A tribute to Ahmed Kathrada', *Mail & Guardian*, 29 March 2017.
15. Cited in 'President Zuma reshuffles cabinet', South African Government News Agency, 31 March 2017.
16. Cited in 'President Zuma has gone "rogue" – Hogan', eNCA, 31 March 2017.
17. Richard Poplak, 'The long goodbye – Gordhan and the anti-Zuma resistance hack the Kathrada memorial', *Daily Maverick*, 1 April 2017.
18. Ahmed Kathrada, *Memoirs* (Cape Town: Zebra Press, 2004), p. 303.
19. Poplak, 'The long goodbye'.
20. Tanisha Heiberg, 'Zuma says marches against him highlight racism', *Moneyweb*, 10 April 2017.

Index